SUPERVISION of INSTRUCTION

SUPERVISION of

Second Edition

EXPLORATION SERIES IN EDUCATION
Under the Advisory Editorship of **JOHN GUY FOWLKES**

INSTRUCTION

Glen G. Eye Lanore A. Netzer

UNIVERSITY OF WISCONSIN
MADISON

Robert D. Krey

WISCONSIN STATE UNIVERSITY
SUPERIOR

HARPER & ROW, PUBLISHERS
New York, Evanston, San Francisco, London

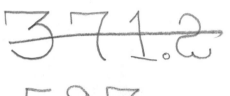

Supervision of Instruction, Second Edition

First Edition

Standard Book Number: 06-041951-2

LIBRARY OF CONGRESS CATALOG CARD NUMBER: 74-168356

Contents

Foreword

Those who are beginners as well as those who have spent many years in studying the purposes and processes of administration well may be intrigued with this book. It deals with the heart of all efforts to provide a sound educational program. Supervision always has had the responsibility of encouraging maximum accomplishment in both learning and teaching. This work is focused particularly on the administrative responsibilities to the instructional program. Many books on administration deal mainly with the non-instructional tasks, and many books in supervision deal only with the non-managerial tasks. Both, however, tend to deal with esoteric tasks which constitute ends rather than means.

The refreshing and refreshingly different aspects of this book are the amalgamations of instructional and managerial concerns as integral parts of administration. Here administrative responsibilities are defined in terms of directing and controlling, stimulating and initiating, analyzing and appraising, and designing and implementing. These tasks are not only administrative in nature but also supervisory in intent. This intent of administrative or supervisory behaviors must be focused upon instruction. Thus, this work is a challenge not only to superintendents and principals, but also to supervisors, directors, coordinators, and teachers in their efforts to improve teaching.

As a long-time student and practitioner of administration, I recommend this book as an appropriate redirection of administrative purposes, as well as a guide to those who constitute the instructional arm of administrative services. The authors have developed procedures for conducting and evaluating the energies expended in instructional responsibilities, and they have tested these procedures in the field. Those who wish to question their own professional efforts will find in this book not only an incentive for increased purposeful activities, but also an opportunity to structure and appraise their own behaviors as instruments for instructional improvement.

The updating characteristic of this second edition is much more than a juggling of content or improved word choice. The first two chapters now put supervisory service in a context of people as well as of program and the variable context is observable in the discussion of processes. Other new materials are equally pertinent to the present demands for quality in educational outputs.

My long association with the authors confirms my commitment of confidence in their careful study of the relationships between administrators, supervisors, and teachers. They reflect an inspired appreciation of their years as teacher, principal, supervisor, or superintendent in both the elementary and secondary fields, as well as university professor. A complete devotion to quality instruction is and always has been an overriding concern to the authors of this book, and they would be the first to invite others with similar interests to offer and share their helpful suggestions. Their humility in offering a "design" for a program of supervision has set the stage for the new era in the improvement of instruction.

John Guy Fowlkes

Preface

This book, in second edition, continues the earlier design of presenting a study of the *purposes, patterns, participants, processes,* and *products* of the supervision of instruction. These five categories of supervision were selected for the following reasons:

1. They are the more important categories of an extremely complex phase of education.
2. They provide a logical basis for analytical and developmental study.
3. They provide elements that are quite discrete in nature even though there may be gray areas of overlap and numerous interrelationships among them.
4. They are of sufficient importance individually to merit independent study.
5. They commit the authors to a high degree of effort in developing a structured consideration of each as well as of a total program of supervision.

This book is not intended to be a manual of specific supervisory behaviors. Supervisory functions in school situations are different in organizational patterns, in traditions, in avowed educational purposes, and in environmental expectations. Experienced professional personnel who are involved in the supervision of instruction and who have achieved a high degree of maturity in organizational and operational activities are not in need of a book that presents the "tricks of the trade," and a book offering the "tricks" of supervision can become a liability not only to experienced supervisors but also to those who may aspire to serve in a supervisory capacity. The person with a solid understanding of the *purposes, patterns, participants, processes,* and *products* of supervision can apply his talents to the situations at hand and develop an individual program of supervision that might be termed "custom-built" for a particular school situation.

The development of a "custom-built" program of supervision should not violate the idea of establishing guidelines in logical and proper relationship. In planning the individual program, then, attention would be given to the selection of, and interrelationships between, those *assumptions, principles, objectives, criteria,* and *procedures* which would constitute a developmental approach as opposed to a Procrustean design. This program is designed to encourage a high level of professional leadership and should not be accepted or used as a prescriptive source either of task or behavior selection. It is intended to offer assistance, direction, and stimulation to those performing supervisory functions as they make selections of supervisory behaviors from the many alternatives available.

The authors are concerned mainly with helping professional personnel achieve insights into the supervisory processes, specific training in the identification of assumptions, and experience in the development of statements of principles that will lead to self-directed and appropriate supervisory performance. It is not their intention to impose upon any student a preconceived and rigid concept of supervision which would determine the nature of supervisory practices in all schools where this particular philosophy is accepted. Nor are they interested in developing a cult around a particular pattern of supervision. Rather, they are dedicated to the possibility of assisting intelligent and professional energetic individuals to achieve insights into the improvement of instruction and an understanding of their responsibility for it and of the interrelationships necessary to produce school programs that are characterized by continuous development.

The authors do present statements of assumptions, principles, objectives, criteria, and procedures, and can defend them within the patterns of use and relationships presented here. Another person might want these modified and/or extended in a manner which, for him, is more logical and helpful. It is well that such should be possible; however, one should do it providing that he is willing to take the responsibility for the interrelational consistency sought in this presentation.

This book, then, should serve as a source of suggestion and direction to

1. The *administrators* who want to survey responsibilities for leadership in the instructional program.
2. The central office *directors of service* related to and supportive of the instructional program who want to keep teaching and learning as the focal point of their particular service agencies.
3. The *supervisors of instruction* who want the technical services to

the instructional program to be appropriate, effective, and developmental.

4. The *teachers* who must make the choice of accepting or resisting supervisory efforts.
5. The *laymen,* many of whom tend to oversimplify the educative function of a school by identifying with isolated personal school experiences and fail to appreciate and understand the complex teaching-learning process.

The organization of the materials in this book is clearly set forth in the table of contents. The only comment made here with respect to format relates to the questions which are often submitted in college textbooks and placed at the ends of the chapters. It is hoped that after the student has read a chapter, he will be inclined to use the questions to explore its subject matter more extensively. The authors of this book also want to encourage scholars to extend their knowledge through discussion and contemplation without being limited to the confines of the chapters. The bibliography has been selected to assist the students in this purpose. The questions usually found at the end of a chapter, however, here will be found within the text of each chapter. It perhaps will be more helpful to have the questions at the point where they might encourage cross-referencing, through problem attack, to other parts of the book and to the work of other authors. These questions and directions are also intended to stimulate the student to question frequently his own consistency of understanding supervisory functions and of his emerging plans for a supervisory program.

Acknowledgment is made for the many substantial contributions of professional colleagues and associates to the development of this book. Appreciation also is expressed to many graduate students of the authors who have positively and patiently worked through the many years of changing syllabi from which the outline of this book emerged. A keen sense of appreciation is extended to Shirley F. Heck, Dolores A. Reihle, and Myrna M. Toney for creative editorial assistance and Nancy N. Neiland for the faithful typing of the manuscript. A final and personal acknowledgment of the years of encouragement, editorial and typing contributions, and delightful associations is extended to Lucile Eye and Geneva Krey.

Glen G. Eye
Lanore A. Netzer
Robert D. Krey

Part I

THE PURPOSES OF SUPERVISION

Part I includes a presentation of the purposes of supervision cast in substantive contexts and undergirded by precise definitions of terms. The contexts are located in people and in programs. The definitions are relevant to the general dictionary sense of the words but the terminology focuses the meanings upon the tasks and functions of supervision. Above all, the authors seek to achieve practicality by making the theoretical concepts serve the practitioner through identifiable contexts of action and clarity of language.

Purposes are not treated in list form. They constitute the focal point or points which should give direction and pertinence to the interrelationships of definition, theory, and agencies of change. The overlay of this approach to the study of supervision is the heuristic intent to commit purposes, theories, and change techniques to a continuous process of evaluation and development through the optimum involvement of all professional staff members.

The development of a custom-built supervisory program necessitates a continuing improvement program. This is the "local sufficiency" concept for the cooperative administrator-supervisor-teacher effort because they must observe the protocol of their developments even as such developments emerge from the states of identification, selection, and application.

The program of supervision must possess, and be possessed by, those purposes which carry beyond mere planning for change to the implementation of planned change. Furthermore, the purposes must direct the planners and implementers to testing the soundness of the theoretical bases for proposed changes. The degree of success of planned changes is related directly to the amount and quality of the personal involvement and understanding of the total staff. Theory and practice must be logically compatible and mutually supportive.

The authors offer the four chapters in Part I in full cognizance that they, too, must observe a purpose about purposes and must display the consistent interrelatedness demanded in a program of supervision. The authors' design for the supervision of instruction includes the contexts of existency, the history of design, the design itself, the underlying theory, and some characteristics of change.

Chapter 1 emphasizes people as the context or vehicle of action. The history of supervision is reviewed very briefly only as a basis for illustrating the evolution of the authors' definition of supervision. This definition and its implications are the bases for a design of supervision as presented in Chapter 2. Portions of this design form the bases for each of the succeeding chapters. The steps in the development of the action pattern referred to briefly in Chapter 2 are more fully developed in Chapter 3. Finally, since "improvement" necessitates change, Chapter 4 is devoted to a discussion on how change takes place.

1

The People Context of Supervision

Supervision is an interaction between and among people. The nature of dominance, supportiveness, rigidity, openness, and all of the other adjectives which might describe the nature of this interaction do not change the fact that any definition of supervision must take into consideration the phenomenon of people influencing people. Supervision can take place in almost any type of human enterprise because most rational activities involve people. Whenever more than one person is involved, interaction in the form of some type of established relationship is inescapable.

Human purpose normally is evidenced in interactions. These purposes often are not held in common. In such instances, the tasks of supervision are made more difficult. Supervision also might be made more difficult by the variations in the personality of the person involved. The purposes for which people interact may be individually determined, identified as a result of competitiveness among the defined group, or supplied by an agency, force, or condition outside the group in action.

Education represents the kind of group activity that has many of its organizational purposes determined by people outside the professional group responsible for directing those activities which promise to achieve the purpose. The purposes which normally guide the action and interactions of people become systematized into sequential relationships which are intended to bring about this realization of purpose. The

How would you respond to a person who says that he does not believe in supervision?

structuring of activities usually is identified by the name "program." Thus, in the consideration of supervision we have at the outset the fact that interaction of people is a common phenomenon and that this interaction is highly influenced by the program which, in large part, has been predetermined. The program, then, represents a structuring of activities to serve a purpose. Whenever such a structuring takes place, it seemingly demands that the interaction of the people involved become systematized. The structuring of the program in schools usually is referred to as the program of instruction.

The systematization of the interaction of those responsible for operating within the structure of the program is called "supervision." The term "administration" is a broader term and involves many functions not characteristic of supervision because supervision is a subsystem of the larger system identified as administration. It becomes obvious, then, that supervision has two contexts: one may be said to be *people* and is dealt with in this chapter; the other is *program* and is dealt with in Chapter 2. The remainder of the book deals with the system most promising in merging these two contexts. If the merging is successful, there will be a high degree of harmony among the people and satisfaction with the program. The responsibility for giving direction to the process of merging *people* and *program* is held by a person (supervisor) who initiates many activities while performing the function of supervision. The primary concern of this chapter is to explore some of the kinds of phenomena which are of major significance to the people context.

VARIATIONS OF DEFINITION

Terms, functions, phenomena, and other aspects of human activities are subjected to definition almost without exception. The things that dominate the specifics of a definition vary among people as well as among that which is defined. Definition of terms is an attempt to achieve mutual meaning which may be communicated and which will establish purpose through encouraging commonality of pursuit and giving significance to an experience or a product (see Chapter 2). This does not mean that the point of reference by which a term is defined assures that the differing points of view will harmonize. Differing points of reference resulting in conflicting definitions of the same term may also engender conflict in the merging of behaviors. An example of varying referent points for defining may be found in the definitions of the term "supervision." One person might perceive supervision as inspection and tend to seek compliance of members to the group patterns. Another may perceive it as persuasion and, while still accomplishing the same outcome, still seek compliance with behaviors and outcomes of the group purpose.

Differences in referent points often are found among certificated and non-certificated (classified) workers in the organized educational effort. The layman may have still a different point of reference for definition than does the professional. These differences could be grounded in the purpose which each sees as appropriate to the activities presumably subsumed in the term. The layman is more inclined to view inspection as the rewarding form of supervision because it leads to a compliance with those outcomes which the layman believes schools should espouse. The professional, however, may view those outcomes as a global target by which the individual can express the expertise subsumed in his professional training and certification.

The employer and the employee may also have differing referent points for the definition of supervision. The employer may see effectiveness or efficiency as the dominant purpose of supervision. The employee subjected to this idea may see supervision as the enforcement of protocol. The referent points of the two groups may not be particularly pliable with respect to achieving commonality of direction of behavior as might be desired by either the employer or the employee contingent. If a system is required for the achievement of agreed-upon global purposes in group activity, then some agreements must be achieved which will give viable relationships between those who would declare the appropriateness of activities in relation to the appropriateness of purpose. Effective communication is required if this is to be achieved. This requirement makes obvious the fact that there must be some link existing between the employer and the employee, the layman and the professional, the supervisor and the supervised, if activities and behaviors are to be brought into proper agreement with the accepted purpose of the group structure.

The maintenance and improvement of learning activities are major purposes for those who would influence classroom teachers. This means that the function of supervision includes the responsibility for bringing about a merger between the expectations of the lay or public controlling group, the professional workers in the school, and the accepted purpose of the group enterprise or system called the school.

IS IT AN "IT"?

Some may consider it irrelevant to be concerned about whether supervision is a person, an activity, an organization, a process, or a function. However, it makes a substantial difference to those who try to describe the processes and purposes of supervision as to whether it is considered as being one or the other of several distinct types of entity. The same issue can be raised with respect to many other activities. An appendectomy, for instance, is not a doctor. It is the process by which the doctor applies his professional skills to the removal of an offending part of the body. In a similar vein, the pilot is not the flight. The pilot is a highly skilled person who can take a piece of complicated equipment and move people and things from one place to another with great speed and safety. It may seem unnecessary to argue whether surgery is an it, a person, a process, or a product. On the other hand, the doctor can save life by whatever happens between him and the patient when the human body develops some dysfunctional parts. It may be of little consequence as to whether the pilot or the plane or the weather conditions are the more important elements of the phenomenon of moving rapidly from one geographic location to another. On the other hand, the successful pilot has a splendid record of applying his professional expertise to the business of transportation. The pilot is a person, but the procedures by which he brings together the efforts of people and complicated equipment become a process—or, if you please, a function of bringing together the person, the matériel, and the purpose. The processes for either the doctor or the pilot for accomplishing the desired outcomes depend upon the proper functioning of specialized knowledge and skills. The concern, then, is one of function.

A function is purposeful action. Supervision is purposeful action. Supervision can give purpose to action. Supervision may be the establishing of purpose which gives direction to action. The supervisor, as an actor, may be dependent upon other persons and certainly upon other matériel and conditions for the achievement of individual or group purposes. Seldom can the supervisor be an actor enjoying the full independence of a person who is wholly self-sufficient and whose purposes do not involve those of others.

Supervision is a function, and it is a function in somewhat the same manner that the term "function" is used in mathematics. In mathematics, function is a way of talking about a mathematical quantity whose value depends upon the values of other quantities. Thus, the supervisor is a person who performs a function which applies some specialized type of knowledges and skills in order to bring people, matériel, environment, and purpose into a desired relationship. The desirability of the relationship usually is evaluated in terms of a product. It is important, therefore, to see supervision as a function. Much of this importance resides in the fact that, when supervision is viewed as a person, the purpose of the group effort may centralize its focus upon the independent self-actualization of the person bearing the title of supervisor. Developing a program of supervision in that context would be developing a design by which one individual or one group of individuals in the organization might involve other people with other purposes and consequently dominate them for a personalized and non-institutional goal. If the supervisor is a person who can achieve the dominance of institutional purposes, then his self-actualization becomes secondary or at least dependent upon another value, namely, the program outcome. If we view the individual as possessing sufficient nobility to maintain an institutional purpose, then supervision must be a *function* because we have one value depending upon another. This logic seems to allow no other alternative than to declare supervision a function and to analyze and explore the processes from this point of view.

CAUSES OF AMBIGUITIES

The mere fact that the previous discussion dealt with the question of whether supervision is an it, a person, or a process gives testimony to the authors' belief that there have been substantial ambiguities regarding the definition and description of supervision. The obscurities, indistinctnesses, and variations in the meanings of the terms used in the definition or even in the discussion of the processes of supervision indicate that ambiguities do exist. These ambiguities may have developed from a variety of causes, not the least of which must be the simple neglect of the task of definition. There are hazards involved in defining which many people prefer to avoid. When a term is defined—particularly if the definition is published—it must stand for continuous re-evaluation by those who may have a variety of purposes in evaluating the definition.

Neglect, then, is perhaps the kindest way to describe the major cause of ambiguities, but there are others. Personal biases may be founded in the previous experience of the individual or the result of a consciously developed philosophy of life and professional activities. If a person has a particular personality characteristic that leads him to find satisfaction only in exercising his dominance over others, he probably will define supervision very much as a control mechanism. If, on the other hand, his personality characteristics support him in the desire to accomplish group purpose, he may be more inclined to see supervision as the process by which people interact successfully to reach known purposes. If he is a person who feels insecure with respect to his own talents, he will define supervision in a way that will protect his own unique way of finding satisfaction in his personal and professional life. The distaste for confrontations on the part of many people would lead to a particular way of thinking about the purpose and process of supervision. If confrontation is consciously avoided, supervision is likely to be defined in terms of the interactive process rather than in a manner that would commit the person to accountability in terms of the outcomes measured in reference to the stated purposes of the organization in which he works.

There are many *ifs* that might be used by way of defining the causes of ambiguity, but perhaps these are enough to suggest what generates them. Perhaps the more common cause of ambiguities is simply the result of compromise. The person who has a particular personality characteristic or pur-

What experiences have influenced your perception of supervision?

pose in professional life may find that he comes into conflict with the purposes of others and neither can achieve satisfaction without yielding a bit of his own. The compromise, then, results in a vagueness of the concepts of supervision and the activities related to it. It has long been stated that if enough compromises are made, the original statements are watered down to the extent of universal acceptability and become almost completely meaningless.

The purpose of this book is to lead from a definition of supervision through a process of supervision to an acceptance of accountability for the outcomes of the institution in which supervision finds its place as a function.

REWARD VERSUS FUTURISTIC ORIENTATION

The *people* context of supervision cannot avoid a consideration of the people who enter the ranks of the supervisors or of those who draw conclusions about the ones who do. Many school systems perhaps have contributed to improper speculations as well as to unfortunate practices by making the assignment to a supervisory post a reward for faithful service. This obviously has led to the notion that, somewhat apart from qualifications for a particular post, there are certain seniority claims that individuals may present and presumably use as a means of succeeding to that post.

The assumption involved in seniority claims is that a person has earned a reward or that a person, by virtue of success as a classroom teacher, develops some expertise in being able to pass judgment upon others. This assumption leads to the inevitable conclusion that there is no specific type of training necessary to become a supervisor. The tenability of this conclusion easily can be brought into question but it does not remove the practical fact that positions in supervision have been filled on the basis of such assumptions. The notion of reward to the faithful has never been, in any type of complex system, the proper basis for assignment to leadership positions. Faithfulness is a worthy virtue but it does not bear a high correlation to skill in performing leadership behaviors.

A reward that sometimes occurs—and it is closely related to the characteristics of faithfulness—is the reciprocity that may be elicited in the selection of a supervisor. There is some belief on the part of administrators, particularly chief executive officers, that the history of past faithfulness is a relationship that can be continued profitably into the future by placing the faithful in positions with leadership responsibilities, but still subordinate to the executive. This reciprocity notion, however, embodies some hazards for the chief executive. Reciprocity denotes a situation in which the subordinate will continue his loyalty to the superordinate but will resist similar reciprocal invitations to his own subordinates, thus diluting the loyalty to the superordinate. Faithfulness will not take care of public accountability nor of status with the professional staff in a school system on the basis of reciprocity benefits. Here again the reward type of basis for making assignments to supervisory positions may be satisfying personally both to the superordinate and the new supervisor, but it nonetheless fails to measure up to an assurance of the kinds of services that supervision is supposed to deliver.

Another type of practice that has not been particularly productive is that of using the assignment to a title position, such as supervisor, as a means of bypassing the salary schedule provisions. This makes it primarily a staffing and budgeting expediency. The convenience of the budget and the desire to hold an excellent teacher by paying above the salary schedule are quite unrelated to the kinds of talents that should be demanded from those who are assigned to supervisory tasks.

These "hang-ups" in the practices of the past cannot possibly stand as good administrative procedures if the focus is placed upon the clarity of the goals that should characterize the accomplishments of supervisors. Goal clarity is a responsibility of the chief executive and goals must be absolutely clear to those who accept supervisory positions. If the goals are clear and well-chosen, there will be a basis for the supervisor to select the processes by which the goals will be achieved and, at the same time, the superordinate will have a basis for establishing the criteria by which accountability will be determined (see Chapter 2). The futuristic orientation attending goal clarification is by far the better basis for viewing the kind of talent needed in supervisory positions. Goal clarity and the processes of achieving systems of accountability inevitably lead to a specialization of staff requirements. These specializations should be stated clearly in the job specifications and appropriate sums of money should be allocated to the elements of qualification that successfully meet the descriptions of the task or position. Supervision, then, must be viewed as a specialization within the area of providing the direction of and leadership for the instructional program. If seen in this manner, the specializations both for the performance on the job and for the preparatory programs for those who would become supervisors can be clearly and successfully identified.

What criteria would you wish used if you were selected for a supervisory position?

BUREAUCRATIC OBFUSCATIONS

Bureaucracy normally embodies some inferences or overtones that are unpleasant or undesirable. There are many and varied concepts of administration but practically all of them have some reference to the hierarchical levels demanded in the management of any complex organization. The superordinate's concept of administration makes a difference as to the kinds of assignments given to supervisors and the expectations held for them. Most important, however, and basic to all of the varieties is the concept of function that is held by the superordinate, the supervisor, and the professional teaching staff.

The concept of the function of the supervisor basically should be that of doing those things which influence people to provide a better instructional program for the pupils who commit their learning potential to the educational system's direction. A declaration of such noble proportions does not take one to the specifics of the behaviors required in order to perform the function of supervision. If the function is seen primarily as a status recognition type of existence, then, in all probability, the influence will be at a minimum. If, however, the function is so defined that the direct outputs of supervision can be identified in their relationships to the influences upon the teachers and the instructional program, a much more practical view of supervision is taken. One of the difficult concepts to establish or to unravel, however, relates to whether a supervisor has authority and power and, if so, to what extent and for what purposes.

A continuing responsibility exists in any complex organization to assess the distribution of authority. Authority need not be of the feudal type; put more positively, it could be the possession of esoteric abilities which are essential to the purposes of the organization. Speaking with authority does not necessarily mean that one must impose his will upon another. Specialized skills and knowledges may be so highly respected that they, in themselves, constitute the authority. Authority is not of a police type when supervision is the topic of consideration. When a supervisor depends upon authoritarianism as the only means of influencing people rather than by the use of superior skills and knowledge, the conclusion can easily be reached that the compensation allocated to such a position is for incompetence rather than for competence. Arriving at this position raises the interesting potentials of the so-called Peter Principle.[1] Regardless of whether the popularized notion is accepted—that is, that everybody in a bureaucracy tends to move up to his point of incompetence—it must be recognized that the purpose of administration is not to bring about such a phenomenon. Many people interested in the instructional program will choose not to move on into the higher levels in the hierarchy of control but rather will seek out that point at which there is the self-experienced sense of contribution to the educational program. To take the cynical point of view that the contribution is of less consequence than personal satisfaction with a position is no more realistic than to revel in the disgusting proportions of the Peter Principle.

Many of the references to the "establishment," and to the Peter Principle as characteristic of the "establishment," can be explained better in terms of the stylistic and standardistic references of the people who perform at any level of specializa-

[1] Lawrence J. Peter and Raymond Hull, *The Peter Principle* (New York: William Morrow and Company, Inc., 1969).

tion. There are conflicts between those who want to do their own thing and those who see the institutional purpose and goal as predominant in the obligation of the individual in the complex organization. Those who are stylistic in their nature tend to feel that their own judgment is of superior quality and that to yield to the judgment of another is a sign of weakness. Those with standardistic orientations value the professional associations that they have, either among their colleagues on a school staff or through membership in an organization, and tend to use these associations as their point of reference. It becomes even more obvious as to the nature of the individual if the matter of deference is considered, which is somewhat more absolute than selecting desirable referent groups. Deference means acceding to the judgments of another. There is nothing in this phenomenon that prevents the individual from making an assessment of another person's competence to merit the confidence of the individual who assigns deference to that person. It does, however, bring about certain strains upon the bureaucratic organization and, therefore, constitutes obfuscations when, within the same staff, there are some people who seek the stylistic reference and others who are happy with the standardistic. The conflict between the two often results in a loss of benefits to the purposes of the organization. This does not mean that the schools should be made up entirely of one or the other. Perhaps the greatest need is to recognize that a bureaucracy has been characterized, even though it is changing in character at the present time, as a means of structuring the efforts of many people in a wide variety of related and conflicting purposes (see Chapter 6).

Within the global purposes of the school there are many short-term, narrowly focused goals proper for individuals to pursue. It is also recognized that the pursuit of these goals must bear some systematic relationship to each other. At the present time no one knows how to get along without orderliness in a complex relationship. It is incumbent upon the leadership of the organization to stimulate the members of the group—particularly the subordinates in the line organization—to accept the responsibilities of institutional goals and to stimulate those conditions which bring about satisfaction for both the stylistic and the standardistic types of people.

WARINESS ABOUT ESTABLISHMENTARIANISM

The above discussion indicates some of the kinds of stresses and conflicts that develop within the structural arrangements for any complex group activity. Educational systems certainly come within this level of group activity. There are so many jokes about management and about the establishment that the popularized notion may lead many to assume that without controls life would be beautiful. Such a rule cannot be applied to any activity with success. A busy intersection may seem to be a highly structured place where people are forced to observe the traffic lights, which thus regulate or restrict their behavior. Conversely, the same corner during a period of maximum traffic movement but without the lights should provide these same persons with the maximum degree of freedom. However, observations indicate that traffic comes to a complete halt and the indecision and fear of all drivers involved results in a maximum freedom that constitutes a maximum loss of privilege. Perhaps this is not an exact parallel to the things that happen in an educational system, but it behooves those who work in a large, complex organization to ask themselves what would be the force that causes individuals to coordinate their movements and activities if there were no directional controls (see Chapter 5).

The notion that the establishment is all bad is wholly unfounded when a reasonable degree of logic is applied to it. Perhaps the feeling against management and the establishment might be unscrambled a bit if each person in the organization could re-evaluate the focus of his own loyalties. This means that each needs to determine whether he really wants to accomplish his assignment in the school organization and, if so, whether his loyalty to purpose can bring about sufficient tolerance for accomplishing it in the midst of many other people and activities.

One of the difficult elements of group action is to keep in proper focus the processes by which school activities are carried on and the conditions which make it possible for these processes, whether control or privilege, to be successful. Perhaps the problem is neither in the pre-service training nor in the in-service experiences but rather in encouraging staff members to separate the singular process of control from the universe of conditions necessary to the success of the enterprise. In the current scene, negotiation is viewed as one of the means by which there can be better equating or balancing of privileges among the various hierarchies in the organization. This might be called negotiated power. Here again it should be recognized that power is power regardless of who is wielding it. Teachers may feel just as constrained by the actions of their negotiating organization as by the establishment. This could be called a sort of "crossing-over syndrome" in which the subordinates in the organization wrest controls from the administration and establish a new controlling segment within the organization. There is no more assurance of purity when the control shifts to the hands of the subordinates than when it was allocated to the establishment (see Chapter 10).

The purposes of supervision perhaps can be served better by recognizing that in the *people* context of supervision, all of these kinds of conflicts and struggles are going on. Knowing this, perhaps one can work out his own personal logic and psychological stance which will permit him to do the things he wants to do and to be somewhat philosophical about the demands of orderliness. Perhaps even more important than attributing all of these hang-ups to the control mechanism is to recognize that any control can be palatable or objectionable, depending upon the nature of the people who inhabit the control post as well as the nature of the people being controlled. This is equally true at the superordinate as well as at the subordinate levels. It is well to move to the consideration of what pathologies may develop in the position incumbents and to explore the therapies that might be helpful.

EVOLVING PATHOLOGIES

Those who occupy positions in the upper level of the hierarchy of control in an organized effort often are attributed *power* which accrues as a result of position or status. The mere fact that most people view position and status as defining expectations in the exercise of power has an effect upon those who hold such positions. If everyone expects a person to wield power, it is a temptation for that person to live up to the expectations. If the purpose of the person in position, in this case a supervisor, should be that of realizing a personal desire to exercise power and authority over others, then the institutional objective has been displaced by a personal one. This is the hierarchical disease that may attack those who are assigned to administration and to supervisory positions.

Should a person be required to choose between personal and organizational goals?

Anyone in a group activity who has opportunities for influence over others has a potential or present problem in maintaining a balance between personal objectives and institutional objectives. If personal objectives become obsessive, then the pathological condition can be one in which the afflicted person is a detriment to organizational efforts and particularly to those who are subordinate.

A second aspect of pathology is the *routinization of activities* for a group of people in which routinization itself becomes the major criterion of success. Each administrator and each supervisor must have the ability to organize his own efforts and the efforts of others. Coordination becomes one of the demands of the responsibility. It is tempting to accomplish coordination through a series of unyielding requirements so that the future of the supervisor might be viewed with certainty of prediction as to how those in the organization will operate. When routinization becomes a major purpose as well as the major criterion for measuring contribution, then the formalization has crystallized to the point where little freedom of activity is left for those who hold subordinate positions (see Chapter 13).

A third aspect of pathology in the supervisory position is that of *seeking security at any cost*. Here, again, a type of disease similar to that indicated as self-realization through authority and power is in evidence. Security becomes a personal objective and could displace the institutional purpose.

When this displacement occurs, the educational system no longer is maintained as a means of achieving the education and development of the pupils—which is claimed as the focal purpose of the total enterprise—and becomes instead an instrument by which an individual can assure his continuance of status through dominance over other aspects of the organization (see Chapter 11).

A fourth pathological characteristic that often develops among those who hold positions of authority and status is what may be called *endemic feudality*. The displacement of institutional goals by personal goals of those in a power position can develop into a posture of feudality almost as it was conceived in the Middle Ages. In this case, the individual at the "top of the pyramid" or in any of the intermediate management positions develops a conviction that certain privileges accrue to the individual holding a certain position purely because it is held. An extended aspect of this attitude is that, because privileges were assumed, deference was expected on the part of the subordinates. It is only necessary to view some of the simple conveniences found in the offices of those who hold the higher-echelon positions in the bureaucratic structure to identify the evidences of this assumed feudality. The term "endemic" indicates that everything about the position and the deference shown to it are also encouragements to the position-holders to feel this sense of essentiality to the group activity and to act that way eventually.

Can you identify other pathological characteristics of supervisors?

None of these four elements of pathology is to be considered as the most serious nor as the total of those that might happen. Rather, they are a sampling of what might happen. The hasty conclusion can be drawn that feudality is endemic in nature and people accede to the authority of position over others in succumbing to pathological developments. New and better ways must be found to select not only the people who can resist these kinds of temptations but also those who can maintain a proper sense of balance between their personal objectives and their institutional obligations. In this modern age of correcting, most anything that happens—whether it is happy or unhappy—leads to some of the corrective measures that hold promise in meeting the pathological threats on the part of those who hold supervisory posts.

THERAPEUTIC MODES

Most of the pathologies that develop in an educational system can be cured by some serious scholastic applications. The first suggestion for therapy is *to acquire more knowledge about causation*. All persons, even those who develop the pathology of wanting security at any cost, have let a proper purpose become cancerous. Everyone needs to have some notion of his right to find out what will happen as a consequence of efforts expended. The primary contribution of therapy here is that of focusing less on self and more on others who are essential to organizational effectiveness. The supervisor should spend substantial time in wondering how his every act will affect the others in the school. A regulation, for instance, may be essential to an orderly relationship in a complex of activities, but the choice of regulation must be weighed in terms of its support of orderliness and its cost to the creativity of subordinates.

A second therapy may be achieved by giving more *attention to the inducement–contribution status of the superordinates and subordinates.* This does not imply that professional people should not be induced by salaries or negotiated working conditions, but that a *part* of the inducement may be those reinforcing activities which can be stimulated through organized operations. This is particularly in evidence when the inducement is intended to be a psychological reinforcement between the superordinate and the subordinate. A word of commendation and the visibility given to an individual's success are as essential as rewards as are preferences in room assignments, new encyclopedias, and other material considerations. A balance must be achieved in that the person receiving inducements must offer some commitment to a contribution in his role of subordinate. This negotiation can take place in one-to-one conferences or it can take place at the negotiating table. The notion emphasized here is that there should be a continuous and reciprocal relationship between the supervisor and the supervised. This approach tends to force a consideration of the contribution of each individual as a team member rather than of the contribution of the individual standing alone (see Chapter 7).

A third therapeutic mode is found in the *predictability of relationships.* There is the old story of the teacher who said that his supervisor was the most even-tempered person he had ever known. He explained this by saying that the supervisor was mad all the time. It can be supposed that even undesirable characteristics are more tolerable when predictable than when unpredictable.

A more positive outlook is disclosed when people work together in planning, implementing, or evaluating the instructional program. Such activities may have virtue primarily because the outcomes are predictable. The general ground rules by which people work together are extremely important whether they have or have not been formalized into a code. A leader leads because the led have confidence in his ability to take the organizational enterprise to a successful outcome. Confidence is built by previous experiences with success and no credential can take the place of it (see Chapter 11).

A fourth form of therapy is that of *mutual recognition of interdependence.* All group enterprises are acknowledgments of the essentiality of diversifying specializations. Each person has his task and each task contributes to the organizational outcome. The pathology of thinking that each one can move alone is a serious one. In the previous section the accusation was pointed primarily at the superordinates. It must also be recognized that the subordinates need to develop a sense of interdependence and mutual contributory activity with superordinates. Teachers, in general, have a tendency to believe that if they were left alone, everything would be wonderful. Probably the most unhappy teachers in any school system would be those who were completely independent because then all the managerial and supervisory services would be withdrawn and each person would have to be self-contained. It is well to think through the nature and extent of interdependence that can be achieved and that would be desirable in the school operation (see Chapter 9).

A fifth type of therapy is that of *visibility*. The probability is that upper-echelon staff achieves visibility with little effort and, eventually, it may become pathologically troublesome. The therapy is in seeking to keep others, particularly subordinates, in prominent visibility. Supervisors, however, must instill in the teachers the willingness to cooperate in providing evidence worthy of visibility because they work in the classrooms which usually are out of public view. Visibility of contributions and successes can become one of the best ways of initiating and pacing the improvement programs of an educational system.

What type of therapy would you suggest for the pathological characteristics you identified in response to the question on page 14?

A sixth and final item selected as an example of therapy is the *guarantee of consistency* in achieving decisions through the choice of commonly seen alternatives. This is perhaps the best therapy against the development of power for power's sake and security at any cost when considering the relationships between the superordinates and subordinates. Few questions have only one answer. Most challenges have alternative ways of achievement. The supervisor who can provide alternatives rather than single requirements probably will be offering wholesome therapy both for himself and for the teacher.

MAINTENANCE DEMANDS

The preceding two sections dealt with what might be called the illnesses that attack supervision and some suggestions for appropriate therapy for such illnesses. Here, a more positive approach is taken in the consideration of the maintenance of an organization in its *pursuit of the goals* which shaped it as an organization. An organization's goals must exist; an organization designed for an unknown purpose seldom accomplishes anything that merits its continuity.

Closely related to organizational goals is what might be called the *battle against ambiguity*. A major problem is to get the organizational goals stated in such a manner that they communicate approximately the same concept to all people. Many organizational goals are the results of compromise.

Compromise often is the process of forcing the specifics into generalities until they achieve a state of ambiguity that makes them acceptable to all parties, including those of conflicting points of view. Citizenship is an example of the ambiguity in a school goal. This has long been a goal of the schools, yet the current milieu of diversity and conflict about how one can express his obligations to his nation dramatizes the vast array of conflicting concepts with respect to citizenship. It is difficult to assume either that a universal instructional program can be designed or that an evaluation program can be developed which could prove the excellence of an instructional program with respect to this particular organizational goal. The school is confronted with the necessity of trying to take this one term and to develop it into something that at least a majority of the school staff as well as the supporting public could accept. It is utterly unfair to commit teachers to using an organizational goal of this type if the supervisory and administrative staffs do not give some assurance to the teachers that a degree of unanimity exists in the supporting public which would make it safe for the teachers to teach citizenship at all.

The third type of maintenance responsibility is that of *achieving a balance between certainty and diversity*. There were declarations earlier that security was desired and that predictable relationships were good therapy for those who wanted to feel free to proceed along the lines which they deemed the best way to accomplish their employment responsibility. Thus, the problem is to maintain a system of controls which would assure that institutional goals are pursued, that coordination among a diversity in staff purposes and functions would assist that pursuit, and that achievement of the goals would be realized without depriving the individual teacher of an undue amount of freedom.

A fourth element in maintenance is the *diffusion of power*. If some therapy as indicated above is successful in dealing with those who choose power as a personal goal regardless of institutional goals, then the next logical step would be to distribute the power. This is accomplished in part through delegation, but often the delegation is not related to the types of accomplishments specified in the organization's goals. If the superordinates tend to judge the quality of the delegated activities in terms of process rather than of outcome, then the person receiving the delegation of power loses the discretion that gives him a sense of freedom and a chance to choose alternatives in applying his own intelligence to the tasks at hand. A part of the unresolved problems in the school organization is that of getting a successful relation of confidence to make decisions on the occasions when decisions must be made. The assumption of the past is no longer tenable, namely, that those who hold a higher position in the hierarchy of the power arrangement are competent to make decisions over those things deemed primary tasks of subordinates. In this age of greater and greater specialization, it is more and more incongruous for any one person to assume that he is competent to make decisions in many different technical areas.

The fifth and final maintenance suggestion to be included here is called the *strategies of co-alignment*. This is another way of saying that coordination must be achieved. The word coordination is burdened with the traditional meaning that it is achieved through the imposition of controls. The strategies of co-alignment indicate a greater respect for the diversity of functions required of highly technical staff and the distribution of power to the points at which decisions are made so that, consequently, the diffusion of power is a diffusion of decision points. An important function is the analysis of the relationships of those people who need to be kept in co-alignment. The procedures by which this can be done do not necessarily imply a power structure nearly so much as they imply a negotiation through analysis for people to relate their own activities to measurable outcomes in their first-line pursuit of a purpose and in their second-line relationships to coordinate functions (see Chapter 8).

PLANNING FOR CREATIVE ACTION

A major challenge to supervision is that of providing the kind of support to the teaching staff that not only will permit but also will encourage teachers to act creatively in fulfilling the teaching function. When this has been done, few teachers will have occasion to register complaints about an "establishment" that is inflexible.

One item of support for the creative act can be identified as *generalized certainty*. This means that subordinates have an increasing competence to predict the consequences of their own acts without deviating from what a superordinate might require. Some of the things that might be done to give this assurance are to make certain that all teachers know that (1) the evidences of success will be rewarded, (2) deviations from agreed plans or goals will be subjected to analysis rather than immediate penalty, and (3) failure does not mean immediate dismissal but invites first a shared responsibility for the analysis of what may have gone wrong. The staff must know that, when plans are made, supporting assistance will be available and no one will be deserted once the implementation process has begun. If generalized certainties exist, the staff must know, too, that the rejection of any particular plan on the part of an individual will not occur unless there is objective evidence at hand which would influence the judgments made jointly between the two parties concerned (see Chapter 11).

A second type of support for creative action is what might be called *contingency controls*. The teacher's chance of success may be dependent upon the origins of the expectations and accountabilities imposed upon him. If these come from a board of education, the teachers must know whether there are diverse expectations and whether they can be attempted safely. It is a responsibility of supervisors to make certain that a controlling board has sufficient unanimity of expectations so that it will not result in confusion for the teaching process or in reprisals upon the teachers in the absence of satisfactory multiple outcomes on the part of the pupils. It is not a matter of wild speculation to declare that even the expectations and systems of accountability established by school administrators and supervisors themselves may be far short of sufficient unanimity to give proper support to the teachers (see Chapters 7 and 8).

Because teachers are subjected to evaluation, there must be a declaration on the part of the supervisors as to what patterns will be followed. An evaluation of teaching in terms of its product rather than of its process is very difficult to achieve. Problems related to which textbook or which method of reading should be used are appropriate subjects for debate but not for evaluation. These are *processes* of teaching. More relevant to the worth of the teaching–learning act would be a determination of the goals for any evaluation that might take place. There are goals of evaluation that apply at the developmental level of any new plan. This is called formative evaluation. Once the instructional plan has been put into operation, it needs to be pursued for a period of time during which there will be diagnostic evaluation or what might be called analytical evaluation. When there has been sufficient time for the teaching and supervisory staff to be assured that the plan is good, it is put into operation, and, after the lapse of more time, it then is subjected to a rigorous operational or summative type of evaluation. No teacher should be subjected to any of these types of evaluation without the supervisors, the administrators, and the controlling boards giving full assurance that the supporting public will not misinterpret the type of evaluation used and, consequently, draw conclusions that are unrelated to the purpose of evaluation. The positive result phobia that seems to attack the whole teaching profession as well as the supporting public is a problem for the teachers that has not received ample attention from their superordinates in the school system. If it is a developmental program and evaluations indicate that the program is only acceptable in part, the teacher must be protected against the unwarranted and unsupported conclusions that the teaching is bad. Supervisors must not permit teachers to be buffeted by the notion that anything new must be right the first time. The purpose of supervision is not nearly so much that of maintaining the status quo as that of maintaining the status rights of teachers (see Chapter 15).

Are directing and controlling essential supervisory processes regarding support for creativity?

A further support for creative action in the classroom would be for the supervisors to recognize that the teacher is only one element controlling the quality of the output in terms of learning within the school. Curricular content, environmental impacts, operational procedures, and instructional materials are items which should be evaluated in terms of their impact (influence) prior to the times that the teaching processes are assessed. In other words, when the pupils are not doing well in a particular classroom, a supervisor well might establish the habit of saying, "Let us check out all other possible culprits before we point an accusing finger at the teacher." In this way, the teacher is protected until it is established beyond doubt that the items of support required for successful teaching and learning were present prior to the appraisal of the teacher's competence to teach. These contingency controls, if administered successfully, can offer the teacher a security which tends to release creativity in the teaching act (see Chapter 15).

Another item of support is what might be called *selected reinforcements.* Those who believe that a superior officer need only offer a word of commendation or be seen patting a subordinate on the back, regardless of the activities involved, are misjudging the relative intelligence or stupidity of teachers. The backslapper is an object of disgust. Selective reinforcement means that, when a major accomplishment is evident, major attention is given to the recognition of it. The routine, day-to-day, nice little things that people do merit no more than just the acceptance of what any person would be doing, and to make more of them is only to emphasize the fact that the supervisor himself has a poor level of perception of aspirations of the teaching–learning act (see Chapter 14).

A concluding note on support for creative action is the suggestion for a new position in the school organization. It is that of the *instructional auditor.* No one questions the advisability of having a financial auditor. Everybody knows that those in the business office are supposed to keep a record of receipts and to have a full accounting for their disbursements. The financial system is easy to check, yet we have specially trained and licensed auditors to do it. An instructional auditor might help focus the emphasis upon the kinds of inputs that are required for the instructional system and provide a better focus upon the outcomes that rightfully are expected. This would do much to keep emphasis on the product rather than on the process by which the products are achieved. A fair speculation is that teachers, if they knew the nature of the instructional auditing system, would be helpful in providing the evidence (which exists in abundance) to assure the supervisors, the administrators, and the supporting public that the purposes of the school as an institution are being achieved satisfactorily.

This chapter has been devoted to the people context of supervision. A program context of supervision is presented in Chapter 2. The merging of people and program purposes is the desired outcome of the many activities initiated by the person (supervisor) responsible for giving direction to the process of merging. If the merging is successful, there will be a high degree of harmony among the people and there will be satisfaction and success with the program. The remainder of the book deals with the design (model) most promising in merging these two contexts of supervision.

2

The Program Context of Supervision

A people context of supervision permits an examination of the humanistic elements which result in the various and vagarious natures of supervisory programs. People seldom function in isolation, however, either physically or psychologically. They operate as members of some environmental system. There needs, therefore, to be some framework or program which will identify the participants in a given system, establish functional patterns of action, and identify the processes necessary to select the appropriate purposes and to achieve the desired outcomes or products of that system. It is with these thoughts in mind that the development of a definition and program design for the study of supervision is presented in this chapter and applied in the remainder of the text.

AN HISTORICAL PERSPECTIVE

Historical backgrounds often are used as proper references for the discussions of contemporary issues. The chronology of supervision of instruction is found in the historical treatments of American education and the development of many important functions of the public schools. The present contexts for the study of supervision have roots in the earlier philosophies, theories, and practices of school organization and pedagogy. As there have been no exhaustive treatises published on the "History of Supervision," historical treatments of supervision must be found in the literature of administration specifically or of education generally.

Rather than a detailed chronology of developments in the history of supervision in American education, short summary statements of historical references and inferences are included in this chapter. The reader could go, with greater profit, to the publications of competent historians for complete backgrounds (see references 3, 4, 6). For the purposes of this chapter, historical data were drawn upon only to provide support for the development of the working definition and the program design for supervision.

The purpose at this point is to explore the relationship of the concepts of administration and supervision as they have developed in American schools over the past three centuries. The historical perspective is limited to the published definitions from several periods of our history. A study of the statements of concepts and definitions which appear in the literature, practically from the beginning of organized government in this country, presents some interesting views of the functions of supervision as they have been conceived from decade to decade and from century to century. There is little doubt that the first recorded definition, as well as the last, is concerned with the improvement of the lot of the citizens by providing an appropriate impact upon the younger generation. There is no clear-cut distinction from period to period insofar as either the personnel or the functions of supervision have been concerned. For practical purposes, the following four periods, each of which seems to contain some dominant and uniquely characteristic place and purpose of supervision, are suggested:

1. The period of *administrative inspection,* 1642–1875.
2. The period of *efficiency orientation,* 1876–1936.
3. The period of *cooperative group effort* in the improvement of teaching and learning, 1937–1959.
4. The period of *research orientation,* 1960 to the present time.

What historical periods are suggested by other authors?

In the belief that it would be profitable to identify and understand the significant characteristics of their relationships to the present, salient features of each period are identified.

The Period of Administrative Inspection, 1642–1875:
Observance of the physical plant, pupil control, and teaching process by inspection of laymen and professionals.

The first supervisory concepts and behaviors were characterized by inspection. This function, as in the case of the business management of schools, usually was carried out by laymen. When an educator became the supervisor or the director of instruction he was called the "inspector." This term still is in

How do judicial- and executive-type functions differ?

use in some areas but it, too, is passing out of the educational vocabulary both as a title and as a function. The concept of inspection or regulation, however, is still being identified by teachers and administrators as a function of supervision.[1] The functions of the "inspector" were more judicial than executive in character.

The early definitions of supervision clearly indicated that the major function of the supervisor was to make judgments about the teacher rather than about the teaching or the pupils' learning. Decisions were made on the basis of what the supervisor or inspector thought he saw. The nature of the remedy always seemed to be that of displacing or replacing the teacher. Among the many early definitions are found terms such as "taking into consideration," "order and decree," "inspect," "visitation and careful examination," "oversight," and "readjustment." Even though these words are taken out of context, they imply a rather stern and forbidding relationship between the supervisor and the supervised, or the inspector and the inspected. Many of the definitions imply that the chief remedy for a failing school system or classroom was that of replacing the teaching personnel.

Inspection was related largely to managing the school and meeting the requirements of the prescribed curriculum rather than to the improvement of instructional procedures. The records of the Governor of Massachusetts Bay Company (1642) indicate that each town's community leaders must force parents to be responsible for their children's learning. The City of Boston (1709) established a committee of inspectors to "visit ye School."

A few scattered definitions can be found which carry the implication that the function of supervision was beginning to be more than inspection for control purposes. A reference from as early as 1709 suggests that there was need for consultation and advisement with the teachers for the improvement of instruction. In 1835 a reference was made to the need for working with teachers from the mental health standpoint. While other such declarations can be found, the concept of supervision as an aid to the teacher was not well established until about 1920.

The Period of Efficiency Orientation, 1876–1936:

Pressurized influence on teaching procedures by experts who were efficiency oriented.

The impact of business practices and ethics upon education was strong. The visibility of rapid industrial development and the underlying management identifications made precision and efficiency the guiding stars of most public enterprises. The effects of these business and industrial orientations for

[1] J. Fred Overman, *Perceptions of the Role of the Instructional Supervisor in the State Department of Public Instruction,* unpublished doctoral dissertation (Madison: University of Wisconsin, 1968).

the schools are well defined both by Callahan and by Curti.[2]

Supervision during this period remained generally an inspectorial function which was related to the instructional program of the school. Administration continued to be concerned primarily with business management. The concepts of supervision and administration, however, were changing and the functions were expanding. In supervision emphases were being placed on the functions of aiding the teacher for the improvement of instruction while administration was developing into a more educationally inclusive position. The supervisor and the business manager became responsible to the chief administrator. In some communities, positions such as the two mentioned above remained as line offices, while in others they became staff offices. The position of business manager seemed to persist as a line office longer than the position of supervisor. This probably developed because, with the advent of the business manager position, the superintendent was considered as being primarily in charge of instruction. The supervisors, then, became responsible to the superintendent of schools when this position became so designated.

An additional situation requiring recognition is that there continued to be one business manager in a school system in contrast to an increasing number of supervisors. In a sense, the duality in administration was continuing with a business manager and a superintendent of instruction, but the nature of the dual relationships was changing as the concept of supervision evolved.

Who serves as the instructional leader in your school system?

The lay inspection of the schools gave way to professional inspection and, as this occurred, the nature of supervision assumed new characteristics. A full-time supervisory position meant time and advisement with teachers for the improvement of instruction that had been advocated but not realized in earlier decades. Practically every definition generated in this period includes the point that supervision exists for the purpose of the improvement of instruction.

The attitude of the supervisors toward the supervised eventually seemed to change. There was more use of the language that is current when talking about a friendly atmosphere, a helpful relationship, or a situation in which corrective measures are instituted with environmental conditions as well as personnel obligations being the objective. It is quite possible that those who were responsible for assuring the public about the quality of education became aware of the many environmental factors even though they had developed very few understandings and techniques for correcting them. During this period of warming relationships between the supervisor and the teacher, words are found such as "conference," "instruction," "advice," "improvement," "constructive," "influ-

[2] Raymond E. Callahan, *Education and the Cult of Efficiency* (Chicago: University of Chicago Press, 1962); and Merle Curti, *The Social Ideas of American Educators* (Paterson, N.J.: Pageant, 1959), pp. 203–260.

What effect did this have on supervisors?

ence," and "growth." Here, even though taken out of context, in our current literature those words carry meanings of more considerateness in the relationship between people. These terms gradually appeared in the definitions which have been extracted from the literature over a substantial period of time.

The mounting educational responsibilities of the schools during this period also gave impetus to the cooperative and coordinative aspects of administration and supervision. These concepts, however, were more apt to be found in the literature than in practice. The movement toward the lessening of autocratic relationships between the supervisor and the supervised led to the third period, namely, "cooperative group effort."

The Period of Cooperative Group Effort, 1937–1959:
Cooperative group effort constituted both means and ends in the change process.

The cooperative and coordinative aspects of school administration became more than theory during this period. While the research in group dynamics promoted the concepts of social processes, the "push" to make these theories of behavior operational was derived from the force of expediency in meeting community expectations. In this period, there is found the generous use of words such as "coordinating," "integrative," "creativity," "stimulation," and "democratic relationships." These words have been used often and appropriately in the definitions developed during this period. Toward the middle of the century, it was evident that a balance in school operations demanded that the business manager be responsible to, rather than coordinate with, the superintendent. The office then developed a title—for example, assistant superintendent for business affairs. Also, the multiplicity of administrative tasks made it essential that other services be treated similarly. This increasing number of tasks for the chief administrator grew out of the demands of district consolidations, increasing enrollments, teacher shortages, classroom shortages, bond issues, and additional pupil services. Enlarged schools and school systems, along with the shortage of adequately prepared teachers, also increased the need for supervision of instruction.

The inclusion of fine arts and extracurricular activities in the total curriculum was followed by an emphasis on foreign languages, mathematics, science, and guidance. This expansion of the curriculum created a need for still more supervisors. When fine arts and physical education also became a significant part of the curriculum a new aspect of supervision was created—namely, special-area supervision. The number of areas covered by these positions recently increased with the development of emphases on depth and quality instruction in all academic areas. There also is evidence indicating that the number of special-area supervisors has increased much more rapidly than has the number of general supervisors. This breadth in supervisory needs has made cooperation and coordination of paramount importance.

The increase in the total number of positions in both general and special-area supervision made cooperation and coordination essential. In the larger school systems it led to the designation of an assistant superintendent in charge of instruction. The functions of this position were to bring about cooperation and coordination in all phases of instruction. The general and special-area supervisors often became responsible to this officer. In small school systems without an assistant superintendent in charge of instruction, the general and special-area supervisors continued to be responsible to the superintendent. When some superintendents were unable to find the time to bring about cooperation and coordination within the supervisory staff, these responsibilities were allocated to a general supervisor or an assistant to the superintendent. This assistant has been designated by various titles, including "curriculum coordinator." In school systems where the total supervisory program is not coordinated in and by the central office, the expected benefits of supervision may be lost.

The Period of Research Orientation, 1960 to the Present:
The melding of personnel relationships and research attacks on the solution of problems in achieving instructional expectations.

The combination of technological advancements, competition with foreign nations in space research, and a public awakening to the necessity for financial contributions to intellectual enterprises are among the factors that have encouraged the development of an environment in which problems are solved more through study than negotiation. The operational aspects of many private and public organizations have been subjected to systematic study. School administration and, consequently, supervision are being studied with increasingly improved research procedures and professionally inspired vigor. The scrutiny of supervision has moved beyond the earlier head-counting type of surveys into more sophisticated efforts to determine the nature of and reason for the interrelationships among persons and situations.

Today emphasis is placed on the *total* process in school administration, which includes all the responsibilities involved in the school operation. Because of the increasing number of these responsibilities, the chief administrator has become concerned largely with decision-making, including the allocation of tasks to the various offices within the system.

Identify research reports which illustrate this trend.

The period of research orientation in the solution of interpersonal and intersituational problems as well as the movement toward the development of improved organizational operations have had an attendant use of characteristic words and expressions. Some of these terms are "role perceptions," "situational factors," "instrumentation for data collection," "empirical study," "experimental and control factors," and "hypothesizing." Added to these expressions might be an array of more technical terms originating in the literature of statistics and experimental design. Almost any professional publication will yield evidence of the general interest in, and respect for, the processes which make the current period one of research orientation.

An Emerging New Period for the 1970's?

An exciting approach to supervision and administration is now emerging which may eventually evolve into an identifiable new period. Increasing demands for accountability in terms of achievement of purposes and the resultant products of supervision along with depreciation of the bureaucratic concept previously applied to educational systems created a desire to seek new methods for accomplishing program and system goals. Educators again have turned to business and industry for guidance in the management of systems. A new period in the changing concepts of supervision may well be called the "period of system analysis."

A word of caution might be appropriate regarding the designation of a title for this new period now appearing on the horizon. Many of the salient features of the "period of research orientation" as identified in the previous section would seem appropriate in identifying a "period of system analysis." Some words commonly used in a system analysis approach to supervision include "input," "output," "control," "feedback," "evaluation," "planning," "budgeting," and "analysis." Many of the terms associated with the systems approach to supervision are found to be characteristic of the current period. The possibility exists, therefore, that this "new" concept for the study of supervision may be only an extension of the "period of research orientation" with more emphasis on *one* process—that of analysis—and on a more practical method for viewing the patterns of and the participants in educational systems.

The definitions of administration and supervision through many decades show parallel changes. These similarities give credence to the point of view that the two functional areas are highly integrated, or rather, that each is a part of the other.

Most people in education are aware that administration during the past fifty to seventy-five years has assumed increased importance not only in the minds of professionals but also in the minds of the supporting laymen. Because the definitions of administration have characterized the definitions of supervision, the inference can be drawn readily that administration and supervision have been closely allied with respect both to purposes and processes.

Administrators and supervisors always have been expected to make judgments, which, in the main, have been conditioned and determined by the particular value pattern(s) possessed by those who make them. The more closely administrators and supervisors are allied in their functional responsibilities, the greater the probability that both will base their judgments on similar value patterns. The study of the definitions of administration and supervision reveals the similarity of positions, purposes, processes, and products. It seems to follow, then, that the incumbent of each office probably would be choosing professional behaviors in highly comparable contexts of responsibilities, expectations, value patterns, and sources of satisfaction.

A POINT OF VIEW

Name authors of the past two decades who have typed patterns of supervisory behavior.

Definition helps in the identification of the characteristics of a particular phenomenon. Students and writers in the field of supervision have dealt both with definitions and with types of supervision. The designation of types tends to identify particular concepts of supervision. A particular concept, however, carrying a descriptive label, is not as discrete in actuality as the "simple life" devotee might wish. The best that can be said of categorization is that it takes the most outstanding or dominant characteristics which constitute the center of a cluster of characteristics called, as a totality, a "category."

The author of a definition may ask other competent professionals to place his definition of supervision into one or more categories. It would be revealing for a person with a basic commitment to democratic behaviors to discover that his definitions of supervision give other people the notion of autocracy because of the amount and application of authority in one or the other or both. The need for the use of authority is wisely and properly found in democratic supervision. The important point here is that the use of authority may not be the issue but rather the capacity of the stated definition to communicate the author's position and intent. The desirability of developing definitions as cues to concepts and probable behaviors is clear. The care with which such statements should be developed cannot be overemphasized.

One caution must be offered. In an attempt to develop a program around a working definition, any outsider's classification of concepts should be used only as a suggestion for the selection of behaviors. This would prevent making a statement of categories restrictive in purpose when it should serve for studying the various functions and techniques of supervision. Consistency may be achieved through the study of a working definition of supervision by suggesting a pattern for a custom-built supervisory program. Statements of categories of supervision are helpful in the analysis of plans and functions but are of questionable value when used as prescriptive guidelines for the choice of behaviors, and consequently have not been presented here. The reader, rather, is directed to various sources if he believes the categorization to be helpful.

The literature contains so many definitions of supervision that have accumulated through history that the value of collecting them may be questioned. Each one, however, does bear some element of uniqueness. In all probability, the defense for so many different statements is that each author develops one for the purpose of giving his own presentation a focal point that will lead to consistency and completeness of treatment. Similarly, the working definition used in this volume is particularly well suited to the approach presented.

While the given definition may be in sharp contrast to some present-day practices, it is firmly grounded in the democratic philosophy. A study of the definitions of administration and supervision is one method of showing the validity of the idea that supervision is an integral part of administration even though it has lost the clarity of well-defined, functional relationships.

What is your definition of supervision?

Supervision in the context of the given definition cannot be considered a recent development either in theory or in practice. It developed through many decades in an evolutionary manner. The past two decades, however, have imposed changes that are more revolutionary. Recent changes, or at least the social stresses and incentives that produce change, demonstrate how environmental pressures bring about the redeployment of personnel, a juggling of staff functions, and the evolvement of new definitions of position. Such changes, based more on decision by expediency than advanced planning, are the result of exploding numbers of pupils and employed personnel, expanding curricula, multiplication of educational or school services, the complicated patterns of human relationships, and the financial concerns associated with these conditions.

This particular definition may be accepted as a *working definition* and each reader should retain an awareness that he is invited to develop his own definition of supervision. Thus, the following should serve as a catalytic agent in the development of a consistent and comprehensive supervisory program:

Supervision is that phase of school administration which focuses primarily upon the achievement of the appropriate instructional expectations of educational systems.

Those who choose to view administration and supervision as discrete and coordinate entities rather than as a unified service will find the above definition unacceptable. Those, however, who view administration and supervision as related areas of educational systems may use it as a starting point for reviewing functional relationships from the standpoint of historical development, operational assumptions, and behavioral characteristics.

The purpose of defining any term is that of giving clarity and precision to its meaning. Any definition can be expanded, interpreted, and reworded until it takes on the meaning of other definitions that initially may appear to be quite different. The above definition is no exception to treatment of this nature. It is presented with the particular selection of words which facilitates an exploration of the assumption that administration and supervision exist in a close relationship within a single area of educational functions. The definition is based upon three assumptions:

1. Supervision is a phase of administration.
2. Supervision is concerned with the appropriateness of instructional expectations.
3. Supervision is that phase of administration which has particular pertinence for the expectations (products) of educational systems.

These assumptions are revealed in chronological order in the statement of the definition and involve only those functional aspects concerned with the basic relationships of administration and supervision. The assumptions dealing only with supervision will be presented in detail in Chapter 3.

A PROGRAM DESIGN

The definition developed for the purpose of this text is:

Supervision is that phase of school administration which focuses primarily upon the achievement of the appropriate instructional expectations of educational systems.

This definition suggests a structure for supervision with its major categories to which attention will be given in this text. An examination of the implications of this definition for a program context of supervision leads to the selection of five major categories of study for designing, implementing, and evaluating a well-rounded program of supervision of instruction. These categories are *purposes, patterns, participants, processes,* and *products,* as shown in Figure 2.1.

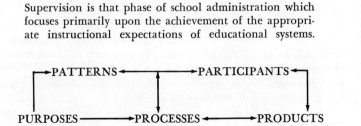

Supervision is that phase of school administration which focuses primarily upon the achievement of the appropriate instructional expectations of educational systems.

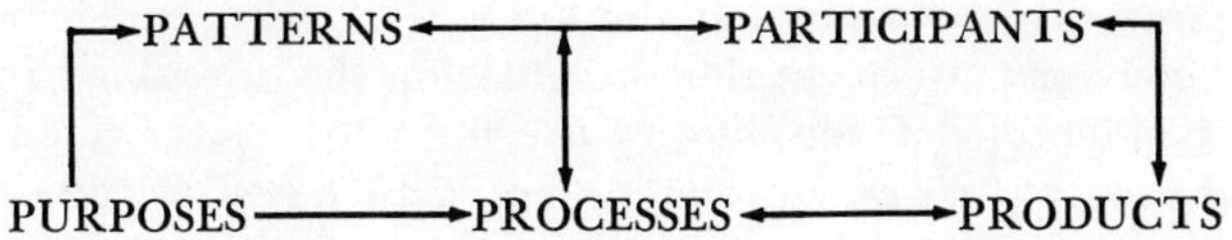

FIGURE 2.1
Major Categories for Study of Supervision

Unusual hazards may be invited by establishing a given number of parts or categories of a total organized activity and declaring that these operate in a fixed relationship. Some venturesomeness, however, is appropriate in suggesting a flow of attention. Therefore, discussion of a total operation proceeds with precision to the exclusion of its parts. The suggestion follows that the planning efforts directed to the five major categories move from *purposes,* to *patterns,* to *participants,* to *processes,* to *products.* As indicated in Figure 2.1, however, a duo-directional relationship exists between and among the categories, thereby suggesting that they cannot be treated as mutually exclusive in a program for the supervision of instruction. These categories are used for the convenience of dividing the contents of this book into five parts, each part dealing with those aspects of supervisory concern which are best related to that particular category. For those who may be uneasy about the interrelationships of the five categories, it is suggested that a glance at the model concluding this chapter might be reassuring with respect to the authors' concern with those interrelationships existing in a well-planned, well-designed program of supervision.

Purposes of Supervision

Attention now turns to a more complete consideration of these five categories, the first of which is *purpose.* Most people have a purpose or many purposes which give direction to the particular behaviors characteristic of their day-to-day and year-to-year activities. Purposes are expected to give consistency to behaviors. Any purpose is established in an environment of purposes and can be either antagonistic or supportive of the purposes of others.

In planning any particular phase of a program for achieving the appropriate instructional expectations, no person can ignore the relationship of his purposes to those already attributed by society as the reason for the establishment of educational systems. In this sense, then, any agent of a community responsible for directing a part or all of the educational system must select his purposes in conformity with or in relationship to the community's overall social purposes.

Similarly, the selected purposes of supervision must harmonize with the goals of the controlling agent. As supervision is considered a phase of school administration, these purposes must be appropriate to those of the administrative service of the educational system. Each phase of the educational system must have its unique purposes, but these must have referent compatibilities. The consistency of the interrelationships of purposes may be assured if the analytic attack may be called the behavior pattern. In this presentation the behavior pattern will be identified as the *action pattern.*

The action pattern proposed here is anchored to the stated definition and to the implementation of the purposes of supervision because purposes constitute the basic guidelines for developing all aspects of the program. This action pattern involves the developmental steps of identifying and stating *assumptions, principles, objectives, criteria,* and *procedures.* These steps are presented in graphic form in Figure 2.2.

The identification and definition of the *assumptions* from which other statements stem constitute the basic ingredients for the individual as he declares, analyzes, and plans. The assumptions may constitute the accumulation of traditions, beliefs, prejudices, and aspects of the personality which exert a profound influence upon behavior. It must be recognized, however, that the identification of one's own assumptions, regardless of the purposes for which they are to be used, is not easily accomplished. The reason for this difficulty, perhaps, is that effective skills of introspection often are not fully de-

Utilize the action pattern in defining and implementing one of the purposes of supervision.

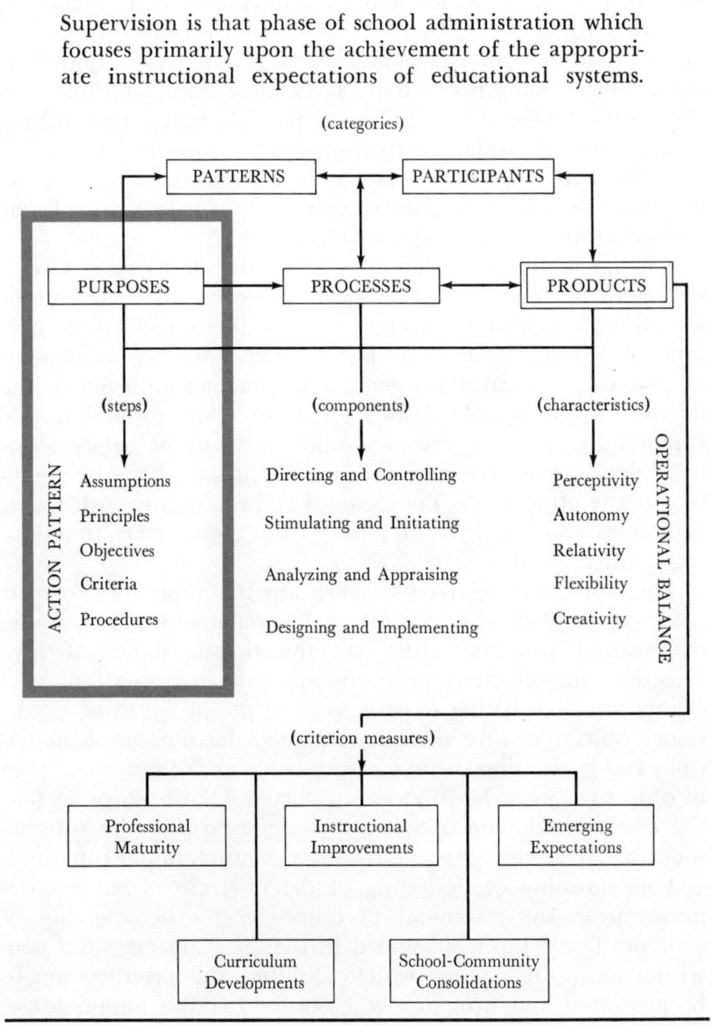

***FIGURE 2.2* Sequential Steps in the Action Pattern for Defining and Implementing the Purposes of Supervision**

veloped. There are few external measures which can be used to discover what only introspection can achieve.

This wholesome respect for assumptions has led to a statement of the assumptions used by the authors in developing the descriptions, discussions, plans, and evaluative suggestions appearing in this text. These assumptions are presented in Chapter 3. The emphasis persists, nevertheless, that each person or group of persons must develop his or their own set of assumptions (see Chapter 3). Those given here are not prescribed for the use of others but presented for the purpose of achieving consistency within this total presentation. The establishment of assumptions should be an integral part of the development of a program of supervision.

A scrutiny of a personal list of assumptions should serve the need for determining the number and character of the *principles* which are to be developed (see Chapter 3). Here again the principles must be consistent with the basic assumptions or they are most likely to be inoperative in the planning and execution of a program involving the selection of behaviors and the interrelationships of people. As assumptions are better when supported by facts, they may "graduate" to the status of principles. It is quite possible that a person may be able to cast aside his assumptions at some point and restate them in terms of principles. It is not necessary, however, to pursue this development of assumptions into principles as a responsibility of the major enterprise.

Principles, in turn, should lead to the development of a statement of *objectives*. The term "objective" is used here as something much more specific than the larger concept of purpose. Principles serve somewhat the same purpose as policies in that each constitutes a general statement supported in the degree of fact required and gives direction to action (see Chapter 3). The objectives should serve in the selection of more detailed behaviors on the part of the supervisor or operative at any other level. They should be in harmony with stated principles and should contribute to the appropriate functioning of the enterprise.

List some supervisory and educational objectives which clearly identify the separate but supportive functions.

The objectives referred to here are the supervisory objectives rather than the general and specific objectives of the educational program. Just as educational objectives give direction to the selection, organization, presentation, and evaluation of learning experiences for pupils, so must supervisory objectives give direction to the selection, implementation, and evaluation of supervisory behaviors. These two types of objectives must be in close supportive relationships so that the educational objectives may be achieved and the supervisory objectives may serve the appropriate directional functions.

The planning or designing of the program of supervision moves from the statement of objectives to the selection of *criteria*. The criteria subsumed in the criterion measures constitute the point against which activities and products are to be measured and provide the bases for making judgments.

With the establishment of interlocking relationships between assumptions, principles, objectives, and criteria, the planners may move to the *procedures* of supervision (see Chapter 3). They then may proceed more specifically to the selection of those behaviors which will constitute the program of supervision.

These steps which have been suggested for implementing purposes at least through the planning stage constitute an *action pattern* for a program of supervision. In fact, the action pattern can be used appropriately for each of the five major categories of supervision as separate and independent entities. Such use of the action pattern can be followed productively even though its use here has been that of application to those behaviors more closely related to the declaration of purpose because this is the foundation upon which a design for a supervisory program is developed.

Patterns and Participants of Supervision

The development of a design for a program of supervision moves from a consideration of purposes to the *patterns* and *participants* so that the purposes as declared can be implemented. The patterns and participants of supervision as related to the five categories of study are shown in Figure 2.3.

The definition indicates that supervision is a phase of school administration. On the basis of the more common structural patterns, the question immediately is raised as to whether the supervisor shall occupy a line or a staff position in the school system. Most students of structural patterns acknowledge that line and staff positions cannot be defined without some overlapping of functions or areas of activity. Perhaps the more important point to be made here is that supervision in the diagrammatic sense "counts down" from the administration of the school rather than "extends up" from the instructional areas of school service (see Chapters 5 and 6).

Supervision, more specifically, might be considered that phase of school administration which deals with the quality control of instructional service. In this context, supervision can be identified as a subsystem providing a specified service in the educational system.[3] The functional planning, for instance, is an important task of administration. It deals with instructional as well as non-instructional service. Planning may be directed toward the selection of instructional materials, toward building site selection, or toward the development of accounting procedures. Under the definition of supervision, however, it ought to be impossible for a superintendent of schools to deploy the time and efforts of the supervisory staff to deal more with the managerial functions of administration than with the instructional aspects of the school. Even though

[3] Kathryn V. Feyereisen, A. John Fiorino, and Arlene T. Nowak, *Supervision and Curriculum Renewal: A Systems Approach* (New York: Appleton-Century-Crofts, 1970), p. 30.

supervision is assigned quite specific tasks within the area of administration, it must be primarily an instruction-focused service within the total responsibilities of administration. Furthermore, supervision should not be considered a specialized type of service that can be rendered better by an agency unrelated fiscally or legally to the local school organization.

Are the titles appropriate to the tasks of the position incumbent in your school system?

The patterns of supervisory functions are related not only to the position titles within the educational system but also to those persons who will achieve or have achieved such titles. The place of supervisory function, therefore, is related to the incumbents of such positions as well as to the positions. In this instance place is irrevocably attached to the concept of position and identifies the participants in the fulfillment of the functions.

The identification of the *patterns* in the total school organi-

Supervision is that phase of school administration which focuses primarily upon the achievement of the appropriate instructional expectations of educational systems.

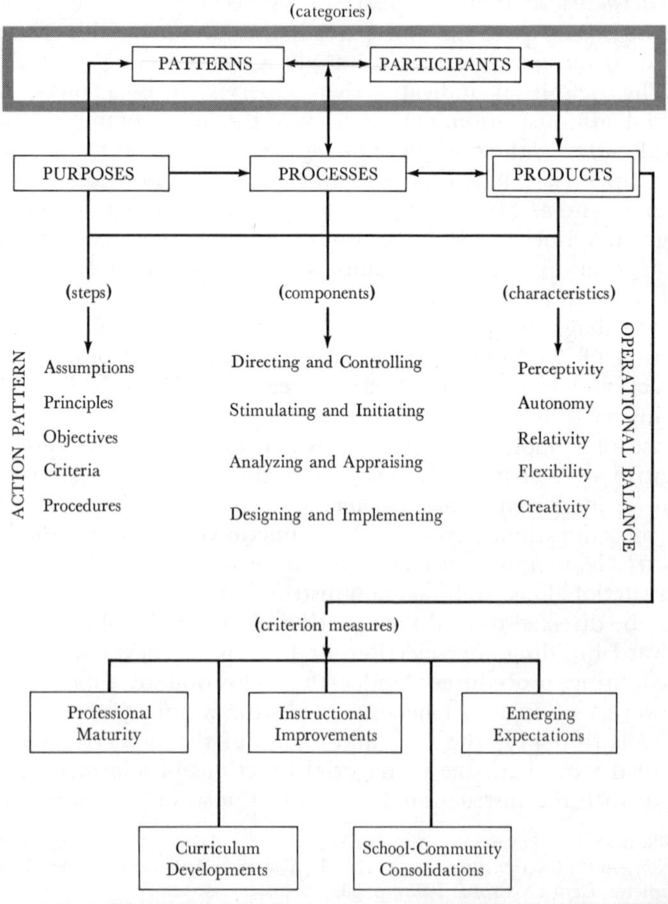

***FIGURE 2.3* Patterns and the Participants for the Programs of Supervision**

zation in which the *purposes* of supervision shall be achieved leads directly to a concern for the identification of the *participants* in the supervisory activities (see Figure 2.3). Contrary to the popular notion that supervision involves primarily classroom visitation, the total of the functions of supervision constitutes a much broader array of activities. As so often is true in staffing both public and private enterprises, there seems to be undue emphasis upon those aspects of the responsibility which result in overt activity and are subjected to the recognition and observation of others. It is quite conceivable that administrative and supervisory functions which are easily exposed to view are of no greater significance than some appropriate reflective activities which cannot be put in the showcase. A more careful delineation of the differences in these types of behaviors and performances will be considered in the chapters dealing with the processes of supervision (see Chapters 13–16).

All members of the system probably could be credited with performing some supervisory functions regardless of the specificity of the definition of supervision. It is doubtful that many of them would devote an equal percentage of time to these functions. It becomes a matter of identifying the functions appropriately allocated to the supervisory program and of associating with these functions the persons and their titles which have been established in the particular school system. The tendency to change the names of position titles in the program, as from supervisor to consultant, too often has not been accompanied by a comparable change in the purposes and functions of either the offices or the incumbents. The mere change of title does nothing other than change the designation of the position. If accompanied by appropriate changes in function, the change in title may be justified. On the other hand, a change of title might be appropriate in order that the title may represent more nearly the functional responsibilities of that position.

The identification of the *participants* in the functions of supervision leads immediately to a query regarding the appropriateness of the numbers of such offices and officers in school systems of various sizes. The guiding principle in determining the appropriate numbers of supervisory staff members is that the functional expectations of the program must be in harmony with the number of incumbents of positions who are expected to fulfill the tasks as designed for a particular educational system (see Chapters 9–11).

Processes of Supervision

The purposes of supervision, when appropriately selected, lead to the identification of the location of supervision in the administrative design and to the identification of the types and numbers of persons who should participate in the program. Assuming that the planning of the supervisory program has included these requirements, attention can be turned to the matter of the *processes* involved. The processes are shown in their relationships to the other categories of supervision in Figure 2.4.

The processes of supervision have constituted the central focus of most of the literature in the field. This, perhaps, is understandable because there is a tendency for any functionnaire to seek whatever help is available in achieving the purposes of his position by selecting the appropriate procedures (see Chapters 13–16). Consequently, many of the textbooks in supervision have dealt almost exclusively with specific techniques. The present authors attempt to hold consistently to the idea that the whole program of supervision should be custom-built for each individual educational system. This means that at no point should the authors dictate the specific

FIGURE 2.4* *Components of the Processes of Supervision

Supervision is that phase of school administration which focuses primarily upon the achievement of the appropriate instructional expectations of educational systems.

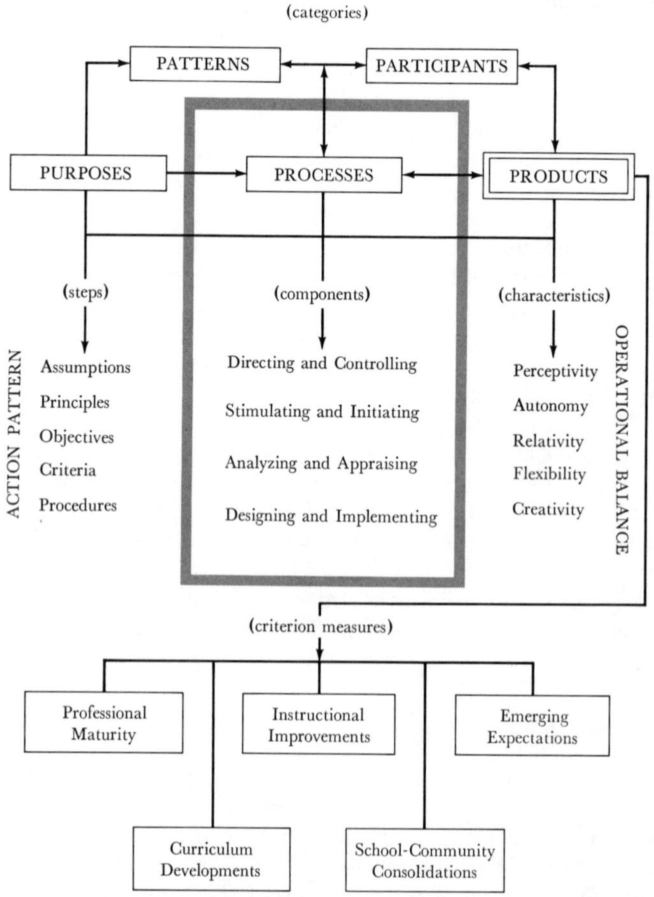

behaviors that should characterize supervision. They accept responsibility, however, for offering suggestions as to how the processes of supervision might be more effectively chosen and implemented. One of the best ways to achieve the wise and independent selection of processes is to assume an environment for planning the proper relationships between the purposes, the patterns, and the participants.

Reference again should be made to Figure 2.2, which indicates that the order of planning or designing a supervisory program starts with purposes. Such a beginning is sound from the standpoint of the procedural needs for ordering the design of a program. In the processes of supervision, however, there is a very direct relationship between the purposes, the processes, and, as will be discussed later, the products. As the figures in this chapter illustrate, there also are interrelationships among the processes and the patterns and participants.

Just as supervision may be explored by categories, so may the processes be scrutinized by their component parts. These parts are closely related to the component parts of administration. The boundaries of autonomy and authority in the case of supervision, however, may be indicated in such a way that a distinction is made between supervisory and administrative functions. The purposes of the discussion as presented here seem to be served better by the selection of four component parts of process, each a distinct aspect of school administration. Thus, it is possible to consider the processes within the discussion of each component part. These components, as indicated in Figure 2.4, are *directing* and *controlling, stimulating* and *initiating, analyzing* and *appraising,* and *designing* and *implementing.*

The relationships between and among the pairs of words designating the components and what is involved in each component will be discussed in Part IV. It is emphasized at this point that the processes of supervision as indicated here, in and among the four component parts, are related to a total design of a program of supervision rather than to the selection of the behaviors for or by an individual supervisor.

Identify the components most often used by your "supervisor."

An appropriate designation of function could be made by "specialization within the specialization" of supervision. This would mean that some supervisors might be more concerned with and more adept in the processes of analyzing and appraising. Those who are to pursue this specialized function with confidence and competence would require specific training in the areas of psychology, measurement, and statistics. On the other hand, other members of the supervisory staff might be more capable in those aspects of process which are more closely related to the stimulating and initiating of activity on the part of individuals in a group enterprise. Thus, the components of the processes of supervision may indicate a team enterprise. The administrative organization of an educational system suggests a team effort in that, under the superintendent's direction, some personnel may be concerned with business management of the system, some with the physical facilities, and others with the instructional program, as is the case for those who carry the designation of supervisor. Just as there is an *action pattern* for developing the design of a supervisory program, there is a directional consideration in the concern for the total of the processes of supervision. This concern is expressed in terms of those characteristics which imply *operational balance.*

The items of concern in establishing the operational balance of a supervisory program are what might be called the characteristics of the behaviors of the participants involved in carrying out one or more of the components of process (see Chapter 12). These characteristics were selected because of their appropriateness for maintaining balance in the multifarious tasks of the supervisory processes. They are *perceptiv-*

Supervision is that phase of school administration which focuses primarily upon the achievement of the appropriate instructional expectations of educational systems.

FIGURE 2.5 Operational Balance in the Processes of Supervision

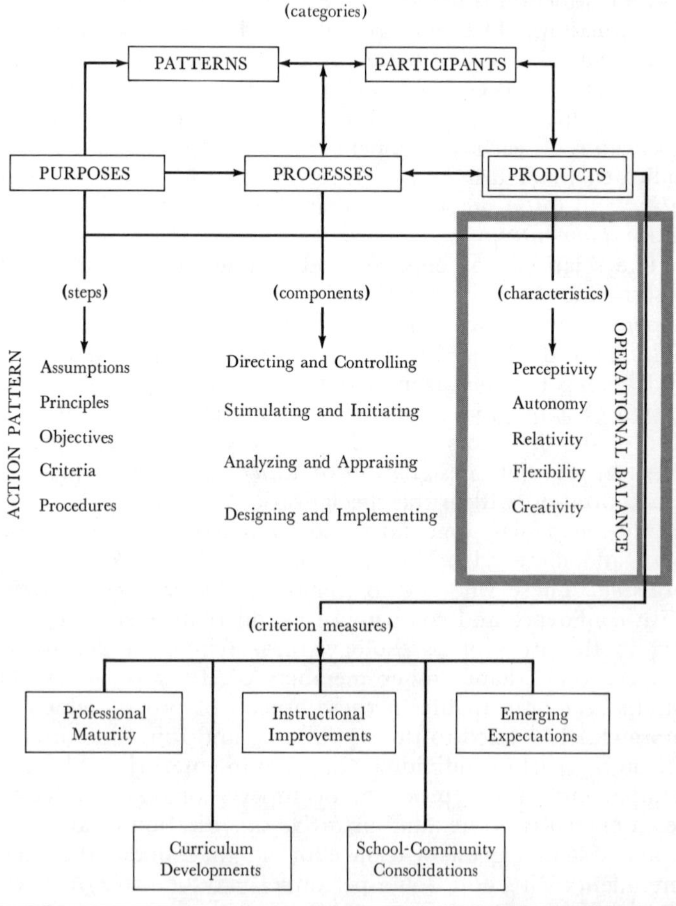

ity, autonomy, relativity, flexibility, and *creativity,* as shown in Figure 2.5.

A list of characteristics of an operation may be developed but usually it is recognized that any one characteristic cannot be dominant for all of the behaviors. So it is with this list of characteristics. Each would assist in establishing an operational balance in the processes of supervision. Each characteristic stands in a definable relationship to all the components of process and, in turn, carries a different weight in influencing the behaviors involved in achieving any component or any combination of components at any particular time. A more detailed discussion of the purposes and an application of these characteristics constituting the operational balance are presented in Part IV.

Products of Supervision

The development of a statement of purposes, patterns, participants, and processes in the design of a supervisory program must have a focal point or concluding state. This focal point is designated appropriately as *products.* The products are: professional maturity, curriculum developments, instructional improvements, school–community consolidations, and emerging expectations. The products and the relation of the products to the other categories of supervision are shown in Figure 2.6.

A distinction too often omitted in the literature of supervision is that the products of the supervisory program are not differentiated clearly from the products of the instructional program. Some may hold, and rightly so, that the only end product of the whole educational system is to be found in pupil development. This need not be argued, but there remains the possibility that those holding the one-product notion may use it as a vehicle for evading an evaluation of *all* the expected products of the supervisory program. It is possible to identify the anticipated products of supervision just as it is possible to develop a statement of the purposes and the processes of supervision (see Chapters 18–22). Any inclination or persistence in evaluating supervision and/or administration in terms of the overall product of the school—namely, the education of youth—can result in an overt attempt to escape the responsibility of evaluating the totality of either the supervisory or administrative service.

What challenge does this present to administrators and supervisors?

Among these five areas of products there are two that are primarily related to instruction. These are *curriculum developments* and *instructional improvements.* This, of course, requires that any evaluation concerned with the products of supervision be heavily weighted in the direction of the improvement of the instructional program. At the same time, it should be recognized that two of the areas of products deal with the professional maturity of all staff members and with the relationship between the school and the community.

Professional maturity ranges beyond the specific teaching skills of the staff member. It suggests an opportunity for a concern for the working conditions and the welfare provision for members of the staff. This maturity is supportive of quality in the curriculum and instructional methods, which in turn relates to the major purpose of the school, the education of youth. It deserves, however, some consideration apart from the direct relationship to the instructional program and is given this consideration in Chapter 18. Professional workers in any field are entitled to some concern for themselves as persons and should not have this concern limited to their performance in working toward the declared and expected outcomes of the educational system.

The concern for relationships between the school and the community is referred to as *school–community consolidations.*

Supervision is that phase of school administration which focuses primarily upon the achievement of the appropriate instructional expectations of educational systems.

FIGURE 2.6* *Products of Supervision

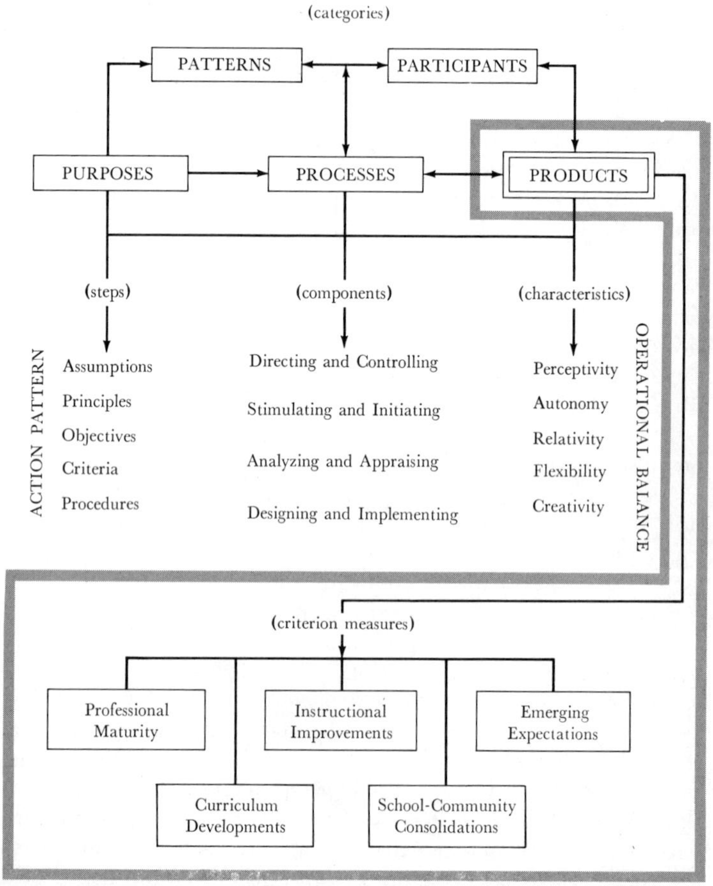

The term "consolidation" is intended to carry a meaning for supervision that goes beyond the meaning of the term "public relations." Supervisors seek to increase the extent to which a school and a supporting community can achieve common purposes and common understandings in the process of education, as well as the ways in which the schools, parents, and other interests in the community can be coordinated and consolidated into a combined effort for the development of youth (see Chapter 21).

The fifth supervisory product, *emerging expectations,* presents an opportunity to invite each school system to declare that some member or members of its staff shall be responsible for studying the social horizon. This study, insofar as it is humanly possible, should anticipate the demands that may be made upon the school at some time in the future (see Chapter 22).

Each of these products of supervision is presented in detail in Part V. Just as operational balance was emphasized in the selection and execution of the processes of supervision, so there must be breadth and balance in the identification of their products. The point of emphasis here is that both supervision and its results must be subjected to evaluation in terms of the areas of products that can properly be allocated as functions of supervision. Any evaluation of these products must be in terms of the purposes of the supervisory program as established at the time the program was designed. The total design for the program of supervision is presented in Figure 2.7. It is here that all the various parts of the supervisory program discussed above are assembled into one design, with the optimum relationships indicated by the various line arrangements, directive arrows, and terminology.

A chronological study of the definitions of supervision and administration within their total context indicates that (1) definition of function precedes practice; (2) in the process of change, wide variations exist in the perceptions of the functions; and (3) throughout the history of American education, supervision has never been divorced from administration. This review, then, gives rise to the following conclusions about the relationships of administration and supervision:

1. Supervision is a phase of administration.
2. There is a dichotomy of function in the administration and supervision of educational systems.
3. There are known gray or overlapping areas in the categorization of the two functions.

Contemporary definitions of supervision, as stated at the outset, have come about by evolution. Greater change appears to have taken place in the second quarter of this century because of the pressures of the expediencies of modern times. Although definitions facilitate the analysis of phenomena and the communication of ideas, they should not be permitted to displace the utility of assumptions, principles, objectives, and criteria. They must be used as catalytic agents in program design. The uniqueness of a definition is found not in its differences from other definitions, but rather in its stimulation of clarity in thought and statement. The authors' definition, in addition, has dictated the identification of purposes, patterns, participants, processes, and products in a design for the supervision of instruction.

Each of the remaining chapters of this book deals with some specific segment of this total design of supervision which can be identified in the model, Figure 2.7. It is hoped that the model itself will be the object of frequent reference as the reader studies the specific elements in this particular design. The purpose of frequent reference to this model is to keep each of the specific segments of supervision in its proper place with respect to the other segments. In other words, the

FIGURE 2.7 A Design for a Program of Supervision of Instruction

Supervision is that phase of school administration which focuses primarily upon the achievement of the appropriate instructional expectations of educational systems.

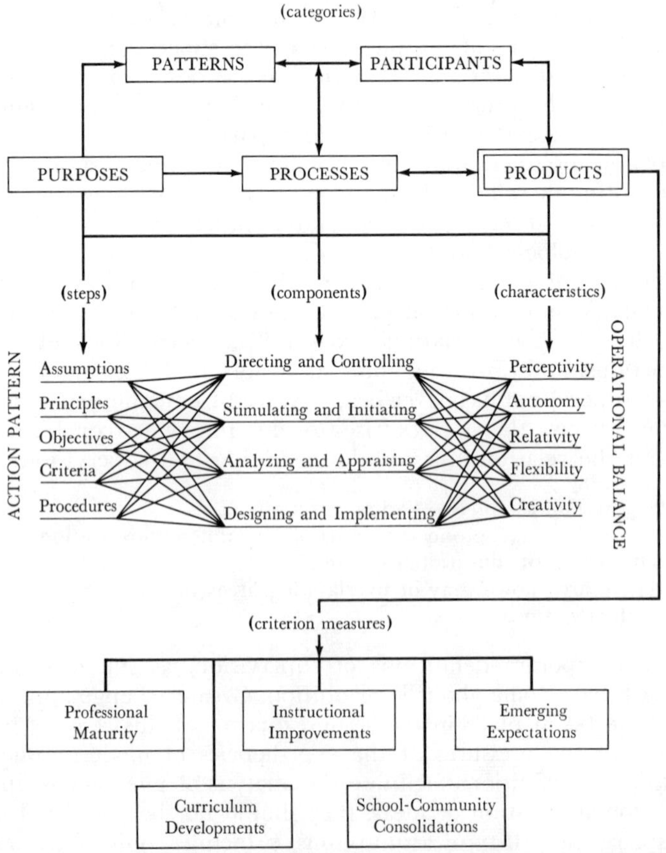

characteristic of relativity should be operating on the part of the reader as he attempts to achieve the interrelationships of the various parts of a custom-built program of supervision of instruction for an educational system. The remaining chapters constitute the test of quality and uniqueness of the working definition:

Supervision is that phase of school administration which focuses primarily upon the achievement of the appropriate instructional expectations of educational systems.

SELECTED REFERENCES

1. Ayer, Fred C., *Fundamentals of Instructional Supervision.* New York: Harper & Row, 1954.
2. Bartky, John, *Supervision as Human Relations.* New York: Heath, 1953.
3. Button, Warren, "A History of Supervision in the Public Schools, 1870–1950," unpublished doctoral dissertation. St. Louis: Washington University, 1961.
4. Butts, R. Freeman and Lawrence A. Cremin, *A History of Education in American Culture.* New York: Holt, Rinehart and Winston, 1953.
5. Callahan, Raymond E., *Education and the Cult of Efficiency.* Chicago: University of Chicago Press, 1962.
6. Campbell, Ronald F., Luvern L. Cunningham, and Roderick F. McPhee, *The Organization and Control of American Schools.* Columbus, Ohio: Charles E. Merrill, 1965.
7. Cremin, Lawrence A., *The Transformation of the School: Progressivism in American Education, 1876–1957.* New York: Knopf, 1961.
8. Curti, Merle, *The Social Ideas of American Educators.* Paterson, N.J.: Pageant, 1959. Pp. 203–260.
9. Deutsch, Morton and Robert M. Krauss, *Theories in Social Psychology.* New York: Basic Books, Inc., 1965.
10. Eye, Glen G. and Lanore A. Netzer, *School Administrators and Instruction: A Guide to Self Appraisal.* Boston: Allyn & Bacon, 1969.
11. Feyereisen, Kathryn V., A. John Fiorino, and Arlene T. Nowak, *Supervision and Curriculum Renewal: A Systems Approach.* New York: Appleton-Century-Crofts, 1970.
12. Johnson, Richard A., Fremont E. Kast, and James E. Rosenzweig, *The Theory and Management of Systems.* New York: McGraw-Hill, 1967.
13. Knezevich, Stephen J., *Administration of Public Education.* 2nd ed., New York: Harper & Row, 1969.
14. Leeper, Robert R. (ed.), *Role of Supervisor and Curriculum Director in a Climate of Change.* Washington, D.C.: Association for Supervision and Curriculum Development, National Education Association, 1965.
15. Lucio, William H. and John D. McNeil, *Supervision: A Synthesis of Thought and Action.* New York: McGraw-Hill, 1969, 2nd ed.

16. Miller, Van, *The Public Administration of American School Systems.* New York: Macmillan, 1965.
17. Netzer, Lanore A., Glen G. Eye, Ardelle Graef, Robert D. Krey, and J. Fred Overman, *Interdisciplinary Foundations of Supervision.* Boston: Allyn & Bacon, 1970. Chapter I.
18. Overman, J. Fred, "Perceptions of the Role of the Instructional Supervisor in the State Department of Public Instruction," unpublished doctoral dissertation. Madison: University of Wisconsin, 1968.
19. Tuttle, Frederick, "The Theory of Supervision of Instruction, 1875–1920," unpublished doctoral dissertation. Yale University, 1942.
20. Wilson, L. Craig, T. Madison Byar, Arthur S. Shapiro, and Shirley H. Schell, *Sociology of Supervision.* Boston: Allyn & Bacon, 1969.

3

The Action Pattern for the Development of a Theory

Philosophizing and theorizing about the functions and practices of supervision appear far removed from the "touch-and-go" situations which require immediate decisions on the choice of postures and behaviors. It is easy to claim that no two situations are alike and that the responsible leader must be alert and "fast on his feet" if he is to meet the requirements of his position with firmness and finesse. After successfully meeting increasing numbers of critical challenges, a leader develops a sense of confidence and evidence of his skill to perform with increasing consistency. Proficiency improves with experience, but it must be thoughtful experience where cognitive behaviors are involved. Thoughtful experience will lead away from consistency in the form of routinized behavior and toward consistency in the form of methodological attack on problems. Consistency becomes the result not of averaging experiences but of a series of successful and varied experiences. These experiences, whether or not verbalized, constitute the theoretical bases of behavioral choices. Thus, theory is inherent in or an integral part of supervisory planning and performance.

There are many different school situations, many different types of supervisors, and many varied supervisory practices. Variations in practice prove neither that supervision is lacking in theory nor that theory would result in more universal approaches to supervision for the various school situations. Speculations about the variations in practice occur primarily

What is the function of theory?

because of the lack of a common theory for supervision. A theory, even though held in common, will in all probability lead supervisors to widely divergent practices in particular school situations. On the other hand, it should be recognized that a genuine comparison of the differing supervisory practices, an analysis of one or more of them, and the process of planning for improvement would immediately become dependent upon sound theory.

Many current practices probably developed initially out of an alert professional worker's need for arriving at immediate decisions which would be palatable to his colleagues and the supporting public. This is called decision by expediency. Expediency *per se* is not necessarily bad. It has a potential weakness because it is not anchored in theory, and, lacking that anchor, it could easily lead to situations in which the practice should not have characterized the post and could not be called sound practice. On the other hand, many intelligent supervisors who have proved their success through years of identifiable accomplishments might be unable to verbalize on the theory underlying the success of their supervisory practices. Paradoxical as it may appear, theory can exist and lead to the selection of excellent behaviors even though the person who is acting upon the theory may be unable either to identify or describe it.

Theory has an important function in the evaluation of current practices and, more importantly, in the development of new and better practices. Theory evolves from, or crystallizes the verbalization of, the basic assumptions, principles, observations, and notions that are held about a particular type of phenomenon or area of activity. When these are collated in an orderly manner so that they constitute a constellation of supporting ideas and evidence, the theory is identified. On the basis of this theory, a model can be developed which will illustrate the theoretical concepts. This allows the practitioner not only a verbalized organization of his ideas but also a design for his plan of action. The popular aversion to acknowledged theorizing probably stems from the practical inabilities for and antipathy to organizing and verbalizing ideas rather than from any illusiveness or magical nature of theories. It may be that contact with theory is avoided because, over the years, it has been the basis for developing a pseudo caste system within professions relying heavily on the intellect.

Why are people generally becoming more tolerant of theory?

The profession of teaching in particular has been beset by the common attitude that only a certain kind of member—usually the college professor or someone hoping to achieve visibility as an intellectual—is capable of dealing with theory. Other professional workers—the "plebeians"—are not supposed to be equal to understanding, discussing, or applying theory. They are supposed only to be practitioners. Perhaps the members of each "caste," in their efforts to defend themselves or to achieve a sense of personal worth, help to build a barrier between theory and practice. The unfortunate result is a common assumption dominating the thinking of many educators at the college and the field position levels that he who is highly theoretical cannot be practical and he who is highly practical need not be theoretical.

There is no intention here of imposing a theory of supervision upon the reader. The choice of theory or theories is the prerogative of the individual member of the profession. One need not accept another member's theory in part or in whole, but one is professionally and ethically responsible either for accepting the theory of another or for developing one of his own.

This chapter deals primarily with the assumptions, principles, and objectives of and about supervision and their interlocking relationships with the criteria for measuring the achievement of those objectives in relation to the procedures used in accomplishing the objectives. The reader, while choosing not to accept this particular pattern of theory, may still use it as a vehicle for creating or developing a theory or creating a model that will support the design of an improved supervisory program in his own situation.

The specific behavior of an individual is the result of a choice of behaviors. The person who insists that he has reacted or behaved consistently over the years might deny that he has been in each instance exercising the opportunity of choice. Such determined insistence that choice was not operative and alternate behaviors non-existent seldom withstands careful analysis. Inherently involved in the choice of behaviors are assumptions, principles, and objectives even though they have not been verbalized and recognized by the individual as guides in his selection of behavior. Most people are able to give some reasons as to why they act as they do. Careful questioning of the individual as to why he chose a certain way of behaving often reveals the nature of these basic assumptions, principles, and objectives whether they have been stated or not. Further inquiry often reveals that these assumptions, the identified principles, and the so-called known facts form a pattern that, for this individual, constitutes his theory with respect to meeting the responsibilities at hand.

Some persons may insist that their judgments and behaviors are based upon intuition. There have been some very unfortunate experiences with short-term leaders who have made this claim. In many instances, decisions based upon intuition prove disastrous not only for the individual but for many other people who may become embroiled in the consequences of those decisions. Intuition makes little demand upon the reasoning powers. It appears to be somewhat of a sixth sense which guides decision-making regardless of the many factors that might be involved. However, persons arriving at decisions in this manner still use as a basis a set of values which they may or may not be able to recognize or to verbalize. Just as in the case of behaviors based on reason but chosen in an environment requiring the displacement of reason by ex-

Identify some leaders of this type.

pediency, so may the behaviors based on intuition be molded by the demands of expediency as well as by personal caprice. Behaviors based on reason may be readily subjected to analysis and appraisal. Behaviors based on intuition require the skills of an inclination to introspection if an analysis is to be made which will reveal the appropriateness of the choice of behavior. In both instances, through evaluations and verbalizations there will develop eventually the constellation of assumptions, principles, objectives, and criteria which will constitute a theory that may have been used, even though not identified as such at the time the choice of behavior was made.

An organization of ideas or behaviors into a theoretical design does not necessarily produce a permanent model. A theory and a model remain static only so long as they represent current thinking and serve current needs. Modifications and alternate designs must not be interpreted to mean that a prototype was not appropriate to the situation or useful to the designers at the point of development. It does indicate that the designers may recognize the need for a change or a modification because of altered situations, or because new information exists which was not available earlier. A theory or a model which continues to represent circumstances appropriately over an extended period may not need to be redesigned so long as it can be applied satisfactorily.

The development of a sound theoretical basis for supervisory practices requires an ability on the part of the supervisor to scrutinize his own actions, to identify his own motivations, and to verbalize his own value patterns to the end that he will be in a position to view, explore, and evaluate the factors involved in his choice of behavior. This ability of self-analysis, to be sure, is enhanced by the power or facility of verbalization.

Compare the definitions of these terms for the action pattern as found in references 1, 2, and 3 at the end of the chapter.

This chapter should assist persons engaged in supervisory activities to develop their skill in supporting a theoretical foundation for the selection of supervisory behaviors through verbalization. Discussion will be centered around the relationships of assumptions, principles, objectives, criteria, and procedures and will be referred to as the *action pattern*.

ASSUMPTIONS

An assumption is a declaration of a supposition which does not require supporting evidence but which is based upon a knowledge of practice, experience, and/or deliberation.

The term "working philosophy" has come into use in order to emphasize the need for a demonstration of the practical aspect of a well-developed statement of beliefs and purposes. Such statements often are referred to as theory. This theory has significant value when it is developed as a systematic organization of ideas or statement of beliefs. This statement has, or rather becomes, the formulation of certain observed phenomena as relationships which have been verified to some degree.

If the statement of philosophy or theory is couched in very general terms, it becomes difficult for the average person to translate it into action. The general statement can become a working philosophy when it is translated into the more specific terms of given operational areas, such as school administration, supervision of instruction, curriculum development, and guidance. These specific statements for any given area may become the core of beliefs sometimes called the *assumptions.*

How does the popularized notion of an assumption compare with the definition here?

Assumptions should have more substance than the notions or hunches that seem to constitute intuition. Assumptions, even though they do not require supporting proof, must be based upon some background knowledge obtained from practice, experience, or the reported deliberations of others who have a right to express themselves in the particular area of beliefs under consideration.

What is the life expectancy of an assumption?

Leadership in a democracy has been defined by Knezevich in this way: "Leadership is . . . concerned with human energy in organized groups. It is a force which can initiate action among people, guide activities in a given direction, maintain such activities, and unify efforts toward common goals." [1] One of the means of identifying and solving problems related to supervision is that of helping people to analyze their own behaviors for the purpose of discovering why they behave as they do. At this point, it is most probable that assumptions will be the factors that are identified. They may be stated and defined as known and proven facts. If they can be successfully defended, so much the better. It is unfortunate, however, when anyone is permitted to delude himself with the idea that he is operating on known principles and facts when, in reality, he has based his behavior on assumptions for so long that he fails to recognize them as such. Again, it is emphasized that for a given operational area there can be no one set of assumptions that can be supplied by a federal or state office, a university, or the authors of text and reference books. All of these may be helpful in developing the constellation of assumptions, principles, objectives, and criterion measures that can be applied to situations, problems, and purposes at the local school level, but it is the task of each local school system to develop a set of basic assumptions for each phase of the local operation. These, of necessity, will need to be in agreement, for, as they are combined, they will make up the working philosophy of the school system.

The assumptions about the supervision of instruction enumerated here are neither prescriptive nor absolute. They constitute the specific beliefs of the authors at this point in time and evolved with their general position on the definition, func-

[1] Stephen J. Knezevich, *Administration of Public Education,* second edition (New York: Harper & Row, 1970), p. 95.

tions, and relationships of supervision. The reader is invited to establish his own pattern just as the authors have established theirs. In order to present a discussion with internal consistencies and to develop a pattern for a supervisory program, these assumptions must be stated. Therefore, the assumptions about the supervision of instruction used in this book are:

1. Productive, democratic supervisory relationships require that all involved personnel (a) hold each other in mutual respect, (b) recognize the need for diversification of tasks, and (c) possess the capacity for finding individual satisfaction while sharing many control functions with others.

2. Theory and practice are mutually reinforcing in the achievement of professional expertise.

3. The major function of supervision is that of influencing situations, persons, and relationships for the purpose of improvement.

4. Planning is supported by systematically applied analysis in accomplishing program improvements.

5. Planning without implementing encourages professional impotence.

6. Load–quality relationships must be considered in the expectations for teaching and supervisory personnel if desirable change is to occur.

7. Supervision is a specialized phase of administration.

8. The limits and boundaries of supervisory authority, autonomy, and responsibility are defined by individuals and groups who can influence the organization and who also possess varying degrees of authority, autonomy, and responsibility.

9. The establishment and maintenance of the structural and operational patterns that encourage cooperative and coordinative behaviors are equally weighted responsibilities of superordinates, peers, and subordinates.

10. Supervision of instruction and curriculum development must be cooperative and coordinative operational functions.

11. The contributory and supportive functions of supervision include those policy determinations and implementations that deal with the improvement of the instructional program and its influential environments.

12. Many personal and situational factors influence behavioral status, change, and mobility.

13. Supervision encompasses the processes of directing and controlling, stimulating and initiating, analyzing and appraising, and designing and implementing those behaviors directly and primarily related to the improvement of teaching and, consequently, to the improvement of learning.

14. Professionalization is a result of individual and group maturation.

15. Professional personnel should be evaluated with specific reference to the declared primary expectations of the position occupied.

16. Leadership in evaluating major and minor trends in the social, economic, physical, and ethical environments in terms of the potential effects upon the instructional program is a responsibility of personnel assigned to the supervisory functions.

17. The evaluation of the effectiveness of supervisory personnel is a responsibility of the chief administrator and should be accomplished as an integral part of a known system-wide plan of output accounting.

18. The appurtenances of superordination do not include rights and privileges withheld from the statuses of subordination.

19. Credentialism and status symbolism are endemic pathologies in the traditions of bureaucracy that may be controlled through selected therapies.

What are your assumptions about supervision?

The above list constitutes the authors' major assumptions about the supervision of instruction. Each assumption is discussed as its appropriateness dictates in order that its meaning may be communicated more adequately and that it may be put in the appropriate context. Some of the assumptions are discussed in greater detail than others. The purpose of discussing any particular one is to show its relationship to the principles and practices discussed at various points in this text.

The first assumption expresses the optimum with respect to the favorable conditions for interpersonal relationships regardless of the situation in which they take place. The optimum or ideal, however, need not be barren of all suggestions of practicality. It stands, rather, as the ideal in providing the conditions for productive, democratic supervisory relationships. Those who have worked together, even for long periods of time, take for granted that the conditions of this particular assumption do exist and do persist. It is quite doubtful that any person could know the extent to which he is held in respect by another unless he were to take some special steps designed particularly to discover the nature and the extent of that respect. Likewise, even though a person may claim that he extends his respect to others, the test may come when a crisis period arrives in which a conflict of interests exists and decisions must be made which will influence the productivity of the enterprise.

The halo effect characteristic of a particular position sometimes does not come into the complete awareness of the person occupying the position. For example, two teachers may have had long experience working together as colleagues and peers. When one is promoted to the position of supervisor or principal, it is often evident that the particular type and quality of friendship existing prior to the change of status does not persist in the new relationship even though the positional status of one is altered. The traditions resident in the environment in which personal relationships exist may not permit them to be otherwise. If the previously expressed relationships of friendship—both personal and professional—tend to change, there is reason to suspect that the nature of mutual respect might have changed in a similar manner.

The human inclination is to seek a sense of personal worth in individual recognition rather than in group recognition. This is not to say that individuals should not be recognized and rewarded for excellent performances even though they are contributing to the larger enterprises of a group. The problem is that such recognition and satisfaction should be gained by each member of the group on some occasion so that all may be reasonably tolerant of the one who has the acclaim of the moment. The essential element is that of recognizing the unique contribution of each member to the productivity of the total enterprise. As part (b) of the first assumption indicates, all members of the organization should recognize that there is a need for diversification of tasks. Each person contributes to the desired organizational goals and each person must recognize the need for the contribution of the specialty of other members.

Part (c) of the first assumption concerns the capacity of the individual to find satisfaction and a sense of personal worth in a group enterprise. It is easy to proclaim that one is most happy when the total operation of which he is a part gains the marks of success. The depth of this feeling is often revealed when there are conflicts of interest which need to be resolved in the group enterprise, or when there are cases in which recognition may be given by the supporting public or by colleagues to a particular person for a singular achievement. The music supervisor, for instance, must fulfill the requirement of the administration that a public presentation be made by the pupils for the benefit of the parents. In all probability, during preparation for the program many of the other teachers will be called upon to relinquish individual pupils or small groups for rehearsals. Yet, on the occasion of the presentation, the acclaim of the supporting public is generally focused upon the music supervisor as though he had accomplished the entire program alone. The music supervisor well might acknowledge the acclaim by sharing the honors with his colleagues who have been working just as devotedly behind the scenes. The failure of this individual to acknowledge these contributions means that he took advantage of the opportunity to be in the spotlight and failed to reveal that his greatest satisfaction is in a group enterprise.

Other instances might be cited to indicate the nature and intent of the first assumption. Other assumptions related to the conditions of productive, democratic supervisory relationships might and possibly should have been stated. The one stated, however, supports the purposes of this discussion and holds possibilities for the inclusion of many concerns to be explored in the area of supervision of instruction.

In the second assumption, there is a more extended statement which indicates the nature of the intent and content of the assumption. Theory and practice are not to be considered separate and unrelated entities. Practice is the implementation of theory. The theory is the storehouse and the stimulator of knowledge acquisition which is used to substantiate present supervisory practices or to develop new practices and techniques to meet the requirements of a given situation. When each practice and technique is grounded in a theory developed by the local system, the two will be mutually reinforcing to the extent that the achievements are of a desired professional quality. Elements of the theory, however, may be more advanced than the practices. Constant research should be carried forward in the development of ideas and theories that are not yet totally suitable for application in practice.

While theory and practice should be progressing on parallel tracks, the theory track always will be ahead of the practice track. The amount of difference or discrepancy, however, will depend upon the procedures. If research continuously is used to develop theory and if practices constantly are being evaluated and changed in reference to that theory, the extent of the difference will remain about the same. If theory and practice are developed independently or with alternating emphases, the differences become greater and often out of proportion. This brings about a condition between theory and practice which cannot be considered to be mutually reinforcing. The frequent occurrence of this condition has created the idea among many that the two are discrete entities. This idea of their relationship is rationalized by reason of expediency and immediacy, which means that practices are put into operation with little or no regard for the underlying theory. The behavior which results in this condition is not considered to have achieved professional expertise.

Can a behavior be good in theory and bad in practice or vice versa?

The disregard for theory may be related to timing or it may be more closely related to lack of knowledge and inability to verbalize the theory that is known. The remaining sections of this chapter present some specific suggestions for developing a theory of supervision that can be used as a basis for practice. The theory is made up of the assumption, of principles related to this assumption, and of the objectives to which the principles are related. The theory, when based upon these relationships, should lead to the wise selection of the behaviors which constitute supervisory practice.

The third assumption is used for the purposes of illustrating the development of the related underlying theory. The remaining assumptions are discussed at other points in the book where they provide the focal point for the consistency of treatment and for demonstration of the practical application of the theory being described.

PRINCIPLES

The second step in the development of a basic philosophy is the statement of those *principles* which are inherently related to each assumption. As the tenets of a philosophy are made more specific by the development of a set of assumptions for each area, so are the assumptions made more specific by the development of the principles suggested by each one.

Abstracted dictionary definitions of the term "principle" are: (1) the ultimate source or origin that causes something; (2) a fundamental, primary, or general truth, a motivating force; (3) a guiding sense of the requirements and obligations of right conduct; and (4) a law or rule of conduct which may be used in deciding choice of conduct.

A working definition of supervision was submitted in Chapter 2 for the purpose of using it as a focal point for the discussion of the administrative function called supervision. This definition is not necessarily better than a definition developed by any other person. It was selected for the purpose of providing an element of consistency in the total presentation of the topic under discussion. In a similar manner a working definition of principle is submitted here:

A principle is a general statement describing a persisting relationship between two or more phenomena which gives direction to action.

The working definition is derived from the dictionary definitions, but the wording is chosen for its adaptability to the needs of this discussion. At this point it might be well to observe that the definition suggests the criteria by which statements can be judged as principles. These criteria are:

1. Two or more phenomena which can be identified.
2. A persisting relationship between these phenomena.
3. A form of statement which gives direction to action.

How would you *define the term "principle"?*

The principles presented here or in other publications and those developed by the practitioner might be subjected to the test of these three criteria (see references 1, 2, 3, 6, and 7). In the literature of supervision and administration, as well as in general discussions, the term "principle" often has been used synonymously with "objective," "rule," "law," and "assumption." The degree to which they overlap is determined by the person who is directing his thinking to a discussion of the terms. In other words, definitions may possess some uniqueness to the person using them.

Recognizing that there may be considerable overlap in meanings, it seems a matter of orderly thinking to attempt a differentiation of the major characteristics of the various terms. The concern here is with the term "principle." To assist in drawing distinctions between this term and others, it is suggested that the three criteria be applied successfully to each statement of principle before it is accepted as an underlying principle of a basic assumption. The differentiation between principle and assumption can be borne out by the application of the criteria for a principle given above to any of the basic assumptions presented in this chapter. If the contention here is sound—that such a differentiation can be made by use of the criteria—then none of the assumptions stated earlier should meet the conditions of the criteria for a principle. On the other hand, the method must meet the requirements of the criteria in all respects. As stated earlier, the third assumption is used as the vehicle for exploring the ways in which assumptions lead to statements of principles and principles in turn suggest objectives.

The question now asked is, "What principles are suggested by assumption number three?" Many principles might be developed from it. There is no intent here to present a list; to do so would conflict with the basic philosophy of this book, namely, that the program of supervision should be custom-built for the particular school system. The principles presented are illustrative of the type that the supervisor might want to draw from a basic assumption as stated above.

Some illustrative principles suggested by this assumption are:

1. Relationships between situations and persons must be manipulated [2] if change is to occur.
2. The relationships between situations and persons should be subjected to manipulation.
3. The manipulation of relationships between situations and persons should result in desirable, rather than undesirable, change.

Now apply the three criteria for establishing a principle to the three statements above. In the first, the two phenomena are *situations* and *persons*. The persistence of the relationships of these two phenomena is supported by the research reports in the areas of psychology and sociology. The statement also gives direction to action in that a person accepting this principle as a means of choosing supervisory behaviors must recognize that his tasks and functions will be related to the manipulating of relationships between situations and persons if changes are to occur. In the case of the second principle the two phenomena are *relationships between situations and persons* and *manipulation*. In the third the two phenomena are *manipulation of relationships* and *desirable change*. In

What other principles are suggested by this assumption?

[2] "Manipulate" may be defined as "to manage or utilize skillfully." *Webster's Seventh New Collegiate Dictionary* (Springfield, Mass.: G. &. C. Merriam Co., 1965).

the second and third the evidence of the persisting relationships of the phenomena is to be found in the reports of competent people who have studied psychological and sociological characteristics of change as implied in the statement of principle. As in the first, principles two and three give direction to action in that the person accepting the principle commits himself to a particular array of behaviors to the exclusion of others.

The supervisor who wants to maintain the status quo will not find in principles of this nature any backing for his lack of desire or effort to bring about change. The assumption which leads to the statement of these principles cannot be espoused comfortably by a person who sees the purpose of supervision as "holding the line" as opposed to quality control in terms of ever-improving outcomes. If the third criterion of a principle is sound and is used, it can lead in only one direction when applied. This direction will be that of determining the behaviors appropriate to the conditions or relationships of phenomena noted in the statement of principles. Behaviors have as their focal points the objectives which the individual establishes for himself. If the principle gives direction to action, it gives first of all direction to the selection of objectives.

OBJECTIVES

An objective is the identity or definition of a goal accepted as the object of achievement.

The principle is not a description of action although it does give direction to action. The *objective,* on the other hand, becomes more specific as the directive of the action. The dictionary definitions of the term "objective" suggest the following: (1) a perceived object as distinguished from something existing in the mind; real, actual; (2) something aimed at; and (3) receiver of the action; objective case. A statement of an objective indicates the object of achievement or what is to be done, what should be done, or what a person is going to do. It is the real, the tangible, the specific directive to action or actions suggested by the principle. As each assumption gives rise to the selection and statement of a set of principles, so does each principle give rise to the selection and statement of a set of objectives. In this way there is a direct line from an assumption to several principles and from each principle to a number of objectives.

The relationship between assumptions, principles, and objectives derived from the third assumption became a starting point for illustrative purposes. It was indicated that this assumption could suggest a number of principles. Three principles were offered at the appropriate point. To carry through the illustration, principle number one is used to show that objectives are derived from the principle.

The following objectives might serve the illustrative purpose of the type that might be related to this principle:

1. To prevent either the situation or the person from remaining constant in the change process.
2. To avoid making self the dominant situational element that affects staff members.
3. To arrange situational and personal elements in some order or priority.

What other objectives might be related to this principle?

If this assumption and the principles suggested by it are accepted, the reader has committed himself to the analysis as suggested in the first objective. The supervisor who approaches his supervisory responsibility with the thought that he must always preserve the image of the status leader who can impose his will upon his subordinates will not find the illustration acceptable. If he were to perform in the manner suggested, his assumptions and his principles would need to be substantially different. The extreme authoritarian might accept the third assumption but adapt the principle in the direction of making himself the leader by authority only—in which case the supervisor would be primarily concerned with the objective of determining what kind of behavior on his part would most quickly cause the subordinate to submit to his will. Such behavior would be impossible under the assumption, the principles, and the objectives of the illustrations used here.

The supervisor needs to study carefully the personality needs of his individual staff members as they go about meeting the requirements of their teaching duties in the particular situation. It takes a minimum effort to identify some of the situational elements that have high esteem in the minds of teachers. Some staff members let it be known very quickly that they operate on a schedule of precision. To them the elements of precision in the total school operation are more important than most any other aspect of the school operation. Other teachers may be less concerned with precision and be much more concerned with the balance of curricular offerings as they impinge upon the product of the school, namely, the education of the pupils.

Can a group objective be achieved by striking an average of the individual objectives?

The objectives as indicated above constitute the specific direction for action. The number of objectives that a particular supervisor wants to develop may depend upon the amount of time that he has, the particular aspect of the supervisory program under development at the moment, and the expectations placed upon him by the central office. The significant thing for the supervisor to keep in mind is that the objectives are important in the selection of his supervisory behaviors. The absence of objectives would put him on the basis of judgment, decision, and behavior selection by bias, expediency, or intuition. It is conceivable that objectives selected and used for a period of time may prove to be unprofitable or wrong. In this case the faulty objectives must be discarded and others developed which will give direction to improved supervisory action.

Behaviorists would not find the form of the selected illustrations acceptable as statements of objectives which could be achieved or evaluated. The approach to a correct form for writing objectives will not be debated. Anyone so inclined should feel free to use the behavioral approach to writing objectives for the supervisory program. It is the authors' belief that various forms for writing objectives may be appropriate for the various purposes for which objectives are established. The behavioral objective includes the performance criteria established for a given objective. The plan here is to establish the desired goals and then establish the criteria which will assist in the evaluation process.

CRITERIA

A criterion is the referent point or condition which can serve as the basis for evaluation.

The degree to which the objectives have been achieved is measured against a standard called a criterion. The *criteria* usually tend to cluster in an area of measurement or of accomplishment termed the *criterion measure*. For instance, the specific criteria or standards may be selected with respect to the following measures:

1. The economy of operation.
2. The internal power structure of the school.
3. The conformity to the known psychological or sociological constructs.
4. The effect upon leadership patterns.
5. The descriptive area which encompasses a group of interrelated objectives.

What criteria can you suggest for these criterion measures?

The illustrations of criterion measures presented in the following pages are of the fifth type. The criterion measure is recognized for its convenience in prescribing the specific criteria or questions which test products within a reasonably controlled area of concern. This is offered as a device which may circumvent the attractive temptation of rendering judgments in global-type terms.

Try developing the A-3-a criterion measure and appropriate criteria for a selected situation in Figure 3.1.

The individual practitioner must establish the criteria by which he will judge himself, or a superordinate will establish the criteria by which the supervisory program will be evaluated. Criteria are sometimes described as referent points of testing. As each principle suggests a set of objectives, each objective suggests a set or sets of criteria. These criteria may be in the form of simple statements or questions, depending upon the form of evaluation that has been devised. Figure 3.1 is designed to illustrate the criterion measures and criteria which might be selected to evaluate the achievement of the objectives which have been established on the basis of the first principle developed from the third assumption.

PROCEDURES

A procedure is the systematic arrangement of behaviors designed to accomplish a stated objective.

Supervision is not a procedure by which a person launches his efforts from a declared point in time and place to a pattern of no return. It is a process more like scaling a cliff; for survival, each step must be linked to a previous purchase. Thus, the relationships between assumptions, principles, objectives, and criteria provide the bases, direction signals, and stimulations for choosing a pattern of supervisory *procedures* that possess validity, consistency, and influence. Each practitioner perceives himself as going about his work with a defined and identifiable method. Method normally is viewed as a systematic arrangement of purposes, technical skills, and artful procedures (see Chapter 17). The method of supervision is a most important end product of the orderly observance of the various steps in the accepted action pattern.

What procedures would you suggest to assist in the achievement of the objectives illustrated, in view of the principles and criteria listed for assumption three?

A discussion of the nature of an assumption was presented earlier in this chapter. The composite illustration for the third assumption with its possible derived principles and, in turn, objectives and criteria were dealt with rather extensively. The composite illustration, Figure 3.1, may clarify the relationships involved in developing procedures from an action pattern.

If this chapter has communicated its content successfully, it is understood that the three assumptions discussed specifically were only the first three of a list of nineteen which relate generally to the entire book. It will be impossible to deal with the others in the detail that has characterized the treatment of the third assumption. Remember, however, that the suggested relationship of principles and objectives to that assumption was submitted only for illustrative purposes. As already indicated, it is believed that a good supervisory program must be custom-built. This means that the suggestive materials offered here should facilitate the development or adaptation of a set of assumptions, principles, objectives, and criterion measures unique to the individual supervisor and his particular school system.

The assumptions in the list of nineteen are discussed at appropriate points in those chapters to which they bear the closest relationships. For instance, the twelfth assumption (that behavioral status, change, and mobility are influenced

FIGURE 3.1
Example of the Use of the Action Pattern

SUPERVISION IS THAT PHASE OF SCHOOL
UPON THE ACHIEVEMENT OF THE
EXPECTATIONS OF

ASSUMPTION NO. 3

The major function of supervision is that of influencing situations, persons, and relationships for the purpose of improvement.

PRINCIPLES

A. Relationships between situations and persons must be manipulated if change is to occur.

B. The relationships between situations and persons should be subjected to manipulation.

C. The manipulation of relationships between situations and persons should result in desirable, rather than undesirable, change.

OBJECTIVES

A-1. To prevent either the situation or the person from remaining constant in the change process.

A-2. To avoid making self the dominant element in making decisions.

A-3. To arrange situational and personal elements in some order of priority.

CRITERION MEASURES

A-1-a. Measurable results of change in both the situation and person indicate the degree of achievement of objectives.

A-2-a. Decisions are made in terms of educational considerations as opposed to personal desires.

A-3-a.

CRITERIA

A-1-a-(1) Situation: A committee report on budget allocations for audio-visual aids is turned in at the end of the school year. This report is issued as a central office directive.

(a) There are suggested changes in the procedures over last year.
(b) These changes create new teaching problems.
(c) The procedures simplify management.
(d) The teachers accomplished the changes to the new procedures.
(e) There were identifiable compromises between the directive and teaching procedures.
(f) The compromises occurred in sufficient volume to cause revision of the plan.
(g) Compromises have been achieved through a change in the plan as well as in the teaching procedures.

PROCEDURES

A-2-a-(1) Situation: Schedule and room assignments are announced for the local school system.

(a) Load preferences are given to some individuals or groups of teachers.
(b) Room assignments are made on a seniority basis.
(c) There are regularized procedures for presenting, receiving, and adjudicating complaints.
(d) Pupil welfare constitutes the central focus in resolving differences in opinions.
(e) Differences in opinions are resolved with freedom from fear of reprisals.

A-3-a-(1) Situation:

A-1.
A-2.
A-3.

by many personal and situational factors) is closely related to the content of the three chapters of Part III which deal with the participants in supervision.

Work out a similar example for one other assumption.

The action pattern developed in this chapter now becomes the basis for an exploration of other assumptions. Practicality will be served better if actual situations are used and if the illustration becomes the operational decision of the individual supervisor who is fulfilling the responsibilities of his position.

Illustrative or operational application related to assumptions, principles, objectives, and criteria become sterile if there is no vehicle for initiating and implementing change. It has been stated several times and in various ways that improvement implies change. The supervisory plan that is well-grounded in theory still remains dependent upon the technical skills that translate it into action and change. The involvements in the techniques of change are discussed in Chapter 4, "The Management of Change."

THE ACTION PATTERN

An assumption is a declaration of a supposition which does not require supporting evidence but which is based upon a knowledge of practice, experience, and/or deliberation.

A principle is a general statement describing a persisting relationship between two or more phenomena which gives direction to action.

An objective is the identity or definition of a goal accepted as the object of achievement.

A criterion is the referent point or condition which can serve as the basis for evaluation.

A procedure is the systematic arrangement of behaviors designed to accomplish a stated objective.

SELECTED REFERENCES

1. Ayer, Fred C., *Fundamentals of Instructional Supervision.* New York: Harper & Row, 1954. pp. 29–49.
2. Briggs, Thomas H. and Joseph Justman, *Improving Instruction Through Supervision.* New York: Macmillan, 1952. pp. 126–142.
3. Burton, William H. and Leo J. Brueckner, *Supervision: A Social Process.* pp. 44–64, 70–88.
4. Deutsch, Morton and Robert M. Krauss, *Theories in Social Psychology.* New York: Basic Books, Inc., 1965.
5. Eye, Glen G. and Lanore A. Netzer, *School Administrators and Instruction: A Guide to Self-Appraisal.* Boston: Allyn & Bacon, Inc., 1969. Chapter 8.
6. Franseth, Jane, *Supervision or Leadership.* Evanston, Ill.: Row Peterson and Company, 1961. pp. 21–29.

7. Hicks, Hanne J., *Educational Supervision in Principle and Practice*. New York: Ronald, 1960. pp. 25–48.
8. Knezevich, Stephen J., *Administration of Public Education*. New York: Harper & Row, 1970, 2nd ed. p. 95.
9. Lucio, William H. and John D. McNeil, *Supervision: A Synthesis of Thought and Action*. New York: McGraw-Hill Book Co., 1969, 2nd ed. pp. 143–148, 228–236.
10. Netzer, Lanore A., Glen G. Eye, Ardelle Graef, Robert D. Krey, and J. Fred Overman, *Interdisciplinary Foundations of Supervision*. Boston: Allyn & Bacon, Inc., 1970. Chapters I and III.
11. Wilson, L. Craig, T. Madison Byar, Arthur S. Shapiro, and Shirley H. Schell, *Sociology of Supervision*. Boston: Allyn & Bacon, Inc., 1969. pp. 63–75.

4

The Management of Change

The manner of stating definitions of supervision differs, but regardless of the date of origin or procedures implied, the declared and implied intent of the service is to bring about change that results in improvement. A review of Chapter 2 reinforces this summarizing statement. Among the categories of supervision, as noted in Chapter 2, are *processes* and *products;* these two items emphasize the fact that change leading to improvement is of major importance. The suggestions for the development of a theory of supervision, as detailed in Chapter 3, focus upon decisions about outcome, thus denoting movement from one status to another. Improvement is a result of change. Those charged with management responsibilities must have the foresight, sense of purpose, and technical competence to establish control over change which possesses relevance to institutional objectives. It seems appropriate, then, that a consideration of the management of change should be included in this part of this text.

A list of assumptions about the supervision of instruction was offered in Chapter 3. Among them were two—the third and the fourth—which relate primarily to the connection between the supervisory task and the process of change. These assumptions are:

3. The major function of supervision is that of influencing situations, persons, and relationships for the purpose of improvement.

4. Planning is supported by systematically applied analysis in accomplishing program improvements.

Each practitioner or theorist in the field of supervision should (1) accept these assumptions, (2) alter them, or (3) determine those assumptions which are pertinent as the basis for his own behavior. The particular point to be noted in the third assumption is that it is just as important to consider situations as to consider persons and relationships in the process of improving the instructional program. In the fourth assumption, there are two primary characteristics, design and implementation. To date, researchers and practitioners have paid more attention to the process of designing change than to the process of implementing change. The two are related intimately in the process of the improvement of instruction. There is a further implication, that these processes must be based on analysis if improvement is to occur.

Why?

TYPES OF MANAGEMENT

The techniques in the processes of designing and implementing are considered in Part IV. This chapter is concerned primarily with the supervisor's or leader's responsibility for determining the methodology, direction, and control of change. The assumptions involve some rather specific responsibilities in the process. The history of instructional leadership indicates that it has been easy to ignore those assumptions which commit a leader to specifics. They have been omitted in favor of broad generalizations about the process and the direction of change. Many educators have not taken advantage of the research which has been done on the anatomy of the change process. Supervisors, however, are becoming more adept at making use of research evidence and in sharpening their own preferences for fact-supported as opposed to subjectively based generalizations. The emerging trend favors demonstrated research competence which encourages the rejection of judgments by social expediency.

The confirmed status leader, on the other hand, seems inclined to initiate change by stating the desired goal and giving a simple illustration of the process by which the goal can be achieved. The people in the lower echelons of the school establishment often find amusement in observing their leader's wealth of vocabulary and missionary zeal to stimulate performance on the part of others. Such zeal is commendable but the needed accompanying ability is to identify as well as to solve problems.

Zeal, as a technique of leadership, is found on many occasions and in the hands of a great variety of people. The dean or professor of a university, the superintendent of schools, and the principal or the supervisor may or may not have basic knowledge in the area of a particular need for change, but each may have strong opinions about the *need* as a *need*. On the other hand, each may be well qualified in the content and methodology of the area to be changed yet be so pressured by a multitude of activities and responsibilities that there is only time to point the direction and *hope*. They must hope that their followers will expand upon that which they may not know how to do or which they have neither the time nor the energy to do.

In such a situation, a new curriculum in the social studies might be an example. The status leader might give this sort of directive to the kindergarten teachers:

> In the new social studies program that we now will design, the child must become a little citizen who understands the processes of government *at his level.* That is, the kindergartner must see that hanging his hat on a hook is meeting a responsibility set by his governing school community. Thus, the teacher will scale the learning experiences which are appropriate to each grade level. In this way we will have a new social studies curriculum which will accomplish these new goals which have been defined and will achieve that end through the selection of appropriate learning experiences. It is your responsibility and prerogative to plan these experiences for your pupils.

Even though the above statement seems somewhat cynical, it may be presumed that this matter of the kindergartner hanging his hat is to proceed year by year through successive learning experiences to the highest level of abstraction about good citizenship. In this latter case, perhaps, it would not be the kindergartner's hat placed on the appropriate hook, but the hat on the hatrack outside the office door labeled *President.* This is an abstraction that is to be interpreted by some as the issuance of a statement not by the office occupant, but by a spokesman who may not quote but who is known to be close to the throne. The statement by the spokesman may be quoted but is not to be attributed to the chief.

The intellectual distance from the kindergartner hanging his hat on a hook in a schoolroom to the ideas inferred from the hat on the hatrack outside the President's office is long. There are many and devious teaching and learning trails which must be pursued in the area of the social studies. The leader who has established the direction of instructional improvement, even though in a glowing and polished manner, is not communicating much assistance to the teachers or other staff members who have to fill in the details of the learning experiences which would constitute a total program.

There are also instructional leaders who can enumerate most eloquently the many needs for change. Entirely too often, however, the people who so eloquently identify, describe, and establish the magnitude of problems confronting a group conclude with this final summary statement: "Sometime, somewhere, there will be a person who is willing to apply his expertise to the task of finding solutions to these problems." Again, it must be recognized that such leaders do believe in change. In all probability they are convinced that they have a technique for bringing it about. This concept of management, however, is extremely limited in that it is either a matter of stimulating someone else's intelligence to solve the problems or of functioning primarily by pointing the direction either by simple illustration or by declaration of the problems that exist.

The responsibility for initiating and pursuing a pattern of change must never be assumed to be limited to the control of the leader. The followers of any leader in any enterprise make great differences in the types of change patterns established and in the speed with which the old can be cast aside and the new established. Both leaders and followers often pursue the selection of their behaviors in the light of the stereotypes which they hold. Many seem to cling to the stereotypes of the *new* as a cult and others take the same view toward the stereotypes of the *old*. Each of these groups have from time to time been labeled in various ways. The more common designation is that of "modern" or "progressive" as opposed to "old-fashioned" or "conservative." Often these terms are assumed to declare a very well-defined type of person and action. Those efforts in which such a dichotomy of the population is attempted usually have faltered and failed.

Most individuals, as well as most groups, have a terrific amount of overlapping between the positions of the progressive and the conservative. With respect to change, it is interesting and possibly worthwhile to identify the stereotypes associated with each of these categories. Those who hold to the stereotypes of the new are inclined to place high priority on expressions such as "progress," "change," "modern," "stranglehold of tradition," "trailblazing," and "newness." Those who are inclined to be guided by the stereotypes of the old appear to place higher priorities on terms such as "time-tested," "wisdom of the ages," "cultural accretion," "evolutionary process," "solid foundation," "the golden age," or "the good old times." In each case the terms or the stereotypes tend to emphasize fixed patterns of conduct.

Those who hold to the new seem to be restless people, who, when confronted with the fact that they have been pursuing the same pattern of action over a long period of time, become worried lest they are "in a rut." These are the people who perhaps feel that anyone who has been in the same position for a few years is inevitably old-fashioned and in a rut. This way of thinking does not characterize only younger people and newcomers to the profession; many of the older people have spent a whole professional lifetime in skipping from one gadget or plan to another. They perhaps have found great satisfaction in the educational profession, but they have found these satisfactions because it was an occupation that provided them with the opportunity to cast off the old and to seek the new with great facility. These are the people who are inclined to quote such classics as "the reach must exceed the grasp or what's a heaven for." [1] It indicates a preference for the

To whom do you refer and/or defer?

[1] Robert Browning, "Andrea del Sarto," in *Complete Poetical Works of Browning* (Boston: Houghton Mifflin [Cambridge ed.], 1895), p. 346.

new as a criterion measure all on its own. Those leaders who are responsible for initiating and directing change programs will find great facility among those who hold to the ideas expressed in the stereotypes of the new. As a matter of fact, if a school staff had a very high majority of people of this type, the leader might find himself being outdistanced in the process of change without having the opportunity to evaluate that change in terms of any criterion other than that change has been accomplished. Such a criterion is not found in the literature of education as being among the more desirable ones for judging the quality of an instructional program.

Those who cling predominantly to the stereotypes of the old are well anchored in their confidence in the past. These people perhaps feel that few things can be new and, indeed, they have much evidence to support such a position. The gradual revelation of the cultures in the past in any section of the world indicates that many accomplishments preceding our current time were perhaps of equal or greater worth to the very goals which we are now establishing for future achievement. Those who cling to these stereotypes can be just as wrong as those who cling only to the new.

A part of the difference between these two types is that of the choice of pace. It is simple to say that people differ with respect to the speed with which they want change. This is more than simply a preference with respect to pace. It is evidence of a belief in the procedures by which change shall take place. It is not unrelated to the individual's preference for a sense of security as opposed to the fear of insecurity. This is security with respect to:

1. The prestige qualities of one's own ideas.
2. His relative influence or status within a group.
3. The sense of personal worth which he achieves through his image of the way other people see him.
4. His confidence in personal success in an individual or group enterprise which, having been assured in the past, might become endangered.
5. A basic integrity related to the goals selected by the leader and, by whatever means, imposed upon the followers.

Neither those who hold to the old nor those who hold to the new have a basically different feeling about the achievement of security and the avoidance of a sense of insecurity. It is evident, however, that the point of reference for each group is quite different in the perception of the manner by which security can be achieved. For the one group, security is connected to the idea of developmentalism in terms of change to something different than is currently being done. For the other group, it is a strong belief that security is attached to the slower evolutionary process of change.

Among the followers as well as among the leaders there is a third stereotype, that of the *neutral*. The neutral receives little support, respect, or praise from those who hold to the new or the old as a criterion of change. The neutral holds to a stereotype that is represented in this quotation from Pope's "Essay on Criticism": "Be not the first by whom the new are tried, nor yet the last to lay the old aside." [2] Those who hold to the old and the new as the change criterion perhaps would say that the neutral is affectionately attached to this quotation from Pope, but that it ought to be liberally interpreted as, "Let the other fellow stick out his neck. If he is wrong, give him the ax. If he is right, join his parade and outshout him." It is not the purpose here to attempt an appraisal of which of the three groups is the most correct in its attitude toward the process and direction of change. The purpose is to point out that no matter what the enterprise in the instructional program, there will be these three groups. Those persons desirous of managing change would be wise to study first the attitudes toward change held by those whom they seek to influence.

What makes some people more receptive to change than others?

PURPOSES AND VEHICLES OF CHANGE

A distinction is made here between two types of change. Perhaps this distinction is appropriate to any area of activity but it seems particularly applicable to instruction. The distinction is that of whether the change has to do with the *purpose* of the instructional activities or with the *vehicle* by which the goals or purposes are to be achieved. An example of this distinction can be found in *educating for citizenship.* Certainly this, as a purpose of the instructional program, is not new. It has appeared in some form in most of the statements of the purposes of education that can be identified in all of the published works. The purposes of the educational enterprise have been amazingly constant, yet we are inclined to view education as having been a rapidly changing type of activity. In a sense the latter is true, because there have been many changes in education. The changes, however, have not been so much in purpose as they have been in the procedures by which the purposes could be achieved.

Why should this distinction be made?

A brief reference brings to mind the stability of the purposes of education. One might view those as found in Plato's *Republic* [3] or in Herbert Spencer's "What Knowledge Is of Most Worth." [4] In the educational history of this country the *Cardinal Principles of Secondary Education* [5] served for many decades and still is favored by many educationists as providing the proper rubric of the design for an educational program. In 1940, the Educational Policies Commission published *The*

[2] Alexander Pope, "Essay on Criticism," in *The Pleasures of Pope* (London: Hamish Hamilton, 1949), p. 25.

[3] Plato, *The Republic,* O. O. Shorey, trans. (Boston: Harvard University Press, 1935).

[4] Herbert Spencer, *Education: Intellectual, Moral, and Physical* (New York: Appleton-Century-Crofts, 1860).

[5] Commission on the Reorganization of Secondary Education, *Cardinal Principles of Secondary Education* (Washington, D.C.: United States Bureau of Education, Bulletin No. 35, 1918).

Purposes of Education in American Democracy [6] and, in 1961, *The Central Purpose of American Education.* [7] On many occasions these have been used by educators as the standards by which educational change should be designed and by which the quality of the instructional program should be assessed. New statements of the purposes of education always are forthcoming. It is not to be assumed that the above major statements of purpose constitute an exclusive list. Reference need be made only to statements offered by many substantial scholars who have developed their own statements of purpose.

The major publications of local school systems in the area of curricular change have not at any time produced different statements of general purposes of education than those indicated in the above references. The purposes for a particular age group, for a particular grade level, or for a specified subject matter area perhaps have been altered slightly in some instances and substantially in others. It must be conceded, however, that even major change in the purposes of individual aspects of the curriculum has held in focus the less changeable general purposes of education. Many who have sponsored changes in the vehicles of instruction have referred to them as something sufficiently substantial to be considered a change in purpose. An assessment of such claims seldom supports the position of the creator or author of the idea.

In an effort to complete the intent of communication at this point—that is, to establish the difference between the *purpose* and the *vehicle* in change programs—the following list of activities, organizational plans, and educational gadgets gleaned from the past three or four decades of education in this country is submitted. While the classification is not and cannot be perfect, three groups of items are suggested. The first group deals with the organizational attack on the instructional program. Items which can be listed in this category and which are labeled here as the vehicles of change are:

activity school	modular schedule
platoon plan	ungraded block
Montessori plan	departmentalized program
Lancastrian system	parallel tracks

A second category of items believed to be vehicles of change is found in the methods of instruction as well as in the organization of the curriculum. Items indicated here come from the literature of recent decades. In each instance, they were or are proclaimed by many as the innovation for which the educational world had been waiting. Recalled for this list are:

[6] National Education Association, Educational Policies Commission, *The Purposes of Education in American Democracy* (Washington, D.C.: NEA, 1940).

[7] National Education Association, Educational Policies Commission, *The Central Purpose of American Education* (Washington, D.C.: NEA, 1961).

unit method	core curriculum
project method	emerging curriculum
contract method	experience curriculum
laboratory method	creative dramatics
correlated content	town meeting
socialized recitation	team teaching
grouping	individualized instruction
fusion	

In the third group of vehicles, again proclaimed as very significant in the process of change and improvement of education, are:

single textbooks	sound film
multiple textbooks	television
workbooks	multimedia laboratories
stereopticon views	field trips
keystone views	teaching machines
silent film	computer-assisted instruction

List others in each of these three groups.

The purpose of reference in this inventory is not to imply an appraisal of any one of these vehicles of change as being better or poorer than another. Differential worth, no doubt, always has been the case with each plan for change. At this point in the consideration of supervision, it is more important that recognition be given to the heritage of multifaceted change in the vehicles of instructional improvement. In view of the history of the instructional developments in the educational program, it is reasonable to accuse the profession of having succumbed to gadgetry. There is little reason to deny such an accusation, but, at the same time, there is no reason to assume that education is unique in this respect among all of the professions. It also is unnecessary to single out another profession for comparison with education. Any reader may select for his own consideration the changes and efforts to modernize some other profession. In doing so it may be found that other professions are just as guilty or as aggressive as is the profession of teaching.

What is the gadgetry of other professions? Compare with education.

Recognition, however, must be granted to the fact that the gadgetry of any profession seems to be the rallying point for the quacks of the profession. In this sense, all need to be aware of the danger of gadgetry. There have been, there are, and probably there will continue to be "operators" in the educational profession who are willing to single out any vehicle of change and deal with it as though it satisfied all of the professional program needs. The teaching machine is one of the more recent items subjected to exaggerated claims. It is a device that may prove to be extremely helpful in facilitating teaching and learning. Its commercial potential seems to have stimulated its popularity beyond its usefulness in the instructional program as supported by research evidence. The future may hold great promise for it, but, for the present, it would be better for the amateurs in this medium of instruction to withhold accepting it wholeheartedly until the scientists in the field can establish its proper application.

The instructional leader who attaches himself to one of the vehicles and carries it to the extreme becomes one of the quacks guilty of faulty educational leadership. Such people are not limited to those who have a commercial interest in the particular gadget. Many who desire a high level of prestige in the instructional program and the educational systems of our country can be tempted by the opportunities to fancy themselves as modern-day prophets who will cure the educational ills with one device. Interestingly enough, those who are inclined to this method of operation are most likely to take the simple gadget and to do everything possible to make it appear to be so complex that only they and their disciples have achieved mastery of it. The caution offered here is that whatever vehicles are chosen for the accomplishment of instructional change, the road to be traveled—the purpose of improvement—must be firmly established and the vehicles commanded to follow that road.

Relate this idea to the action pattern suggested in Chapter 3.

There always will be the important decision as to whether the new road and the new vehicle chosen shall be accomplished primarily through the criterion of the new or the criterion of the old. In order not to leave the readers too much to the hazards of speculation, the authors admit to a high degree of conservatism in viewing the process of change. This conservatism takes the form of an insistence upon a mechanism built into the change plan that will make analysis and appraisal an integral part of the change procedures. It is well to know the purposes of the present instructional program if the approach to the process of change is to be made in the most valid manner. It is held that the pursuit of change based upon the evaluation of the old need not and should not blind one to the directional signs of new purposes and of new ways of achieving those purposes.

PROCESSES OF CHANGE

Purposes can be analyzed in terms of their social, economic, intellectual, and moral significances. Such analyses can point to the manner in which improvement programs might and should be initiated. The current speculation about the future being a cybernetic age may indeed change both the purposes and processes of education. If it means a change in the patterns for the development of good citizens, such a change in purpose must be accomplished after very careful and thorough consideration by all people who are concerned. It is almost impossible to think of any member of the current population who would want not to be concerned with such a change. Leaders in directing the change in purposes and procedures, however, must come from among the professionals in the field of education. Failure to meet these responsibilities may well cause that leadership to be sacrificed to other, perhaps less competent, agents in the planning of educational change. In

Are changes of behavior related to accompanying changes in values?

other words, educators must give direction to educational change or lose the prerogative to aggressive nonprofessionals.

In order to accommodate those who are somewhat inclined to facetiousness, the following seven ways are suggested as the best means for resisting change:

1. Do not read or think.
2. Consider all others less knowledgeable than yourself.
3. Discredit the judgment and integrity of anyone who thinks your performance unsatisfactory.
4. Assume that you are your own best critic.
5. Insist that there are more intangible than tangible products of teaching and learning.
6. Find a new suggestive name for what has always been done.
7. Brush aside change suggestions as theoretical so that you may continue the pleasant and secure paths of practical mediocrity.

Such ways of resisting change should not become the code of behavior for those who are enamored with the static state. It may be helpful, however, for each reader to assess his own point of view and his own behaviors in terms of some such list of ways to resist change. More importantly and not at all facetiously, the primary purpose of the instructional leader is that of directing sound change in the instructional program. Such a leader must become a scholar of the process of change. Just as it is not enough for the classroom teacher to know only the content of the subject areas taught, so it is not enough for the instructional leader to know only the content of the instructional program of the school. At the same time, the teacher must know the methodology of teaching and learning. It follows, then, that the supervisor must know the methodology of the management of change.

Read Part IV for suggestions on processes of change.

The processes of change have been subjected to much research. It is impossible and impractical to review more than sample types of research reports on these processes in this chapter. Bennis, in a recent publication, suggested a typology of the change process, with the following eight types of change indicated:

1. Planned change
2. Indoctrination
3. Coercive change
4. Technocratic change
5. Interactional change
6. Socialization
7. Emulative change
8. Natural change [8]

In his discussion of the above types, Bennis indicated that goal setting varies in the deliberateness and nondeliberateness of one or both parties in the relationship and that there are varying degrees in the power ratios that may be involved between the leader and the follower in each of the types of change. At no point does he suggest that the typology is particularly precise. He makes this valid assumption: "However, we believe it does provide suggestions as to how 'planned

[8] Warren G. Bennis, Kenneth D. Benne, and Robert Chin (eds.), *The Planning of Change* (New York: Holt, Rinehart, and Winston, 1961), pp. 154–156.

change' can be distinguished from other change processes." The task of the instructional leader, then, is to take the research as reported by scholars such as Bennis and seek the ways in which it can be adapted to the specific instructional leadership tasks encountered at the local school level.

Bass, in *Leadership, Psychology, and Organizational Behavior,* emphasized the following three types of leadership: persuasive, coercive, and permissive.[9] He relates many factors to these types of leadership. His publication is particularly helpful in that he provided 1155 items in the bibliography—most of which are research-based reports. He has related these reports to the various interests in leader and organizational behaviors. The referent discipline in most of the research reported is that of psychology. Publications of this type can be extremely helpful for those who will see their leadership responsibilities in the instructional program as an obligation to become a student of the process of change. Then, on the basis of the opportunities provided in the practical situation, they may make a rewarding adaptation of the research findings.

Cartwright and Zander, in *Group Dynamics,* provided reports from many whose research work is pertinent to the responsibilities of the instructional leader. The work of Jackson is reported as "Reference Group Processes in a Formal Organization." Jackson tested the following hypotheses:

> 1. In any group or organization a person's attraction to membership will be directly related to the magnitude of his social worth.
> 2. The magnitude of the positive relationship hypothesized in (1) will vary directly with the volume of interaction the person has with other members of the group or organization under consideration.
> 3. Where alternative group orientations are possible for a person, his relative attraction to membership in one or another group will be directly related to his relative social worth in the groups considered.
> 4. The magnitude of the positive relationship hypothesized in (3) will vary directly with the volume of interaction the person has with other members of the group under consideration.[10]

Adapt these hypotheses to education.

These hypotheses were supported, but the validity of the generalizations appears to be related more directly than anticipated to the populations, conditions, and contexts. For instance, in the populations studied, Jackson found that the hypotheses were supported for professional people but not for nonprofessional people. He concluded that:

> The research suggests that reference group processes are continually at work distributing gratifications and deprivations in social interaction and modifying individuals' desire to belong. A dynamic view of social structure emerges, with some persons moving in the direction of increased psychological membership, some in relative equi-

[9] Bernard M. Bass, *Leadership, Psychology, and Organizational Behavior* (New York: Harper & Row, 1960).

[10] Dorwin Cartwright and A. F. Zander (eds.), *Group Dynamics: Research and Theory* (New York: Harper & Row, 1960, 2nd edition), p. 122.

librium, and others gradually drifting toward psychological membership.[11]

Another study, reported by Raven and Rietsema, carried the title, "The Effects of Varied Clarity of Group Goal and Group Path Upon the Individual and His Relation to His Group." Among the hypotheses tested were:

1. The greater the clarity of the group situation, the more will the individual be attracted to the group-goal-related task.
2. The greater the clarity of the group situation, the less non-task-directed tension will be experienced by the individual.
3. The greater the clarity of the group situation, the less hostile feelings will be experienced by the individual.
5. The greater the clarity of the group situation, the greater the group-belongingness of the individual.
8. The greater the clarity of the group situation, the more will the group be able to influence the individual.[12]

These researchers summarized part of the study in this manner:

Our hypotheses were, by and large, well supported: Comparing the two experimental conditions, we found that, as an individual, the subject in the clear condition was more interested in the personal task and showed less hostility. As a group member, the subject who had a clear picture of his group goal and group path experienced greater feelings of group-belongingness, particularly as manifested in an involvement with the group goal and in sympathy with group emotions. He was also more able to perceive social differentiation and more willing to accept influence from his group than subjects who were unclear about the goals and paths of their group.[13]

What does this mean for the supervisor?

Fiedler's report, "The Leader's Psychological Distance and Group Effectiveness," summarized his research on this point as follows:

In summary, we have here presented a series of studies which indicate that psychologically distant leaders are more effective in promoting the productivity of task groups than are leaders with psychologically closer interpersonal relations.[14]

A number of generalizations may be advanced to account for these findings; that is, that psychologically closer, warmer relations make it difficult for the leader to discipline his subordinates and that a tendency to become emotionally dependent on one or two group members encourages rivalries and the charge of favoritism. Even though the populations studied by the above researchers do not include professional school personnel, strong and appropriate inferences can be drawn by the instructional leader.

What inferences can you draw from these research evidences?

For the supervisor who chooses to study the process of change, it matters little whether the research in this field

[11] *Ibid.*, p. 139.
[12] *Ibid.*, pp. 402–410.
[13] *Ibid.*, pp. 411–412.
[14] *Ibid.*, p. 605.

proves to be contrary to his traditional notions about the interrelationships of people and the process of change. The extent to which he is willing and able to explore the basic research in this area is a measure of his ability to be an adequate leader in the instructional program where the major responsibility is focused upon the establishment of the procedures of change.

The management of change must involve the consideration of many factors. Among them are the people, the situation which constitutes the environment in which the people work, and well-supported factual information about the process of change. While it is recognized that all of the evidence is not in, and perhaps never will be, with respect to change processes, this does not constitute an excuse for omitting that which is reasonably well established at the present time. The instructional leader who would become a manager of change must discipline himself to recognize all of these factors as a responsibility of his position. He must be able to appreciate a proposal coming from any source which might or might not shake the sense of security of himself or those who depend upon his leadership. He must be able to look squarely at such proposals and raise these questions with himself: (1) Can the proposal be analyzed into some constituent parts, and (2) Can such an analysis be supported by well-established criteria which are serviceable for the instructional program? If the suggestions appear to be those which ought to be tried, what must the leader stop doing that he has been accustomed to doing, and what must he do that he has not done before?

The instructional leader, in finding answers to these questions, may find the best direction in fulfilling the responsibilities of leadership. He must listen carefully to the proposals, rationale for change, and research-supported evidence of those who would help him change to better ways. From himself, he must demand more time for study, more evaluation of established purposes and practices, a great willingness to explore change possibilities, and a stern control over his nonteaching interests which might dissipate many hours of productive potential in the leadership functions related to the management of change.

SELECTED REFERENCES

1. Bass, Bernard M., *Leadership, Psychology, and Organizational Behavior*. New York: Harper & Row, 1960.
2. Bennis, Warren G., Kenneth D. Benne, and Robert Chin (eds.), *The Planning of Change*. New York: Holt, Rinehart, and Winston, 1961. pp. 154–156.
3. Browning, Robert, "Andrea del Sarto," in *Complete Poetical Works of Browning*. Boston: Houghton Mifflin (Cambridge ed.), 1895. p. 346.
4. Cartwright, Dorwin, and A. F. Zander (eds.), *Group Dynamics:*

Research and Theory. New York: Harper & Row, 1960, 2nd ed. pp. 122, 139, 402–410, 411–412, and 605.
5. Commission on the Reorganization of Secondary Education, *Cardinal Principles of Secondary Education*. Washington, D.C.: United States Bureau of Education, Bulletin No. 35, 1918.
6. National Education Association, Educational Policies Commission, *The Purposes of Education in American Democracy*. Washington, D.C.: NEA, 1938. Chap. II.
7. National Education Association, Educational Policies Commission, *The Central Purpose of American Education*. Washington, D.C.: NEA, 1961.
8. Netzer, Lanore A., *et al., Education, Administration, and Change*. New York: Harper & Row, 1970.
9. Netzer, Lanore A., Glen G. Eye, Robert D. Krey, Ardelle Graef, and J. Fred Overman, *Interdisciplinary Foundations of Supervision*. Boston: Allyn & Bacon, 1970, chap. II.
10. Plato, *The Republic* (trans. O. O. Shorey). Boston: Harvard University Press, 1935.
11. Pope, Alexander, "Essay on Criticism," in *The Pleasures of Pope*. London: Hamish Hamilton, 1949. p. 25.
12. Spencer, Herbert, *Education: Intellectual, Moral, and Physical*. New York: Appleton-Century-Crofts, 1860.

Part II

THE PATTERNS OF SUPERVISION

The action pattern for a custom-built program was developed in Part I and progressed from assumptions, to principles, to objectives, to criteria, and finally to procedures. In designing a supervisory program, all effort is directional and the *products* are the central target. This does not imply that the procedures are of little importance; it does imply that supervision without a focal point might be only an intellectual exercise.

Supervision is a functional part of the total administrative service of the school system. It must have an identity in the administrative hierarchy if it is to be supported by the proper directional assistance and if it is to have opportunities for achieving its purposes. It cannot take place in isolation. The precise location in the hierarchy, however, is of less importance than the purposes to which it has been assigned.

Administrative service requires people, an environment, and interrelationships between them. Supervision may be identified by designating positions, by job descriptions, and by its operational functions. This may be done by emphasizing one of the means indicated above or by a balance of all of them. At the very minimum, the identity must recognize the superordinate, subordinate, and peer positions, all of which must be carefully defined. Their interrelationships also must be described.

Structural patterns of school systems tend to show variety, and each is unique. The pattern of a particular system does not change markedly, even though it differs from others.

Supervision, then, must be custom-built and flexible. While the structural pattern normally is static, patterns within it may be flexible. Individuals also may be flexible even though the structure changes little. This is why the literature includes numerous discussions of how a line and staff organization, normally authoritative in its leadership, can be adapted by individuals to democratic relationships. The mere existence of such arguments shows that structural patterns have not necessarily dictated the behaviors of individuals.

To provide a common understanding of the difference between the structural and operational patterns with which this Part is concerned, their definitions are given here:

The structural pattern for supervision is the systematic array of anticipated requisite tasks, appropriate to the achievement of instructional purposes, into a workable arrangement of defined positions with described power or control relationships.

The operational pattern for supervision is the set of observable behavioral characteristics and interrelationships displayed by the position incumbents in a formally organized group.

The term "line and staff organization" has been used so long that often the "and" has been dropped. "Line" and "staff" designate two major areas of position and functional relationships. These distinctions will be recognized in Chapters 5 and 6.

The focal point of staff responsibility and source of staff power is in the line office to which it is attached, usually the central office. This is the legal and philosophical basis of staff power. Staff influence, on the other hand, is more related to individual competence than to legal authority.

Staff positions may have subordinate positions attached to them. Thus, there may be miniature line organizations within staff groups. Each person in a staff position has obligations to his superordinates, his subordinates, and his peers. Most of the functions of staff positions may be classified into the categories of *contributory* and *supportive*. To clarify these categories, the following definitions are offered:

The contributory function of supervision is the performance of those tasks under voluntary or prescribed controls which reinforce the efforts of others in the achievement of results appropriate to the purpose ascribed to the organization.

The supportive function of supervision is the performance of all tasks in a manner and to a purpose that will uphold and strengthen other personnel in achieving the results properly expected of each as incumbent of a related position.

These two functions are discussed in detail in Chapters 7 and 8.

In Part I it was stated that the assumptions held by the

authors would be recalled in later chapters. Assumptions seven and nine are particularly related to Chapter 5; assumptions eight and eighteen, to Chapter 6; assumptions eleven and nineteen, to Chapter 7; and assumptions nine, ten, and eleven, to Chapter 8.

This introduction has been presented to show that patterns for a functional service are found partially in location and partially in the way people perform their assigned tasks. The delineation of this intent is presented in the next four chapters.

5

The Structural Pattern for Supervision

The specific tasks to be performed in a complex organization seldom occur as isolated activities. The individual performer may feel isolated and may even seek separation from colleagues. Separation, however, may be more a state of mind than an organizational reality. When the actions of one person affect the present or potential activities of another person, unilateralness is non-existent and the multilateral consequences are identified easily.

The school system involves the efforts of many certificated as well as classified personnel. The attention here is directed primarily to the certificated teachers, supervisors, and administrators whose specialized abilities must be meshed into working relationships that make all energy and talent serve the purpose of the educational system. The structural pattern is crucial in identifying the conditions which permit and encourage mutually helpful behaviors and which assist in preventing individually destructive behaviors.

The theory of supervision as presented in this book is based upon a series of acknowledged, identified, and enumerated assumptions held by the authors. It was indicated in the introduction to Part II that certain of the assumptions listed in Chapter 3 were related to the various chapters in this section. Each assumption cannot be exclusive with respect to other assumptions or chapters. For the convenience of presentation, however, each assumption appears in the chapter to which it is most related.

Assumptions seven and nine are related to this chapter more specifically than to any other. They are stated as follows:

7. Supervision is a specialized phase of administration.

9. The establishment and maintenance of the structural and operational patterns that encourage cooperative and coordinative behaviors are equally weighted responsibilities of superordinates, peers, and subordinates.

Supervision, then, being an integral part of central office functions, finds its diagrammatic place in the structural charts in close relationship to the superintendent. These assumptions imply that the phase of administrative services called supervision can be performed by either line and/or staff officers and, further, that the important attachment of line and staff personnel to the central office is functional rather than geographic.

A simple exception to this central office focus of staff services, however, is found in the individual school principalship which needs some specialized help for positions such as guidance director, director of instruction, or other designated specialized personnel. In such a case, the assumption does not hold as specifically implied. It indicates, nonetheless, that in the more usual circumstances specialized personnel are attached to the central office, which is the focal point for the structural pattern that is established.

In order to bring into focus more clearly what is meant by the structural pattern as indicated in the chapter title, the following definition is offered:

The structural pattern for supervision is the systematic array of anticipated requisite tasks, appropriate to the achievement of instructional purposes, into a workable arrangement of defined positions with described power or control relationships.

Draft your definition of the structural pattern for supervision.

Since this book deals with only one of the numerous and variously designated positions in the organizational structure, there will be no attempt to discuss other central office positions except as they must be related in both the structural and operational patterns of the services of supervision.

What, if anything, is wrong with "empire-building"?

The temptation to perceive any position, particularly by the person holding that position, as an essential and specialized kind of universe is always present. Position incumbents see their positions in relation to numerous other positions. They may fail, at the same time, to recognize that there is not only a higher level in the hierarchy of control but also a necessity for recognizing the controlled relationships among the various positions attached to the central office. The same statement might be made about any subordinate position. At any level, this type of "empire-builder" would seek to create about himself and his position a coterie of associates, each giving support to his particular esoteric and technical contribution to the operation of the school.

CONTROL SYSTEMS

List some less visible controls.

Control is inherent in any structural pattern whether the enterprise be private or public. The schools are public enterprises which have readily recognized systems of control. Federal laws, regulations, and court decisions constitute elements of control. Some of the controls are far removed from the scene of action which they control. Many are not known or are not recognized as control factors by many staff members either in the upper or lower echelons of the organization. State laws, regulations, and court decisions also have control qualities, normally to a more extensive degree than is true for those of the federal government. Controls can be both regulatory and supportive if so viewed by the persons affected. They can be the sources of frustration for either a superordinate or a subordinate position incumbent if he does not know that they exist. In one instance he may plan his own program of activities within the limits of known controls and in another instance he may experience the starts, stops, and restarts of the trial-and-error method. In any instance, these conditions usually are described as the limits of autonomy; but limits of autonomy must be discovered and declared at each level of operation.

Federal and state controls are policed at the local level primarily by the superintendent. It is his responsibility to indicate the limits of autonomy of the supervisor as well as other staff officers affected by such controls. Much closer than the state and federal controls are those more visible to the local school personnel, inherent in the authority of the local board of education. In most states the local board or its counterpart has the major control over the nature and limits of the autonomy of individual practitioners within the structural pattern. In many situations in which the school board is not acting independently, it is credited with exercising the controls even though it is performing only a ministerial function for another and superordinate legal agency.

The superintendent as the executive officer of the board of education must impose the controls ordered by that board. But he, in the process, exercises some controls of his own design and initiative. These are based upon his insights, knowledge, foresight, ego disposition, and many other factors. The subordinate—in this case, the supervisor—must find the area of activity and responsibility attainable within the interdictions of all of these controls. The controls mentioned above are visible and often readily identifiable as controls.

A type of invisible control, however, is that of the abilities possessed by those who have been employed to fill the various positions in the organization. The supervisor's ultimate success is found in the improved products of the teaching-learning activities. He must depend upon an intermediary—the teacher—to produce these products. Limited ability or limited use of ability on the part of the teacher constitutes a serious control over the supervisory efforts. On the other hand, if the supervisor establishes a purpose or commitment for which he does not have the necessary technical preparation or basic intelligence, he has imposed upon himself a control that is as real as and perhaps more frustrating and devastating than those imposed by other persons. Since the abilities of individuals show great variation, one of the planning tasks of the superintendent of schools in organizing his administrative staff is the wise deployment of available talent. This means that, as the personnel in the various positions change from year to year, it may be necessary to redeploy the available talent. This, in turn, may require a revision of the structural pattern.

IDENTIFICATION OF TASKS

These authors believe that the specific tasks of supervision and other functions of administration can be identified and classified. It should be recognized that, in separating one function from a cluster of functions which are designated by a generic term such as administration, there must, of necessity, be overlap in the categories of classification. In fact, if the assumption is accepted that "supervision is a specialized phase of administration," all of the items classified as supervision must be administrative in nature and parts of the total constellation of administrative functions. Perhaps it would be simpler at this point to indicate that this dichotomy can be achieved if the tasks which are most uniquely supervisory in nature and others which are primarily managerial are identified. Even with these presumed differences in the nature of function, it is impossible to do other than identify the extremes and recognize that between them there is a broad gray area of tasks that might be classified one way or the other.

Classifying or dichotomizing is primarily an intellectual activity. The real purpose of recognizing the differences is to accept the evidenced need for the diversification of tasks in the total operation of the school system. The diversification of tasks is a recognition that a division of labor becomes necessary in the complex operation of the school. The division of labor or the diversification of tasks, then, becomes one of allocating responsibility and authority to certain designated positions. Stated in another way, the diversification of tasks stimulates a redistribution of authority within which the specific nature of supervisory functions may be redesigned. The concern here is with that position designated *supervisor,* or any similar position identified by some other name, with a task description that involves those unique behaviors classified as supervision. Even the most perfunctory look at the school operation should result in the identification of tasks such as teaching duty, guidance service, curricular development, cocurricular direction, management of school property, accounting for school finances, keeping of official records, preparing official reports, community relationships, and mutual professional assistance, along with as many others as one would care to enumerate. The more extended and detailed this list becomes, the greater the overlapping of the categories in the assigned responsibilities of each individual.

If the identification of tasks is confined to large categories, then in most instances it will be possible to identify a person and a position in specific classifications. An example is found in the area of guidance and counseling. Most school systems need some specialized assistance in guidance and, when a school system becomes large enough, some coordination of the various facilities and talents within the system becomes necessary. At this time a director of guidance probably should be appointed. The director of guidance enters the position with a relationship to many people other than those directly concerned with guidance and counseling activities. A similar situation can be found in the various other types of supervisory needs. If the supervisor should be one of those in the special areas, such as music, the particular tasks and behaviors for that particular position can be identified and the responsibilities can be enumerated. The authority could be granted to carry out the kinds of tasks delegated to the position. This does not mean, however, that the music supervisor should operate a private enterprise with little responsibility for coordinating his activities with the many other operational aspects of the school system. It is necessary that the place of the music supervisor be identified in the hierarchy of positions called the structural pattern. It is equally necessary that the relationships of his position be identified, enumerated, and described so that the incumbent may work in harmony with other operatives within the structure.

How does the provision for the diversification of tasks encourage or discourage "empire-building"?

The structural pattern, then, is the device by which each functionnaire can assess or be apprised of his place in this hierarchy. At the same time, the pattern must indicate the systems of communication—up, down, and across—in the organization. The more vividly the superintendent can clarify these interrelationships, the greater the probability that his efforts to staff for all the responsibilities in the administrative area will be achieved.

How are structural patterns and administrative procedures related?

Structural or organizational charts too often are drafted as though they were something apart from the actual operation of the school system. They seem to be a sort of insignia of administrative status rather than a functional instrument for establishing and facilitating the relationships between people for the achievement of a common goal. Whenever possible the two concepts should be kept together or, at least, presented in such a manner that each individual position incumbent can see not only the structural pattern but also the interrelationships available to him. Working conditions, as well as working effectiveness, are facilitated if each staff member knows the systems of appraisal, review, and appeal. These, in addition to the types of communications systems characteristic of the organization, encourage the staff to move forward coordinately and cooperatively as a team constituting the administrative and supervisory staff of the school system.

ASSESSING THE PATTERN

One of the primary problems of the superintendent is to develop a structural pattern in a manner that he and his advisors believe will achieve the best system of relationships. In this sense, the superintendent has the same problem as a gardener. The gardener cannot plant the seeds, then fail to attend them during the growing season if he expects a harvest as envisioned at the time of the planting. Neither is a superintendent able to strike off at one point in time a pattern that will remain adequate through a long tenure in office. It is not merely a problem of the changing purposes in education which call for different or additional specialized services that must be provided in the form of staff positions. The instructional program is involved in the changing purposes of education which, in turn, demand new and special personnel in the area of supervision. The structural pattern also must be updated to accommodate changing school purposes and procedures. Assuming that the school purpose or purposes have not changed over a substantial period of time, however, the superintendent still is unable to coast along in organizational peace in the belief that the structural pattern remains constant and adequate until some substantial purpose of education changes.

How often should there be a formal evaluation of the structural pattern? What evaluative criteria should be used?

The superintendent must keep the structural pattern compatible with the original and central purpose for which it was established. The constant checking of the composite administrative pattern is necessary in order that the operational patterns that evolve might not contradict the intent of the structural pattern.

The ways in which the operational patterns may change the structural pattern is the subject of Chapter 6. Suffice it to say at this point that there must be eternal vigilance on the part of the superintendent in keeping the central purpose of the organization as the central point of effort in structural assessment. Failing to do this will result in the destruction of a pattern which may have been originally designed wisely and proudly.

UNIT RELATIONSHIPS

One of the most difficult problems in designing the structural pattern is that of determining the relationships between the central office unit and the individual building unit. This can be called the problem of *centralized* versus *unit* control (see references 1, 2, 3, 5). There are basic assumptions about formal organization which help to detail the relationships between the various offices. Personnel problems cannot be solved by the structural pattern alone. The solution of the personal and personnel problems that evolve can be given a favorable environment through a suitable structural pattern in which people may work out day-to-day relationships. It is to be recognized, however, that the statement of general working relationships between a central office staff member, such as the supervisor of elementary schools, and the individual elementary school principal is no more than a part of the environment. Many opportunities should be provided for members of the administrative and supervisory team to have face-to-face meetings regarding what their position interrelationships should be with respect to the performance of their respective tasks.

What would be the effect on the structural pattern if supervisors were attached to the principal's office?

Theoretically, authority rests in the line office. No matter how one may rationalize or argue the theory that the supervisor as a staff officer possesses no authority in his contact with the teacher, the practical situations seem to deny it. The supervisor stands as a person ready to supply the teacher with a specialized type of help. The structural chart would show this relationship as a dotted line rather than as a solid line. The charts detailing the organizational relationships have oversimplified the many complexities that are involved in the relationships between people. Even though the superintendent might declare that the supervisor did not possess authority over the teachers and even though the supervisor agreed with this, in most instances his every contact with a teacher would be, in the teacher's perception, an authoritative contact. It is in this sense that the formalized chart cannot control, determine, or direct the day-to-day interrelationships between central office staff members and the individual classroom teachers. Even though the supervisor tries to exercise no authority or control over the teacher, the teacher's perception of his possession of authority and control will cause the teacher to react in about the same manner as if the supervisor really possessed them.

The efforts at clarifying the limits of autonomy through charts and patterns, in the sense indicated above, fall short of achieving the operational relationships that constitute the chief purpose for the existence of the structural pattern. There are many subtle control mechanisms available for those who choose to use them and they never have and probably never will be identified in a diagrammatic pattern. These are the simple and complex mechanisms stimulated from a variety of known and unknown motivations which cannot easily be accounted for in the structure of an organization. An attempt, however, is made in Chapter 6 to define and describe some of these.

PLACE OF THE SUPERVISORY POSITION

The supervisory position, ideally, is a staff position attached to the superintendent's office. This staff officer holds at least three basic responsibilities—all accountable to the superintendent. The first responsibility is that of collecting and organizing information about the instructional program which is presumed to be of substantial assistance to the superintendent as he makes the important decisions affecting the program. The second responsibility is that the supervisor should be able to help the superintendent in interpreting the information collected. The third responsibility of the supervisor is to act under the direction of the superintendent in the specialized contributory and supportive activities primarily involved with planning instructional improvements after the proper evaluative devices have indicated the point at which an improvement program should start.

In this third category of responsibility, the superintendent may call upon the supervisor to be available to the individual schools and classrooms for consultation as the plan for change comes to the point of implementation. It is at this point of staff relationships that much of the stress and strain develops between the individual principal and the supervisor. Some supervisors may be unable to restrain their desires to influence others or their personal motivations for ego satisfaction in order to remain in the staff pattern when working with teachers in an individual building. In those cases where the supervisors fail to follow the structural pattern, there is the potential of strife with the building principal. If the supervisor is a particularly aggressive person, it is possible to bypass the principal to such an extent that the function of his office is completely vitiated. More of the aspects of these operational relationships are discussed in the next chapter.

PROLIFERATION OF SUBUNITS

One of the complicating aspects of developing the structural pattern for individual school systems has been that of the proliferation of organizational subunits. There is little doubt about the inclination of people in general to organize for the accomplishment of almost any idea that any one individual conceives. School personnel are among the greatest committee-forming peoples on earth. Schools now have departments, advisory councils, supervisory councils, elected committees, standing committees, *ad hoc* committees, vertical committees, horizontal committees, professional organization committees, special-area committees, and so on to the complete proliferation of almost every functional aspect of a school system's operation. As these subunits proliferate, the problem of structuring them into one pattern with a common purpose becomes more and more difficult.

In few instances is it possible to strike out, in one bold move, all of the organizational characteristics from a school district and to begin anew. The actual problem is to assess continuously the purpose and function of the structural pattern as a pattern. Ideally, the pattern should have a profound relationship to the establishment of an optimum operational pattern. The two patterns, however, need not operate congruently in so far as goodness and badness are concerned. In other words, there could exist a very proper and potentially profitable structural pattern but the school system adopting that pattern might be unwise and employ a substantial number of people who ignore the system-wide pattern and enter into the enterprises of empire-building. The nature of the people, then, can completely vitiate or substantially change the structural pattern.

Perhaps the proliferation of subunits shows that each individual in the total organization has a desire to feel that he is near some point of control. The closeness of that point of control to his responsibilities will possess virtues of inordinate appropriateness in contrast to those aspects of the structural pattern characteristics a little further from his own scene of action.

Structural patterns can be facilitators only if they are made to serve as such. In turn, the structural pattern can become a phobia for that superintendent who does not see the action potential of a static design. Its fulfillment in the operational pattern will determine whether the structural pattern is serving the purpose for which it was designed.

The structural pattern for supervision is the systematic array of anticipated requisite tasks, appropriate to the achievement of instructional purposes, into a workable arrangement of defined positions with described power or control relationships.

SELECTED REFERENCES

1. Castetter, William B., *Administering the School Personnel Program.* New York: Macmillan, 1962. Chap. III.
2. Dalton, Gene W., Louis B. Barnes, and Abraham Zaleznik, *The Distribution of Authority in Formal Organizations.* Boston: Harvard University Press, Division of Research, Graduate School of Business Administration, 1967. Chap. III.
3. Filley, Alan C. and Robert J. House, *Managerial Process and Organizational Behavior.* Glenview, Illinois: Scott, Foresman and Company, 1969. Chap. III.

4. Kast, Fremont E. and James E. Rosenzweig, *Organization and Management: A Systems Approach.* New York: McGraw-Hill, 1970.
5. Knezevich, Stephen J., *Administration of Public Education.* New York: Harper & Row, 1969. Chap. II.

6

The Operational Pattern of Supervision

Chapter 5 dealt with the structural pattern for supervision which constituted the systematic arrangement of duties and relationships between and among the personnel involved in the work of the school. In a sense, the structural pattern is the idealization of the relationships between the people occupying the various positions required in the accomplishment of group purposes. To the extent that it is an idealization of relationships and functions, there is the presumed anticipation of all the variations of demands that might be made by the clientele being served by the system as well as by those directly involved in its operation.

An assumption that the idealized pattern of an organization would be pure and accurate in anticipating the way all people relate to each other and to the tasks of particular positions would be naive. The normal and basic differences in people would mitigate against the achievement of the idealized array of tasks and relationships. Man is confronted almost each minute of every day with some sort of organized pattern of control over his behavior. The traffic laws, with concrete reminders in the form of traffic signs, are presumed to provide a plan by which people will conduct their automotive mobility without interfering with or interrupting others. It is well known that a traffic sign often is not seen by a driver or, if seen, is not obeyed. In some instances the driver may forget momentarily the significance and implication of the directive of a road sign or misinterpret it. On the other

Provide other illustrations of how people react to external controls.

hand, the driver may see the sign, know its significance, intend to observe its requirements, and yet, in the performance of his own duties with respect to it, fail to operate his vehicle in a manner that would not interfere with the rights, privileges, and safety of others. This oversimplified example is used to illustrate how the structural pattern and the actuality of individual behaviors under that pattern may be far from the anticipated congruences.

The structural chart may be beautifully drawn and based upon carefully considered relationships, functions, and controls. Those who occupy the various school positions, however, may fail to see, may see and misinterpret, may choose to ignore, or may see and interpret correctly but fail to perform according to the anticipation of the person developing the systematic array of duties and functions which comprise the structural chart.

The introduction to Part II included the definitions which sought to distinguish between the structural and operational patterns. For the purpose of emphasis, the definition for the operational pattern of supervision is repeated here:

The operational pattern for supervision is the set of observable behavioral characteristics and interrelationships displayed by the position incumbents in a formally organized group.

List some of the other factors.

The central thrust described in the definition is that of setting apart the behaviors of position incumbents from the descriptions of the positions in terms of anticipated tasks which are to be found in the defined structural pattern for supervision. The concern now is with the people who occupy the positions—their characteristics, personality needs, ambitions, concepts of themselves, and many other factors which condition behavior. These factors differ from person to person. There is little hope for achieving a structural pattern so universal that it would guarantee the similar or common behavior of different people when assigned to a specific position. This is not to suggest that a structural pattern is not useful because of the variations in the people who hold the positions. Rather, it is to indicate that the structure provides only broad guidelines within which the personal variations may be kept within those bounds acceptable to institutional purposes and within the limits that can be tolerated by colleagues.

In Part I it was indicated that each step in the development of a program of supervision followed an "action pattern." It was emphasized that all decisions with respect to the structural pattern had their beginnings in the assumptions held by those who create and direct its operation. From the list of assumptions held by these authors (see pp. 52–53), numbers eight and eighteen relate particularly to the operational pattern:

8. The limits and boundaries of supervisory authority, autonomy, and responsibility are defined by individuals and groups influencing the organization who also possess varying degrees of authority, autonomy, and responsibility.

18. The appurtenances of superordination do not include rights and privileges withheld from the statuses of subordination.

Authority, autonomy, and responsibility are not easily communicated in a structural chart. The chart can encourage what may be considered inherent to the definition of authority, autonomy, and responsibility. It remains, however, for the devisor of a chart to describe what is meant by the inferred relationships in terms of authority, autonomy, and responsibility. The implication to be drawn from the two assumptions above is that a structural diagram must be supplemented by descriptions of operational guidelines which, preferably, should be drafted cooperatively by the affected personnel.

The chief administrator in a school system is the superintendent. This position of authority has its origin in the board of education and the laws of the state. Even though the structural chart or pattern is approved by the board of education or even though the origin of the pattern was fixed by state statute, the superintendent still must make those determinations which give character to the operation of the school as an organization. The conditions under which work shall be done must be defined for each position and for the interrelationships between positions in each school system. Further, the position responsibility requires frequent assessments as to whether the people in the organization are conforming to the plan and to an acceptable perception of the operational relationships that constitute the operational pattern.

KNOWLEDGE ABOUT POSITION

The above discussion of structural and operational patterns facilitates a move to the consideration of what might happen to a person approaching a first assignment to a supervisory position. The initial assignment is considered at this point because of the critical nature of the position for the person accepting it. The new supervisor must have had some personal motivation in making himself available to the employing officer who had a supervisory position to fill. This personal motivation is not easily assessed. Motives should never be assumed by another party except as specific information is available from the one who is to occupy the position.

Personal motivation, however, may have many implications for the way in which the person will perform as a supervisor. If the supervisory position has been accepted because it is seen as a way to achieve the prestige which has not been realized as a classroom teacher, the performance may indicate a need to satisfy a desire to gain recognition. The motivation, on the other hand, may have been a desire to possess a position of influence or control over other persons. This desire may have been stimulated by resentment at having been controlled. On the positive side, the motivation may have been the desire to see the instructional program changed in a direction in which the ideas impressed upon others would result in better learning opportunities for pupils. In any case, the person may have been driven by a sincere conscience. A wish to exercise influence or control in order that a particular concept of instruction may be followed might cause one supervisor to have less flexibility than another who wants to impose particular facility for the techniques of measurement upon his staff. In either case, the control over the supervised might be equally firm, but it might have differing implications for the effect both on the morale of the teacher and on the flexibility of the instructional program or the solution of instructional problems which may be identified.

Devise interview questions designed to gain information about the operational relationships of a position.

Regardless of the personal motivation of the person accepting a supervisory position, reliable knowledge should be sought about that position. It is at the point of recruiting and accepting positions that many of the basic understandings of the structural pattern should be clarified for those about to become incumbent of a position in a school system. It is equally important that the employing officer indicate to the candidate the nature of the relationships that are considered most desirable in the school system. The applicant should be given the opportunity to decide whether it is possible to work creatively and profitably under such conditions.

Instances of supervisory positions being created in a school system by the decree of the superintendent of schools are well known. This often has been done without the previous knowledge of the teaching staff. Sometimes such decrees have been issued without prior warning to other members of the administrative and supervisory staff. In such cases the first person to occupy the new position, whether he is from within or from outside the system, accepts a more difficult role. If the other members of the staff who become colleagues in the total enterprise must accept the newcomer without warning, there is little hope that they will have any basic understanding of the purpose and function of this new position. This easily could lead to antagonism on the part of those intended to be influenced by the new position and its occupant. An environment is created which has serious implications for the operational patterns which can or might be established. In situations of this type, it is obvious that the superintendent has failed to follow those known administrative procedures which might have given both the purpose of the new position and the new occupant of that position a reasonable chance to become a functioning part of the structure and an acceptable and positive part of the operation of that school system (see reference 5).

The superintendent, on the other hand, may have laid the groundwork exceptionally well. Previous consultation may have been held with the entire staff regarding the need for services not currently provided by the array of existing positions. Other consultations with his colleagues about the tasks of the new position as well as of the characteristics of the person to be assigned may have been included. All of these things may have been communicated effectively to the applicant. An acceptance by the applicant, according to all reasonable rules of conduct, then means a commitment to the major aspects of both the structural and operational systems. Under these conditions the occupant of this position assumes the tasks in a favorable environment.

How can position evaluations become part of the in-service program for the total staff?

During the first year of the supervisor's experience in the position, the concepts of the evidence of success will begin to emerge into prominence. These concepts may make substantial differences in the degree to which an honest personal commitment to the structural and the operational patterns has been made. If there is a compelling nature to show "results," the supervisor will seek types of behavior and influence upon the program that are the most visible in a short period of time. This may or may not prove satisfactory to the superintendent and to other colleagues in the school system responsible for creating the position. Frequent opportunities to communicate with the superintendent should be available. The purpose of this communication would be to make frequent assessments of the extent to which the system patterns have been kept in proper relationship. At no time and at no point can there be, nor should there be, complete congruence between the structural and operational patterns. The congruence of the relationships should mean that they are mutually supportive but not in a sense that one could or should determine the detailed nature of the other.

What expectations of the superintendent encourage this haste for visible outputs?

How often should the degree of congruence between patterns be assessed? Explain.

The attention given here to the new supervisor has been for the purpose of illustrating the kinds of problems involved in the interrelationships of the structural and operational patterns. It is not to imply that an experienced supervisor going to a new position or remaining in a position over a long period of time does not have problems comparable to those described above. Frequent assessments with and by the superintendent are as important for the experienced supervisor as for the beginner.

The operational pattern has greater mobility with respect to drift and change than does the structural pattern. The structural pattern is static and the operational pattern is dependent upon individuals who possess great variability in behavior; thus, the two patterns are substantially different in nature. Consequently, the experienced supervisor has some hazards not encountered by a new supervisor. The more important difference is that the experienced supervisor becomes entrenched in a confidence resulting from previous actions. This, in its extreme, is probably what is meant by saying a person is "in a rut." On the other hand, there is no need to assume that an experienced person lacks the capacity to make adaptations or major changes.

CLARITY OF PURPOSE AND FUNCTION

The need for clarity of purpose and of function cannot be over-emphasized. The chief purpose for establishing a structural pattern is to clarify tasks and relationships between various persons involved in the organization's operation. Clarity of purpose and function is not achieved at any one point in time and held inviolate by all parties involved over an extended period. Purposes may change in actuality or they may change in the perceptions by which people hold them. In either case clarity may be lost for those not involved in planning the operations of the school system. Others can be little involved when the change in purpose is the change in the perception of the purpose by one person. Unfortunately, the change in the perception of purpose may take place so gradually that the individual nurturing such change may not be aware of it. A frequent review of purpose and function is important not only for the supervisors but also for the superintendent who must maintain the efficiency and effectiveness of the structural and operational patterns.

One point of stress between the structural and operational patterns is that involving the status connotations of the various positions. Specifically, such a problem is presented in achieving and maintaining the proper working relationships between the general and the special-area supervisors. In many school systems, the supervisory program originating in the central office is headed by a general supervisor, a director of instruction, an assistant superintendent in charge of instruction, or some other position designation which implies a similar function. This person has a corps of supervisors working under his direction. In a sense, the staff officer—the general supervisor—has some line relationships to the special-area supervisors by whatever position designations they are given. Sometimes it is extremely difficult for the general supervisor to remember that, while there are line or command relationships to the supervisory staff working under his office, such relationships may not carry over to the line offices such as the principalship. Another aspect of the problem in operational relationships is that, with other officers in the same echelon, the general supervisor has a coordinative function not quite comparable to the narrowness of coordinative responsibilities of the special-area supervisor. The degree of comprehension of coordination may cause some rift in the smooth operational relationships of the general and special-area supervisors. This occurs not so much as a matter of status but as one of communication in the maintenance of the originally established purpose.

In the case of elementary and secondary school supervisors, there often is a status problem as well as an organizational one. The concept of the educational ladder in the organization of education seems to preserve some undesirable and unsavory status implications. It is sometimes difficult for the structural relationships as described in the chart to be realized in the operational relationships between the elementary and secondary school supervisors because of the prestige perceptions held by both educators and lay people.

Another type of problem involved in the achieving of profitable operational relationships is that of harmonizing the tasks and the procedures of the different members of the central office staff even when they have achieved a common perception of purposes and functions. An example of this operational problem is that of the school psychologist and the general or special-area supervisor. The one focuses on the individual pupil while the other is more concerned with the teacher's success with all pupils in the class. The person who is most keenly aware of this lack of coordination is the classroom teacher. The general or special-area supervisor establishes the minimum expectations to be realized by the pupils in a particular class. This becomes of serious import to that teacher, because achieving these expectations may be a determinant of salary, promotion, retention, or other items of security and professional advancement. The school psychologist, on the other hand, may be studying some individual cases in which a certain type of therapy is preferred. He may be pursuing the expectation declared as an approved function for his position and also may be pursuing the achievement of this function within an operational pattern that appears acceptable. For example, the therapy deemed wise by the school psychologist might involve keeping a particular child with a problem in the regular class. This may occupy much more time on the part of the teacher than profitably can be given to one of thirty or more pupils. Both the psychologist and the supervisor may have a common purpose with respect to assisting the teachers to accomplish maximum outcomes in terms of pupil learning. The teacher, however, is then confronted with the choice of pursuing the advice and urgent request of the school psychologist, whose concern is with the therapy of the pupil under consideration, or of the supervisor, whose concern is with the output expected for the whole class.

What problems are involved in coordinating the work of instructional and non-instructional supervisors?

The teacher in the above situation is torn between two proper obligations. Each supervisory officer is working within the defined function and expectations for his position. Each is intent upon establishing good operational relationships and the intentions are sincere and appropriate. On the other hand, the tasks of the supervisor result in the teacher being influenced by two superior officers whose divergent expectations create a serious and frustrating situation. It is easy to declare that a third or fourth person should resolve this conflict for the teacher and that the principal of the building is the most appropriate party to harmonize the expectations of the two supervisors, but the solution does not come so easily. In fact, it is one of the unresolved problems in both structural and operational patterns. Time must be granted

Who is responsible for coordination between various supervisory personnel? Why?

for the resolution of conflicts of this nature. At least recognizing the nature of the problem is the first step in its solution. Recognizing it as something not in violation of the operational pattern is wholesome and might contribute to its solution. An operational problem cannot be declared resolved even though it satisfies those in the supervisory or administrative positions. At no time should such problems be considered solved until the teacher has been prominent in the solution.

Another persisting and serious problem in achieving a good operational pattern might be termed "the soft and the strong hand on the same person." An illustration is that of the supervisor and the line officer, both of whom relate to the classroom teacher and have common concerns with respect to the success of the classroom activities. In the descriptions of the structural pattern, it is recognized that the staff officers have only consultant or advisory relationships to the classroom teacher. On the other hand, the principal of the building stands in a more authoritative or control relationship. The responsibility of the principal is to serve in an administrative fashion in so far as the school regulations are concerned. The principal must do the policing for the superintendent, for the board of education, or for the intent of the state statutes. This puts the principal in quite a different position from that of the supervisor or the consultant. The supervisor or the supervisory function is not to police the operation of a school to make sure that the intent of a superior organizational status is observed. It is simple for the individual teacher to look upon the supervisory function as the soft and supporting hand of a friendly person while at the same time seeing the hand of the administrator as hard because controls and sometimes sanctions must be exercised by that person.

Further discussion of the problem involved in this type of situation is presented in Chapters 7 and 8, in which the *contributory* and *supportive* functions of supervision are the points of concern. For the purpose of this chapter, the problem can be resolved simply but inadequately in terms of seeking the remedy in two forms. First, there must be continued effort on the part of the superintendent to make certain that the functions of the various positions have been carefully defined and that these definitions have been communicated, understood, and accepted by all members of the teaching, administrative, and supervisory staffs. The more clearly these functions are understood or perceived, the more probable it is that the teachers will not react as indicated above—namely, by feeling that the supervisor's hand is supportive and the principal's restrictive. A second way in which this operational problem may be resolved is also in the hands of the superintendent. Eternal alertness to the operational relationships of the various members of the supervisory staff as well as the various members of the administrative or line positions is essential. These persons must hold each other in a mutual respect based upon a common understanding of function. This should be achieved through their sincere desire to support the total operation of the school system rather than to realize personal and immediate goals to the disregard and possible destruction of the opportunity for others to achieve their goals in the organization (see Chapter 9). In pursuit of this condition, the superintendent must do the enforcing at the central office level just as the principal must be responsible for enforcing the approved procedures in the individual building.

SATISFACTION OF PERSONAL NEEDS

One of the fundamental rules in the operations of a large and complex organization such as a school is the need for satisfaction of individuals at all levels. Satisfaction is not realized in similar or comparable experiences for all members of the staff. What constitutes satisfaction for each individual is inextricably interwoven in the personal background of experience and sense of values, self image, and desire for a sense of personal worth. That which accomplishes this for one person may not accomplish it for another; yet, regardless of what is required for this satisfaction on the job, it becomes an important aspect of the operational pattern of a system.

Most people seek a sense of personal worth, and this causes a search for assurance that a contribution to the enterprise at hand has been made. It is well for all administrative, supervisory, and teaching staff members to remember that this desire for a sense of personal worth is also a problem for their colleagues at all levels. The superintendent is no exception, even though looked upon by members of the teaching staff and the subordinate administrative officers as the one person whose personal needs for satisfaction can be accommodated easily. This is rationalized on the basis that the superintendent has ready access to the board of education and that his continued employment by the board indicates that he has no status problem as an intermediary between the members of the staff, the board, and the people in the community. As a matter of fact, few teachers see the superintendent in an intermediate position at all, at least not to the extent that they see themselves in an intermediate position between the parents, the children, and the school administrative and supervisory staff.

Perhaps the genius of administration is in being able to establish structural and operational patterns which will make it possible for the maximum number of position incumbents to achieve a sense of personal worth. The superintendent's greatest assurance that such can be accomplished is through the careful definition of position expectation and the pursuit of proper analysis and appraisal of the behaviors of each person in a particular post. With the minimum of personal flexibility, the superintendent may be able to offer rewarding reinforcements to staff members at all levels in the achievement of this sense of worth. The sense of worth for each person will be involved in the images which they have of themselves. The image held by each individual will, in all probability, be most potent when he sees himself held in high esteem by his colleagues in teaching, supervisory, and administrative posts (see reference 2). At any rate, the problem of the operational pattern as recognized here is primarily that of perceiving, influencing, and reinforcing the best elements in human relationships.

INTERPERSONAL RELATIONSHIPS

Some of the problems of interpersonal relationships may be found in the goals held by individuals and the goals approved by the group. There are many different sources of goals and many different ways of describing them; consequently, mere reference to a difference between individual and group goals could lead to some misunderstanding. The point here is that the individual goal is that sought-for achievement by the individual through his own effort as opposed to his individual efforts to achieve the goals established by the group. Group goals are those goals agreed upon by the individual members of the group; for example, the goals selected by the third grade teachers as opposed to the group goals which might be called the system-wide expectations. The individual's personal goals and the individual's efforts to achieve the institutional goals sometimes come into conflict. One of the more promising ways of resolving these conflicts is through the process of identifying, analyzing, and discussing them.

It is axiomatic that each successful individual in a complex organization must possess some capacity for adaptation and change. If it is difficult to change modes of behavior, or even the goals which are sought personally, some adaptation must be made to a group enterprise in which others find it less difficult to effect change in behavior and purpose. One of the major contributions of the administrative and supervisory staff is to recognize the characteristics of interpersonal relationships and to exert influences toward the development of the more encouraging, supporting relationships between colleagues at any level and across all levels (see references 3, 5).

SANCTION SYSTEMS

The structural pattern, no matter how well designed and described, cannot accommodate all of the aspects of the operational relationships. The operational pattern normally is strongly influenced by a combination of the motivational characteristics and behaviors of the people involved. One of the procedures used by various administrative officers—and sometimes improperly appropriated by supervisory staff members—is that of developing sanction systems, or the use of rewards and penalties. Sanctions assume many forms—formal and informal, agreed upon and not agreed upon, legitimate and improper. There is little use in arguing that sanction systems do not have a place in the structural and operational patterns. If, without a sanction system, one can devise a way of achieving adequate conformity with any degree of assurance, then certainly it should be used. There is no desire here to encourage the probability of anarchy merely because there now is no sure way of maintaining those controls which will achieve the purpose of an institution without a sanction system. There must be some enforcement and reinforcement system available if cooperative and coordinative action is fostered.

Sanction systems often are developed jointly by several levels in the organizational hierarchy. Suggestions that members of a faculty read in the professional literature—that supervisory personnel should possess no powers over other staff members but should maintain only a consultative relationship—are somewhat short of realistic. The fact that a staff officer is attached to a line office is sufficient cause for any teacher to perceive authority in the officer even though this possession is denied. So long as a teacher perceives the authority as existing, the reaction to the supervisor will be the same as though the authority were really possessed.

A practical consideration is that the degree of authority, control, and power of rewards or penalties attached to each position should be discussed frequently and, as nearly as possible, subjected to rigorous definition. The effects of the sanction system developed by colleagues and peers should not be overlooked. In this instance, the teacher cannot accuse the supervisor or the line officer of having imposed a sanction system. Similarly, the staff officers cannot claim that the line officers have imposed a sanction system upon them when such a system exists between and among colleagues and peers. In its simpler form, this type of sanction system might be identified in the case of a teacher who has become interested in developing some new course content or teaching method. In seeking to implement this idea, the teacher may do considerable overtime work and perhaps spend some of his own money securing material or equipment not within the possibility of the school budget. Because of this, however, the teacher may become a target for jeers, criticism, and avoidance on the part of his fellow teachers. This is not infrequent in many school systems. The problem here is that of dealing with a situation in which the individual is being controlled by his colleagues rather than by the superstructure of the organization. All of this is a part of the operational pattern. Its remedy or its

Identify other instances of colleague control.

use for positive purpose becomes that of (1) identifying, (2) discussing, and (3) resolving cooperatively the problems which are engendered.

The sanction systems imposed by colleagues and peers might be termed the informal systems. There are also well-established formal sanction systems in almost all school organizations. Some people, perhaps, would choose not to classify these as sanctions; rather, they are seen as proper requirements for getting large numbers of people to work together harmoniously and rewardingly toward the institutional goals. Such a posture is mostly a matter of semantics. Most schools do have policies, rules, and regulations intended to offer suggestions and even to constitute controls over the behavior of members of the staff. In so far as policies, rules, and regulations achieve such control, they become instrumental in establishing the operational pattern of administration.

The perennial problem is that of determining the wisest procedures in establishing those elements of a system which help it to pursue an established purpose, yet to stimulate its various personnel to work harmoniously and creatively. Some prefer that policies, rules, and regulations be so general that the individuals operating at each level will have the maximum autonomy in contributing their own talent to the institutional enterprise. On the other hand, some hold to the view that the policies may be general, the rules a little more specific, and the regulations extremely specific in order to serve as guides for any member of an organization in selection of an appropriate behavior. The hope is that the selected behavior will be rewarding from the institutional point of view and satisfying to the individual in that he gains the reinforcements which are at the command of those directing the operational pattern.

IMPLEMENTATION OF THE PATTERN

There is yet another type of operational pattern problem to be discussed in this chapter. This is not to imply that one might not continue identifying and pursuing the various problems in operational patterns until a complete catalogue had been achieved. Such is not the intent here and the limitations of space make it necessary that only this one more type be considered. The problem is that of making a distinction between those efforts which are involved in the development of a plan for change and improvement and those developed for the implementation of that plan. This brings the consideration back to the inherent and intended relationships between the line and staff officers. It is within the intent of a structural pattern that a supervisor or director of curriculum be asked by the superintendent to direct the instructional developments of the school system, first in assessing the quality of the learning, and second in planning the appropriate changes which would lead to more effective learning. This becomes an assignment to the supervisor. Suppose that the supervisor succeeded in marshaling the most appropriate help from the members of the faculty at all levels and in developing a design for improving the instruction in the assigned area. This effort would have required insights that might be worthy of praise. It would have tested the ability to organize the efforts of people and would have challenged insights into the process of planning as well as into the content of the area under consideration. Eventually, the design would be completed and submitted to the superintendent's office as a proposal. The superintendent then might have this proposal screened by people who had not been involved in its development. He might send it back to the supervisor and the committee for reappraisal in light of some of the suggestions offered. When the task is completed and the design approved, the implementation of the proposal is in order.

At this point, the superintendent may choose to implement the proposal for change through the line officers. This means that the superintendent would advise the building principals about the plans and direct them to proceed with implementation in the various schools. The supervisor now has committed a product of labor, ingenuity, and emotional attachment by one person to someone else for implementation. This is generally difficult for the staff member to accept. It is a contradiction of human nature to invest time, effort, and concern in the creation of a plan which, if it is to be used, must be implemented by another person. There has been too little attention given to this complexity of line and staff relationships in the educational operation. It has been resolved to substantially greater limits in governmental or military services and in industrial organizations. The authors are not inclined here to try to explain why an educational organization is so different. In fact, they are unable to make this explanation.

How does the supervisory objective change between the completion of a plan and its implementation?

The situation is comparable to that of a playwright who may have published a most acceptable play and achieved a magnificent contract for its production. On the other hand, there is little inclination to allow the playwright to direct the production for stage presentation. It is true that there are few playwrights who would be good directors. The playwright, however, is always available to interpret the intent of the writing. This availability may be helpful to the director, but few directors will permit the playwright to be in a position to overrule the technical decisions about the production except as the specific provisions of the contract between the producer and the playwright may provide automatic controls.

The superintendent, then, has the important and difficult task of stimulating staff officers in the process of developing designs for change and yet preventing their complete discouragement when plans are turned over to line officers for implementation. It may be possible for him to achieve a reasonable compromise or, if not compromise, a method for coordinating the line and staff officers in the operational pattern through his own procedures of evaluation. The purpose of evaluation is that of determining whether the plan has resulted in improvement so far as the instructional program is concerned. The superintendent has the responsibility for frequent in-service reminders about operational relationships for his line and staff officers. When the superintendent discusses in-service improvement activities with his administrative and supervisory personnel he must remember that most line and staff officers, while seeing the necessity of improvement activities for teachers, often do not accept improvement stipulations as applicable to themselves. Thus, the term, if applied to all personnel, requires that the superintendent offer frequent directives which lead to frequent reassessment of the operational pattern of the school. When the operational pattern is wholly unacceptable or when it has drifted in a direction that will defeat the purposes of the school system, the superintendent is responsible for exercising the discipline needed to correct the undesirable situation. In this sense, he is responsible for a sanction system which must be applied to his own line and staff officers. Supervision must follow an operational pattern that will accomplish the assigned functions and must develop this pattern in close relationship to the structural pattern.

The operational pattern is an important factor in determining the extent to which supervisory behavior is supportive among colleagues. The implications of this influence of pattern are discussed at greater length in Chapter 8.

The operational pattern of supervision is the set of observable behavioral characteristics and interrelationships displayed by the position incumbents in a formally organized group.

SELECTED REFERENCES

1. Allport, Gordon W., *The Nature of Prejudice.* New York: Doubleday, 1958.
2. Association for Supervision and Curriculum Development, *New Insights and the Curriculum,* Yearbook. Washington, D.C.: National Education Association, 1963.
3. Association for Supervision and Curriculum Development, Yearbook, *Perceiving, Behaving, Becoming.* Washington, D.C.: National Education Association, 1962.
4. Association for Supervision and Curriculum Development, *To Nurture Humaneness: Commitment for the '70's,* 1970 Yearbook. Washington, D.C.: National Education Association, 1970. Part III.
5. Homme, Lloyd, "A Modern Concept of Motivation," in Lanore A. Netzer, *et al., Education, Administration and Change: The Redeployment of Resources.* New York: Harper & Row, 1970. Chap. III.

6. MacMillan, Velma J. "A Study of Procedures Used in Establishing New Intermediate Administrative-Supervisory Positions in Public Schools." Unpublished doctor's dissertation. Madison, Wisconsin: University of Wisconsin, 1970.
7. Olmsted, Michael S., *The Small Group*. New York: Random House, 1959.
8. Tagiuri, Renato and Luigi Petrullo (eds.), *Person Perception and Interpersonal Behavior*. Stanford University Press, 1958.

7

The Contributory Function of Supervision

The substance of this chapter is related functionally to the content of Chapter 5, which dealt with various aspects of the structural pattern for supervision. One assumption is inherent to the content of this chapter, namely, that supervision is a *staff*-type function. Supervision is a function and that function may be performed by any and all personnel.

There are many school systems in which it is difficult to draw a sharp distinction between the line, staff, and teaching functions. The assumption is imposed here upon the area of supervisory tasks in order that the description of the contributory function might be better achieved. The title of the chapter itself would indicate that the supervisor is contributing to another person or another function. This is precisely the direction that the discussion is to take.

The definition of the contributory function of supervision, as presented in the introduction to Part II, is:

The contributory function of supervision is the performance of those tasks under voluntary or prescribed controls which reinforce the efforts of others in the achievement of the purposes ascribed to the organization.

The definition specifies that the contributory function is directed toward the tasks being performed by others. It applies sharing activities to the task and is unrelated to the bureaucratic location or the hierarchical levels of the contributor or the receiver. This universality of assistance is consistent with the expanding concept of supervisory service.

Another element which should be discussed briefly is that the tasks are performed under voluntary or prescribed controls. When the task is performed under voluntary control, an assignment by the supervisor has been assumed and full authority and responsibility have been granted in the performance of the task. It is primarily a matter of a definition of the degree of autonomy deemed appropriate by the supervisor that is authorized by the officer in the control position. A task performed under prescribed controls means simply and directly that the person making the assignment designates or delineates the limits within which autonomy may be exercised. As the autonomy of the individual performing the task is restricted, it can be considered nothing other than a prescribed control over that person. In either the voluntary or the prescribed control type of activity, the function itself is a contributory one.

The assumptions from the list presented in Chapter 3 most related to the content of this discussion of the contributory function are:

11. The contributory and supportive functions of supervision include those policy determinations and implementations that deal with the improvement of the instructional program and its influential environments.

19. Credentialism and status symbolism are endemic pathologies in the traditions of bureaucracy that may be controlled through selected therapies.

The significance of these assumptions is that, whatever the administrative task and function may be, the supervisor has contributory and supportive contributions to make. Rather than assume that the supervisor is an independent agent in the determination of policies with respect to the instructional program, he or she is recognized as a contributor to policy formulation in a supporting role to the administrative officer. Even though the policy may deal exclusively with the concerns of the instructional program, the final determination of such policy is in the hands of the superintendent or of the board of education. This, of course, represents those areas of policymaking which are left to the autonomy or discretion of the local school district.

There are many policies in which the supervisor might be little involved in the department or even in advising with respect to determination or implementation for the good reason that such policies may touch the instructional program only very lightly. There is, however, a direct concern of the supervisory staff in those task and policy areas primarily concerned with the instructional program. The superintendent of schools may choose to give full authority and responsi-

List several policy areas in which the supervisor has a primary and secondary concern.

bility to the supervisor for policy developments, determinations, and implementations in the instructional program. Again, it is implied in assumptions eleven and nineteen that the supervisory staff will be more involved in advising with respect to policy determination than it will be involved in policy implementation which is beyond the communication stage. The implementation of policy is more properly the responsibility of the appropriate administrative officer in each individual school unit.

CLASSIFICATION OF ADMINISTRATIVE FUNCTIONS

Compare the several lists of functions reported by Knezevich.[2]

The past decade records a marked development in the clarification of systems concepts as they relate to administrative structure and operation.[1] The definition of systems facilitated the exploration of subsystems, and these definitions and explorations supported the early efforts to categorize the major functions of administration. The various lists of categories or classification systems present several points of difference but, at the same time, possess many elements of clear agreement. Each student of the field may properly elect his favorite list. These authors chose to use the terms offered by Johnson, Kast, and Rosenzweig.[3]

The definition of supervision presented in this book indicates that it is a subsystem of administration. Supervision, then, should identify clearly with the specific categories of function in administration. It consequently "gets a piece of the action" in those administrative functions, but the amount of involvement in each functional area will vary from category to category.

An example of this varying amount of involvement is found in the administrative task of the selection of a site for a new building. There are some tasks in selection falling within each of the major functional areas. The degree of involvement in each area will vary. Site selection requires planning, organizing, communicating, and controlling—each in its appropriate degree. Supervision will find its contributory function in advising the administrative staff about those elements in site selection which have an important impact upon the instructional program. The supervisor, for instance, might be much more concerned, and should so express this concern, about the environmental factors of the site which might result in classroom interruptions, thus deterring the achievement of a highly effective instructional program. If the site were located

[1] Fremont E. Kast and James E. Rosenzweig, *Organizations and Management* (New York: McGraw-Hill, 1970).

[2] Stephen J. Knezevich, *Administration of Public Education* (New York: Harper & Row, 1969), Chapter 2.

[3] Richard A. Johnson, Fremont E. Kast, and James E. Rosenzweig, *The Theory and Management of Systems* (New York: McGraw-Hill, 1967, 2d ed.), pp. 121–127.

near a factory which produced noise in such amounts that classrooms on the industrial side of the building would experience certain types of interruptions and diversions of attention from the instructional pursuits, the supervisor must express his judgment on this aspect of its suitability.

Decisions will need to be made with respect to the nature of the ground and the structure beneath its surface. This is a concern involving engineering responsibilities and there must be adequate information for advising the administrators in such non-instructional matters. Normally there is a population study made prior to the selection of a school site. This involves some technical procedures in population analysis and prediction. The supervisor rarely becomes involved in these studies in so far as numbers of people are concerned. If, however, the character of the predicted population changes substantially with respect to its culture, its outlook, or its vocational interests, this becomes of major concern to the supervisor because the character of the population may have some definite influences upon the type of instructional program needed.

While the supervisor is performing his functions of advising the administrative staff in planning, he may at the same time be asked to take major responsibilities in putting into effect a communication system related to site selection and building planning. The responsibility here might be for the supervisor, at the direction of the administrative officer, to communicate adequate and accurate information to the members of the professional staff. It is the superintendent's responsibility to assess the particular qualifications of his various associates and to deploy their time and effort to the best advantage of the task at hand.

Should an instructional supervisor resist assignment to executive functions such as budget-making, purchasing, and school site selection?

CONTRIBUTORY TASK INVOLVEMENTS

The above illustrations involve an administrative task area that demands minor involvements of the supervisory staff. There are other task areas in which the supervisor will be called upon to accept major responsibilities. One such area is that of the selection of teachers, supervisors, and administrators. It has often been said that the first and most important responsibility of the board of education is to select its chief executive officer, the superintendent of schools. With equal force, it has been declared that the first and most important responsibility of the superintendent is the selection of the teachers who will preside in the classrooms and the choice of officers who will occupy the posts needed to carry forward the purposes of the school system. Technically, the board of education is the only legal authority for entering into a contract with a teacher. Most boards wisely delegate the matter of selection to the superintendent who, in turn, may share this function with various members of his organization.

Just as the board of education must be the agency for entering into a contract, so the superintendent must be the responsible agent for making the final decision on the persons who will be recommended to the board of education for employment. Behind this decision in the appointment process are many activities that take place and which give assurance to the wisdom of the decision. It is in this array of activities that supervisors find their appropriate share of the larger administrative function. Several contributory tasks selected from this array of activities are discussed in some detail on the following pages.

Selecting Staff

Wise selection will depend materially upon the manner in which the procedures of selection are developed. The development of position descriptions has proved helpful in the identification of appropriate candidates for a particular position. A position description needs to be drafted for each post to be filled. It is not enough simply to say that a position is open in the science department of the junior high school. Such meager information given to a placement bureau will elicit little assistance in the identification of appropriate candidates. The persons more closely related to the ongoing tasks and responsibilities of the position are in the most favorable place for developing the description. If a position is open in the field of science in the junior high school, the specific area of science needs to be indicated. The general type of content included in the courses should be specified. If there are teaching methodologies preferred, they should be described. If there are specialized items of equipment to be used that require special competency, they should be indicated. If there are non-class expectations placed upon the person employed, the candidates should know this at the time of the announcement of the vacancy. It would seem, then, that the position description constitutes a portion of the selection process that might be left as the exclusive responsibility of the supervisory staff.

In addition, there should be a statement of the position specifications which indicates in some detail the nature of the qualifications and characteristics of the person that the district would like to employ for the position. Here again, the person closest to the scene of action is the best one to develop these specifications. It might be a function of the principal of the building, of the department head, or of the supervisor. The communications between the individual school and the central office can be facilitated if the supervisor is given the responsibility of serving as liaison between the two. As the liaison, he can organize the expression of judgments of the various people involved, including the teachers who will receive the new colleague. These judgments can be summarized for the use of those officers who are involved directly in the screening

Develop specifications for a vacant position in your school system.

of candidates and in determining the one to be recommended for employment.

Another part of the selection process in which supervisors might be involved is that of interviewing candidates. Knowing the descriptions of the position and the specifications considered most desirable for the person to be employed, the supervisor is in an excellent position to determine the suitability of the candidate for a particular position. It is not suggested here that the supervisor be the only interviewer. Of the several who interview the candidate, the unique position of the supervisor, in relationship to the individual schools and the instructional program, constitutes a strategic position to have the judgment well received and weighted heavily in the final selection process. The supervisor not only can provide good information about the candidate as based on his interview but also may become somewhat of a specialist in the assessment of the information that can be related to the suitability of candidates. Many school systems have a personnel officer who coordinates the selection procedures and does much of the assessment of qualifications. Even where there is a personnel officer attached to the superintendent's office, the supervisor still might provide discriminating advice to that officer by way of assessment of various items of information about the individual candidates. Weightings often are assigned to certain items of information about candidates. The supervisor can be useful to the selecting officer in this important responsibility of administration. Here, then, is one major task of administration in which there might be much involvement of the supervisor in the administrative functions.

The supervisor might also offer help to the central office in establishing the descriptions, specifications, and information about candidates for other supervisory positions that are to be filled. Any person on the staff ought to be concerned about the character and qualifications of those who are to become his colleagues.

Another important item in the area of selection of staff is that of identifying the persons who are to be assigned in their first administrative posts. It appears that in too many instances the selection of an assistant principal has become more or less a perfunctory decision. There may be various motivations for the selection and various criteria used for the particular appointments that are made. Assistant principals, nonetheless, become principals. In view of the fact that over three-fourths of the superintendents of schools in the United States have found their way to that position of leadership via the school principalship, it must be conceded that assignment to an assistant or vice-principalship in any school must be viewed as an invitation from the central office to become motivated to higher positions in the hierarchy of administration (see reference 6). Failure to take extreme care in the selection of those first assigned to an administrative position gives assurance that the reservoir from which more potent leadership positions are to be filled will include a dangerous supply of mediocre possibilities.

Single-handed control over the selections to first administrative positions on the part of the superintendent may provide a situation in which the criteria related to the social relationship aspects of administration dominate other criteria which are more important to the instructional program. For instance, a principalship candidate of limited or average intellect might do well in relating to people and in organizing his own and other people's efforts. His intelligence may be adequate for the routine aspects of administration. However, a person who becomes principal of a school and possesses only limited or average intelligence will not provide stimulating leadership to teachers who have sharper minds. The supervisor or the supervisory staff, then, stands in the unique position of being able to help the superintendent in assessing the qualifications of people who are to be assigned to various administrative posts, but particularly those who are receiving such an assignment for the first time. The supervisors are almost certain to give greater emphasis to those criteria related to the teaching-learning program than they would to the managerial and public relations type of criteria which may be weighted more heavily by the superintendent. This is not a criticism either of the superintendent or of the supervisory staff; it simply represents the dominance of their interest which probably led to many currently held positions. There is strength in this diversity of perception of criteria in that, by working together, there is greater probability of achieving a wiser balance between the various criterion measures.

How do the certification qualifications for the principalship differ from those for the teacher?

Assigning Staff

Another area of involvement of supervision in the administrative process is the assignment of staff to specific positions. This includes transfers from section to section, grade to grade, course to course, or building to building. As in many functional areas, the supervisor constitutes the best liaison agent between the individual school and the central office. The supervisor brings to the central office information about the situation in which teachers find themselves working. Some teachers work more effectively in one type of school than they do in another. It is important, then, that someone study the situational factors and see what impact these have upon the individual teachers with their unique sets of values and personality needs. An excellent teacher in one situation might be a mediocre teacher in another. The majority of superior teachers, of course, have sufficient adaptability to be successful in a variety of assignments. On the other hand, some situations develop in a manner that a high degree of frustration eventually might limit the tenure of the teacher in the school system or in the teaching profession. Thus, attention needs to be given on a system-wide basis to the deployment of personnel to the particular situations and locations in which they can perform to best advantage. The unique programs in some schools involving a particular type of activity call for the cooperative efforts of a number of teachers. This means, then, that someone must be in a position to survey the personnel in an entire school system in order to accomplish the wisest selection of persons for the cooperative effort. In these days of increasing interest in team teaching, the matter of the appropriateness of persons for teams comes into sharper focus. The supervisor, who works closely with teachers in the classrooms, with individual building principals, and with the central office, is a logical person to assist in the identification of those who can join profitably in team efforts.

What is the key policy on the transfer of staff? Why?

Another type of concern that might be allocated to the supervisor is that of evaluating the work load of each teacher. Involved in every assignment is this matter of load, not only in terms of the number of pupils involved or the number of preparations but also in terms of the type of pupils and the type of preparation. Too often it has been simplified, if not oversimplified, to the point that only two or three factors are considered in assessing load. These factors usually have been the total number of pupils assigned to the classes and the total number of hours taught. It is assumed that, with an equalization of these two factors, loads have been equalized among all members of the staff. It does not take much insight into the educational process to know that this is wholly inadequate. Those subjects and/or grades in which there is more paper-reading certainly command a greater number of non-teaching hours than those in which all of the work is done in class or in a laboratory. Those who offer laboratory courses often are not given adequate time for preparing the laboratory facilities and equipment for their classes. There needs to be system-wide policy and control with respect to load assessment. Thus, again, it appears that the supervisor is a logical person to direct the efforts in load assessment and equalization.

Another aspect of assignment and load is that of working conditions. Someone in the system needs to be particularly sensitive to working conditions regardless of the outcomes of collective bargaining provisions. Building principals are heavily involved in managerial functions related to scheduling activities, arranging transportation schedules, supervising lunch facilities, directing attendance programs, maintaining good community relationships, and carrying out the reporting functions as detailed by the superintendent's office, along with many other non-instructional types of activities. The supervisor is in that unique position of being able to keep emphasis on those facets of administrative service which are more directly related to the teaching and learning situations.

Administrative officers often, through their own systems of communication with teachers, have been the cause of many classroom interruptions. An assessment was made as to how many times a specific class was interrupted during the first three weeks of school. There were many days in which the teacher and pupil activity was interrupted ten or twelve times (see reference 1). Simple mathematics indicates that, in this situation, the teacher seldom had as much as thirty minutes of uninterrupted teaching time and, in turn, the pupils had few instances in which their learning activities were not interrupted within each thirty-minute period. On the basis of an analysis of some tape recordings of entire class periods, it was discovered that it normally took from three to five minutes after an interruption for a teacher to get the pupils back to work again if, indeed, they ever got back to where they were prior to the interruption. There are many class interruptions other than those permitted or instigated by the administrative officers. It is even more imperative, then, that as interruptions have several sources, they be assessed carefully by someone primarily concerned with instructional purposes. This seems to be properly the supervisor of instruction. This is another instance in which the supervisor finds many specific contributory tasks within a major category of administrative responsibility. The degree of involvement of supervision in each of the different categories of administrative function may vary but the supervisor fulfills the concept of the definition in that supervision is a subsystem of administration.

Inducting Staff

Since World War II, much more attention has been given to the induction of new staff members than had been done previously. This constitutes another administrative functional area in which the supervisor has substantial involvement. The induction process essentially begins with the announcement of a vacancy. In the discussion above, it was indicated how the supervisor might function profitably in description and specification phases of the selection process. In so doing, the supervisor is already involved in the induction of new staff members into the school system. Much more needs to be done with induction than simply to develop position descriptions and specifications and to make wise selections, even though these are items of major importance. Once a person has entered into a contract with a local school board, a series of activities should be set into motion. These activities, in series or in isolation, need planning and implementation. Because the successful induction of a new staff member, particularly one entering a teaching position, has serious import for the quality of the instructional program, the supervisor properly might accept substantial responsibilities in developing and directing the induction program. Well-planned induction programs have been described in a number of publications, and there is no need here to elaborate on what the specific activ-

Would it be a proper function of supervisors to accept full responsibility for an induction program?

ities should be. Suffice it to say at this point that the efforts of staff members as well as people in the community must have some stimulation and direction if those efforts are to result in successful induction activities (see reference 2).

The time is long past when the perception of the supervisory function is that of inspection, yet to this day many people seem to think that they ought to leave the new teacher alone until he "gets his feet on the ground." This means that many of the new teachers are not visited by a supervisor, a department head, or a school principal during the first two or three months of school. Several surveys have indicated that many teachers, not only those new to a school system but particularly those new to the profession, were not visited during the first half of their first teaching year. It seems logical that if there is any time when there should be frequent, continuing, and expected contacts between the supervisory and administrative officers and the new teachers, it would be during those first weeks of school. Much of the management routine is new to the person, even though he may be experienced in teaching. There is little doubt that if the control of the class is lost during the first weeks of school, it is extremely difficult to regain that control and confidence no matter how many potential teaching qualities a person may possess. An involvement of the supervisory staff in the induction of new staff members, then, is both a wise expenditure of supervisory time and a guarantee that the school district will benefit from the talents of the new employee. This is another administrative area in which the supervisor assumes a heavy contributory responsibility for the successful implementation of the function involved.

Describe the major elements in an induction program.

Evaluating the Instructional Program

The evaluation of the instructional program calls for a high degree of technical assistance. While it is the superintendent's responsibility to give assurance to the board of education that the quality of the instructional program is satisfactory, he is unable and perhaps unqualified to establish and direct a full-scale evaluation program. This constitutes the superintendent's quality control concern for which he properly is held by the board of education. The superintendent, then, must turn to those on his staff who have the unique abilities, skills, and insights which will provide a comprehensive and adequate evaluation program. Here again, it seems evident that the supervisor as a representative of the central office will work through the individual building principals in establishing and carrying out the evaluative procedures. The supervisor is an appropriate officer to initiate the process and give direction to it. The implementation of the administration of specific evaluative instruments may fall to other appropriate officers, but planning and coordination is a primary concern (see Chapter 15). The supervisor is one of the most appropriate line or staff officers to provide this planning and coordinative service.

The superintendent may ask the supervisor to perform other functions of administration which are attendant to the evaluation of the instructional program. Information needs to be given to the teachers relating the true state of affairs with respect to the quality of the instructional program. Assurance needs to be given to the board of education and to the community with respect to the findings of the evaluative program. The superintendent, then, may ask the supervisor to perform some of the administrative tasks of communicating and influencing as listed among the major categories of administrative functions (see Chapter 21). The communicating and influencing responsibilities of the supervisor will be restricted in purpose and scope as directed by the superintendent. The supervisor performs these supervisory functions as a part of the overall administrative operation.

Planning Instructional Change

The supervisor, as the one who is best able and best qualified to establish the program of evaluation, can identify those points of weakness in the instructional program at which an improvement effort should be established. This is a part of the problem of interpreting the data at hand. This interpretation should lead directly to pertinent suggestions for corrective measures. These measures constitute the improvement program and the supervisor has major involvement in it. The supervisor is the logical person not only to identify the points where improvement is needed but also to organize and direct the ability of an entire staff to the solution of the problems at hand. Solutions usually appear in the form of a plan for change. Planning for change is more than a casual responsibility (see Chapter 4). Many plans are so inadequate that they never lead to change; they simply stand as ideas about change rather than as directing agents for the specific changes that should be effected. An assessment needs to be made, then, of the plans that are developed. The evaluation of a plan *as a plan* seems to require certain types of specialized insights and abilities (see Chapter 19). It is proper to expect the supervisor to bring these insights and abilities to his school position. His service could be one of assuring good quality not only in the process of planning but in the products of the planning effort. It is the supervisor's responsibility to determine the type of involvements of the various offices and officers in the instructional program which would bring about maximum positive results in the planning efforts. Coordination is one of the major administrative functions. Again, the supervisor is contributing to the realization of this administrative function by assisting the superintendent in many of the specific tasks involved in it.

In the implementation of change as well as in the development of plans, the supervisor can be very useful in the briefing sessions with the various officers. The implementation of a plan requires more than a simple directive from the central office indicating that a plan is being presented and that all professional employees are expected to pursue it (see Chapter 16). Once a good plan is available, the process of implementation requires the ingenuity and efforts of everyone in the school system. Each person must have his particular role defined and interpreted in relation to the changes proposed. When a plan has been developed and implemented, it must be evaluated after an appropriate length of time to determine if it brought about the type and quality of change desired. This evaluation becomes one of the unique contributory functions of the supervisor.

There has been no effort in this chapter to list all of the specific contributory task involvements of supervision. The five indicated for illustrative purposes were (1) selecting the staff, (2) assigning the staff, (3) inducting new staff, (4) evaluating the instructional program, and (5) planning instructional change. Personnel responsible for developing the custom-built program of supervision for a particular school system will need to consider these tasks along with others of import to that system.

A declaration was made earlier that supervision is a function and that any one or all members of the administrative, supervisory, and teaching staffs may be required to perform this function. This chapter has been limited to the contributory function of those staff members called supervisors. The observations directed to the supervisors apply with equal pertinence to other officers. They, too, have contributory functions.

By popular perception, teachers are the major recipients of supervisory efforts. It is conceded here that most supervisory efforts are so directed—and properly so. It is not conceded, however, that teachers are without supervisory responsibilities. *They have many,* and, having such responsibilities, they must perform some of the tasks of the contributory function. The teachers' responsibilities, because of their unusual contributions to supervisory obligations, are discussed in detail in Chapter 11.

The contributory function must be supportive toward those to whom it is directed. The supportive function is discussed in Chapter 8 and may be considered an extension of contributory function.

The contributory function of supervision is the performance of those tasks under voluntary or prescribed controls which reinforce the efforts of others in the achievement of the purposes ascribed to the organization.

SELECTED REFERENCES

1. Eye, Glen G., "The Importance of Decreasing Classroom Interruptions," *American School Board Journal,* June, 1955.
2. Eye, Glen G. and Lanore A. Netzer, *School Administrators and Instruction.* Boston: Allyn & Bacon, Inc., 1969. Chaps. IV, V, and VI.
3. Johnson, Richard A., Fremont E. Kast, and James S. Rosenzweig, *The Theory and Management of Systems.* New York: McGraw-Hill, 1967, 2d ed. pp. 121–127.
4. Kast, Fremont E., and James E. Rosenzweig, *Organizations and Management.* New York: McGraw-Hill, 1970.
5. Knezevich, Stephen J., *Administration of Public Education.* New York: Harper & Row, 1969. Chap. II.
6. Stewart, Harold G., "Criteria Used by Superintendents in the Selection of Beginning Building Principals in Certain Wisconsin Schools." Unpublished doctor's dissertation. Madison: University of Wisconsin, 1963.
7. Thompson, Barbara S., "A Study of the Synchronization of Behaviors Related to Selected Tasks of Elementary School Supervisors and Principals." Unpublished doctor's dissertation. Madison: University of Wisconsin, 1969.

8

The Supportive Function of Supervision

The discussion presented in this chapter is closely related to Chapter 6, which dealt with the operational pattern for supervision. In Chapter 6 there was detailed from various angles the fact that, no matter how carefully the structural pattern might be developed, the various positions represented in that pattern have to be appropriately staffed.

An individual brings to a position unique qualities, values, and motivations which make substantial differences in the way each position serves the purposes and interests of the total organization. Structural and operational descriptions include more than simply detailing the major tasks or functions of a position. The manner in which individuals go about the performance of those tasks and functions makes the major difference as to what the outcomes of that service might be.

The content of this chapter is designed to indicate the ways in which supervisory personnel may behave in proving to be not only performers in the designated function, but also the overall supporters of the operation of a school system by reinforcing the tasks, responsibilities, and behaviors of other line and staff officers. The definition of the supportive function as presented in the introduction of Part II is:

The supportive function of supervision is the performance of all tasks in a manner and to a purpose that will uphold and strengthen other personnel in achieving the results properly expected of each as incumbent of a related position.

Thus, the supportive function includes not only the behaviors of the supervisory personnel in the performance of designated tasks but also their attitudes toward others as they go about the performance of their tasks. It is impossible for one supervisor to assume that he can go about his business, pay no attention to the work of other supervisors, and have no effect on the outcomes of their efforts. The fact that all are attached to the central office and are intended to perform a definable service to the overall operation of the school system makes it undesirable for anyone to work in isolation. Merely to ignore the services of another supervisor is to destroy a part of the effectiveness of that supervisor.

SUPPORTIVE TASK INVOLVEMENTS

The position of the authors with respect to supportive functions as a responsibility of individual supervisors is consistent with the declared assumptions about supervision presented earlier. Assumption number eleven, presented in Chapter 3, is related to this chapter. That assumption indicated that both contributory and supportive functions of supervision involved the supervisor in certain types of policy determinations, particularly those which are related to the instructional program. There are two other assumptions in the total list which are related specifically to the subjects under discussion in this chapter. These assumptions are:

9. The establishment and maintenance of the structural and operational patterns that encourage cooperative and coordinative behaviors are equally weighted responsibilities of superordinates, peers, and subordinates.

10. Supervision of instruction and curriculum development must be cooperative and coordinative operational functions.

In each of these two assumptions, the words "cooperative" and "coordinative" were used. These assumptions deal with items of concern which cannot be called a delineation of specific tasks or functions but rather are concerned with the behavioral characteristics of the position occupants. The behavioral characteristics are related closely to the types of outcomes that might be realized.

No person within the central office can operate in isolation. It is possible, however, for any one member or several members to operate independently, but operating independently and in isolation have quite different connotations as one looks at the total operation of a system. Cooperative people are those who have accepted a common goal and set about achieving it through contributing their own specific and unique talents, abilities, and skills to the achievement of that goal. Those who are coordinative in their behavior have immediate goals that are not the same, yet each may pursue the immediate goal for which he is held responsible without interfering with the efforts of other staff members in accomplishing their immediate goals (see Chapter 12). It is assumed in either cooperative or coordinative types of action that there is an overriding global purpose for the school system which must be considered as acceptable and be accepted by all members of the school personnel. In the sense of seeing the global purpose of the school system, all efforts of school personnel must be cooperative because they are pursuing a common goal. In another sense, there are short-term goals which, when combined to move toward the common goal, make it possible to perceive workers pursuing their assigned immediate goals independently but in a coordinative relationship.

What are some individual goals that can be harmonized with those of the school system?

Inherent in assumption number nine is the belief that a supervisor of instruction and a director of curriculum cannot be presumed at any point to be working toward different goals. One particular aspect of instruction might be more related to methodology and the other to the arrangement of the various learning experiences into what is termed a curriculum. The time is long past for profitable debate on the issue of whether methodology can be separated from content to be taught. One aspect of the teaching–learning act does not proceed successfully while another stands still or retrogresses. They are tied together in the learning experience and both must progress or retrogress at the same time. It is recognized in the statement of this assumption, however, that the two major tasks involved in the teaching–learning experiences can be subjected to a dichotomization. This is evidenced in those school systems where one staff officer carries the designation of supervisor of instruction and another is director of curriculum. They cannot be seen as separate entities, but neither can they be seen as other than each representing an important phase of the administrative responsibilities of a school system.

Illustrate the dichotomy with several tasks carried out by these two positions.

Note again assumption number ten. Inherent in this assumption is the expectation that the superintendent of schools will accept the responsibility for establishing, encouraging, maintaining, evaluating, enforcing, and exercising other controls over his central office personnel as presumed in his responsibility. Other stated assumptions have indicated that the superintendent is the focal point of the school organization with respect to the personnel's decision-making prerogatives. He must also be responsible for the types of working relationships that are developed and maintained as well as for the organic structure of the school's operation. Several supportive tasks selected from the array of possible activities are discussed in some detail on the following pages.

Reinforcing

What is the responsibility of the individual who is unable to harmonize personal and organizational goals?

One of the most important supportive functions of the supervisor is that of reinforcing the leadership efforts of colleagues in the school organization. Leadership in its simplest definable state implies the influencing of others. The process of influencing may be extremely complex. Influencing others means the changing of goals for those who are to be influenced. Changing goals is not always easy for the individual to accomplish, even though he might be a willing participant to the effort. By definition, each member of the organization has some responsibilities for leadership. The inclination of the staff or line officer colleagues to oppose, ignore, or support the efforts of another becomes an important factor in the leadership efforts of each.

Classroom teachers are well aware of the interrelationships of the members of the central office. It is folly for central office personnel to assume that teachers will not be aware of any intra-staff conflict that may exist. It is not necessary for one person to differ openly with or oppose another person in order to affect the outcome of the other's efforts. Even though the central office is far removed from many of the individual buildings and the classroom teachers of those buildings, there is little hope that strife will not be known. It long has been recognized that teachers within a building cannot oppose, ignore, or support each other without even the youngest of the pupils being aware of the characteristics of such interpersonal relationships.

What are the next steps if a staff member wishes to pursue a point of view that has been rejected by his superordinate?

There are ways of resolving differences of opinion and it is the responsibility of the superintendent to provide these opportunities for the members of his central office. The differences should be resolved prior to any effort that carries the central office personnel to the point of attempting to influence the individual building personnel. The individual member, if unable to impose his wishes or beliefs upon his colleagues at the central office level, must accede to the decision of the majority or to the decision of his superior officer. The individual, having had the opportunity to present a point of view, then must be willing to accept the fact that his point of view did not prevail and he must become a supportive member of the central office team. To do less would point to his lack of qualifications for central office attachment of any type.

Another area of reinforcement, although not so closely related to leadership efforts, is the matter of supporting the more acceptable and enlightened pressures that may be directed to the school by noncertificated but responsible lay people, who constitute the creating and supporting public for the school system and who need to receive the same respect achieved among the members of the staff. Should differences of opinion develop between the school and community, there are opportunities for resolving them and the superintendent becomes the agent responsible for initiating this effort. There is little point in any supervisor assuming that, if a critic of the school's program in the community is to be received properly, he should not handle this with all the respect that he would request from his superior officer. This is not to imply that a supervisor or any member of the professional personnel must yield to any demand made by a layman from the supporting public. The reference here is more to the attitude that is taken toward the suggestions which might come in the form of pressure (see reference 1). Even in the form of pressure, the public is entitled to fair consideration and should not be subjected to ridicule by the supervisor as contacts are made with the various members of the teaching staff. Quality education is difficult enough to achieve and there is little point in creating schisms between the classroom teacher and the supporting public so that the objects of all the effort—the children—lose confidence in the school and thus have their educational opportunities undermined.

Interpreting

The supervisor is an interpreter of central office regulations and directives. The superintendent of schools is the proper authority for issuing those official directives which establish the limits of authority and autonomy for the various certificated and classified employees of the school system. A good directive depends for its effectiveness upon the extent to which it is well communicated. The types of communication media most often used by the central office are the written directive and the verbal statement, which may be presented in large or small groups. The wise superintendent normally briefs the central office on the more important items and purposes of the directives, discussing the implications and intent prior to the time of release to the teachers. Many speculate that the superintendent is fortunate if even fifty percent of the content of his directive will have communicated to all members of his staff what he intended to have communicated. Thus, familiarity with these releases from the central office on the part of the supervisory staff becomes essential in supportive activities. The supervisor, as he makes contact with the various building representatives as well as with other members of the central office, is in a position to be helpful in interpretation when asked about the intent of a directive. Supervisors must not cast off this responsibility with some flippant remark such as "It was not my directive, and why should I be able to interpret it?" The subtle insinuation may be that the supervisor knew better but was not consulted. This peculiar quirk of the personality of the individual is a most unfortunate one to find among the employees of a school system.

Some consideration should be given to the serious question

of what the supervisor's ethical responsibility is in interpreting and supporting central office directives when he is not in agreement with them. Such a situation could mean that the superintendent's leadership functions were thwarted. The supervisor who opposes the intent of a directive should have an opportunity to discuss with the superintendent and other colleagues in the central office whether the differences in opinion might be resolved. Again, if the supervisor is unable to establish his point of view with the superintendent, he has no choice but to recognize the fact that the decision-making process requires a focal point and that decisions must be made. The supervisor is hardly in a position to discredit the orderly processes of operation in the school system merely because an opinion has not been accepted. The opportunity to present opinions is assurance of a place in the democratic process and an individual has a right to expect this privilege. When there is failure to impose his point of view, the staff member must accept the professional responsibility of supporting the officers whose decision powers are dominant in the subject at issue.

How can regular briefing sessions assist in the supporting role?

Correcting

Various types of controls must exist in order to assure the proper relationships among people involved in a common enterprise. It is not the purpose here to discuss the characteristics of these various types of controls. It is, rather, to indicate that a thorough understanding of the controls which exist usually makes it possible for persons to work at a higher level of efficiency and effectiveness. The controls that are exercised over the employees of a local school system have their origin either in the statutes of the state, the decisions of the courts, the actions of the local board of education, or the prerogatives of the superintendent.

At each level in the hierarchy of control, there is the possibility of delegating additional prerogatives of control actions to subordinate positions. Thus, the supervisor, under his own initiative and making his own decision, may set up certain types of controls for those who are subject to his direction. When these controls exist, it is because the superintendent of schools permits their existence. The supportive function of the supervisor with respect to control factors, then, is first that of determining in his own mind what controls exist, and second, that of identifying in the behaviors of others evidence of failure to understand either the incident or the characteristics of the controls. A misconception of the control factors may be equally as damaging as the existence of an improper control agency influencing the behaviors of others. The supervisor is supportive of his superiors when accepting the propriety of control over himself and supportive of his subordinates when alleviating the generalized resistance to regulatory actions. This is particularly true for the members of the teaching staff whose comprehension of the nature of the controls and of the extent to which they are implemented may or may not stand as operating factors in achieving the assignments of each individual concerned.

Motivations for personal advantages or causing the supervisor to misinform others about the responsibilities of control actions ought to be cause for dismissal. This constitutes not only a dangerous element in the operation of the school system but also constitutes unethical conduct.

Acknowledging

The supervisor is supportive when acknowledging the successes of other staff and teaching colleagues. If one supervisor finds a colleague achieving success and being recognized for it in a particular area of responsibility, applause and encouragement should be given to that colleague. Those who are stimulated to envy, antagonism, and opposition should be provided little opportunity to continue as members of the staff.

The supervisor, above all, should emphasize recognition of the successes of classroom teachers. In so many ways the classroom teacher is performing the most important task in the total school organization. Nevertheless, much of the teacher's work is done with little public or colleague recognition and the position has little prestige compared to that of administrative and supervisory offices. There is the problem of public acknowledgment, for instance, when news releases are made about the successes of individual teachers. Teachers resent, and perhaps properly so, having line and staff officer names attached to the story. The newsworthy incident may have been accomplished by the excellent and major effort of the teacher alone. The balance of contributions should be recognized in the public acknowledgment of the teacher's success (see Chapter 21).

Not to be overlooked among the responsibilities of supportive-type functions is that of giving public acknowledgment to the importance of the non-instructional services performed by the various people in the school organization. Too many jokes have been made about janitors, even to the point of indicating that janitors perhaps do more of the detailed supervision with respect to the evaluative function applied to teachers than do the supervisory and administrative staffs. It is important that schools have good services in the non-instructional areas. These areas are contracted by the directors of the system because they are considered essential to the successful operation of the school. It is not unreasonable, then, for the supervisor to consider that the supportive function be extended to janitors, bus drivers, cafeteria workers, and stockroom clerks.

Resisting

There is often an inclination to include in a chapter of this type an extensive list of "do's and don'ts." In general, the intent has been to offer positive suggestions with respect to the supportive function of supervision. At this point it may be well to introduce one or two negative suggestions. The first is to develop a resistance to the urge to be an empire-builder. This term has been used in many connotations, but it usually carries a fairly clear concept of a person who wishes to collect for himself all of the functions that might be directly or even remotely related to the responsibilities of his office. An empire-builder is one who gets great satisfaction from the possession of controls over other people and programs. The empire-builder may judge his own success by the number of people that he can bring into his area of endeavor and under his direction. The empire-builder also would be willing to see other empires tumble if that would contribute to his own sense of prestige. It is somewhat hazardous to give examples from specific subject areas in the negative situations as indicated here. There is no intent to indicate by the choice of example that any subject or supervisory area is more prone to empire-building than any other. The example to be used here is that of the field of science.

During recent years there has been a great increase in the popular and professional concern for the science programs in the schools. This has been closely and properly identified with the general concern for national security. The machines and facilities of defense require scientific knowledge to an extent that was not true a few decades ago. In order to secure competent people to man the defense facilities, increasing knowledge is needed in the fields of mathematics and science. This constitutes a tempting situation for a supervisor of science. He easily could become an empire-builder at this point and say "science at any price." Science at any price might mean the usurpation of a budget to the extent that other important subject areas might be neglected. The need for new equipment might be demanded on the basis of the interest of national security and in the federal recognition of the importance of this teaching area. Other subject areas might have to exist with little or no support for their improvement possibilities and needs.

Another example of empire-building potential is in the field of music, which represents the dominant interest and concern of the supervisor of music. Music, along with some other subject areas and activities, lends itself well to public presentation. Many communities become extremely attached to and dependent upon entertainment provided by the school music program. The community may be proud of its marching band, its concert orchestra, and its superb soloists. The temptation is for the music teacher and supervisor to consider this a demand from the supporting public much as a politician may claim that his election is a dictate from the people. The teacher and supervisor may be properly enthusiastic about popular recognition of their area, and they are stronger staff members because of the devotion generated by it. On the other hand, this enthusiasm must not be carried to the point where they are unable to see this subject as one contributor among many facets of the total enterprise of the school system.

A second negative caution suggested here is that of ego-centered motivations. This, of course, cannot be separated from the motivations that lead to empire-building. In essence, it is an expression of concern for the individual who has chosen not to build empires but rather to direct his own behaviors primarily toward the satisfaction of his own personal needs and desires. The supervisor of this type is the one who may emphasize the *unique* in anything that he is doing, even to the exclusion of the old which had already proved itself serviceable. Supervisors of this type are inclined to dramatize change even though the proposal of change might constitute basically the reintroduction in a new form of that which had been done previously. This is most tempting in the area of curricular proposals. Few curricular proposals identify the uniqueness of the new material being introduced. As a matter of fact, it is almost impossible to read a curricular guide and identify in the content what has been introduced as change and what had been taught previously.

The ego-centered motivation causes the person to attempt to identify himself with the contributions of others. In its simplest form, it is expressed in terms of an insistence upon one's name being attached to news releases or to being included in the pictures taken to inform others about the new enterprise—usually that which is going on in the individual classroom. Occasionally, a supervisor can be found who institutes competitive action with his colleagues. Competitiveness is shown when one staff member gets attention and recognition for having instituted or directed some worthwhile and successful enterprise in the school, and this becomes the reason for a colleague to develop another plan that would possess attention-getting characteristics. The attention-getting innovations in a school system are not necessarily improvements. The wrongness of the motivation denies the probability that the innovation was needed. When innovation is brought about by this motivation, it is only good luck that causes it to result in an improvement of the teaching–learning opportunities.

How can evaluation be used to identify empire-builders?

Recognizing

A final and positive suggestion to the supervisor who would recognize supportive functions in his position is that of cultivating the ability to recognize differences between the executive, the advisory, and the judicial functions of all personnel. There is some inclination for each person, regardless of his motivation—some proper and some improper—to impose his beliefs, his desires, and his purposes upon others. This temptation leads to the urge to issue directives or to give advice which borders on command—sometimes out of enthusiasm for the innovation itself and sometimes for the sheer pleasure of feeling like an executive. There are executive functions to be performed. These executive functions should exist for no purpose other than that of achieving the purposes of the organization. The advising responsibility constitutes one of the most important tasks of supervision. There are many people who can profit from the suggestions and advice of the supervisor. The judicial functions of supervision come into play primarily in the responsibilities for evaluation of the program and for the evaluation of staff members for whom the supervisor has some assigned jurisdiction. This judicial function, however, should not extend to areas which are not the direct responsibility of the supervisor. Such extensions occur when the supervisor makes judgments about the quality of the superintendent's decisions and reports such judgments to other people. It is supportive when the supervisor, judging adversely the superintendent's decisions and directives, goes directly to the superintendent as the proper place to offer his criticisms and suggestions.

How can supportive types of behavior be encouraged by all personnel?

The assistance given to other people in achieving proper concepts with respect to all personnel in the school organization is a supportive responsibility of the supervisor. The development of adequate concepts of executive decisions, of advisory services, and of judicial expression at any level becomes a responsibility of the supervisor in his supportive role in the school system.

Develop a list of ways in which a teacher can be supportive of supervisory personnel.

The closing paragraph in Chapter 7 indicated that teachers have a unique contribution to make through their contributory functions in the supervisory program. A similar point of view is held with respect to the teacher's supportive functions in the supervisory program. The uniqueness of these contributions is discussed in detail in Chapter 11.

The supportive function of supervision is the performance of all tasks in a manner and to a purpose that will uphold and strengthen other personnel in achieving the results properly expected of each as incumbent of a related position.

The contributory function of supervision is the performance of those tasks under voluntary or prescribed controls which reinforce the efforts of others in the achievement of results appropriate to the purpose ascribed to the organization.

The operational pattern for supervision is the set of observable behavioral characteristics and interrelationships displayed by the position incumbents in a formally organized group.

The structural pattern for supervision is the systematic array of anticipated requisite tasks appropriate to the achievement of in-

structional purposes into a workable arrangement of defined positions with described power or control relationships.

SELECTED REFERENCES

1. Bass, Bernard M., *Leadership, Psychology, and Organizational Behavior*. New York: Harper & Row, 1960.
2. McGregor, Douglas, *The Professional Manager*. New York: McGraw-Hill, 1967.
3. Netzer, Lanore A., Glen G. Eye, Ardelle Graef, Robert D. Krey, and J. Fred Overman, *Interdisciplinary Foundations of Supervision*. Boston: Allyn & Bacon, 1970. Chap. III.

Part III

THE PARTICIPANTS IN SUPERVISION

The purposes and patterns of supervision are discussed in Parts I and II, respectively. The purposes are inherent in the definition of supervision given in Chapter 2. The patterns are suggested by the attachment of supervision to administration, which is based on a structural pattern and tempered by an operational pattern. The three chapters of Part III are devoted to the participants in supervision.

Individuals in any group effort are influenced by other people, and these influences can be termed supervision. It follows, then, that all professional employees in the school organization are both supervisors and supervised. All members of the school system are influenced and, therefore, supervised by their superiors, their subordinates, and their peers in the organization.

Although comprehensiveness of program is a consideration in supervision, the classroom teachers are the focal points in most supervisory efforts. Like central office personnel, teachers are influenced by their superiors, their peers, and other individuals and groups within as well as outside the formal organization of the local school system. Attempts to influence the certificated personnel are not limited to employees of a school system. Lay persons and groups try to exert influence and, when they are successful, the result is supervision. Because individuals who supervise are diffused within the community, it seems practical to look upon supervision as a function to be performed rather than as a person to be identified.

Administration is an organizing service to provide educative experiences for a community's youth and supervision is a phase of that service. It perhaps is unfortunate to use a term such as supervision as a title for any person when that term actually indicates a function. Titles of various positions seldom describe accurately the functions of those positions. Thus, it is required that attention be given to their specific functions before determining the extent to which supervisory functions are being performed.

Supervision takes place at the local level but is influenced by local, state, and national officials and by others providing supervisory services to which a school system may be committed. Those who have continuing relationships with the persons supervised probably will exercise the greatest influence upon the instructional program. Change in structural patterns leads to numerous changes in the functions of regional and state supervisors. The numbers of pupils and teachers make a difference in the time any one supervisor can spend with an individual teacher. It is practically impossible for state supervisors to spend enough time with individual teachers to provide helpful leadership or evaluation. State supervision is provided for the purpose of improving a local administrative service rather than for performing a specific service in the local system. The state supervisor can help administrators in local districts assess their programs and outcomes. Federal supervision is a more generalized influence, channeled through state departments of public instruction.

The twelfth assumption found in Chapter 3 is most closely related to this Part. It states:

Many personal and situational factors influence behavioral status, change, and mobility.

The purpose is to call attention to the fact that changes must be focused both on the participants of the educational program and on the conditions and environment in which the education takes place. The time is past when improvement is considered a result of identifying and dismissing weak teachers. Emphasis now is placed upon selection of those who will be admitted to the profession and upon the conditions for maximizing their competencies.

Also related to Part III is the eighth assumption, which states:

The limits and boundaries of supervisory authority, autonomy, and responsibility are defined by individuals and groups influencing the organization who also possess varying degrees of authority, autonomy, and responsibility.

This assumption identifies the influence of participants at various levels inside and outside the formal organizational structure of a school system. For the participants in supervision it is not enough merely to know *how to supervise*. The participant, on the receiving end, will be influenced more if he knows the techniques of *being supervised*. Some of the problems and advantages to be observed, studied, and used in order that supervision may have multidirectional support are discussed in Chapters 9, 10, and 11.

9

The Allocation of Supervisory Talent

The creation of positions and the description of the functions to be performed by holders of those positions do not give assurance that the incumbents have the talents needed to achieve the purposes for which the organization exists. Neither is it sufficient merely to describe the characteristics of the person desired for a particular position. Such a description will provide little assurance that the available talent has been identified and assigned to the right place, or that conditions have been created which will encourage the most effective use of that talent in the organization. The development of the selection processes for filling positions, the best arrangement of those positions for providing coordinative activity, the description of the tasks to be performed, and the qualities of the people who will perform them only constitute the first step in the allocation of supervisory talent to its best advantage.

Structural and operational patterns were discussed in Chapters 5 and 6, respectively. The nature of the allocation of talent as discussed in this chapter is properly and closely related to the chapters in Part II. The concerns at this point go beyond the mechanical aspects of organization and the considerations of the various ways that functions are performed.

The prime purpose of this chapter is to explore the ways in which the talent selected for specific posts and for specific purposes can be allocated in such a manner that it will be consistent with the best interests of the organization and make it probable that these interests will be served in the performance of the person possessing the talent. The administrator, responsible for the development of a structural pattern and for staffing the posts in that pattern, is concerned with more than the simple mechanical fitting of personal specifications to job specifications.

ORIGIN OF TALENT

Policies of making promotions only from within the organization present the problem of being limited to the qualifications existing on the staff, which may or may not be adequate for the demands of a particular position and its array of functions. The common error in complying with these policies is that of assuming that *uniqueness* is a general quality in a person. In other words, it can be and often is assumed that a person who has been innovative and who has made unique contributions in his teaching responsibilities at a particular class level or in a content area will be equally inclined toward innovation and uniqueness when given other responsibilities. There is, however, no assurance at all that a science teacher who has merited distinction for his work in the teaching of chemistry in the high school will make even an average special-area supervisor if given the responsibility of influencing the whole science program in the school system. In the same manner, there is no assurance that the most effective elementary school teacher in a school system would perform at the same high level if taken from the teaching post and placed in the position of elementary school supervisor. The demands of the supervisory position are different from the demands made upon the classroom teacher. They may be no more difficult or no more complex, but simply different from those required of the teacher.

Identify some demands on a supervisor that a teacher does not have.

The person responsible for the staffing of a school system should not assume that talent transfers unchanged when a person is moved from one position to another. On the other hand, the evidence of talent exhibited in the teaching position is based, in part, upon superior mental qualities and educational insights. It may be one of the most promising factors in the identification of talent for a supervisory position. The assumption should not be made, however, that superior performance in one type of work will give assurance of superior performance in another. The superior-teacher criterion as a basis for the selection of persons for administrative and supervisory posts long has been recognized as hazardous and misleading in resolving staffing problems.

A successful student counselor may not possess the characteristics required to succeed in directing other counselors in a system-wide counseling program. Similarly, with some safety the generalization can be made that an excellent special-area supervisor might not be a satisfactory general supervisor or director of instruction. This generalization may be extended to the more rigidly defined administrative positons; namely, a good department head might be inappropriate for the principalship and the experience in the principalship may contribute little toward the success of the same person in the position of the superintendent.

Those who look beyond the existing staff in a school system to find talent for the various positions and functions have a limitation located more in themselves than in the candidates. They must evaluate candidates not known at first hand from the present school organization and on the basis of other types and sources of data. The problem of identifying the talent potential of those who might be available for the various positions remains the same, but the selection procedures differ. Whether selecting from within the staff or from outside the school system, the superintendent is seeking primarily a uniqueness in educational preparation, experience, and personal characteristics which will serve the best interests of the school system.

Can the findings of reference 1 apply to the supervisory staff?

As school systems become larger in membership, they become more complex in organization and operation. The complexity of the various systems demands diversification of tasks and creates a demand for individuals with differing talents. The size of the organization, then, is one factor to consider in identifying and allocating supervisory talent.

SIZE OF ORGANIZATION

The terms "small" and "large" are defined in reference to the numbers of people involved in the operation. The smallest organization, perhaps, is the group of two who possess a one-to-one relationship, yet one of them may possess a position of status authority. This situation might be found in a two-room school in which one teacher is senior to the other, and one either presumes or has been assigned the title of head teacher or principal. There are few two-teacher schools left; consequently, any discussion about the virtues or deficiencies of the group of two seems to be of little profit. There are, of course, many one-to-one relationships existing within the larger organizations, but in general things are much more complicated at the organizational level. Schools are presently characterized by increasing numbers of people. There are more pupils and more teachers. As the number of both increases, a central office organization begins to evolve.

Complications of titles, positions, status, and prestige come more and more into evidence as the school system grows in size. There is one thing that seems to be held in common by schools of all sizes—the teachers always are shown diagrammatically at the bottom or end of the structural pattern. There is perhaps good reason for teachers to be referred to as the "Indians" in the school organization. The old cliché of having more chiefs than "Indians" loses some of its facetiousness in the face of some organizational practices. When the top management or administration becomes more concerned with the superstructure than with accomplishing the purposes of the organization, the teachers perform the tasks of the "Indians." The "Indians" are as often forgotten in the schools as their real counterparts were forgotten as a responsibility of the government that assumed jurisdiction over them. It is unfortunate when administrative and supervisory posts are created and maintained for the satisfaction of the ego of those in the higher echelons of control. In these situations, the allocation of talent is a missing factor or is displaced by an ego-urge that contributes little to, if it actually does not deter from, accomplishing the purposes of the school. Specialization in this sense has been used to serve the persons holding the positions rather than the purposes of the organization for which and in which they have been created.

As schools grow larger the result to be expected is that of greater division of labor which, of necessity, encourages specialization of position and personnel. As this specialization develops more and more positions, the hierarchy of relationships becomes more and more complex. Also, as it becomes larger and as the hierarchy of control becomes more complex, those in the lower echelons have more and more difficulty in clearly understanding the expectations of those in the higher echelons. The intermediate positions often are those of specializations in techniques required at the operational level and may not possess the facilities or specializations that are needed to effectuate a good communication system.

A phenomenon that attends largeness and complexity is that of the assignment of prestige, values, and qualities to the higher-echelon positions. The increase in prestige qualities of a position makes it more desirable to those farther down in the organizational line who have urges for upward mobility and, consequently, a competitiveness within the ranks develops. There is no reason to fear this type of competitiveness unless those who define the position vacate their responsibilities of defining the specializations needed and of selecting the talent appropriate to the position. This means that the individual interested in moving up in the hierarchy must develop a specialization appropriate to the position he seeks. He must develop this specialization while maintaining the evidence of competence in his nonspecialized tasks or in his specialized task at a lower level. Thus, talents may be lost or gained, depending upon the actions and decisions of those holding certain positions in the hierarchy of control.

How can you harmonize the urge for upward mobility and professional competence?

As the organization increases in numbers, and thereby in complexity, the individual titles of positions may lose something in the precision of the function described while at the same time gaining the rewards of prestige and status. It is tempting for a position holder at any level to see his prestige and status grow as he increases the number of people under his direction and control or the number of functions to be credited to his particular specialization. In this process of seeking prestige and status, always the potential in a position, the seeker may forget that he has limits in span of attention. If the particular specialization is intended to provide specialized assistance to those under the position's influence, the failure to provide that leadership and direction will result in lowered prestige for the position. In other words, the ego-urge of a person to gain prestige through increasing numbers of people and functions within his responsibility invites failure for himself purely because he is overcommitted and does not have the opportunity, even though of his own choice, to provide that which the position demands.

Control, similarly, is affected seriously as one seeks to increase the numbers of people and functions under his influence. Control loses its essence of visibility as the number of people to be controlled increases. This control, or the essence of control, is lost because, as the number of people to be controlled increases, the person in the supervisory position is unable to provide or to exercise the controls which have to be applied to such a great variety of persons and talents. The ultimate outcome of exceeding a span of attention and control, as well as the inability to increase the controls over increasing numbers of people, results in a diffusion of perceptions of the purposes of the control agents. The type of person being discussed at this point, the empire-builder, is often his own agent of failure. He exceeds the commitments that can be met by one person, particularly by himself, and therefore is unable to fulfill the perceptions of his service and the expectations of his office. The result is that both the person and the position are downgraded. Part of the reason for this is that the increasing numbers of people unable to make direct and personal contact with the supervisor become disinterested in the services of the office. The expectations for that position become more and more ephemeral as a centralized agent and more the expression of individual preferences.

Frequent assessment of the real and the idealized characteristics in each line and staff position is appropriate. This reassessment requires a new look at the position—the perceptions held of it; its state of actual prestige among superiors, peers, and subordinates; and, finally, whether the position with the specialized person assigned to it is serving the purpose declared at the time it was created as a part of the organization.

IMPLICATIONS OF SPECIALIZATION

A popular notion, which is supported by convincing evidence, is that the large organization tends to lose sight of the importance of the individual, particularly of those who are not in the top hierarchical positions. Further, the largeness factor seems to encourage the inclination to share fewer decisions with all members of the organization and to concentrate the control with a few people in the higher echelons of the administrative organizations. There is a strong feeling among those who are not in the small control group at the top to feel that freedom has been lost in the process of becoming large and that, having lost this freedom, there is less opportunity for creativity in meeting their particular assignments. Some may argue that creativity is not desirable except at the higher levels of administrative control. Others may debate the beneficial effects of creativity at any level in the organizational structure.

What are the pros and cons of this issue?

An inappropriate comparison is that of the classroom teacher, who is presumably at the end of the organizational line, with the factory worker who has a semi-skilled, assembly-line task which must be performed with a high degree of precision. Teaching and assembly-line work are not comparable tasks. The many statements of comparability between schools and industry in this respect probably have done a disservice to both. Regardless of the nature of the need for commonality and conformity at one level and creativity at the other organizational level, expectations flow through the various positions to those who are performing the main tasks required in accomplishing the purpose of the educational system. It may be a moot question as to which end of the organization requires greater specialization.

As school systems have become larger in size, there has been an inclination to increase the employment of "specialists." The small school may have little need for a business manager. The teacher, having limited requirements for instructional supplies, may depend on the principal to make one stock-purchasing foray which would meet the needs of the school for an entire year. This is not so easily done when dealing with hundreds of teachers and pupils in a large school system. A purchasing specialist becomes both a convenience and a necessity as school systems grow larger. The business manager represents a specialization just as does the supervisor of music, the director of curriculum, or the teacher of reading.

One of the great misfortunes in staffing the school system is that of having too little respect for the needed specializations. Specialization is not achieved simply by giving a title implying specialized service to a position, then filling the position with one who does not possess those abilities presumed in the title. When non-specialists are assigned to specialized services they are not able to meet the expectations of the employer, their colleagues, or the people of the supporting community. Many have observed that a person who has accepted a position for which he is not qualified sooner or later supports his ego and defends his inabilities by blaming someone else for his failure to fulfill the demands of that position. Thus, a supervisor who does not possess the specialization presumed in his title is likely to blame either the superintendent of schools or the principals of the individual buildings for his own lack of progress in supplying leadership.

There is some evidence to support the idea that the higher the degree of specialization implied by a particular position and possessed by the position holder, the greater the probability that such a person will be free to go about his work with little concern for the controls imposed from the higher levels in the hierarchy. A supervisor who does not have the specialized knowledge and techniques required for the position will find himself little respected and considered unable to supply the needed assistance in solving the various problems that confront the school organization. The superintendent may employ such specialists and use them to perform those administrative and supervisory functions for which they have not developed sufficient specialization. It is an error, either for the superintendent or the persons working under his direction, to presume that there is a pyramiding of specializations needed all along the line from the classroom to the central office and that the superintendent possesses all of these specialized abilities. If the superintendent were so talented, he might employ almost anyone, or almost no one, for specialized positions because he would be able to make all decisions and to give all directions required of these specializations.

What is your perception of a staff officer whose competence does not support his position?

The person accepting a supervisory position who does not possess the level of specialization required by that position is subjected to consequences of the assumption of equal rights in making judgments on the part of those both above and below him in the hierarchy of the organization. This means that the talent needed for the position has not been identified and is not exemplified in the person assigned to the position. Thus, the allocation of talent on the part of the superintendent represents failure in one of the areas of specialization that he, as chief administrator, is presumed to possess—namely, the identification of talent and the assignment of that talent where it is needed in the school organization.

Perhaps the outstanding example of lack of respect for specialization is in the attitude of laymen toward the classroom teacher. The layman seems to assume that almost anyone can teach school, at least in the elementary grades. It is evident in the expressed attitudes of many people that they assume that anyone who can read can teach reading, and that anyone who can manipulate numerals can teach arithmetic. Those involved in the responsibility of the teaching profession know that this is not the case and that the layman is overestimating his own specialization with respect to the requirements of the skills and techniques for teaching children. The point here is in the perception of the layman toward what he has never identified as a specialized skill. The teacher has the problem that his skills are not held in awe by the parents of the pupils, and consequently he is not recognized as possessing specialized skills. This is the same sort of situation that exists between the teacher and the principal or the teacher and the supervisor when the teacher does not see in the principalship or in the supervisory position the requirement for a specialization of talent. Where specialization is required, it is essential that the person who possesses it make it observable to those who should have a respect for it. This places the responsibility upon the administrators and supervisors for giving evidence to the fact that administration and supervision is a specialized service, that the positions are filled by people who possess the specialization, and that their specializations do make the work of the teachers in the individual classrooms more effective.

In the literature of education over a period of many decades, there has been an inclination to dichotomize the personnel in a school system, particularly at the administrative and supervisory levels, as being either generalists or specialists. No one has ever described particularly well what is meant by a generalist. The status and security of the specialist are more hopeful in that he is presumed to be limited in his area of technical competence and to be working only with those who have a similar specialized interest. Often he works with those who are so poorly prepared in his special area that they are dependent upon him for assistance. The supervisor of music, the supervisor of science, or the guidance director are some whose specializations are now quite easily identified and generally appreciated. Science teachers will accept assistance from the science supervisor who is competent in the field of science if he is able to offer some specialized assistance without which the individual would not be able to function.

How do your perceptions of general- and special-area supervisors differ?

The misfortune in terminology has fallen primarily to the lot of the generalist. No one seems to know for sure about what the generalist is general. Some infer that a generalist is one who knows a little bit about a lot of things but not much about anything. There has not been an inclination to define the generalist as a person who has that technical ability or specialization to coordinate the diverse elements of a broad program of studies. He is not credited with being responsible and having competence in the selection and interpretation of the goals of education. He is not seen as a person who is particularly adept in identifying societal needs or in leading a school staff in establishing a social philosophy which would give guidance to the nature and quality of the instructional program. He is not seen as a person who has specialized in studying the principles of teaching and learning. Nor is he seen as a person who can provide technical help in the evaluation of the progress toward achievement of the overall goals of education accepted by the school system and by its supporting community. This lack of the proper definition of the term "generalist" is now a tradition that has performed a disservice to positions such as general supervisor, director of instruction, and director of curriculum.

Part of the reason for this lack of or improper definition of the generalist may be in the staffing practices that have characterized many school systems, namely, that anyone might be deemed a generalist and, therefore, assigned to those positions which did not require a high degree of technical competence in the fairly narrow area of a specific subject. If this reason for the low state of the term "generalist" in education is accepted, then it can be corrected only by the selection of that talent which can make more observable the special services to be rendered through those positions indicating a broader responsibility than that of the special-area supervisor.

As indicated above, the lack of specialization would more likely cause conformity to the rules, regulations, and wishes of the top echelon of control. This means that the structural pattern has been extremely inconsistent in its operational characteristics because of this lack of wisdom in the allocation of talent. On most of the structural charts, the generalist is higher in the scale of control in the structural pattern than the special-area supervisor, yet the special-area supervisor often is held in higher esteem. If there is anything to the logic of a structural pattern which establishes levels of control over people and aspects of the program, then the operational relationships as described above are reversed to that which was intended in the organizational design. When top supervisory positions are filled by people who possess the talent to meet the expectations of supervision, the traditional lack of respect for the generalist position will improve. In other words, as one possesses higher-level talents in a specialization, one gains greater freedom from the organizational controls and earns the right as well as the opportunity to be creative in his work.

The hierarchy of control is less confining for those offering increasingly esoteric services which are essential to the large-group enterprise. Autonomy is both earned and granted. It is earned in the sense that, as one develops the higher level of competence, there are fewer people who may presume to exercise control over him. Autonomy is granted in the sense that the people in control of the employment and assignment of persons to positions express a respect for a high level of specialization and thereby grant the autonomy that seems to attend it. Even though the service to be rendered is highly esoteric, it must still be essential as a contribution to the achievement of the purposes of the system or the organization (see Chapter 12). One cannot become specialized merely to be specialized, that is, to make specialization obvious and then to expect insulated freedom because of that specialization. Specialization earns autonomy only when it constitutes an appropriate use of essential talent for the purpose of the organization.

DELEGATION OF AUTHORITY AND RESPONSIBILITY

An increase in numbers of workers in an organization as well as an increase in the complexity of the relationships make a division of labor necessary if there is to be a proper delegation of functions and proper use of specialization. This delegation of functions often is referred to as a delegation of authority and responsibility. There was an old maxim in school administration that "you can delegate authority but you cannot delegate responsibility." A number of people have challenged this as an acceptable principle of administration. To delegate authority without holding a person responsible for his actions is no more realistic than to delegate a responsibility without the authority to carry out the task. The increasing size and complexity of school systems have made it quite evident that one person at the apex of the administrative pyramid cannot continue to assume the responsibility for what occurs in all parts of the system. The superintendent of schools cannot be expected to stop third graders from throwing snowballs on their way home from school. Yet the principle of delegation that has come out of a past in which organizations were smaller, their purposes fewer, and their organizational relationships less complex cannot be carried forward into the current situations. It means that delegation must be a delegation of responsibility as well as of authority. Superintendents in middle-sized school systems—however middle-sized is defined—find it difficult to release their personal attachment to and envelopment by responsibility. Boards of education make it difficult for them to dispose of the assumption of possessing absolute authority and responsibility and the consequent expectations with respect to the office. The superintendent often has said, "If I must be responsible for the mistakes that are made in the school system, then I want to make them." Often, he has done so.

What would it mean for teachers to accept full responsibility for pupil progress?

A superintendent will enjoy longer and healthier service in a particular superintendency if the members of the board and the supporting public make it possible for him to delegate responsibility as well as authority. Delegation, however, cannot be a one-way proposition. It is not enough for the superintendent or the principal simply to declare that functions are delegated. Without the acceptance of the delegation, a function is no more delegated than is communication complete until both parties achieve a common understanding.

A supervisor has the problem of accepting delegations from the superintendent or other appropriate administrative officers. If the delegations are entirely foreign to his technical competence, ability, and talent, the expectations placed upon him are improper and invite failure. In protecting his own personal sense of success as well as the recognition of it by others, a supervisor must be aware of the talent that he possesses and, consequently, should contribute his assistance to the delegating officer in making the proper allocations of functions. Acceptance or rejection of delegations becomes one of the important facets of allocating talent where it can be used best in achieving the purposes of the school system.

The effects of accepting too many functions are serious. On the other hand, the effects of accepting too few are equally serious. If one has too little adaptability or flexibility to deviate somewhat from his major specialization, he may find that he is less appreciated by those in the higher echelons than he would desire. The acceptance of the wrong tasks is perhaps the more serious hazard for the supervisory staff member. During this period when schools have been increasing rapidly in size, there have been instances in which supervisory staff members have been asked by superintendents to assume new, strange, and improper functions. It appears that superintendents have been unable to employ competent administrative assistants with the same ease with which they have been able to employ supervisors. The result has been that many superintendents have called upon the supervisors to perform some administrative functions that are not closely related to their professional preparation and experience. For example, a supervisor who has been asked to direct the process of budget-making or to take responsibilities in planning new buildings may be committing himself to some tasks in which he does not have the technical competence to perform with the degree of success that would reflect favorably upon both his position and his competence as an instructional supervisor. The problems of avoiding the acceptance of too much, too little, or the wrong tasks are a matter of responsibility both for the administrative staff making the assignment and for the individual accepting the assignment (see reference 4).

What are some functions that are inappropriate for supervisors?

The 1961 Annual Report of the Cambridge, Massachusetts Superintendent of Schools provides a very simple, direct, and high-quality contribution to this problem of delegating and accepting functional commitments.[1] This report to the school committee includes descriptions of several positions. Its uniqueness is that it specifically and overtly commits the headmaster of a school to ". . . final responsibility for . . ." various functions. Here is an indication that this community has recognized that there must be the delegation of responsibility as well as the delegation of authority. The duties of the headmaster are spelled out in some detail and it can easily be seen that the occupant of this position possesses final responsibility for the itemized functions. Other positions are described, but the degrees of responsibility are not indicated so specifically as they are for the headmaster. In those positions, it can be assumed that the functions are to be performed with the appropriate degree of authority being delegated but that the responsibility for the success or failure of the performance of the function rests with the administrative

[1] John M. Tobin, Superintendent of Schools, *Annual Report of the School Committee and the Superintendent of Schools* (Cambridge, Massachusetts: 1961).

supervisory office to which the person assigned these functions has been attached. In this sense there is a dichotomy—and a proper one—between the line administrative officers and the staff officers attached to the various line positions.

The Janesville, Wisconsin school system developed one of the more complete and detailed differentiations of staff functions that can be found. Its development, cited at this point, is particularly pertinent to the organization for instructional control, direction, and improvement. The allocation of functions to position can be done in an arbitrary manner by an administrative officer. The Janesville system, however, approached the definition of position functions by means of wide staff participation in the declaration of perceptions rather than by arbitrary administrative assignment. There were twenty-five task areas which were subjected to identification by the role that each administrative and supervisory officer would assume in carrying out the tasks. In analyzing the various tasks under these categories and looking particularly for the point of decision, it was found necessary not only to look at the type of activity as found in the task categories but also to consider its functional nature. There was a task category as well as a function category, because several functions might be needed for the completion of one task. By a function category is meant the type of classifications assigned to administrative functions that appear in many of the standard texts on school administration. The publication of the results of this school-wide study carries the title *Allocation of Administrative Functions*.[2] Even though it was a more laborious procedure for allocating functions, the probable accuracy and acceptability of descriptions are sufficiently encouraging to warrant this approach. It is important to recognize that such an effort to improve understanding of functions of positions does not serve a school system for all time. In 1967 a revision of the original document was issued and nine additional positions were included. A further indication of a need for continual evaluation of such operations is provided as a result of a new study initiated in that school system in 1968 to reassess the allocation of managerial functions. This illustration should be sufficient to alert those concerned with delegation of tasks to the persisting problem of appropriateness as systems become larger and as the specialized demands on the participants are altered.

What conditions might initiate a similar study in your school system?

MAXIMIZING TALENT

The larger and more complex the school system becomes, the greater the concern for the specializations required for the management of that system. The problem of numerical adequacy of the staff then becomes an extremely pertinent

[2] Fred R. Holt, *Allocation of Administrative Functions* (Janesville, Wisconsin: Janesville Public Schools, 1963, 1967, and 1970).

issue. It is recognized that the staffing of schools in a period of rapidly growing student population is an increasingly difficult problem. Lay people as well as educators focus attention primarily upon the need for more teachers and for more classrooms. The overriding problems to be solved are dominantly those of quantity. The concerns for classroom teachers and classrooms become so demanding that insufficient attention is given to the matter of staffing the supervisory and administrative positions. It seems appropriate to raise the question about the staffing of administrative and supervisory positions as these are primarily concerned with the quality control services of the school system. The primary concern is that of determining whether the change in the ratios of various staff positions to pupils and teachers as well as load expectations may cause major changes in the functions designated as supervision. In the light of the definition of supervision as used by these authors, it is proper to raise the question: "Do the ratios among personnel involved in the processes of supervision make it possible to carry out this type of supervision at a satisfactory level?"

The question might well be raised as to what the optimum should be in the teacher–supervisor ratio. This has not been determined with any degree of certainty. It only can be speculated that when the ratio reaches one supervisor to over 600 teachers, the nature of the supervisory contacts, relationships, and impact would be quite different from when the ratio is one to fifty. This is not to suggest a criterion but rather to raise the question as to whether sheer numerical relationships may result in substantial changes in the nature of the supervisory services that may characterize a school system.

How would you decide whether the numerical ratios of personnel in your school system were adequate?

This brief indication of a concern for adequate talent for supervisory services within a school system raises the following questions:

1. To what extent have the changing pupil populations brought about changes in the purposes, functions, and procedures of supervision?
2. To what extent have the added services imposed upon the schools brought about changes in the purposes, functions, and procedures of both supervision and administration?
3. Have the increasing burdens placed upon administrators resulted in a shift of supervisory time from supervisory functions to administrative functions?
4. Have there been changes in the allocation of responsibility and authority?
5. In what ways may the procedures used in the evaluation of teachers be affected by increasing the ratio of supervisors and administrators to teachers?
6. Has the increase in the percentage of special-area supervisors resulted in an uncoordinated impact upon the improvement of the instructional program?

An encouraging example of the recognition of the delineation of tasks of appropriate commitments in terms of quantity and type is to be found in the publication *Staffing Schools for Essential Services,* published by the Philadelphia Area School Study Council.[3] The unique contribution of this publication is the recognition that the quality of services to be performed is related to the number of persons provided for staffing those functions. In the various functions and services indicated, there are a number of functions indicated as *superior, adequate, transitional,* or *initial.* In each instance there is indicated the numbers and types of staff members needed to perform these services at the level of proper expectation. Attention is called to the fact that the Council was cognizant of the need for relating the number of assigned and assumed functions to appropriate staffing needs. The implied caution is: one person can adequately perform a given number of tasks, but an excess in the assignment of tasks well might result in less than an acceptable performance.

The solutions to problems related to allocation of talent rest with the superintendent of schools and other administrative and supervisory staff members. The efforts of many people are required over a long period of time. Even then, there must be frequent reassessments if the services of supervision are to keep pace with the demands that are being made upon educational services at the present time and as they may be anticipated for the future.

In considering the allocation of supervisory talent, there is proper concern for the provision of, as well as the acceptance of, the conditions that nurture the development and use of talent for its proper purposes. It is the responsibility of the central office to provide those working conditions which include primarily the assignment to posts where the expectations are appropriate to the talents of the persons placed in those positions. In making assignments, the reverse of the previous statement also must be realized. The talent sought should be that which seems to meet most completely the expectations of the position. But, having made the selection of the person, it is incumbent upon the administrative staff, as well as the supervisors, to create working conditions that permit the talent to fulfill its proper expectations. This is a joint responsibility of the person making the selection and the allocation as well as of the person being selected and allocated. References related to conditions influencing these situations have been made in Part II.

The responsibility of selecting the proper allocation of function appropriate to the individual cannot be left entirely to the central office administrator. The superintendent is entitled to assistance from the supervisors both in the assessment of talents and in the assignment to positions where the unique talents available are most appropriate and where they may be put to their fullest realization.

[3] Leon Ovsiew, Executive Secretary, Philadelphia Area School Study Council, *Staffing Schools for Essential Services* (Philadelphia: Temple University, 1957).

A further responsibility is that of recognizing and accepting the extent of participation to be expected from all whose specialized contributions will have an impact on the system or organization. The participants and the influence of participation are discussed in Chapter 10.

SELECTED REFERENCES

1. Carlson, Richard O., *Executive Succession and Organization Change: Place-Bound and Career-Bound Superintendents of Schools.* Chicago: Midwest Administration Center, University of Chicago, 1962.
2. Eye, Glen G. and Lanore A. Netzer, *School Administrators and Instruction.* Boston: Allyn & Bacon, 1969. Chaps. IV, VII, and VIII.
3. Holt, Fred R., *Allocation of Administrative Functions.* Janesville, Wisconsin: Janesville Public Schools, 1963, 1967, and 1970.
4. Netzer, Lanore A. and Glen G. Eye, "What Is the Supervisor's Position in the School's Program?" *Wisconsin Journal of Education,* January, 1962, pp. 8–9.
5. Netzer, Lanore A., Glen G. Eye, Ardelle Graef, Robert D. Krey, and J. Fred Overman, *Interdisciplinary Foundations of Supervision.* Boston: Allyn & Bacon, Inc., 1970. Chap. VI.
6. Ovsiew, Leon, Executive Secretary, Philadelphia Area School Study Council, *Staffing Schools for Essential Services.* Philadelphia: Temple University, 1957.
7. Tobin, John M., Superintendent of Schools, *Annual Report of the School Committee and the Superintendent of Schools.* Cambridge, Massachusetts: 1961.

10

The Realm of Participation

Increasing numbers of individuals are requesting, demanding, and acquiring greater degrees of participation in those affairs about which they are concerned. This occurs most frequently when there is some feeling that those persons charged with authority and responsibility are not exercising their function properly or in the best interests of all members of the system. This phenomenon is evident in many aspects of today's society and, therefore, it is not peculiar that similar behavior is characteristic of members of educational systems. This phenomenon embodies some of those factors to which reference is made in assumption twelve—specifically, influences upon behavioral status, change, and mobility. The relationship between behavioral status and participation can be identified readily. A person allowed to participate in matters of professional and personal concern may consider himself more valued than one who is not permitted to participate. Similarly, an individual who participates when permitted may be considered by others to be more valuable to the system than the individuals who do not participate when permitted.

Participation must also be considered in relation to behavioral change. It is logical to assume that, when change is expected in a person's behavior, individuals should become involved or participate in those activities and decisions which will influence the direction, degree, or type of change. Also to be considered is the fact that involvement, or participation itself, is likely to influence development or change of behavior.

Mobility is related to participation. The individual who constructively participates in a system within his environment is apt to move upward in the hierarchy of his system, in the esteem with which he is held by his colleagues, or in others' perceptions of his contribution to the system. The same person may be increasingly mobile in facility to move to positions of greater prestige, salary, or responsibility. Conversely, a person prevented from constructive participation may be prevented from the benefits of mobility accorded other members of the system. The individual who is permitted to participate and does not, or who participates to the detriment of others, may find himself mobile in a downward direction, both in his own system and to other systems.

The discussion in Chapter 9 pertained to the synchronization of talents of participants and the function of positions within the patterns as presented in Part II. This chapter is devoted to *participation* more directly as it relates to the operational patterns and the contributory and supportive functions of supervision. Participation as it concerns individuals and situations beyond the realm of the structural patterns of a school system is explored.

IDENTIFYING THE PARTICIPANTS

An initial consideration in identifying those participating in the function of supervision would be an examination of the structural pattern of the local school system. When charted, it is readily recognized that the board of education is a dominant participant. This participation is prescribed by law and it is unique in that the board can participate legally only as a group—that is, the individuals of this participating group may not act officially as individuals. This might be considered collective participation as opposed to individual participation. The assumption is imposed that each member acts in a reasonable and responsible manner. Collective participation incurs some responsibilities and results which would differ from the responsibilities and results of individual participation. This group acts collectively in decision-making, in policymaking, and in delegating supervisory responsibility and authority. All the tasks of the positions in the structural patterns of a school system are performed as a result of delegation from the board of education. Their participatory function, then, becomes that of assisting in establishing the appropriate purposes and patterns for the organization and in sponsoring the processes necessary to the achievement of the desired products. Because legal supervisory participation originates with this body, the participatory function described will be delegated along with the delegation of other tasks.

The administrative-supervisory personnel constitutes the group of certificated employees most frequently associated with supervisory interactions. It is, consequently, this portion of the structural pattern of a school system toward which the major efforts of this book have been directed. Significant in identifying this group of school employees as participants is the realization that they become one of a number of groups participating in the total supervisory program. They possess some major responsibilities and authority not characteristic of other groups in the system.

The teaching personnel, however, are participating to a greater extent now than ever before. Certain aspects of participation by this group are of the collective or negotiated type and are, in a sense, comparable to the legal mode of the board of education. There are, nevertheless, many occasions in which teachers participate in the supervisory function as individuals, for example, in developing innovative techniques.

Parents and students and other sub-publics wishing to influence the educational system also become participants in the processes of supervision (see Part IV). The extent of their participation is regulated by desire and ability as well as by recognition of them by the "establishment." There is additional participation by the supporting public expressed in the form of laws and court decisions. The court decisions may result from some action initiated by one of these individuals or groups who wish to participate in formulating policy or in making supervisory decisions.

Manufacturers and publishers of educational equipment and materials become participants by influencing the actions of other participants. This situation may be detrimental to the local school system if the profit motive is permitted to dominate the educational purpose. Curriculum developments and instructional improvements may be regulated unduly by these participants, for instance, if textual materials are allowed to dictate the curriculum and instructional methods rather than serving as a support to those methods developed in the local school system. Computer programs can dictate the curriculum of a school system when the system participants become enamored of the tool or the means of instruction at the expense of being concerned with the resultant curriculum and final product in terms of what children study and learn. The important point here is that responsible people must know the type and extent of participation which suppliers can offer to support the purposes of the educational system.

Educational technologists are another group of participants, and they are fairly new to the scene. These participants originate mainly in the business field, although some are "dropouts" from the traditional fields in the educational profession. They believe that there are more appropriate methods of accomplishing the purposes of our school systems. The idea of "contract education" is so new that complete supportive or evaluative information is not yet available. The experiences of school systems such as Gary, Indiana in contracting with the Behavioral Research Laboratories of Palo Alto, California will help to determine whether these types of participants have greater impact than the more traditional participants in achieving the goals of education.[1]

There is evidence to indicate that business and industry, as participants, are struggling to develop answers to educational problems. Inexperience and failure to solidify their efforts with those of the educational profession have resulted in a lack of hoped-for progress for such participants as Raytheon, General Learning Corporation, and MIND, Inc.[2] The point is not that these participants have no contribution to offer the educational scene but rather that they have fallen short in recognizing the fact of participation which they, themselves, have been trying to achieve.[3]

The purpose here has been to identify the many individuals and groups who are potential participants in influencing the efforts of the local school system. To the extent that they participate in the processes which lead to some impact on the instructional program they become participants in supervision. It is, therefore, this consideration which provides the basis for attention to the broad realm of participation.

What other participants can you identify and what are the directions of their efforts?

TYPES OF PARTICIPANTS

The many participants in supervision may be typed or subjected to categorization. The typology considered here is in reference to the personal characteristics of the individuals in any of the recognized groups of participants.

Presthus has identified three types of individuals as they relate to group activity. His classifications have pertinence in categorizing the people who work in the organizational society. He identified these three types as the upward-mobiles, the indifferents, and the ambivalents. He described the characteristics of the upward-mobiles in this way:

> The upward-mobiles are typically distinguished by high morale; their level of job satisfaction is high. Indeed, the process and criteria by which they are selected insures that they will have an unfailing optimism. The reasons for this are clear. They identify strongly with the organization and derive strength from their involvement. Their dividends also include disproportionate shares of the organization's rewards in power, income, and ego reinforcement. As we have seen, subjective inequality is a built-in feature of big organizations and is rationalized on the basis of equality of opportunity. Power is easily justified by those who have it, since it confirms daily their right (achieved in fair competition) to possess it. The

[1] James Cass, "Profit and Loss in Education," *Saturday Review,* August 15, 1970, pp. 39–40.

[2] Elliot Carlson, "Education and Industry: Troubled Partnership," *Saturday Review,* August 15, 1970, pp. 45–47ff.

[3] Stephen J. Knezevich and Glen G. Eye, *Instructional Technology and the School Administrator* (Washington, D.C.: American Association of School Administrators, 1970).

upward-mobiles will not, therefore, seriously question a system that has proved its rationality.[4]

Few participants will be in an organization long before they have identified the upward-mobiles. These often are referred to as the "apple-polishers." They are seldom those who seriously question proposals made by the supervisor if the existing and successful rationale is challenged. Many supervisors, even though aware of the presence of this type among the people with whom they work, are hesitant to give up the personal satisfaction of the overt expression of acceptance. This is not to suggest that the supervisors should have no need for a sense of security, prestige, and admiration but rather that, when a supervisor succumbs to this type of influence, he may displace the institutional goals and the supervisory objectives in favor of personal aggrandizements.

Describe situations in which persons have responded to upward-mobiles.

The upward-mobiles, on the other hand, can be participants who offer much zest for work, enthusiasm for innovation, and constancy of leadership support. The negative connotations indicated above are points of caution rather than suggestions for avoidance. An awareness on the part of the supervisor of the characteristics of the upward-mobiles is the first and most effective step in channeling talent and enthusiasm to productive and acceptable outcomes. Following this first step in making advantageous use of this type is the responsibility of the superior officers to provide a communications system which will avoid the lack of depth-perception of the upward-mobiles and achieve a comparable and enthusiastic support from those who are not in this category.

The indifferents are described by Presthus in this manner:

> The indifferents are those who have come to terms with their work environment by withdrawal and by a redirection of their interests toward off-the-job satisfactions. They have also been alienated by the work itself, which has often been downgraded by machine processing and by assembly-line methods. This dual basis for alienation must be recognized. In industrial psychology the main effort has been to compensate for the deadening effect of the work itself by providing a happy work place. Less attention has been given to alienation from the job itself.
>
> We are not speaking here of pathological kinds of alienation, but of modes of accommodation that often seem basically healthy. The typical indifferent has rejected majority values of success and power. While the upward-mobile strives for such values, obtainable today mainly through big organizations, the indifferent seeks that security which the organization can also provide for those who merely "go along." Such security seeking varies in accord with the demands of personality. One individual may have been taught to expect more than life can reasonably offer, and anxiety and frustration follow as his unrealistic claims are discounted. Another may have learned to expect less; he may refuse to accept success values or to compete

[4] Reprinted from *The Organizational Society* by Robert Presthus by permission of Alfred A. Knopf, Inc. Copyright © 1962 by Robert Presthus. pp. 167–168.

for them. This role is encouraged by such bureaucratic conditions as hierarchy, oligarchy, and specialization.[5]

Many supervisors have complained that there are always one or more participants who, when a proposal is made, are likely to say, "We did that years ago and it didn't work," or simply, "It won't work." Perhaps more often they will simply say nothing. They show little interest and little response either in their acceptance of an idea or their pursuance of a plan. Many of them may do acceptable work, so acceptable that they could not be dismissed, but yet they do not contribute to those goals of the leadership of the school system that are designed to bring about an instructional program having the mark of superiority.

Explain the positive effects credited to the indifferents.

Presthus described the ambivalents as follows:

> One important qualification is required. Despite his inability to meet bureaucratic demands, the ambivalent type plays a critical social role, namely, that of providing the insight, motivation, and the dialectic that inspire change. The upward-mobile honors the status quo and the indifferent accepts it, but the ambivalent is always sensitive to the need for change. His innovating role is often obscured because the authority, leadership, and money needed to institutionalize change remain in the hands of organizational elites. Nevertheless, few ideals or institutions escape his critical scrutiny. In his view custom is no guarantee of either rationality or legitimacy. This perception is sharpened by his inability to accept charismatic and traditional bases of authority; rationality alone provides a compelling standard. Certain personality traits underlie this critical posture.[6]

He elaborated further with respect to the ambivalents as follows:

> The ambivalent ordinarily plays a specialist, "cosmopolitan" role. He honors theory, knowledge, and skill. Socialization as an independent professional often blinds him to legitimate organizational needs for control and co-ordination. Believing explicitly that both motivation and expertise come from within, he resists bureaucratic rules and supervision. Attempts to impose standards from without are seen as presumptuous and denigrating. As a result, there is always a gap between his self-perception as an independent professional and the galling realization, punctuated daily by the organization's authority and status of differentiation, that he is really an employee. His skill authority is not always recognized, even though it is perfectly clear that his technical judgments have been decisive. The managerial facade with which he is confronted confirms his belief that hierarchical authority is often specious. This tension between skill and hierarchical authority is aggravated by the organization's subjective criteria of seniority and obedience. In sum, the bureaucratic situation is inapposite to his personal and professional values.
>
> The heart of the ambivalent reaction is a tenacious self-concern. Most events are perceived by the ambivalent in terms of himself; personal goals are usually primary. His own experiences and skills

[5] *Ibid.*, p. 208.
[6] *Ibid.*, p. 258.

seem unique; and when his career expectations prove unrealistic, as they often do, he may invoke humanistic themes to buttress his claims for preference. In terms of an earlier distinction, we may regard the ambivalent as an idealistic, independent personality. Unable to achieve distinction on the organization's terms, he may adopt idiosyncratic alternatives, a reaction encouraged by the erosion of qualitative standards. If he aspires to artistic achievement he may assume a bohemian role. If adequate discipline or talent frustrate his intellectual claims, he may again enlist conventional substitutes. But since majority values usually prove irresistible, such behaviors are unsatisfactory to him. Sensitive, emotionally undisciplined, an individual in a mass society, he is perpetually out of step.[7]

Earlier reference was made to the situation of the brilliant person on the teaching staff whose supervisor is dull and to the various combinations tending toward the more favorable situation of a brilliant supervisor and a brilliant teacher. Brilliant minds are, as the ambivalents, less likely to be satisfied with the simple rule-of-thumb conformity that makes for peaceful individual relationships. The ambivalents, however, are credited with being the type in organizational efforts that bring about the more promising innovations. It is a challenge to the supervisor to order his feelings and his purposes in his position so that he can accommodate situations in which the ambivalents may be perpetually questioning the position, logic, and direction of supervisory effort. On the other hand, personal relationships can be established in which differences of opinion possess the potential of being the crucible in which ideas are refined, declared, and implemented. This is not the promise of a peaceful life in a position either for the supervisor or for the supervised. Both should focus away from personal conflict or the relationships of individuals and concentrate upon those things which are to be accomplished in the educational program. The ways of progress may be stormy and noisy, but they will be sure and proper.

What other designations could be used to categorize the participants?

The benefits in categorizing the participants are not in the stereotyping that may result but rather in assisting the participants in understanding some of the actions and reactions of other participants. Better understanding of the behaviors of other individuals should result in improved working relationships and in improved contributions from those who wish to be considered participants in supervision.

IMPACT OF PARTICIPATION

Psychologists, sociologists, and other educators have explored the benefits of participation to societal improvement. Occasionally, this has been done with some qualifying conditions. Benne presented his idea in the following statement.

[7] *Ibid.*, pp. 259–260.

> . . . the principle of participation by all persons affected by a social policy, as equals, in the processes by which such policy is formulated and reconstructed has been approved as a (if not the) central norm of democratic operation.[8]

The two conditions emphasized in the statement are that (1) those affected by the policy should participate in formulating it, and (2) the participants should be treated as equals. Some types of participants may have difficulty in treating all other participants as equal. This may be especially true for the incumbents of positions at those levels in the structural pattern which either are or are not perceived to be "above" those in other positions. Those participating need to make some contribution if they are allowed to participate. Nearly three decades ago, Koopman, Miel, and Misner listed five basic principles of democratic administration in which they emphasized the need for and the advantage of allowing people to participate in all enterprises in which they have some ability, interest, need, or concern.[9] It seems that school administrators have not always heeded these "words of wisdom," to the detriment of many members of the profession and many school systems.

The impact of participation on improvement of the instructional program has been investigated and reported by researchers in education. Johansen reported the positive effects of teacher participation in activities associated with curriculum development in terms of improved curricular implementation.[10] Positive relationships between teachers' perceptions of their participation in planning and evaluating curricular implementation activities also were identified by Krey.[11] In the same investigation it was determined that while participation in these events resulted in a positive effect on curricular implementation, the teachers perceived themselves to be relatively insignificant as participants in planning and evaluating these activities.

Emphasizing the positive aspects of involvement, Teague reported that "experience has demonstrated quite clearly that teachers will spend time and effort on programs they helped

[8] Kenneth D. Benne, "Democratic Ethics and Human Engineering," in Warren G. Bennis, Kenneth D. Benne, and Robert Chin (eds.), *The Planning of Change* (New York: Holt, Rinehart & Winston, Inc., 1961), p. 142.

[9] G. Robert Koopman, Alice Miel, and Paul J. Misner, *Democracy in School Administration* (New York: Appleton-Century-Crofts, Inc., 1943), pp. 3–4.

[10] John H. Johansen, "An Investigation of the Relationships Between Teachers' Perceptions of Authoritative Influence in Local Curriculum Decision-Making and Curriculum Implementation," unpublished doctoral dissertation (Evanston, Illinois: Northwestern University, 1965), pp. 196–197.

[11] Robert D. Krey, "Factors Relating to Teachers' Perceptions of Curricular Implementation Activities and the Extent of Curricular Implementation," unpublished doctoral dissertation (Madison: University of Wisconsin, 1968).

plan, participated in, and had an opportunity to evaluate." [12] In his study of in-service education programs, Wesner recognized that involving teachers to improve or change the curriculum was important.[13]

Supporting these educational studies are investigations and reports in other fields. Bass and Leavitt reported "a strong positive relationship between participation in planning on the one hand and morale and productivity on the other." [14] Participation in the process of change ". . . results in higher production, higher morale and better labor management relations," according to Coch and French.[15]

What is and what is not participation must be a concern of those attempting to involve responsible organization members in improving instruction. Allport gave a bit of caution when he stated:

> Activity alone is not participation. Most of our fellow citizens spin as cogs in many systems without engaging their own egos even in those activities of most vital concern to them.
>
> When the ego is not effectively engaged the individual becomes reactive. He lives a life of ugly protest, finding outlets in complaints, strikes, above all in scapegoating; in this condition he is ripe prey for a demagogue whose whole purpose is to focus and exploit the aggressive outburst of non-participating ego.[16]

Have you been connected with an activity in which there was no ego involvement? Describe it.

This admonition reemphasizes the importance of restricting participation to individuals who have some concern or ego involvement with the activities undertaken. A further attack on the problem is that much activity may not be participation at all in that there may be lack of goal orientation toward which the participation is directed.

With the recognition of the need for and impact of participation in achieving improvement in the instructional program, it is imperative that the administrative-supervisory staff has an understanding of the perceptions of those concerned with the implementation of new programs. An example of the type of data-gathering device which may be useful in scanning the local scene regarding curricular implementation is the instrument utilized in the investigation by Krey, to

[12] Wayne Teague, "An Evaluative Analysis of the In-Service Program for Teachers and Administrators in DeKalb County, Georgia," unpublished Ed.D. dissertation (Auburn, Alabama: Auburn University, 1962), p. 50.

[13] Gordon Eugene Wesner, "A Study of In-Service Education Programs for Secondary School Teachers in Selected Large-City Systems," unpublished Ed.D. dissertation (Lawrence: University of Kansas, 1963).

[14] Bernard M. Bass and Harold J. Leavitt, "Some Experiments in Planning and Operating," *Management Science,* IX, July, 1963, p. 584.

[15] Lester Coch and John R. P. French, Jr., "Overcoming Resistance to Change," in Eleanor E. Maccoby, Theodore M. Newcomb, and Eugene L. Hartley (eds.), *Readings in Social Psychology* (Chicago: Holt, Rinehart & Winston, 1958), p. 250.

[16] Gordon W. Allport, "Psychology of Participation," *Psychological Review,* LIII, May, 1945, p. 126.

which earlier reference was made. The original instrument with the analysis of its development is found in a publication by Eye and Netzer.[17]

Another interesting view of the impact of participation is found in the nearness or remoteness of the participant to the purpose for which the participation takes place. This concept is illustrated diagrammatically in Figure 10.1. The relative distance between various organizational participants and the realization of the purpose for which schools exist—pupil learning—has a bearing on the impact of involvement or participation for each member identified. The diagram shows that the teacher's primary impact is on the pupil and the principal's primary impact is on the teacher; consequently, the impact of the principal's effort on pupil learning is secondary in nature. The impact of the effort of the supervisory personnel is diffused, because a supervisor's primary impact may be on the superintendent, the principal, or the teacher at any given time and for any given situation. At another time, the supervisor's efforts may be diffused over all those position incumbents. The impact on pupil learning is in either case remote in relation to the other positions in the structural pattern. It is important, in reference to this design, that individuals within the organization, as well as others wishing to influence education, understand this concept in relation to the impact of their participation on pupil learning. This should assist in preventing participants from becoming disillusioned or misled in terms of the results of such participation and attempts to influence the products of school systems.

How could your perception of the impact of your efforts influence your work?

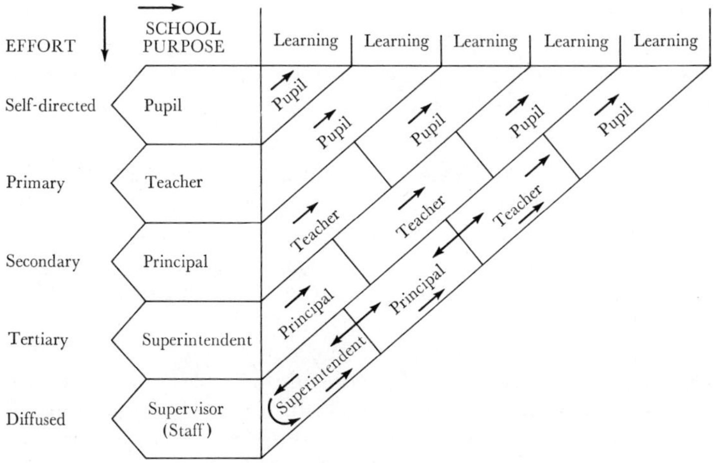

***FIGURE 10.1* Nearness–Remoteness Impact Scale for School Purpose Realization**

[17] Glen G. Eye and Lanore A. Netzer, *School Administrators and Instruction: A Guide to Self-Appraisal* (Boston: Allyn & Bacon, 1970), pp. 276–292.

CONNOTATIONS OF SUBORDINATION

Subordination, as a term, can evoke distasteful implications for the participants who use the term and for those to whom the term is applied. The root of the term "ordinal" signifies the arrangement of things or persons in some priority order. The prefix "sub" indicates a lower status. Thus, the term indicates that some persons in the organization are of lower status than others. Whether or not the reader finds this definition satisfactory, it is true that in a hierarchy the participants in the organization are of different ranks or statuses. The hazard is in the inference that some participants are of lesser importance than others.

The fact persists, nevertheless, that inherent in a structural pattern is the concept of subordination. Everyone in an organizational structure is subordinate to another subordinate. The board of education is subordinate to the supporting public or client group, the superintendent is subordinate to the board of education, and so on "down the line." The positive implication is that everyone is accountable or should be accountable to one or more other position incumbents. Difficulties are apt to arise when the structural pattern requires a subordinate to be accountable to more than one superordinate. Especially difficult is the situation in which a subordinate is required to be accountable to two or more superordinates who have conflicting desires or goals. Filley and House presented two propositions regarding chain of command and unity of command. They were stated as follows:

How are the lines of authority clarified for your school system?

1. Organizations with a clear and single flow of authority from the top to the bottom are more satisfying to their members, and realize more effective economic performance and goal achievement than do organizations without a single clear flow of authority.

2. Violations of the principle of unity of command result in decreased satisfaction for the recipients of commands, and in decreased organizational effectiveness.[18]

Participants in supervision, therefore, must accept the role of subordinate and demand the same clear lines of authority for their subordinates as they desire for themselves. As subordinates, the participants also become recipients of supervisory action. This is discussed at greater length in Chapter 11.

Essential to acceptance of a position in the organizational hierarchy is the acceptance of the connotations of and the label of subordinate and the concomitant obligations. If an individual cannot bear this responsibility he has no right to accept such a position, nor should he expect to become a participant in supervision. Considering that those accepting positions in school systems are attuned to accepting the connotations of their positions, it is then imperative that some

[18] Allen C. Filley and Robert J. House, *Managerial Process and Organizational Behavior* (Glenview, Ill.: Scott, Foresman & Co., 1969), p. 300.

thought be given to the issue of the obligations of a subordinate.

A primary requisite of a subordinate is to have self-confidence in the adequacy of his professional preparation. Undergraduate and graduate degrees in the area of specialization are not sufficient evidence or support for adequacy in this respect. With the rapid increase in the total stock of knowledge, self-discipline becomes essential to identify, secure, and continue to study those areas demanded by the role of the participant at a given point in his professional career.

Knowledge and acceptance of a participant's position expectations are required. He must deal with the expectations of the people in the community, the superordinates, the peers, and the subordinates. It is prerequisite to know these expectations if they are to be acknowledged and accepted. If the expectations are inappropriate, an attempt should be made to alter them so that they become appropriate and agreeable to all concerned.

The knowledge and understanding of the processes of administration and supervision provide insights which permit organizational members to improve the quality of their participation as subordinates. Teachers who have attended graduate courses in administration and supervision have exhibited modified and improved concepts and perceptions of their superordinates. Only an understanding of the origin of control, authority, and responsibility can assist in promoting better intra-staff relations.

The broad view of subordination as discussed here is recommended strongly. Important is the realization that superiors are not the only members with expectations for the participants. Peers and subordinates also hold expectations and controls over the behaviors of the participants. These expectations and controls should not be viewed only in the negative way that some subordinates appraise them. A subordinate who understands the problems inherent in organizational management will welcome legitimate expectations and controls as necessary to his own freedom to operate satisfactorily.

Recognition of the contribution of specialized assistance is another mark of a subordinate with understanding of a properly functioning organization. Every professional worker needs open-mindedness in accepting advice from a specialized and esoteric field not represented in his basic competencies. He must know when to seek assistance and he must be encouraged to do so. Seeking help from specialists should not be viewed as a sign of weakness in preparation; a greater inadequacy in performance would be evidenced by the subordinate who requires assistance and either does not recognize or refuses to admit his need. A word of caution is offered, however, in regard to "specialized assistance." The reference need not be limited to those of narrowly defined esoteric capabilities. It is vital to recognize and search for the needed guidance from any participant who may have some contribution to make. An illustration would be that of the principal or supervisor who asks for assistance from outside the organization in regard to a specific area of study rather than recognize the talents possessed and the contributions to be made by some of the teaching personnel. The structural pattern of an organization indicates a diversification of tasks which needs recognition by all participants.

A subordinate also needs to be realistic in his claim for support. This requires admitting mistakes and accepting the consequences of his actions. Some subordinates act as though they expect a continuous utopia in working conditions, facilities, and resources. The participant should not claim support from his superiors, peers, and subordinates which is contrary to the type of support they are able to provide. Claim for support inherently suggests the requirement of discipline for those who make such claim. To expect otherwise would indicate that a subordinate is unduly intolerant of mistakes.

Discipline elicits thoughts of correcting or changing the behavior of others. In this respect, consideration must be given to the value of positive as well as negative connotations. Suggestions are positive when they clarify purpose, structure relationships, and improve individual behavior as interpreted through institutional rather than individual purposes and goals. Negative suggestions may be helpful if protective. They may reinforce improved behaviors when they protect the individual in conforming to legal and regulatory requirements; they may also contribute to the allocation of time, energy, and ability in accomplishing meritorious outcomes. Imperative, too, is the procedure of self-evaluation in terms of achieving organizational goals.

The ultimate desired outcome of participants contributing to and supporting the attainment of established purposes is that of achieving a team operation. The participant who recognizes and values the knowledge and assistance of another displays the intelligence that recognizes that his own strength becomes stronger through utilizing the strengths of others. The subordinate at any level will fall short of his innate potential if he refuses to see himself strengthened by the reinforcing efforts exerted by others. The essence in the art of subordination is found in the individual's willingness and ability to join, voluntarily and with purpose, the strengths of his superiors and peers with his own unique qualities of insight, foresight, and performance. The progressive refinement of this art is a badge of professional maturity.

What other obligations have been placed upon you as a subordinate?

TEAMING AS A CONCEPT OF PARTICIPATION

Reference has been made to the necessity and desirability of achieving a team operation. The notion that any one participant possesses more knowledge than the combined membership of the group is as obsolete as the little red schoolhouse. Although a person may accept this precept, he may continue to function as the omniscient overseer. The persistence of this phenomenon may be related to security (see Chapter 11) or may result from the participant's perceptions of authority, power, and influence. Filley and House discussed the macrocosmic and microcosmic views of authority, power, and influence as they relate to the participation of organizational members.[19] The macrocosmic view refers to the power and authority inherent in the various positions of the structural pattern (see Chapter 5) and prescribed in the job descriptions for the organization. Influence and power, which organizational members may possess to affect the behaviors of superordinates and subordinates, is included in the microcosmic view. The participant who disregards the contributions of his colleagues is ignoring the microcosmic view of power, authority, and influence and consequently cannot be so successful as the one who utilizes the talents and abilities of all members in achieving organizational goals.

Expanding the concept of the microcosmic view of power, authority, and influence, the implications for delegation must be considered (see Chapter 9). It is necessary to identify and recognize the contributions of others in delegating responsibility and one must be willing to delegate the authority commensurate to the task. The participant who perceives himself or his position as the only tenant of authority or responsibility will be unable to delegate properly. Consequently, he will not view teaming as an appropriate approach to the achievement of goals. According to Ardrey, this individual may view any participation in performing the duties of his position as an attack on or a challenge to his territory of operations, and he will thereby combat any effort to share responsibility and authority.[20]

The committee is an example of teaming, because the designated body is assigned to solve some problems, to complete a task, or to develop plans. In this teaming effort the talents of the committee members will be used either individually or combined to accomplish their goal. Some rather serious misuses of the committee have been evidenced in administrative-supervisory behaviors. Too well known is the situation in which a committee is assigned to make recommendations for overcoming a problem when the superior officer has already made his own decision as to the solution. This type of behavior cannot be considered as teaming by any stretch of the imagination. The officer is protecting his territory as surely as is the person who makes his decision without appointing a committee.

All the criteria applying to the delegation of authority and responsibility should be utilized in appointing committees.

[19] *Ibid.*, pp. 55–65, chap. III.

[20] Robert Ardrey, *The Territorial Imperative* (New York: Atheneum, 1966).

The key in appointing and delegating is that of selecting those participants who are able to make a contribution to the task assigned or delegated. The contributory function was discussed in Chapter 7. The charge to supervision is to direct and guide the efforts of those who wish to, and can, contribute to the proper channels and to desirable goals. It is not enough to want to participate; the participant must have something appropriate to contribute. The subsequent charge to supervision is that of providing support to those who contribute as a result of the assignment or delegation (see Chapter 8).

When would teaming not include members outside the structural pattern of a school system?

A look at *teaming* as it pertains to improvement of the instructional program directs attention to the tasks to be accomplished as they pertain to the contributions to be made by the position incumbents of the school system. This may be expanded to include those members outside the structural pattern of an organization who may influence, direct, or control the efforts of the other participants. The concept itself implies the recognition of the contributions of the people who are concerned with, influenced by, and helpful in accomplishing the tasks of school operations.

Figure 10.2 contains a matrix designed to aid in identifying the contributions of the various participants to the accomplishment of different tasks. The team in this illustration includes the teachers, principal(s), supervisor(s), superintendent, board of education, and lay contributors. This team membership could be and would be modified to identify the appropriate team for a given school system. Task categories selected for the illustration include curriculum and instruction, operational management, business management, community consolidation, supra-agency coordination, accountability, and a category called "others," to allow for necessary additions. This list of task categories could be modified to suit individual desires. Interpretation and use of the matrix are aided by graphical differentiations such as dots, wavy lines, and straight horizontal lines. The dotted lines represent the major areas for contribution by a given team member. The wavy lines represent areas in which the team members should have a contribution to make. The straight lines represent areas in which a team member should be least concerned in deference to his major contribution. Using this codification, the matrix identifies the supervisor(s) as placing his major contribution in the category of curriculum and instruction in deference to other contributors in the other task categories. Also identified are the other team members who will have something to offer in the area of curriculum and instruction, namely, the teacher(s), principal(s), superintendent, board of education, and lay contributors. The type, extent, and method of contribution must be clarified for and acceptable to each team member. A similar team plan should be designed for the participants in the other task categories.

The concept of teaming demands clarification of role de-

FIGURE 10.2
Teaming in School Operations

TASK CATEGORIES	The Team					
	.1 Teacher	.2 Principal	.3 Supervisor	.4 Superin-tendent	.5 Board of Education	.6 Lay Contributors
1. Curriculum and Instruction	1.1	1.2	1.3	1.4	1.5	1.6
2. Operational Management	2.1	2.2	2.3	2.4	2.5	2.6
3. Business Management	3.1	3.2	3.3	3.4	3.5	3.6
4. Community Consolidation	4.1	4.2	4.3	4.4	4.5	4.6
5. Supra-Agency Coordination	5.1	5.2	5.3	5.4	5.5	5.6
6. Accountability	6.1	6.2	6.3	6.4	6.5	6.6
7. Others	7.1	7.2	7.3	7.4	7.5	7.6

(dotted) major area of contribution — (horizontal lines) areas of concern — (wavy lines) area for contribution

scriptions for the team membership. The distinct contribution to be expected from a given participant is not always known. Thompson reported this fact and its effect on total team effort in "A Study of the Synchronization of Behaviors Related to Selected Tasks of Elementary School Supervisors and Principals" [21] (see instrumentation in Appendix B). She stated that "principals and supervisors who have job descriptions synchronize their behaviors more than those incumbents who do not have one available." [22] Thus, clarification of roles should result in more effective and efficient task performance. The difficulty in many school systems in identification of tasks, especially for supervisors and principals, has been a source of frustration for those team members as well as for others. In reference to this point, Thompson concluded that "those incumbents who were involved in the development of their job descriptions were more likely to synchronize behaviors with their colleague(s) than if they had not been involved." [23] She also stated that "if no (job) description was available, the interviewees were not sure how they were evaluated, or if, in fact, they were evaluated at all." [24] This may be a reason, however negative, that some people in administrative-supervisory positions resist the idea of developing job descriptions. They argue that the organization changes so much that by the time the roles are defined there are new descriptions needed. While this problem may exist, it all the more requires delineation of tasks to help the participants in a growing organization understand their positions and those of the other members. Some have also argued that someone in the organization will do the job that needs to be done so why be so worried about identifying the individuals responsible. It is suspected that these resisters to role definitions are resisting accountability to a greater extent than they are resisting the responsibility of describing position tasks. The idea of teaming as a concept of participation is not likely to be successful in a school system in which the members of the team do not clearly understand the contributions to be made by the individual participants as group members.

PARTICIPATION BY CONFRONTATION

Inherent in participation, as it refers to behavior of members within a system, is the obligation to become involved with other members of the system. Participation has been viewed as a positive factor in achieving organizational goals.

[21] Barbara S. Thompson, "A Study of the Synchronization of Behaviors Related to Selected Tasks of Elementary School Supervisors and Principals," unpublished doctoral dissertation (Madison: University of Wisconsin, 1969), p. 176.

[22] *Ibid.*, p. 177.

[23] *Ibid.*, p. 179.

[24] *Ibid.*, p. 180.

A component of involvement—that of conflict—remains as a real threat in any enterprise requiring teamwork. Conflicts that arise need to be resolved if involvement or participation is to continue as a positive force for the organization. One method for resolving organizational conflicts is in the form of confrontation.

Confrontation is not a comfortable concept for many people. The term implies identification and recognition of weaknesses, either within an individual, a group, or the system itself. Those more inclined to "sweep under the rug" or "whitewash" individual or system failures will not find confrontation an acceptable concept. These individuals perhaps are the same as those who are uncomfortable about accountability. Those in management positions today are finding that both confrontation and accountability are becoming increasingly real as facts of life. The two connotations, indeed, have many common relationships in process and in purpose.

Situations requiring confrontation may range from the simple act of two people trying to resolve a personal disagreement or misunderstanding to the complexities of professional negotiations or collective bargaining. Confrontation has been recognized as an effective method for solving organizational problems. The confrontation meeting has been found to be useful in analyzing management team difficulties and in planning improvement. The chief benefits are in the time saved both in meeting and in the solution of problem situations.[25] If confrontation can be used as a tool to eliminate problem areas within an organization, it can be viewed as a positive means of participation which could be utilized by educational systems.

What do you see in the term "confrontation" apart from negotiation?

Participation by confrontation can be used as a continual method for achieving accountability within an organization. This is especially true if this approach is applied in reference to organizational purposes and products rather than in reference to personalities. Confrontation also requires an attack on the problem situation as opposed to the social, bull-session type of participation that is found to be repulsive to participants interested in getting a task accomplished. This might be viewed as the "coffee vs. analysis" approach to accomplishing the tasks of a local school system.

Perhaps some of the less effective methods used by administrative-supervisory personnel in solving system problems have been a factor leading to the currently popular type of confrontation identified either as professional negotiation or collective bargaining. The confrontation existing in this situation identifies the participants as belonging to one of two camps—administration or teachers. The unfortunate implication that results from this type of forced confrontation is that these two factions are not members of the same instructional

[25] Richard Beckhard, "The Confrontation Meeting," in Warren G. Bennis, Kenneth D. Benne, and Robert Chin (eds.), *The Planning of Change* (New York: Holt, Rinehart & Winston, 1969, 2d ed.), pp. 478–485.

In your experience, has professional negotiation strengthened or weakened the professional team?

team. A further development is that of one group acquiring participation at the expense of the other or a substitution of control from one group to the other (see Chapter 1). The more serious problems have been identified as "the procedures and tactics being employed in the process and the nature of the items that are placed on the bargaining table." [26] The positive aspects of professional negotiation are related to participation; that is, teachers have felt the need to negotiate their position in participating in the making of decisions and policies concerning those matters affecting them. It might be assumed that inappropriate administrative-supervisory techniques have been the instigating element in the posture of teacher groups regarding negotiations. In reference to this, Stone suggested that "teachers were not reacting negatively to the basic tenets of the bureaucratic educational organization, but rather to the excesses of the organization or the pathologies involved." [27] The failure of each group to recognize the professional contribution to be made by the other, however, voids the positive nature of the concept of participation or teaming. It would appear that it is in correcting this condition that supervision can find its greatest challenge in dealing with professional negotiations.

The scope of participation through negotiations has included policy formulation and decision-making regarding curriculum, methods of instruction, staffing, organization, and evaluation, as well as wages, benefits, and working conditions. Many of these negotiable items are related to the instructional program and consequently affect supervision.[28] To the extent that negotiations contribute to goal achievement, the beneficial aspects cannot be denied. The process has had some negative overtones which cannot be considered as contributory to the attainment of system goals; nevertheless, to the extent that negotiation achieves rightful participation by all concerned parties, the process can be advantageous. Demanding complete authority at the expense of the participation of other legitimate contributors does not seem to be in the best interests of the school system but rather resembles the type of anarchy evidenced by those in our society who believe that they know best what is right for everyone else. There is no intent here to criticize teachers or administrators as a group; instead, it is to identify pathologies involved which may be as easily identifiable with one group of participants as with another group. Evidence is available to support teachers' ac-

[26] William H. Lucio (ed.), *The Supervisor: New Demands—New Dimensions* (Washington, D.C.: Association for Supervision and Curriculum Development, National Education Association, 1969), pp. 32–33.

[27] Howard L. Stone, "A Conceptualization of Professional Autonomy in the Context of Emerging Negotiated Relationships," unpublished doctoral dissertation (Madison: University of Wisconsin, 1970), p. 297.

[28] William F. Young, "Curriculum Negotiations: Present Status—Future Trends," in Robert R. Leeper (ed.), *Supervision: Emerging Profession* (Washington, D.C.: Association for Supervision and Curriculum Development, National Education Association, 1969), pp. 238–241.

tions in negotiations professionally. In his study on negotiations, one conclusion Stone reached was that "teachers are willing to accede to the legal, recognized authority structure in the resolution of negotiable decision demands and that they do not expect the final resolution of these demands to be consummated outside this structure." [29] This conclusion indicates that teachers as a group are willing to, and indeed do, follow appropriate guidelines in resolving differences between the participants.

Negotiation has been defined as:

> . . . a process wherein the parties come to the negotiating table with divergent points of view about given items and through give-and-take discussion move toward consensus so that agreement may be reached.[30]

It is to this definition that these authors believe educational systems should be directing the efforts of the professional team in resolving their differences. It is only in this way that the concept of participation and teaming can be preserved and developed to the strengthening of the participant as a professional operating in good faith and trust. The individuals and groups demanding participation must expect to be held accountable for their contributions and must be willing and able to devote the time and effort required to participate. Many organizational members may find that they are unable to participate in their new roles and may need to accept representation by other participants. It is possible, then, that the decisions resulting from this representation are not any more acceptable than were decisions made prior to the time of representation. Only a protracted period of time may provide the information necessary to determine whether professional negotiations or collective bargaining result in improved professional relations in reference to participation.

Another example of participation by confrontation is that of sensitivity training or T-group experiences. This type of confrontation is similar to the previous types discussed in that the participants become involved in dealing with problems about which they are concerned. The difference is that the major thrust of this type of confrontation is psychological in nature. An increased awareness and acceptance of one's own behavior and the behavior of other group members is the major goal. Clark, in his paper on interaction, stated that increased understanding of one's own behavior and of the behavior of others occurs simultaneously.[31] The resultant understanding of behavior has been helpful, especially to persons

What may be some other positive outcomes of sensitivity training?

[29] Stone, *op. cit.*, p. 279.

[30] American Association of School Administrators, *The School Administrator and Negotiation* (Washington, D.C.: National Education Association, 1968), p. 12.

[31] James V. Clark, "Authentic Interaction and Personal Growth in Sensitivity Training Groups," in Warren G. Bennis, Kenneth D. Benne, and Robert Chin (eds.), *The Planning of Change* (New York: Holt, Rinehart & Winston, 1969, 2nd ed.), p. 406.

in managerial positions. This is perhaps true because the assistance gained in relating to others allows a participant to recognize that each contributor toward a group effort assists the other participants to contribute.

The identification of the participants, some of their characteristics, and methods for participation were discussed in this chapter. The consequences and obligations of participation also were considered, along with some psychological and sociological aspects of participation. In the next and final chapter of Part III, the authors devote their attention to *security* as it may affect the participants in supervision.

SELECTED REFERENCES

1. Allport, Gordon W., "Psychology of Participation," *Psychological Review,* LIII, May, 1945, p. 126.
2. American Association of School Administrators, *The School Administrator and Negotiations.* Washington, D.C.: National Education Association, 1968.
3. Ardrey, Robert, *The Territorial Imperative.* New York: Atheneum, 1966.
4. Bass, Bernard M. and Harold J. Leavitt, "Some Experiments in Planning and Operating," *Management Science,* IX, July, 1963, p. 584.
5. Beckhard, Richard, "The Confrontation Meeting," in Warren G. Bennis, Kenneth D. Benne, and Robert Chin (eds.), *The Planning of Change.* New York: Holt, Rinehart & Winston, 1961. pp. 485–487.
6. Benne, Richard D., "Democratic Ethics and Human Engineering," in Warren G. Bennis, Kenneth D. Benne, and Robert Chin (eds.), *The Planning of Change.* New York: Holt, Rinehart & Winston, 1961. p. 142.
7. Carlson, Elliot, "Education and Industry: Troubled Partnership," *Saturday Review,* August 15, 1970, pp. 45–47ff.
8. Cass, James, "Profit and Loss in Education," *Saturday Review,* August 15, 1970, pp. 39–40.
9. Clark, James V., "Authentic Interactions and Personal Growth in Sensitivity Training Groups," in Warren G. Bennis, Kenneth D. Benne, and Robert Chin (eds.), *The Planning of Change.* New York: Holt, Rinehart & Winston, 1969, 2nd ed. p. 406.
10. Coch, Lester and John R. P. French, Jr., "Overcoming Resistance to Change," in Eleanor E. Maccoby, Theodore M. Newcomb, and Eugene L. Hartley (eds.), *Readings in Social Psychology.* Chicago: Holt, Rinehart & Winston, 1958. p. 250.
11. Eye, Glen G. and Lanore A. Netzer, *School Administrators and Instruction: A Guide to Self-Appraisal.* Boston: Allyn & Bacon, 1970.
12. Filley, Allen C. and Robert J. House, *Managerial Process and Organizational Behavior.* Glenview, Illinois: Scott, Foresman and Co., 1969. Chaps. III and XIII.
13. Johansen, John H., "An Investigation of the Relationships Between Teachers' Perceptions of Authoritative Influence in Local Curriculum Decision-Making and Curriculum Imple-

mentation." Unpublished doctoral dissertation. Evanston, Illinois: Northwestern University, 1965.
14. Knezevich, Stephen J. and Glen G. Eye, *Instructional Technology and the School Administrator.* Washington, D.C.: American Association of School Administrators, National Education Association, 1970.
15. Koopman, Robert G., Alice Miel, and Paul J. Misner, *Democracy in School Administration.* New York: Appleton-Century-Crofts, 1943. pp. 3–4.
16. Krey, Robert D., "Factors Relating to Teachers' Perceptions of Curricular Implementation Activities and the Extent of Curricular Implementation." Unpublished doctoral dissertation. Madison: University of Wisconsin, 1968.
17. Lucio, William H. (ed.), *The Supervisor: New Demands—New Dimensions.* Washington, D.C.: National Education Association, 1969. pp. 32–33.
18. Netzer, Lanore A., Glen G. Eye, Ardelle Graef, Robert D. Krey, and J. Fred Overman, *Interdisciplinary Foundations of Supervision.* Boston: Allyn & Bacon, 1970. Chaps. III, IV, and VI.
19. Presthus, Robert, *The Organizational Society.* New York: Alfred A. Knopf, Inc., 1962. pp. 167–168, 209, 258, 259–260.
20. Saunders, Robert L. and John T. Lovell, "Negotiations: Inevitable Consequences of Bureaucracy?" in Robert R. Leeper (ed.), *Supervision: Emerging Profession.* Washington, D.C.: National Education Association, 1969. pp. 241–244.
21. Schein, Edgar H. and Warren G. Bennis, *Personal and Organizational Change through Group Methods.* New York: Wiley, 1965.
22. Stone, Howard L., "A Conceptualization of Professional Autonomy in the Context of Emerging Negotiated Relationships." Unpublished doctoral dissertation. Madison: University of Wisconsin, 1970.
23. Teague, Wayne, "An Evaluative Analysis of the In-Service Program for Teachers and Administrators in DeKalb County, Georgia." Unpublished Ed.D. dissertation. Auburn, Alabama: Auburn University, 1962.
24. Thompson, Barbara S., "A Study of the Synchronization of Behaviors Related to Selected Tasks of Elementary School Supervisors and Principals." Unpublished doctoral dissertation. Madison: University of Wisconsin, 1969.
25. Wesner, Gordon Eugene, "A Study of In-Service Education Programs for Secondary School Teachers in Selected Large-City Systems." Unpublished Ed.D. dissertation. Lawrence: University of Kansas, 1963.
26. Young, William F., "Curriculum Negotiations: Present Status—Future Trends," in Robert R. Leeper (ed.), *Supervision: Emerging Profession.* Washington, D.C.: National Education Association, 1969. pp. 238–241.

11

The Security of the Participants

The previous two chapters revealed that many persons in a school system are involved in practically every function related to administration and supervision. The efforts of the administrative and supervisory personnel are directed toward the pupils as the school's chief reason for existence. While each member may provide some self-supervision, he is, nevertheless, at various times the primary recipient of someone's supervisory efforts. Because the efforts of so many people are focused upon so many people it is even more important that care be given to the development of wholesome relationships. It is possible to give too much attention to or to "manhandle" certain organizational members if efforts to assist them are not well coordinated. This chapter is designed to explore various factors appropriate to the welfare of the participants.

SECURITY DEFINED

Security may be identified and defined in terms of either its positive or negative characteristics. On the positive side, security means that an individual has a sense of safety and confidence in his current situation which, if good, will be maintained and which, if bad, will be improved. The negative aspect is that security is freedom from those things which, in the mind of the supervised person, constitute a sense of danger —not necessarily a danger to physical existence but rather danger to that person's status among colleagues and to his relationships to those things which are important to him. In this negative sense, security for the participant is freedom from fear of the loss of salary, the loss of an appropriate or satisfactory assignment, the loss of his colleagues' respect and, consequently, the loss of prestige or opportunities such as promotion and retention in the school organization. There are many participants who feel that security is closely tied to the concept of academic freedom. A popular notion is that academic freedom constitutes the absence of interference with a person's thinking as he chooses to think and applying his thoughts to his work in any way that he wishes. In the extreme form of the negative aspect of the concept, however, participants may want to be completely unrestricted and without a sense of responsibility to the organized efforts. The less extreme would indicate a sense of responsibility to their own perception of their creative abilities and opportunities.

One of the primary aspects of security is that of experiencing a consistency in the relationships with others—superiors, peers, and subordinates. In this case, the clarity of the expected relationships constitutes a basic part of the sense of security. It is difficult for a person to work for or with another person when he is completely lacking in any perception of how that person is thinking either about his work or about his relationship to his colleagues or his responsibility to the goals of the organization. Some may see security primarily as a state of mind. This may be supported in some instances, but when a reprisal system exists this is more than a state of mind.

Illustrate security as a state of mind.

The problem of being participants in supervision is different for the administrative and supervisory staffs than for the members of the teaching staff. At the outset, the administrative and supervisory staffs are in what may be called "the driver's seat." They constitute the group identified as being responsible for doing the supervision and, consequently, they direct their efforts toward the teachers as their avenue of school change and improvement. The person who is exercising controls over another maintains an attitude toward those controls that is substantially different from the attitudes of those who are subjected to the controls. The administrative and supervisory staffs have a recognized decision-making role. The persons making decisions are not as threatened by the decisions which they make as are those people who must carry out the decisions or who are primarily affected by them. Nevertheless, the decision-makers have a responsibility to those whom they supervise in terms of the quality of the decisions made. A superintendent is threatened by his own decisions in the sense that those decisions may be reviewed by the board of education. The review made by the board may be after the fact, that is, after the decisions have caused action to be instituted and perhaps completed. If, at this point, it becomes evident that the decision was unsound, the superintendent is confronted with the situation of being evaluated with respect to the appropriateness of his decision-making prerogatives rather than being advised with respect to how he might arrive at the most acceptable or wisest decision.

While teachers are the objects of more supervisory efforts and, therefore, the subjects of more decision-making activity at the administrative and supervisory levels, they nevertheless know about these decisions and almost universally are advised about them rather than evaluated because of them. To the extent that teachers are involved or are participants in the decision-making process, they also would be held accountable. In many ways, teachers occupy a more favorable position than do the superintendent and the principals when evaluations are made about their own activities. The security of the teachers is related closely to the care with which the administrative and supervisory staffs provide adequate communication about the expectations placed upon them. The degree of security sensed by the teachers will depend upon the nature of the sanction system and the vigor or the consistency with which it is implemented by the administrative staff. This makes the teachers' security closely dependent upon the personal characteristics of the administrators and supervisors. This discussion, then, becomes an extension of the situations discussed in Chapter 6.

Another of the major differences between security for the administrative and supervisory staffs and for the teachers is the nature of the expectations placed upon them. A superintendent of schools serving as the chief executive officer of the board of education is in frequent contact and conversation with the members of the board. If he is unable to get a clear idea of the board's expectations, the fault usually can be allocated to himself. If he is not able to elicit from the board members their ideas of how the schools should be operated and their functions in the operation, he has failed in one of the basic responsibilities of an executive officer. The relationship between the board and the superintendent with respect to frequency of face-to-face discussion is matched normally by the frequency of contacts between the superintendent and the principals. This pattern of consistency does not hold between the superintendent and the central office supervisors or between the superintendent and the teachers, or between the central office supervisor and the principals and teachers of the various buildings. As the face-to-face contacts become more infrequent, there is a tendency for other communications media to be neglected and for the clarity of goals and common knowledge of staff expectations to become deficient. The teacher, being at the end of the line in the structural pattern, probably will be less well informed about the institutional goals, plans, and expectations than others in the hierarchy of the organization.

Teachers have a further complication in achieving a sense of security—the probability that there will be more controls over them than over employees of other professions. The teacher has multiple role-definers. While this is common to administrative, supervisory, and teaching staffs with respect to the external or environmental influences in the community, it is mainly for the teachers that the structural and operational patterns do not provide sufficient protection against multiple expectations. There is often little effort at the central office level to coordinate these multiple expectations. An illustration of this multiplicity can be found in the elementary grade school teacher who is committed to the general regulations of the system, the specific administrative directives of the building principal, the requests and expectations of the general supervisor, and the requirements of the special supervisors.

Name some role-definers of the teacher.

An interesting facet of the development of the administrative patterns and practices in the United States is that, over a period of several decades, the school superintendent organizations waged and won the battle to do away with the dual control system at the central office level. This system usually constituted two officers, the superintendent of schools and the business manager, each of whom was coordinate in power and authority and had equal privileges in his representations to the board of education. The superintendent groups are to be congratulated for persistence in this matter of eliminating one of the very undesirable structural aspects in the patterns of the city school organization. Few school systems now have business managers who are not under the jurisdiction of the superintendent. Principals and teachers properly may wonder why, after the superintendents recognized and solved this serious problem of school organization and administration at the central office level, they did not see it as a tactical problem at the building and, particularly, at the individual classroom level. It is just as difficult for the teacher to develop a well-balanced instructional program in the classroom when he must serve at the same time as a coordinator and balance wheel between the various influences and enthusiasms created by the central office and directed toward teachers in the individual classrooms. It is to be hoped that the multiplicity of controls over the classroom teacher soon may be markedly reduced. This reduction would enhance substantially the sense of security possessed by the teachers as one group within the organization, the members of which are participants in and recipients of supervision.

RECIPIENT DEFINED

Any participant in supervision may become at any time a recipient of supervision. A recipient of supervision is one who at any particular time is the focal point of the attention of that staff member who may be exercising some supervisory functions. The recipients are those who are to be influenced by the members of the organizational staff who have some responsibilities for achieving the pre-established goals of the school system.

The recipient is also the person subjected to certain controls which may be issued by other personnel, either verbally or as written directives. The recipient is the person to whom advisory efforts are directed. Finally, the recipient is the person for whom expectations are established. Sometimes these expectations indicate that the object of supervision is to be self-sustaining and self-motivated to improvement.

The question properly may be raised as to what the recipient does receive. At the outset, he is continuously receiving the efforts of others to influence him. He receives the assistance, direction, restrictions, and thwartings of all those who would exercise influence in the school organization. Most of all the recipient receives advice. There are occasions when he receives the products, created within himself, of whatever the systems of compulsion may be to get people to respond to the manipulations of those in the other positions.

The recipient also receives reinforcement on the occasions when his work has gained approbation. This, in turn, may make him the recipient of stimulation to develop innovations or improvements in the duties to which he is assigned. The recipient is the object of evaluative efforts and judgments related to his future in the organization.

All persons employed in a school system are recipients of someone's efforts to influence their selection of behaviors. The superintendent is the object of influence by the board of education, by pressure groups in the community, by the teachers, and by both lay and professional individuals who would influence the instructional program through his office. Assistant superintendents, principals, and central office supervisors are also objects of the attention of other parties and in this sense become the recipients of supervision. To the extent that any of their behaviors are controlled, any or all of these persons may be the object of influence through the process of negotiation.

The list of assumptions upon which this book is based indicates at various points that the superintendent possesses a responsibility to exercise some controls over members of the supervisory staff. To this extent, the supervisors are the recipients of supervision in that they are the objects of the superintendent's influence regarding the methods and manner of their supervising or of the supervisory program which they have developed. The professional associations exercise an influence upon the individual members. Supervisors, for instance, may be members of the Association for Supervision and Curriculum Development. This national organization does stand as a voice of the organized profession in this particular field. Resolutions taken at the national, regional, or state conventions, positions stated by the officers of the Association, and the manuscripts published in the official journals tend to influence those members of the Association who are serving as supervisors and directors of curriculum in the field situations. It is not necessary, then, to think of a recipient as only that person who is receiving the influence of a superior officer who has certain powers of reprisal should the recipient not respond satisfactorily.

Each person receives supervisory efforts when they are directed to him and when he acknowledges the efforts and permits them to influence his behavior as he goes about his duties. The teaching situation remains the most frequent and consistent object of influence in the supervisory program. There seems to be a popular assumption that supervision exists for those influences which it can exercise over others to the end that the teaching–learning situation will be influenced and improved. Any discussion on participants who become recipients of supervision must consider the responsibilities of those recipients.

RECIPIENT RESPONSIBILITY

The recipients of supervision have a great responsibility for their own security. It is not sufficient for teachers' organizations to pass resolutions, apply pressures, negotiate, or plead for assurances that their professional lives shall be dominated by a sense of security. If, as stated earlier, security is in part a state of mind, then the individual is a prime factor in the achievement of this. There is no intent here to suggest the achievement of that sense of security through any sort of real or imaginary tranquilizers. The point is that the teacher cannot and must not demand security as something that can be delivered in a neat package. He not only must put forth effort to achieve the conditions of security but also must provide in his mind the receptivity for this sense of security.

There are numerous ways that the teacher can support or meet his responsibilities for the accomplishment of security as a recipient of supervision. Research in recent years indicates that the understanding of the roles and role expectations of all members of the staff is a potent factor in accomplishing certain favorable program relationships and outcomes. This understanding of roles and expectations is gained through effective means of communication (see Chapter 9). It is not necessarily a completed communication if the superintendent or someone delegated by him provides only a teachers' handbook which presumably indicates the nature of the position responsibility and roles that will characterize the members of the staff in their respective assignments. Teachers must read such a handbook if it is to serve as a communication medium at all. Having read it, they must achieve a basic understanding of the roles of the various staff officers—including their own. It is not probable that an understanding of various roles and role expectations will be accomplished simply through the issuance of a teachers' or administrators' handbook. These understandings must be achieved just as the concepts in the assigned subjects are achieved by elementary school pupils. Learning requires effort on the part of the learners. If the teachers are to accomplish an understanding of roles and expectations, they are learners and their efforts in the learning process become a major determinant of the success of that organization. If the influence of the supervisor is to have a successful impact upon the behaviors of the teachers, there must be some mutual understanding among the participants regarding their respective roles, responsibilities, and expectations.

The popularly accepted prerogative of a subordinate to say unkind things about, do unkind things toward, and be resistant generally to the influence of a superior officer may be appropriate in a facetious discussion of the relationship between a buck private and a sergeant in the infantry, but it is not appropriate for professional people as they establish their behaviors within an organization dedicated to learning. That teacher who substitutes careless criticism of and opposition to the supervisor for honestly seeking to understand the supervisor's role and relationship to his own position is vacating the responsibilities of his position.

The recipient of supervision may meet the responsibility for establishing his own security by making his successful activities more visible. To many this has an unsavory flavor in that it is looked upon as "blowing your own horn." When carried to excess it is an unpalatable trait. The simple point is that one participant has no right to expect another to know of his success in accomplishing his task unless he provides some opportunity for that person to observe or to learn in some other way about the success. There is a more positive than negative connotation in the teacher indicating to a supervisor that a particular piece of work is progressing well and that it would be appreciated if the supervisor would either observe it in process or learn about it through a conference with the teacher (see Chapter 17). From this type of sharing, the supervisor gains a better knowledge of the teacher's work and this knowledge becomes the basis for suggestions and supervisory support. That teacher who, while being successful in the classroom responsibilities, assumes that the supervisor is responsible for discovering it, is neither cooperating with the intent of supervision nor being practical in basic human relationships. The supervisor is not clairvoyant and cannot know what is happening in dozens of classrooms unless he has some specific assistance from the teachers who have the first-hand information available.

The opposite of making successes visible is the practice of reporting the failing ventures. There is the human inclination to attempt in every way possible to conceal mistakes. Educators, like people in any other venture in human relationships, have many instances in which the hopes for a particular activity are not fulfilled. In fact, some efforts may have been dismal failures. The teacher too often, though perhaps justifiably, has taken the position that if the supervisor or administrator knows of these failures, they will become the basis for some form of reprisals. The most powerful form of sanction is in re-employment and salary considerations. This is particularly true where a merit salary policy is in effect. On the other hand, the supervisor is unable to know about all teaching failures, and consequently, unless he knows about the situation, he is also unable to determine how he can be of service. The teacher's security is not particularly sound if based upon his artfulness in concealing and withholding information about his failures. It is probably a much more tenable position to recognize honestly the ways in which he has not met his own or others' expectations and to present all of this information to the supervisor whose responsibility it is to be of assistance.

In discussing the approach to improvement programs in the total system, it is wise to talk from the point of view of identifying the major weaknesses. The weakness in the system becomes the point at which an improvement program can and should be instituted. The same can be said for identifying and instituting improvement in the individual classroom situation. Responsibility for initiating this type of cooperative supervisor–teacher effort lies primarily with the classroom teachers. A teacher has no grounds for complaining about his lack of security when he has failed to take advantage of the services available to help his efforts to become successful. It is probable that a tradition among teachers in some school systems dictates that supervisors have not dealt wisely with many of the teachers who have acknowledged their failures and sought help. It could be that the supervisor did not know what to do about it and, in the process of protecting his own security, may have committed teachers to professional annihilation. Incidents of this type cannot happen frequently without becoming a part of our traditions, and to that extent they become more difficult to eradicate in the process of instituting a proper relationship between supervisors and teachers.

How should supervisors treat teachers' reports of failures?

Periodically, the professional associations go through a flurry of statements of codes of ethics and standards of behavior. These efforts are worthwhile because they may influence some people. Seldom are codes developed which have any provision for enforcement. Human beings seem unable to make codes and to live by them to the extent that they dominate their choice of behaviors. Even though efforts to date have not been particularly successful in establishing and enforcing ethical standards among the members of the teaching profession or supervisor and administrator associations, they are still great needs in the interpersonal relationships of the school organization. Teachers must be ethical in their relationships to their fellow teachers and to their superiors if they expect to achieve any semblance of security in their positions. Unethical conduct should become the basis for removing the security of the individual whether he is a teacher, a supervisor, or an administrator.

There are practical expectations encountered in the relationships between supervisors and teachers which carry some import for the achievement of security. When somewhat overcome by the importance of their positions, administrators and supervisors often tend to expect that, when they exercise their control over a teacher either by direction or disciplinary action, the teacher should appreciate what has been done to him. This is an impracticality in the view that administrators and supervisors seem to develop about their positions. It is a simple maxim that people do not thank superiors for abuse. In other words, people who are hurt or belittled are not likely to subscribe to the worth and dignity of the person committing them to such indignity. An important consideration for the teacher is that a subordinate cannot be abusive, either overtly or covertly, to the superior and expect that superior to respond by high praise and appreciation of the subordinate's position and productivity. It is strange that the simplicity of human relationships at this level has been overlooked so grossly by those people who seek with such contradictory efforts to find the assurances of security in the supervisory and administrative positions. It requires as much skill to be a successful recipient of supervisory effort as it does to be a supervisor who accomplishes the purposes and functions of supervision.

RELATION OF SECURITY TO TALENT

There is a close relationship between the sense of security of a person's experiences and the amount of developed talent he possesses for the fulfillment of the commitments to the position which he has accepted. There is a difference between the weak and the strong administrator and supervisor. The brilliant and talented supervisor will not fear the ingenuity and innovative capacity of the members of the staff with which he works. This supervisor is likely to enjoy the give and take of ideas and points of view. He does not feel insecure about his own ability to compete with the ideas of the staff he is supposed to influence. On the other hand, a supervisor of less intellectual power and technical competence may feel insecure in attempting to influence people he knows are superior to him in ability. He probably would devise some supervisory techniques that possess the proper control factors. He would seek to avoid a situation in which he could be challenged and his lack of ability exposed. This means, then, that the dull supervisor will be more dictatorial with the members of the teaching staff, will permit less latitude in the variations of their programs, and will not permit the teachers to get him into a situation where the security of his position

Why do dictatorial actions seem to offer security?

could be challenged by exposure of his inability to meet the full requirements of that position.

The weak teacher, perhaps, would operate in about the same way in his relationships with the pupils in his class. His sense of security has come from dominating those brilliant pupils who might expose his ignorance were he not to use rigid controls. There are many rationalizations that can be used by the weak teacher, as well as by the weak supervisor, to create what seems to be comparative security and the preservation of a sense of prestige. Obviously, these types of behaviors will never contribute to a strong improvement program in the school.

The intelligent and competent supervisor has many characteristics in common with the intelligent and competent teacher. Greater variations in behavior can be encompassed without their constituting a challenge to his security. This should be a point of consideration in the selection of persons to fill positions. An inferior person with the power of control over others is a much greater potential danger to the participants and to the program than an intelligent person with an equal amount of power and authority. It is conceded that a brilliant person who has improper goals and unsound judgment would be a liability to group operation. These factors, however, are points of consideration whether the individual being considered for employment is a dull or a bright person. Assuming that identification of persons with improper goals and unsound judgment constitutes a common concern in the employment of teachers, supervisors, and administrators, the employer may use basic intelligence and technical competence as a basis for the decision to award employment contracts.

Just as ability and competence affect the attitude toward controls and the use of control devices, so do these factors have substantial influence upon the perceptions that the individual holds with respect to himself, others, and the appropriateness of the interrelationships that are to be established (see Chapter 12). A dull and incompetent person will select his behavior through defensiveness, whereas a bright and technically competent person is relieved of the urgency for self-protection and may direct a greater percentage of his efforts toward the goals of the institution without undue concern for his personal security. These factors also have an impact upon the nature and quality of esteem by which each person is held between and among his colleagues. The person of high ability may be extremely competitive with his colleagues of high ability but the resulting hazard to the accomplishment of the organizational goals is less.

How do intelligent supervisors and teachers create unusual responsibilities for the superintendent?

The superintendent of schools may prefer to have a calm situation and choose to secure it through selecting staff members who are not of top quality in intellectual aggressiveness and in carrying out the tasks of their positions. But the courageous superintendent, placing excellence in education above all other considerations, would seek highly intellectual and highly competent people even though the competitiveness of sharp minds might make the task of being superintendent less peaceful and less comfortable than it would be with a staff of dull, less competent people. The superintendent's policy and practice in this matter is more highly related to the success of the educational enterprise than educational practitioners have been willing to admit.

RELATION OF SECURITY TO PARTICIPATION

The relation of security to talent has been discussed. In similar respects it should be recognized that there is a relationship between a person's sense of security and the extent to which he can or will be a participant in supervision. Cases have been related concerning an individual who, having lost his sense of security—whether real or imagined—was unable to function. This has been evidenced in many situations to varying degrees. It is as true of the psychotic who cannot function or participate in any facet of societal relationships as it is of a child who is afraid to participate in a game because he doesn't know the rules. An opposite example is that of the extremely active individual who is able to participate in a large number of organizational activities because he feels secure in his relationships with others, or the child who is aggressive because he perceives himself capable of accepting any challenge which might arise. It is also noted that some persons become lively participants in order to take from rather than to contribute to the group organization. One might observe that these same people are advancing their personal goals at the expense of organizational goals. A caution here is to recognize that these behaviors can become pathological if carried to extremes.

A personal sense of security, then, must be a concern for those who are being stimulated to participate as well as for those who are providing the stimulation. If an individual lacks a sense of security because of lack of talent to function properly, it should be considered a necessity to influence that individual to improve his talents in reference to the contribution required. When a person is placed in a position for which he is not suited, his sense of security will be destroyed and his ability to participate will be impaired.

The participant whose security is challenged because of the system of sanctions perceived to be in operation will be overly cautious in response to the bid to contribute to the supervisory program. A supervisor may not be free to offer recommendations for improvement when the superintendent is known to be opposed to such proposals. Similarly, the teacher may be reluctant to experiment with novel approaches to instruction in a situation where lack of immediate success may incur the disapproval of the principal.

A not uncommon occurrence is the position taken by administrators and supervisors—and easily perceived by subordinates—to not "rock the boat." The superordinates in this case use sanctions to maintain an "even keel." The subordinates then maintain the security of their positions by not participating.

The reverse order of the relationship between security and participation also needs to be understood. A recipient may perceive his sense of security to be diminished because he is not allowed to participate. An administrator, for example, may not be allowed to contribute to a decision regarding the school calendar when it becomes a negotiable item between the teachers and the board of education. A professionally trained person will appreciate being allowed to participate in making decisions which affect him and to which he can make a contribution. When a teacher is asked to assist in such activities as curricular planning or textbook selection, he will realize that his professional competence is being recognized and he will have a greater sense of security in his position. In the same manner, when principals and supervisors are allowed to participate in such activities as identifying the need for additional personnel and selecting new staff members, they are being identified as being valuable contributors to the organization. An appreciation and realization of these relationships are required if supervision is to be an effective or beneficial endeavor.

OBLIGATION OF SUPERVISION

The primary obligation of supervision is that of possessing an awareness of those conditions which influence participation. This awareness allows a better understanding of the actions and interactions which must be considered in developing a sound supervisory program. The next step is to apply that knowledge in improving those conditions which involve the sense of security, talents, and degree of participation for all the recipients of supervisory influence.

Supervisors should demand appropriate placement of all members of the school systems in terms of the talent which is brought to the organization. This also requires that the person lacking in the ability to function in a position must receive assistance to acquire the necessary talent or, if this fails, to assist him in being realistic in terms of relating his talents to a different, more appropriate position. A related requirement is that of protecting the security of all organizational members so that the influence of another, whether superordinate, subordinate, or peer, cannot go to the extent of destroying their sense of security or their opportunity or desire to participate.

A further obligation is that of reducing those policies and actions, whether deliberate or unintentional, which tend to diminish the security of those who will contribute intelligently to the operation of the school system. Any participant must recognize that the combined talents of the membership should assist him in improvement of the total setting. A participant who perceives himself to be more knowledgeable, or any group of participants which perceives itself more knowledgeable, than the combined organizational membership perhaps is not in the appropriate position and should be assisted in finding an assignment more suitable to its talents.

Participants must be insured of their security within the school system if they are expected to identify strengths and weaknesses. Appropriate supervisory procedures will communicate the consequences to be expected in such situations. It must be acceptable to supervisors to have weaknesses identified by the recipients if they are expected to accept such assistance from the supervisors.

Each participant needs to understand the specific contribution required of his talents in relation to the total instructional program. Recognition of the necessity for diversification of tasks should result in reciprocity of support between and among the many contributors to and the recipients of supervision.

An obligation of supervision is also that of maintaining a balance of behaviors (see Chapters 12–17) to the end that the participants are helped to become increasingly secure in exercising their talents for the good of the organization.

SELECTED REFERENCES

1. Association for Supervision and Curriculum Development, Yearbook, *Perceiving, Behaving, and Becoming*. Washington, D.C.: National Education Association, 1962. Chaps. 6, 7, 8, and 9.
2. Netzer, Lanore A., Glen G. Eye, Ardelle Graef, Robert D. Krey, and J. Fred Overman, *Interdisciplinary Foundations of Supervision*. Boston: Allyn & Bacon, Inc., 1970. Chaps. 3 and 4.

Part IV

THE PROCESSES OF SUPERVISION

The working definition of supervision from Chapter 1 is repeated here: "Supervision is that phase of school administration which focuses primarily upon the achievement of the appropriate instructional expectations of educational systems." This part is devoted to the last phrase in the definition, "the achievement of the appropriate instructional expectations of educational systems." Achievement implies change; supervision is the management of change.

This book is not a manual for supervisors; rather, its aims are to help develop custom-built programs of supervision, and this basic point of view characterizes this part. Also, the emphasis throughout the book, and particularly in this part, is on improvement. Our definition's "expectations" should involve thoughtful change from the old to the new in terms of appropriateness for the demands of the time. Few would hold that our society is so static that education can rest solely on maintaining the old. It remains, then, for supervision to provide the direction and leadership which will improve educational systems.

The implementation of a design for improvement is facilitated when the processes of supervision are understood by all concerned. In comparing various lists of administrative processes, it becomes apparent that eight might be identified with some degree of accuracy. These seem to fall logically into pairs as complementary components. These pairs, as indicated in Chapter 2, are: (1) directing and controlling, (2) stimulating and initiating, (3) analyzing and appraising, and (4) designing and implementing. Chapters 13 through 16 discuss these pairs.

The problem of balance becomes apparent as one confronts the task of analyzing these process components. To counteract imbalance and to present a viable way to study balance, Part IV starts with a chapter on operational balance. In applying an action pattern to the processes involved, the achievement of balance may be identified as the individual supervisor's method of supervision. *Method,* in this sense, is the overall pattern of design and implementation in the program. The specific behaviors of the supervisor may be termed *techniques.*

Five characteristics of operational balance are *perceptivity, autonomy, relativity, flexibility,* and *creativity.* Obviously, they cannot be mutually exclusive. There are overlaps between characteristics. This overlap is comparable to that in the components of process which cannot be isolated or made mutually exclusive; we separate them only for purposes of discussion. These characteristics are discussed in Chapter 12.

Chapter 17 brings together the various characteristics of operational balance and the four major components of process. Thus, Part IV ends with an attempt at a synthesis of the characteristics between and among themselves as well as integration between and among the four components of process.

12

The Characteristics of Operational Balance

Human achievement is determined primarily by the abilities of the individual and the characteristics of the environment in which effort is applied. Each person with his peculiar characteristics must assess the nature of his environment in order to determine the best means of achieving his purpose. In a situation that requires lifting, it is fruitless for one to use up all his energy in pushing. This example is so simple that the lack of balance between purpose, effort, and technique is easily identified. It is not so easy to identify the ways in which balance may be achieved when the elements involved are human beings, each with his own significant aspects of uniqueness. When two or more individuals are confronted with the need to accomplish a single purpose in a social system, the complexities multiply quickly and continuously. The need for balance in all human effort demands little supporting argument. Rather, it requires study of the means of accomplishment.

The purposes of the instructional program may be achieved in many ways; the same is true in achieving the purposes of supervision. The supervisory purposes are intended to influence people so that the purposes of the instructional program may be achieved. If the supervisor develops a way of dealing with the teachers under his influence and discovers that this way is successful, he may become reluctant to adopt new ways of dealing with the same or other people or to modify what has been previously successful. Success gives a sense of security, and supervisors want security. Security is not easily abandoned and a change to different ways of supervising might seem to threaten the supervisor's success and, consequently, his security in position. Some supervisors, on the other hand, may find security in variations of technique as a means of increasing the success potential.

The recipients of supervision—the teachers—differ in many ways, both in their personal characteristics and in their ways of teaching (see Chapter 11). A supervisor who has discovered one or a few successful techniques of supervision might assume that, regardless of the differences in those supervised, the techniques should prove adequate. The differences in recipients, however, make it improbable that a supervisor can devise one technique that will prove successful for all persons and all occasions. Just as a teacher finds that teaching techniques must be varied in order to make different pupils respond favorably, so also have many supervisors found that variation in technique is essential in supervision.

The time probably is past when school systems could tolerate supervisors who went about their work with one dominant criterion for selecting supervisory behaviors. There have been many stories in the history of our schools in which, for instance, a supervisor becomes particularly sensitive about the position of books on the library shelves. In such a case, the "library shelf" criterion would lead the supervisor, when visiting a classroom, to look first at the neatness of the library shelves. If the books were in line, neatly stacked, and presenting a pleasant appearance, the supervisor would, in turn, look upon any activity in the classroom with probable approval. Other supervisors might focus upon other criteria, such as the manner in which the assignments for the next day or the next unit were presented. If the assignments were well done, then all other aspects of the teaching–learning situation would probably have the approval of the supervisor. It is not necessary to multiply such examples to establish the fact that supervisors often have given their supervisory programs an imbalance because of an overemphasis on one aspect of the teaching–learning situation. When this happens, it is obvious that a better balance in supervisory objectives, as well as behaviors, is needed. The ability of the supervisor to vary the ways of going about his task is the essence of balance, just as it is for the teacher who must catch the interest of the pupil in order to support his inclination and ability to learn.

Describe other criteria.

The need for balance among the various parts of a machine or a situation involving human reaction requires some type of control. The gasoline motor has its flywheel to smooth the operation by bringing together in continuous action the force of the explosion in several separate cylinders. The automobile has its regulator, its distributor, and its timing gears in order to transform the power of the fuel into the movement of the gears and wheels which results in transportation under the control of the one who wants to be transported. Other conveyances, with their various types of mechanical power, use ballast and gyroscopes as well as other devices for bringing about a balance between the various forces and means of accomplishing work.

Human endeavor does not have easily available balancing devices with predictable results as do machines. Human endeavor must depend for its balance upon some referent points which can be used to test the contribution of each aspect of the total effort toward the accomplishment of a desired goal. Referent points for some may be what they consider absolute truth; others might use measured achievement; still others use rules of behavior or the characteristics of personal and interpersonal behavior. The latter has been chosen by these authors as the most desirable and useful of the ways of establishing referent points for judging the balance or imbalance of the interpersonal behaviors of the supervisor and the supervised. The recognition of the presence or absence of the characteristics of balance in interpersonal behavior does not constitute a control in the same sense as balance devices in the area of mechanics. It is probable, however, that the knowledge and ability to recognize these characteristics of balance may constitute some control; at the same time, however, they will provide the individual supervisor with the kind of information that could lead him to attain this balance.

IDENTIFICATION OF THE CHARACTERISTICS

Perceptivity, autonomy, relativity, flexibility, and creativity are characteristics of action that appear consistently in the literature of administration and supervision. The frequency of reference led to their selection as relevant to a system of supervisory activities. Each of these characteristics is discussed in a separate section and a working definition is provided for each one. A supervisor is free to reject this particular list of characteristics but, in so doing, should assume the responsibility for developing others that will be useful and productive to his own purposes and assignment.

There is a discussion of the concepts that appear to be involved in the working definition for each characteristic. These concepts are not to be considered as a complete description of the characteristic, nor even as the most significant, because the importance must be determined by the situation requiring supervisory effort. The characteristics listed above bear a direct relationship to each of the components of process discussed in Chapters 13 through 16. The purpose of identifying the characteristics is to provide the kind of checkpoint that will help the supervisor to use the components of process not only in the appropriate supervisory situations but also in the proper interrelationships between and among the four pairs of components.

One device, *one* definition, *one* principle, or *one* of most anything cannot constitute adequacy when dealing with the intricacies of human relationships. Thus, in studying the characteristics of process, some of the characteristics will be closely related to one process in one supervisory situation but have quite a different impact in another situation using the same technique or process of supervisory behavior. There can be no rule of thumb available to the supervisor; no card index will provide a check on the element of balance or the selection of that component most appropriate to a particular problem in each unique situation. The interrelationships between characteristics, components, and supervisory situations are explored in the discussion of the five characteristics of balance.

PERCEPTIVITY

The working definition of perceptivity is:

The sensitivity of a person to the many elements of human personality that must adapt to or change a multitude of environmental forces.

How can a person test his own perception of the expectations he thinks others impose upon him?

Perceptivity, in its simplest form, is the inclination or ability of a person to see what is to be seen and understood in any person, situation, or interaction between persons and situations. Simple tests of long standing indicate that, when two or more people witness the same incident, they are unable to give identical reports. This means that looking at the same thing at the same time does not assure commonality of perception. It is well established, too, that whatever any person sees is tempered by that which he has experienced previously. It is impossible for any one situation to be observed or perceived without some previous experience of the observer influencing his observation of the moment. It is also well established that people vary from day to day—if not hour to hour or moment to moment—in the degree of consistency with which they see situations that are as nearly common as could be arranged. This being true, the supervisor must be continuously aware of the fact that his physical condition, past experience, educational background, knowledge of the perceiving process, and desire for objectivity, along with many other personal attributes, probably determine the degree of consistency with which he perceives similar or identical situations.

Added to this complexity is the fact that the supervisor is observing teachers who probably possess to a degree characteristics like his own. This means that the observer and the observed constitute a highly complex situation in which understanding and mutual assistance are expected to be possible.

There have been many notions about how people react on different days of the week or under different weather conditions. Parents long have charged that the pupils are so tired by the end of the school week that the children cannot be dealt with in the home as easily then as earlier in the week. This is the perception held by parents of their children who are shifting from the rigors of the school week to the presumably more relaxed controls of the weekend home situation. On the contrary, many teachers insist that the pupils display more evidences of fatigue on Monday than they do on Friday. The teachers charge that over the weekend parents have not exercised the proper control or balance of activities—particularly those related to rest. These are the same pupils going into the homes on Friday and returning to the schools on Monday, yet the perceptions of the parents and the teachers seem to differ markedly.

If there are such differences between parents and teachers in observing the same pupils, it may be equally true that supervisors and teachers have many instances and occasions in which each claims objectivity while denying it to the other. The teacher may react as though the book that fell to the floor on Friday—even though of the same weight and at the same height from the floor—does not fall with such noise and disturbance potential as it does on Monday. Supervisors may be far less tolerant about the completion of assignments to teachers if the due date is Friday rather than Monday. These may be small, inconsequential illustrations, but they constitute the potential situational characteristic of determining the kind and quality of human relationships that exist between important persons in the school operation.

The situation perhaps becomes more complex, or at least more difficult to solve, if consideration is given to the fact that physical condition, being one of the determiners of the quality of perception, becomes important in studying and determining the loads of teachers. Tradition dictates that each teacher, regardless of physical condition or energy potential, must teach as many pupils for as many hours per day as does any other teacher. The perceptive supervisor trying to adapt or adjust the teaching load to the physical condition of the teacher is confronted with serious barriers in the form of traditions and negotiated formulae which have been established. Thus, the mere recognition of the fact that the physical condition is an important factor in one's reactions might help the supervisor to establish the interpersonal relationships between and among the physically strong and weak teachers with some greater degree of understanding than if it is not known at all.

Illustrate how various perceptions are related to some actual tasks.

Inferences have been drawn from research indicating that the character of the formal educational program in preparation for teaching affects the inclination or ability of teachers to work in group situations. It has been found that those with a greater part of their teacher education program in the pedagogical subject areas exhibit greater ability to work in groups than do those with a higher concentration in the academic subject areas. Knowing this, the supervisor would perceive the potential participation of elementary and high school teachers somewhat differently. The wise supervisor can spend more time with the secondary school teachers in making certain that the commonality of purpose or goal in working together is established. In working with elementary school teachers, this commonality of purpose is established more easily and the attack on the accomplishment of the purposes might be initiated more rapidly. This can be considered a rule of thumb, but it has implications regarding the perceptivity of the supervisor.

Perceptivity being a sensitivity to persons and situations, it has compelling involvements in the various components of process. Perceptivity in the processes of directing and controlling is essential to the selection of those behaviors which constitute direction and control. Perception is particularly essential in the processes of stimulating and initiating, because it is involved in the psychological aspects of human motivation. In the latter component of process, motivation is one of the more important factors in the processes of analyzing and appraising. Perceptivity is essential if the person directing the analysis and appraisal is to be alert to the various types of data needed and to the selection of appropriate criteria by which the data are evaluated.

What are the effects of the reprisal or sanction system upon the perceptions of role?

Perceptivity is particularly important in analyzing and appraising because it is at this point that the individuals involved may easily be offended unless the one directing such activities has the inclination and ability to keep the purpose of evaluation on the welfare of the student rather than on the discipline of the teacher. Perceptivity is important in the component of designing and implementing. It is here that the creativity of each member of the staff is involved in the design of innovations which will characterize the school improvement program. The stimulation of creativity is a sensitive task. One cannot command another to be creative, yet creativity is one of the outcomes sought by the wise supervisor. The implementation of plans requires a high degree of sensitivity on the part of the person directing the implementation because it is here that the goals and the methods of people are to be changed. People do not easily give up what they have been accustomed to doing. Implementation must move forward, but it must move forward without doing serious injustice to those involved in the change pattern.

Does the extreme nonconformist free himself from the behavioral influences of other people?

AUTONOMY

The working definition of autonomy is:

The free choice of behaviors within those normative restrictions which are voluntarily accepted or over which the individual possesses some power of determination.

Autonomy is not viewed as that characteristic which removes all restraints and constraints from a person as he chooses the behaviors which will constitute his pattern of work. Autonomy, as in the concept of democracy, does not presume that controls shall not exist. Autonomy is not a characteristic that should lead to anarchy. Autonomy must not be made possible for one person by denying it to another. This latter type of relationship develops between two people when one wants to control the other and claims that he must have the freedom or the autonomy to do so, but, in doing so, removes from the person controlled the opportunity to experience his own autonomous activity.

There are limits, boundaries, rules, and regulations for all interpersonal activity. Those who see guidelines as limitations and controls as something undesirable to group activity should neither seek nor accept group activity assignments or leadership roles. Autonomy as a word and as a meaning is related to words such as freedom, independence, dependence, interdependence, and authority. The late President John F. Kennedy, on July 4, 1962, indicated in a public address that this country fought a war of revolution to gain its independence, has fought more wars to preserve that independence, and yet proceeded immediately and continuously after the revolution to draw up a constitution and to pass laws to guarantee the pattern of our interdependence. The laws passed through each succeeding generation constitute the rules and regulations by which people have their interpersonal relationships directed and controlled. This is accepted as a democratic and desirable process. Those in the political arena who want to have autonomy obviously recognize that it is achieved through the controlling agents which make it possible for people to work within known limits, boundaries, and procedures.

How is it possible to exert authority in achieving autonomy?

An individual has some freedom in selecting the nature of the autonomy which he desires by studying the kind of working relationships that exist in the profession or the vocation he chooses. If he finds in one pursuit that the autonomy is not defined and provided in the way and amount that he prefers, he may seek employment elsewhere or choose to work for himself. Even when an individual works for himself he must recognize those rules which establish the proper relationships between the independent enterprisers. Each person who accepts responsibility in an organized group activity must at the same time accept some responsibility to and for the goals of that group. In this sense, a free choice is made. The organization member also has some opportunity to exercise influence in changing the working conditions and relationships in the direction which might better suit his particular inclinations. In attempting to exercise this influence, the group member is seeking to rearrange the conditions and characteristics of the autonomy possessed in the work.

There have been notable inconsistencies, however, among

those who clamor for autonomy and define it rigidly as lessened restraints and increased freedom in choice of activity. Interestingly enough, many such persons want autonomy when things are going well and they are making progress toward the organizational goal as well as toward the accomplishment of their own purposes. When the situation is reversed, however, and the general outlook is bad, the same individual is inclined to seek out that person in the organization upon whom he may be dependent. This shoulder to cry on, in order to be satisfying, protective, and regenerative of a sense of security, must be that of a superior officer in the organization. Thus, the supervisor must be ready to deal with this duality in human nature and expect it will appear among those teachers whom he elects to influence in the processes of supervision. At the same time, the supervisor must be alert to or perceptive about his own inclinations to seek autonomy when times are good and, when times are bad, to yield it readily to achieve needed dependence upon his superior officer, the superintendent of schools.

The teachers of a middle-sized school system recently were canvassed with respect to their expectations of the functions of the building principal. For many of the possible functions, there was a lack of common perception. The one outstanding task on which the teachers could agree was that the principal "should support the teachers even though he knows them to be wrong." The teachers in this school system were known to have exercised a high degree of freedom and autonomy in going about the tasks required in their classrooms. Nevertheless, those teachers who had achieved a high level of autonomy wanted to have the sense of security found in yielding the essence of that autonomy in the face of public attack and criticism. No matter who challenged the teachers, the principal was expected to support them even though he knew he was supporting a wrong position. Teachers and supervisors alike must rethink this near-frivolity in seeing autonomy in fair-weather status as the emerging concepts of accountability are sharpened and invoked in organizational procedures.

How do these inconsistencies affect the location of decision points?

While supervisors may be amused by this apparent inconsistency in the behavior of teachers, they should be sobered by the fact that teachers often indicate a complete lack of confidence in the superintendent's support of the teacher when a difference develops between the supervisor and the teacher. The teachers normally say that "you may always expect the administration group to hang together." They mean by this that an administrator will support an administrator even though he is wrong. If the superior administrator supports the subordinate administrator against the teacher, then in reality the situation is comparable to that in which the principal is expected to support the teacher even when the teacher is wrong. Inconsistency is the word to describe both types of situations. A better understanding of the essence of autonomy perhaps will help both subordinates and superordinates to avoid these types of incongruencies.

The definition of autonomy given above indicates an operation within normative restrictions which are voluntarily acceptable. This means that when a person accepts a position he should know the conditions under which he may pursue his work and he should be able to expect those conditions to remain constant. Autonomy, like democracy, is largely a state of mind. It may be and often is conditioned by the structured controls that exist in the organization. The discussion in Chapters 5 and 6 may carry more meaning at this point if the structural and operational patterns are reviewed with the thought in mind that here basically is the origin of whatever autonomy is realized by the workers of an organization at all levels.

No person can possess autonomy unless he is willing to accept a reasonable definition of it and is able to recognize it when it is possessed. This is similar to the problem of communication. A communication is not complete until the thoughts transmitted by one person are accepted by another person in the same sense as projected by the originator. Thus, a mere definition of autonomy can never be sufficient. An appreciation of it is the better part of the definition.

How can role analyses increase the autonomy of individuals?

Autonomy, as in the case of the characteristic of perceptivity, is involved in each of the four components of process. Autonomy becomes one of the extremely important conditioners of the human relationships that develop and exist as the supervisor goes about the various processes of supervision. Autonomy will not exist in each process and in each situation with uniform force and value. It will be present, however, in each and all of the supervisory situations. It constitutes one of the referents for the supervisor to use in trying to determine whether the supervisory program is in balance with respect to the four components in the processes of supervision and the five characteristics of operational balance.

RELATIVITY

The working definition of relativity is:

The recognition of value and utility of one object, person, or situation as it relates to another with a different set of purposes, processes, and outcomes.

There are numerous aspects of relativity, but perhaps two or three are dominant in most situations. The major problem in using relativity as a referent in assessing interpersonal relationships is the absolute used as the zero-point for making judgments about people and situations. Supervisors vary greatly in the belief that there are some things known with such conclusiveness that they ought never to be questioned. This is the absolute of the absolute. It is as though one had called upon a deity who had provided the ultimate truth and that truth should not be questioned, challenged, or subjected to change. This means that any supervisor who perceives the absolute as the referent point in this manner will be most inflexible in being able to hold any concept other than "conforming activity" as acceptable in any supervisory situation.

Philosophically, it is extremely distressing to many people to realize that there are few things that are known absolutely and for all time. The fundamentalist approach to truth has caused distress among people because it becomes impossible to arrive at any compromise of ideas when one of the two people in a conflict of opinion finds it difficult to compromise on the points of difference. The person who holds to one absolute as the only solution is not in a position to relate his knowledge to the possible knowledge that another may hold.

Closely allied to the problem of the absolute is that of ego-centeredness. Status positions often increase the tendency to ego-centeredness. Supervisors, as status position holders, may unknowingly drift in the direction of ego-centeredness, which means that conclusions are made in terms of one's own judgment. There is little inclination on the part of the ego-centered person to recognize that another might possess that fact or value which could be used as the point of reference in resolving differences. The practical virtue of the absolute or the ego-centered judgment is that it constitutes a reference or standard against which the judgments of evaluation may be directed. If no standards of any kind exist, there will be an inclination to drift one way or the other with the resultant loss of time and opportunities for excellence through indecision.

The essence of relativity is mainly in the ability to see the variations in people and things rather than in the judgment of the rightness and wrongness of anyone in any particular situation or status of behavior. Trying to see things in relationship to other things does not mean that standards are absent. It requires a different kind of standard than that implied in the absolute and in the ego-centered judgment. The alternative to them, however, need not be drift and indecision. Relativity is perhaps better illustrated in the relationships involved in cooperation, coordination, and compromise (see Chapters 5 and 6 and reference 4).

Describe cases when a teacher has been labeled cooperative or uncooperative. What makes the difference?

Cooperation, as shown in Figure 12.1, means that in the school situation teacher A and teacher B each may be teaching a fourth grade group and each may have a common purpose in that both fourth grades are to sing for the parents' program at the Christmas Festival. The teachers have a common purpose in so far as this performance is concerned, but each might go about the training of the pupils for their respective parts in quite a different way. The final test of cooperation would be that the two groups combine and sing well together. Thus, there are two different people but they have a common short-range goal. This short-range goal, to which both teachers have contributed, may then contribute to one of the major purposes of the school program.

Coordination, as shown in Figure 12.1, means that teachers A and B may be teaching separate subjects such as mathematics and physics, and each has his short-range goal. Each wants to develop a mastery of the processes in his respective subject as well as to develop those concepts which would make the content of the subject function in problem situations. Each may pursue his goal directly. The rule of interpersonal relationships in coordination is that each may proceed to his own short-term goal so long as he does not interfere with the other's opportunity to pursue those behaviors which will lead him to his short-term goal. In the case of coordination, the short-term goals may not be held in common but may contribute to the common general purpose of the school system.

Explain how goals differ for cooperative and coordinative actions.

Compromise, whether it be in the cooperative or in the coordinative type of relationships or in the pursuit of short- and long-range goals, is of necessity a yielding on the part of one or both of the parties in his particular point of view. This might be illustrated in the form of the coordinative action in which the physics and mathematics teachers may have been teaching some content which resulted in contradictory learning between the two courses. If, in the teaching of the concepts of ratio and proportion, the mathematics teacher did not establish those characteristic concepts which were needed by the physics teacher, a resolution of the differences would

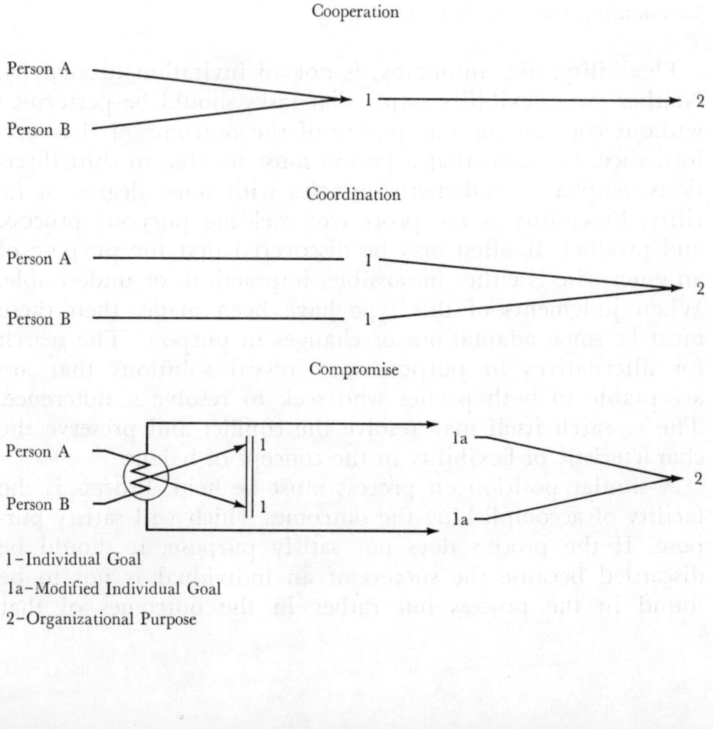

FIGURE 12.1* *A Graphic Presentation of Cooperation, Coordination, and Compromise

have to be achieved. Here, relativity of importance comes into play and each of the teachers must decide whether maintaining his own point of view is more important than sacrificing the learning opportunities of the pupil.

The supervisor's responsibility at this point is to provide an opportunity for the teachers concerned to discuss the results of their differences as they affect the pupils. Compromise is the recognition and acceptance of the proper relatedness of the two courses of action. A part of the supervisor's task is to seek an increase in the tolerance of each teacher toward the differences. Low tolerance for difference does not mean that one would not be comfortable in the presence of another who is pursuing a pattern of activity quite contrary to one's own. It means that one must recognize that differences are not necessarily threatening or dangerous. It also means that as differences are recognized they must be analyzed. If the tolerance for differences can be increased, the patience needed in resolving them is more probable.

How do you decide on the limits of compromise?

Relativity, like the previous characteristics, is important and significant in each of the components of the processes of supervision. These relationships are discussed in greater detail in Chapters 13 through 16.

FLEXIBILITY

The working definition of flexibility is:

The capability of a person or a situation to change patterns of being and behavior by adapting to newly accepted goals, to the different patterns espoused by others, and to the escape mechanisms for avoiding undesirable outcomes.

Flexibility, like autonomy, is not an invitation to anarchy. Neither does flexibility imply that tasks should be performed without concern for the quality of the outcome of that performance. It means that a person must be able to shift directions, emphases, and methodologies with some degree of facility. Flexibility is the process of melding purpose, process, and product. It often may be discovered that the purpose of an enterprise is either impossible, impractical, or undesirable. When judgments of this type have been made, then there must be some adaptations or changes in purpose. The search for alternatives in purpose may reveal solutions that are acceptable to both parties who seek to resolve a difference. The research itself may resolve the conflict and preserve the characteristic of flexibility in the concept of balance.

A similar position on process must be held. Process is the facility of accomplishing the outcomes which will satisfy purpose. If the process does not satisfy purpose, it should be discarded because the success of an individual is not to be found in the process but rather in the outcomes of that process. Flexibility in process is more essential than either flexibility in the establishment of purpose or the assessment of the quality of outcome. Flexibility is a strength when it can be used as a means of probing for a better way. If flexibility is viewed as a means of escaping difficult situations and of moving from one method of doing something to another, then it is not serving the purposes of supervision regardless of the process that may be under consideration.

When is flexibility no longer within democratic action?

Flexibility may be looked upon as the before-and-after of decision-making. One may view a situation with all the facts that can be mustered and feel that a firm decision can be made with confidence. After this decision is made and one must live with the results of it, it may be discovered that it was not as wise a decision as had been envisioned. Flexibility immediately would move the person to a review of the facts which led him to this particular decision outcome. Thus, the before-and-after concept of decision-making becomes highly related to the concept of flexibility. Flexibility as seen in this way is closely related to the selectivity of purpose, process, and product.

A person who can see only one particular way of doing something is not in a position to select from among the many alternatives that are available to him. Perhaps it should be indicated at this point that many people do not see decision-making as the opportunity to *choose* between a number of ways of doing things. Entirely too often, decision-making is seen as the process of recognizing a problem, thinking it through, and arriving at a conclusion. But the thinking-through process, if it is valid at all, must be the process of looking at the various ways of accomplishing a purpose. With each alternative, one tries to anticipate those things which might support it or thwart it. It is the mental review of all of these potentials that brings one finally to the selection of a particular decision as being the most promising because it has more of the supportive and less of the thwartive element. Flexibility is not to be interpreted as the bandwagon-hopping so enticing to many people who have not been able to find the most satisfactory way of accomplishing an accepted task. It is tempting to want to be with the majority. It is tempting to hope to perform in that manner which will garner the favorable recognition of observers and result in prestige status (see Chapters 17 and 18 and reference 4). Flexibility is not intended here to be the fickle pursuit of the pleasant or the successful. Rather, it means pursuing success regardless of the manner in which others may be performing their tasks or solving their problems.

How does the choice to conform or not to conform relate to the concept of flexibility?

Flexibility, like other characteristics, is closely related to each of the components of process. The balance to be established between directing and controlling, stimulating and initiating, analyzing and appraising, and designing and implementing is dependent upon the perceptions of flexibility possessed by the supervisor. Flexibility for the supervisor means the opportunity to select from many more potential decisions than would be true for the inflexible person. The supervisor must assess the particular situation with the people involved and decide which of the components of process might be most appropriate to accomplish the supervisory purpose at that particular moment and in that particular situation.

CREATIVITY

The working definition of creativity is:

The selective capacity of high intelligence, operating with freedom from repressive and suppressive control factors, as it offers direction to the choice of the rewarding alternatives of behavioral purposes and processes.

Creativity is the most complex of the characteristics and the most difficult to describe. It also is hard to recognize in the practical situation. There have been so many perceptions of creativity that it is difficult to filter from many possibilities the practical ones for the purposes of supervision. The perception, perhaps, is revealed in the above definition. If one is freeing himself from repressive and suppressive control factors, he is providing himself an opportunity to use intelligence in arraying the potentials in any situation so as to lead to the best choice of solution. In this sense, creativity is more a process than a product. It is difficult to see how anyone could look at an end product and say that it is creative. To say that it is creative means that the person making the judgment presumes to have had all of the experience of mankind readily at hand and has the ability to recognize similarities and, when none are found, to presume that this is something that has never before happened. Such is not the essence of creativity.

Creativity is not to be assessed in terms of the odd disposition of the creator nor in terms of the oddities of his work or of his work habits. It is not to be used as a haven for what may be called individual whims. It is a highly intellectual activity. It is not the intention here to review the voluminous literature on the subject nor to try to resolve the present-day debates which surround it. Rather, the purpose is to introduce a concept essential to the assessment of balance in the operational pattern. Creativity does not consist of doing something in a way in which the individual has not done it before—for instance, trying a new technique as described in the literature. This might be creative for the author of the article but it is not creative for the person who attempts to emulate that author. Further, it is not in the introducing of innovations to teachers that supervision might be called creative. It is not merely doing something for the first time.

The uniqueness of creativity is in its origin. The inherent ability to originate what has not been originated before is a unique characteristic. All persons are not equally creative, however. They may all possess varying degrees of flexibility that may prompt them to attempt to duplicate and to vary an idea or technique that they have not tried before. This would be a new activity but not necessarily a creative one. The essence of creativity is in the processes by which the abilities of a brilliant intellect are brought to a situation. A mass of information that is well understood and developed into a synthesized whole constituting the solution to a problem or the development of a pattern of innovation is the benchmark of creativity. In this sense, there may be times when that which is originated by the creative individual may nevertheless be a duplication of what has come before. If, however, the individual is highly intelligent and has a high level of information about what has been done before, there is less chance that he will duplicate it precisely.

MacKinnon has presented this concept of creativity very succinctly in the following statement:

> The full and complete picturing of the creative person will require many images. But if, despite this caution, one still insists on asking what most generally characterizes the creative individual as he has revealed himself in the Berkeley studies, it is his high level of effective intelligence, his openness to experience, his freedom from crippling restraints and impoverishing inhibitions, his esthetic sensitivity, his cognitive flexibility, his independence in thought and action, his high level of creative energy, his unquestioning commitment to creative endeavor, and his unceasing striving for solutions to the ever more difficult problems that he constantly sets for himself.[1]

The persons who possess that intrinsic persuasion which stimulates them to create may not all have the drive which gives them the courage of their convictions. This may be related to success, failure, security, and other factors. There is a constant problem with expression versus repression. There is a difference between may and can, and can and will. These differences have been resolved by those people who perform in a creative way. Because creativity is an inherent quality in all persons—but in varying degrees—it cannot be considered a group process. This does not mean that there can be no creative group. It does mean that there is no creative group without some better than average creative individuals in it. The creative ones may stimulate and direct activities which then cause the group to appear creative. Original ideas are products of individuals. On the other hand, the group and its need may give the individual the stimulation to be creative and the opportunity to experience in-

What happens when a group is made up of artists?

[1] Donald W. MacKinnon, Director of the Institute of Personality Assessment and Research at the University of California, Berkeley, "What Makes a Person Creative," *Saturday Review,* February 10, 1962, p. 69.

dividual security in the group as a result of his creativity. Even if a group were formed because all members were highly creative, group actions are still only modifications of unique individual ideas.

Objectives related to creativity need to be developed cooperatively in both the general and specific aspects. This concept is developed by Torrance as follows:

> . . . the following specific goals seem essential: rewarding diverse contributions; helping creative persons recognize the value of their own talents, avoid exploitation, accept limitations creatively, develop minimum skills, make use of opportunities, develop values and purposes, hold to purposes; avoiding the equation of divergent with mental illness or delinquency; reducing overemphases or misplaced emphasis on sex roles; helping them learn how to be less obnoxious without sacrificing their creativity; reducing isolation; and helping them to learn how to cope with anxieties, fears, hardships, and failures.[2]

Even though the above statement is referring to the creativity of children, those responsible for supervision might well take note of Torrance's ideas and develop comparable objectives for teachers.

As with the other individual characteristics of operational balance, creativity is involved in each of the four components of process. Again, each will be related more specifically in the four following chapters.

RELATIONSHIPS OF THE CHARACTERISTICS TO THE COMPONENTS

The definitions of each of the characteristics as presented in this chapter are working definitions. They are stated in this manner because they fit the concept of supervision as developed in this book. As with the list of assumptions about supervision, there is no claim that we have selected the best or presented an exhaustive list. Each person, in turn, either may accept the characteristics indicated here as serviceable in determining the operational balance of other supervisory plans and programs or he may write his own characteristics and select those definitions which would serve him best.

The five characteristics chosen here seem serviceable to the purposes of the authors. There is no reason why other words and other concepts might not be used. It is conceivable that one might want to choose characteristics such as economy, dependency, freedom, sensitivity, validity, deference, substantiation, articulation, accruement, or a multitude of others. It is a matter of selectivity of those characteristics which will give the kind of operational balance sought by the individual supervisor in devising the supervisory program. The important concept is that some characteristics must be observed if

[2] E. Paul Torrance, *Guiding Creative Talent* (Englewood Cliffs, N.J.: Prentice-Hall, 1962), p. 161.

an operational balance is to be assured. These constitute that fly-wheel, regulator, gyroscope, etc., of the only type that is available to assure balance in a supervisory program. It is assumed, too, that all of the characteristics as well as the components of process must operate within the described limits of democratic action and of the policies of the organization in which they take place. They must be in agreement with the objectives of the program.

It is emphasized again that each individual characteristic is more related to one process than to another, but each is related to some extent to all the components of process. The most highly related ones are emphasized for illustrative purposes in each of the four chapters which follow. Autonomy is emphasized in Chapter 13, which deals with the processes of directing and controlling. Perceptivity and creativity are emphasized in Chapter 14, which includes discussions on stimulating and initiating. Relativity is the point of emphasis in Chapter 15, where analyzing and appraising are the subjects of discussion. Flexibility is used for the illustrative emphasis in Chapter 16, which deals with designing and implementing. It is mentioned again in each of these chapters that, even though a characteristic has been singled out for emphasis in developing an illustration, each one has an important but varying part in each of the components of the processes necessary to a balanced program of supervision.

THE WORKING DEFINITIONS

Perceptivity is the sensitivity of a person to the many elements of human personality that must adapt to or change a multitude of environmental forces.

Autonomy is the free choice of behaviors within those normative restrictions which are voluntarily accepted or over which the individual possesses some power of determination.

Relativity is the recognition of value and utility of one object, person, or situation as it relates to another with a different set of purposes, processes, and outcomes.

Flexibility is the capability of a person or a situation to change patterns of being and behavior by adapting to newly accepted goals, to the different patterns espoused by others, and to the escape mechanisms for avoiding undesirable outcomes.

Creativity is the selective capacity of high intelligence, operating with freedom from repressive and suppressive control factors, as it offers direction to the choice of the rewarding alternatives of behavioral purposes and processes.

SELECTED REFERENCES

1. Association for Supervision and Curriculum Development, Yearbook, "Balancing the Roles in Decision-Making," in *Balance in the Curriculum*. Washington, D.C.: National Education Association, 1961. Chap. VIII, pp. 162–194.
2. Association for Supervision and Curriculum Development, Yearbook, "Expectations that Influence Leaders," in *Leadership for Improving Instruction*. Washington, D.C.: National Education Association, 1960. Chap. III, pp. 67–87.
3. Association for Supervision and Curriculum Development, Yearbook, "Dignity, Integrity and Autonomy," in *Perceiving, Behaving, Becoming*. Washington, D.C.: National Education Association, 1962. Chap. XIV, pp. 213–233.
4. Ayer, Fred C., *Fundamentals of Instructional Supervision*. New York: Harper & Row, 1954. Chaps. V–VI, IX–X, XVII–XVIII.
5. Bennis, Warren G., Kenneth D. Benne, and Robert Chin (eds.), *The Planning of Change*. New York: Holt, Rinehart & Winston, 1961. p. 2.
6. Getzels, Jacob W., "Administration as a Social Process," in *Administrative Theory in Education*, Andrew W. Halpin (ed.). Chicago: Midwest Administration Center, University of Chicago, 1958. Chap. 7.
7. Gross, Neal, Ward S. Mason, and Alexander W. McEachern, *Exploration in Role Analysis*. New York: Wiley, 1958.
8. Gruber, Howard E., Glen Terrell, and Michael Wertheimer (eds.), *Contemporary Approaches to Creative Thinking*. New York: Atherton, 1963.
9. Kennedy, John F., *Profiles in Courage*. New York: Harper & Row, 1961, Inaugural Ed. pp. 1–21.
10. MacKinnon, Donald W., "What Makes a Person Creative," *Saturday Review*, February 10, 1962, p. 69.
11. Miel, Alice (ed.), *Creativity in Teaching: Invitations and Instances*. San Francisco: Wadsworth, 1961. (See bibliography on creativity in the appendix.)
12. Torrance, E. Paul, *Guiding Creative Talent*. Englewood Cliffs, N.J.: Prentice-Hall, 1962.
13. Tagiuri, Renato and Luigi Petrullo, *Person Perception and Interpersonal Behavior*. Stanford: Stanford University Press, 1958.

13

The Component of Process: Directing and Controlling

The implications of the definition of supervision as used in this book were presented in Chapter 2. In that chapter, the direction of the discussion and the procedures for developing the theory and design of supervision moved from purposes to products. The logical steps were conceived as moving from a discussion of the purposes to the patterns of supervision and then to the participants in supervision. It was pointed out in Chapter 2 that *patterns* and *participants* were necessary, supportive, and undergirding factors as related to the other three categories, *purposes, processes,* and *products*. Patterns of organization are important and staffing procedures are essential. The intent of supervision is declared in the first category—purpose—and action proceeds from that point to the processes in the operating program of supervision. It is logical, then, to move from processes to products.

The content of Part IV is an analysis of the concepts and a discussion of the program implications of various facets in the categories of process. The characteristics of operational balance needed in a supervisory program were presented in Chapter 12. Following the discussion of the four component areas of process, there is a chapter devoted to the integration of procedures, characteristics, and components. Process remains the most potent link between the purposes of supervision and the anticipated products of the supervisory program.

DEFINING THE COMPONENT

The first component to be discussed is *directing and controlling.* Attention was given in the previous chapter to the reason for considering the components in terms of two words rather than one. It might be well to turn back to that chapter at this point and to think again of the relationship of the two words "directing" and "controlling." Those who are interested in the discussion of words as words might find some interest in trying to determine the extent to which directing is involved in controlling and the extent to which controlling is to be used in the same sense as directing.

The two terms are not intended to be synonymous even though they are used as one component of supervision. It would be a very broad and, indeed, a dangerous assumption to make directing and controlling synonymous. It is even more hazardous to consider this particular component as constituting the total program of supervision. A point was made in the previous chapter that the balance in operation confronts a human tendency to use those behaviors more frequently which prove to be rewarding in whatever sense a reward is appreciated by the individual. Cautions were indicated that persistence in the pursuit of a particular behavior, whether it be in the supervisory program or in any other area of activity, constitutes an overemphasis of one behavior and is tantamount to an assurance of failure, particularly where the activity involved influences other people. Thus, it seems wise to caution once again that the total program of supervision includes other components than the one of directing and controlling. There is need for a balance between the four components just as there is need for a balance in the characteristics of action by which the individual supervisor goes about the tasks of supervision regardless of the involvement of one or more of the components of supervision.

Why is it hazardous to overemphasize one type of procedure?

The authors made a firm commitment to what certainly must be termed the democratic philosophy of change and this commitment was indicated in the first assumption in the list presented in Chapter 3. This assumption indicated that the conditions of fruitful interrelationships between people depended upon *mutual* respect for the necessity of having different people do different things in a group enterprise. It also indicated that the individual must find satisfaction and assurance of personal worth.

Recast the first assumption in a negative form.

The terms "directing" and "controlling" must be given the positive rather than the negative connotation in view of this assumption. By positive is meant that directing and controlling is done for the purpose of making possible the maximum contribution to the purposes of the group activity as well as to directing and controlling those behaviors and situational factors which would make it possible for the individual to experience a sense of achievement. If the negative connotation were used, it would be found in statements which indicate that directing and controlling are necessary because of the probability that the individuals who are serving in subordinate positions might be expected to perform inappropriately or fail to possess either the knowledge or the technical competence to achieve the purposes known and defined by the superordinates. Directing and controlling in this sense would be based upon an unacceptable assumption.

A reasonable generalization is that supervisors work with people who are intelligent and well prepared for their positions. Obviously, this generalization will not apply with equal force in all situations. There are some persons of limited ability who get into the teaching profession and others who possess high potential but do not apply their abilities to the tasks of teaching. The increases in the requirements for teacher certification and in the selective practices and program characteristics of the teacher education institutions steadily promote the probability that those who are employed to teach are of a high level of intelligence, ability, and inclination to make a positive contribution in their teaching service. Supervisors, nevertheless, must be capable of assisting teachers with varied levels of skill—the laggards and the perverse as well as the gifted and willing.

From the standpoint of the definition of the terms, the process of directing implies a line of acting, pointing, aiming, or guiding the activities of others to bring about desirable change. Further, the process of controlling includes the exercising of restraint, holding in check, or regulating behaviors so that the change will be that which is desired. The question of the limits of freedom to pursue these processes places the supervisor in a very interesting, if not a difficult, predicament. When making decisions as a supervisor, there is always the problem of deciding how far to go in directing and how far to go in controlling, yet at the same time to stay within the boundaries of an acceptable definition of democratic action. Bennis, Benne, and Chin offer the following suggestion:

> The predicament we confront, then, concerns method; methods that maximize freedom and limit as little as possible the potentialities of growth; methods that will realize man's dignity as well as bring into fruition desirable social goals.[1]

BALANCE BETWEEN AUTHORITY AND AUTONOMY

The criterion for judging whether the component—directing and controlling—is within the framework of democratic action when being applied is found in the theory underlying the process. If the procedures selected to direct and control actions in implementing a plan were developed in an autocratic fashion, no amount of group activity will make these

[1] Warren G. Bennis, Kenneth D. Benne, and Robert Chin (eds.), *The Planning of Change* (New York: Holt, Rinehart & Winston, 1951), p. 2.

processes other than autocratic. If policies were developed through democratic group action and the procedures were selected in a similar manner to direct and control continued group action, there need be little fear of violating democratic principles.

An illustration of the problem involved in holding to a desirable pattern of choice between directing and controlling follows: The supervisor, at the superintendent's suggestion, traveled at school expense to a nearby state to study machine processing of pupil tests. The suggestion was interpreted by the supervisor, even though not made explicit by the superintendent, to mean that the purpose of the trip was to import the procedures observed. The observed procedures were maturely executed. The supervisor returned to the home school system with enthusiasm for implementing the machine procedures. The halo of superintendent-initiated suggestion emerged in the supervisor as a demand for immediate implementation. The consequent bulletins, directories, and informational meetings were expedited. As might be expected by a noncommitted appraiser, the teachers became increasingly confused, reluctant, and defiant. The cry for a return to "sane" procedures soon reached the ear of the superintendent. The tactics of innovation were evaluated by a representative group of teachers, supervisors, and administrators. The cause of difficulty was quickly diagnosed as an autocratic imposition of procedures upon the teachers. With some embarrassment to the supervisor, but without reprisals, the same supervisor was given a two-year period to prepare the staff and institute the new procedures. The committee pledged support and cooperation to the new attack which would place emphasis on supervisory *direction* as opposed to *control.*

Inconsistencies may develop when one fails to recognize the difference between the control and the autonomy of a group. When autonomy is granted, it may be granted under certain conditions and within the structure of the democratic process. Other illustrations of this type, but dealing with different aspects of the instructional program, might be described but this one seems sufficient to indicate the nature of the dichotomy of concept and practice emphasized at this point.

A person who has the power to grant autonomy of action to the teachers is, at the same time, in a position to withdraw that autonomy. One of the serious problems confronting the supervisor, as he selects those personal behaviors that determine the interrelationships between the supervisor and the teacher, is that of establishing a balance in direction and control. In this sense, the balance is between the supervisor and the teacher rather than the type of balance described earlier between directing and controlling or among the characteristics of the supervisory operation. It perhaps can be explained more easily by using an illustration that must, of necessity, be purely hypothetical. This illustration is based upon the items in Figure 13.1.

It will be noted in the figure that the major tasks to be performed are related to (1) school objectives, (2) course objectives, (3) selection of learning experiences, (4) criteria of satisfactory achievement, and (5) evaluation of outcomes of the teaching–learning act. It might be assumed that these things are involved when the school system arrives at that period in the development of the instructional program when new content is introduced. It will be noted that under each of the major task areas there are two persons indicated, namely, the supervisor and the teacher. In this hypothetical situation the *one* supervisor and the *one* teacher involved must determine the extent to which the supervisor will exercise direction and control and the extent to which direction and control of the factors involved in the curriculum problem indicated shall be allocated to the teacher. The purpose of the figure is to illustrate how control and autonomy shift in dominance from the supervisor to the teacher (or vice versa) as the task demands change. The line (–) without an arrow indicates an even balance between control and autonomy while the line (→) with an arrow shows the direction of dominance. Note particularly the fact that in all task demands each party retains some prerogative. When the arrow points to one or the other, it means that, in points of difference, the direction of the arrow points to the dominant decision-maker. Caution should be exercised in the interpretation of this diagram by recognizing that existing legal prescriptions cannot be the object of transfer of control among supervisors and teachers since both are subordinate to higher controls.

The illustration makes clear that as the tasks become more specific with respect to the introduction of new material in the curriculum, items such as course objectives suggest a shift of control, with less by the supervisor but more by the teacher. In the item of the selection of learning experiences, the supervisor's control is reduced even more and the control of the teacher is increased substantially. This seems logical even though the exact percent of shift varies with the tasks. The teacher gradually increases in the granted autonomy as the item of decision becomes more specific with respect to the teaching–learning act. Those supervisors who would retain the higher percentage in the supervisor's position must be able to demonstrate that they possess greater knowledge about and

Objectives of Education	*Subject Objectives*	*Selection of Learning Experiences*	*Criteria of Achievement*	*Evaluation of Outcomes*
S–T	S–T	S–T	S–T	S–T
50–50%	25–75%	0–100%	75–25%	25–75%
C–A	C→A	C→A	C←A	C→A

S: Supervisor T: Teacher C: Control A: Autonomy

***FIGURE 13.1* Balance Between Control and Autonomy**

skill in the teaching process than does the teacher. Furthermore, the matter of creativity becomes an issue if too great a proportion of direction and control is maintained by the supervisor. Some freedom or autonomy must be granted to the teacher if creativity is to characterize the teacher's work.

The guarantees of quality control as represented in Figure 13.1 are found in the allocation of the predominance of control in the choice of criteria for evaluating achievement. At this point the supervisor exercises dominant direction and control. It seems consistent that the supervisor should devote energy and intellectual capacity to overall objectives and the criteria for judging whether the objectives have been achieved. This preserves the opportunity to fulfill the responsibilities for quality control over the activities and outcomes of the classroom where the teacher is permitted to be dominant in making the decisions about the specifics of teaching. Even though the supervisor might be inclined to maintain a greater control over the specific activities in the classroom, it is almost useless for that supervisor to entertain such hopes. Supervisors are so outnumbered by teachers that they could not possibly make the necessary observations to guarantee that their wishes or orders were pursued satisfactorily in each of the classrooms. Again, attention is directed to the evaluation of outcomes in which the teacher is dominant. It is quite possible that the balance in the control and autonomy here should be about equal. Evaluation of outcomes might well be a cooperative endeavor to the extent of equal responsibility. On the other hand, as in the case of the selection of learning experiences, some might reason that the supervisor has adequate control when that effort is directed to the general objectives of education and the teacher's control is exercised over the selection of learning experiences. The control of the supervisor in the evaluation of the outcomes might well be considered sufficient when the dominant control resides with the supervisor in selecting and stating the criteria by which achievement shall be judged. The teacher, even though dominant in the selection of the procedures for evaluating outcomes, still must satisfy the supervisor in terms of the data submitted when related to the criteria by which those data are judged.

What balance or imbalance in control allocation have you experienced?

The illustration here must occupy a position similar to the assumptions, principles, and objectives of supervision in that it must be custom-built to the real and the practical situation. It is important for the supervisor to give thought to this balance of direction and control and to develop his own set of balances for supervisor or teacher control in each element of the educational program. In the end, the supervisor's success will be dependent upon the extent to which the balance of direction and control between the supervisor and the teacher is achieved and proves effective.

In a sense, the illustration above is an attempt to draw a picture of the difference between self-control and outside control in so far as the teacher and the teaching activities are concerned. This concept of self-control and outside control, as well as its realization in practice, may constitute the difference between creativity and conformity. It is easy to speculate that, if the supervisor maintains 100 percent of direction and control with zero percent allocated to the teacher, the teacher would have only one type of responsibility—that of conforming to the requirements as stated by the supervisor. It seems impractical in a supervisory program and unworthy of a professionally educated person to act in such a manner; thus, the discussion of these unfortunate possibilities will not be permitted to occupy more space in this discussion. Essentially, the problem is the practical one not only of determining the balance between self-control and outside control but also of defining the limits and boundaries of individual choice or autonomy of action.

The above illustration deals with the introduction of some new content into the program for which mastery is demanded on the part of pupils. There are other situations in which different categories might be selected and different percentages assigned to achieve the acceptable balance between supervisor and teacher control. The illustration might cover the type of consideration required whenever any new content is introduced into the teaching program. On the other hand, if the situation under consideration evolves from the necessity of adapting some new regulations of a state department of public instruction, little autonomy could be extended to the teacher. In this situation, the administrator and the supervisor would be performing a ministerial function and would not be permitted to grant autonomy to their subordinates or even to claim autonomy for themselves. The task would be to achieve a balance between the supervisor and the teacher in selecting the means for the implementation of the regulation which might best be made in the light of the particular patterns of organization and operation of that particular school system. If the situation evolved about a plan for a new research attack to discover new facts about the educational program in a highly specialized area, the supervisor might choose to grant a greater responsibility for direction and control to the teacher than he would retain for himself. This is consistent with the concept repeatedly stated that the supervisory program must be custom-built for the school system.

The supervisory program within the local school system should be custom-built for all major situations and problems that require supervisor and teacher attention. If the task at hand is that of analyzing the possibilities or methods of introducing a new plan and of stimulating those concerned with it to become involved progressively in the implementation, then it is conceivable that the supervisor again might be required to play the major or dominant role in the direction and control of such an activity. This relates to the type of area in which there will be an overlap of the components of process. A more specific reference is made to this in

Chapter 14 where the component of stimulating and initiating is the major focus of the discussion. Direction and control are important factors in many of the situations where the major functional intent is that of stimulating and initiating.

The task of revitalizing an established program is another illustrative situation. It is conceivable that the mere fact that the program needed to be revitalized would require greater control and direction on the part of the supervisor. All compartments of school activity, however, may be dichotomized or analyzed in terms of the supervisor's influence. These are only a few of the countless situations that might be cited in which the problems of directing and controlling become a major supervisory concern and in which the autonomy on the part of the supervisor and of the teacher becomes the issue with respect to balance. The supervisor, being the superior officer, must accept more responsibility than the teacher for achieving this balance.

The processes of supervision are directly related to the patterns of leadership that are developed and pursued by the superior officers. It would be impossible to differentiate in the patterns of leadership between the various components. The reason for this is that the components constitute process or the kinds of things that are done to accomplish the purposes established. This means that the persons who are responsible for establishing and directing these processes may use the same kind of leadership tactics in each of the components but in each separate instance might have a focal point for the particular component which dominates the selection of leadership activities.

TYPES OF LEADERSHIP

What are the benchmarks of the wise use of authority?

Directing and controlling are processes of supervision that can be explained in terms of the types of leadership: coercive, persuasive, and permissive. Coercive leadership is the type in which the superior attempts to impose his will upon, and thereby control the behavior of, those who are subordinate to him (see reference 1). Even though the subordinate position is recognized in the hierarchy of control, it is of limited importance in discussing the leadership types because the leader is the one who influences others to perform in a certain way. Sometimes this means changing the ways of those who are led either in terms of the processes of behaviors or in terms of the goals pursued. Coercion is a procedure that does not inherently violate democratic patterns of action. Reference was made earlier to the fact that democracy does not mean freedom to the extent that anarchy might result, but rather that it presumes certain authorities and controls which bring about the desired action. In the democratic group, the definition of what is desired resides more in all members of the group than in those who have gained a position of status authority and control over the other members.

Many times coercion—the exercise of authority or the imposition of one will over another—is essential in democratic action. If a group has decided on a given plan and procedure, the supervisor is obligated to direct and control the actions of everyone in the group within the limits of the plan or to stimulate the group to the selection of new purposes and new directions. In instances of this type, the supervisor becomes the agent of the group, particularly when he has decided to share the decisions with the entire group. Sharing of decisions should not be attempted unless the superior officer intends to respect the decisions made and becomes the agent of that group in implementing the decisions.

Give illustrations of the use of coercion in democratic action.

Coercive leadership is dependent upon power in order for it to achieve the purposes of leadership. Power can be achieved in many different ways. It can be through the recognition of superiority on the part of the person submitting to the power. In this case, the will of the superior officer is in control over the will of the subordinates purely because the subordinates chose to have it that way. In the more typical situations, however, power is closely related to the ability of the person exercising the power to provide rewards and punishments. It may be that the leader exercising coercion as a pattern of leadership may be known to have the potential of rewards and punishment without needing to exercise either. Whether real or imagined, the effect upon those who are led is about the same. The leader, if he depends upon coercion as his method of influencing people, must have more than merely the potential for rewards because he may be called upon to provide them on certain occasions. If he is unable to provide them at the appropriate time, he loses the power and, consequently, the use of this particular type of leadership. A reward is not a reward unless the recipient seeks it as such. It will not be recognized as a reward unless it provides some type of satisfaction or protection from some dissatisfaction on the part of the person who is the object of coercive leadership. Similarly, punishment is not considered punishment unless it withdraws from that person some of the satisfactions coveted by him. It is impossible for a coercive leader to lead those who are unconcerned with any rewards or punishments which might be dealt out by the superior officer—in this case, the supervisor. Theoretically, it means that the leader must possess the power and that the power must be recognized whether rewards or punishments are involved. In either case, the influence on the persons led determines the existence of power.

How can a supervisor stimulate creative behavior through a sanction-supported control system?

The supervisor, as the incumbent, occupies an important status position and may not recognize the fact that the source of his power is, in part, resident in those whom he would lead. The supervisor is ill-advised to assume that the power

How can an individual exercise leadership without a status title?

is inherent in the status position. He is unable to escape the fact that those whom he would lead may hold the key to his permission for leadership. Even though these are some of the characteristics involved in coercive leadership, many people are so emotionally constituted that the kinesthetic experiences of coercion seem to grant satisfaction even though leadership results are not attendant. It is unfortunate if the leader refuses or is unable to see when those whom he would lead are unconcerned about his power potential; he thus fails to see that he may continue with a false sense of being able to exercise power and authority. A person who can no longer perceive his actual leadership powers and accomplishments can no longer be effective and essential to organizational effort.

The second type of leadership involved is that of the persuasive leader. In this type, ability is more important than power. The leader who wants to be persuasive, in the positive sense, in imposing his will upon others must be able to understand the logic by which others select their own behaviors. He must be sufficiently informed and intellectually alert to make counter-proposals to those whom he would lead. The persuasive leader is an indirect or secondary reinforcing agent (see reference 1). He must be able to help those he leads to gain satisfactions and, having gained them, to believe that they were achieved under their own power. The persuasive leader informs, warns, signals, or indicates which behavior is most desirable for goal attainment on the part of those he leads. He must be sensitive to the problems that exist in the minds of his subordinates. He must be able to help his subordinates analyze problems when they are recognized. He must be able to provide suggestions for the solutions to problems and he must have creative plans when change is essential. The persuasive leader, in order to gain and maintain his persuasiveness, must establish a record of success in his attempts to solve problems and to provide suggestions to those who are in the process of solving problems. Confidence in the fact that a person possesses this kind of ability is essential to those who accept persuasive leadership.

The third type is that of permissive leadership. Here again, both power and ability are important to the leader. Perhaps power is the more dominant ingredient. It differs from coercive leadership in the degree to which inhibitions are imposed or reprisals threatened (see reference 1). Reprisals seldom are threatened overtly. If it is presumed by those who are led that the leader possesses these powers but has no intention of exercising them, they then might grant him opportunities for effectiveness in permissive leadership. The permissive leader must exercise the ability of persuasiveness in order to change the goals of the individual and, consequently, group goals so that they may be in agreement with his own purpose. Once the permissive leader has gained the consent or acceptance of his group, he has the added advantage of the power of the group decision in itself. Groups exert pressure upon individuals to conform to the group decision (see reference 4). As in coercive leadership, those who are unconcerned about potential rewards and punishments either in terms of material benefits, working conditions, or prestige will not try to conform to the leader's suggestions. Consequently, permissive leadership for such people fails.

The interrelationship of these three types of leadership involves the question of whether leadership types are mutually exclusive or whether there is not only substantial overlapping but also a mixture of the three. The nature and amount of the mixture are dependent primarily upon the situation and the people involved. The person most successful in influencing his subordinates is that person who can sense which type of leadership is most appropriate to the situation at hand. The supervisor must assess the nature of the problem involved and make decisions as a supervisor just as suggested in the illustration cited earlier relating to the balance between the supervisor and the teacher in the possession of control over a situation. A supervisor will find many opportunities and occasions to use coercion, persuasion, and permissiveness in his leadership role.

There is no intent here to indicate that one or another type is more desirable or more likely to succeed. The emphasis on group dynamics and the democratic process during the past decade has led many superficial and casual students to conclude that coercive leadership is synonymous with authoritarianism and, thereby, undesirable. On the other hand, many have chosen to consider permissive leadership as being synonymous with laissez-faire and therefore presumed it to be undesirable. Such casual persumptions leave persuasive leadership based primarily upon ability as the most popularly accepted type of leadership pattern. All these easy assumptions probably are questionable in about the same degree.

The purpose of leadership is to influence people. Leadership is undesirable when it causes people to perform at less than their ability potential in relation to the purposes of the enterprise to which they are committed. The supervisor well might consider all three types of leadership as being appropriate either alternately or in some combination.

There are many dualities in the nature and practice of leadership. One duality that finds expression in the leadership activities of many people is that of whether leadership means leading or driving. Those who perceive coercion as the major leadership type most probably will see leadership as drivership. The important thing to recognize in all of the clichés involving leadership is the common purpose of influencing people to change their purposes and their behaviors. Because the change of purpose and the determination of behavior necessary to change purpose are something in advance of behavioral change, perhaps there is little use in worrying whether it is called leadership or drivership. In every instance, however, there is the desire to change something in the future of the institutional activity and of the persons who are employed to carry forward the institutional purposes.

How can leadership emerge without the incentive of status position?

Another and more troublesome type of duality is that directing and controlling actions may create dual functions of leadership, namely, that of performing as a leader and, at the same time, causing potential leadership to emerge. In this sense, there is a duality in the purpose of leadership. This unique duality, however, need not be considered one that will deter the quality of or the desirability for leadership. The task of the leader in keeping these dualities in balance is a tremendous challenge from not only the standpoint of democratic action but also that of the human characteristics of ego-involvement.

An illustration of the type of challenge that may be involved for supervisors is that of keeping self-evaluation *by* the supervisor as one of the techniques employed *in* supervision. The purposes of supervision must be constantly in mind and must be the referent point for evaluating supervisory effectiveness. This might help the supervisor to keep the dual or multiple functions of leadership in a proper balance so that the effectiveness of supervision may be satisfactory from the standpoint of the supervisor as well as of the subordinates and the institution served by that supervisor.

CONDITIONS INFLUENCING TALENT

Because the component of the process of supervision occupying major attention in this chapter is that of directing and controlling, it is well to consider some of the kinds of situations which encourage direction and control as opposed to the choice of one or more of the other processes as the means of supervision at the moment. Some of the conditions that encourage direction and control are:

1. *A personal drive for prestige gained through superiority of performance on the part of the supervisor.* This is the ego-centered type of drive and, in itself, constitutes a condition that encourages a high degree of the imposition of the supervisor's will upon the will of those supervised.

2. *The presence of a high degree of control by a legislative or executive board or a superior administrative officer.* This means that the supervisor possesses little autonomy in choosing his type of leadership. This could generate a tendency for the supervisor to feel compelled to conform to the directives or legislation of his superiors. This, in turn, would require that he impose his own controls over his subordinates and that direction and control of only one type would be dominant.

3. *Inept behavior on the part of subordinates that requires a high degree of direction and control.* This, in a sense, would be an undesirable type of control; however, the cause for it is to be found in those supervised rather than in the design

of supervisory operation. It is important for the supervisor to exercise caution, of course, in that behaviors simply different from the ideal perceived in his own mind would be labeled as inept, whereas in another referent situation that might not be true at all. The point here is that, should the supervisor deem his subordinate's behaviors unacceptable, he would be inclined to increase the degree of his own direction and control over the supervised.

4. *Emergency situations.* In the emergency situation prompt action is necessary. The nature of crisis makes it more probable that the subordinates will subdue their own desires for autonomous action and will look to their superior as the person who has the ability to provide guarantees against misfortunes that might come to them because of the emergency situation.

A precautionary suggestion is offered at this point, namely, that supervisors can create emergencies. The emergency might be created because of a delay in taking action on the part of the responsible person. This means that delay resulting from a lack of perception of the actual situation, a lack of knowledge about the situation, or selfish intents on the part of the leader or members of the staff tend to create emergency situations. Because of this possibility, each supervisor should make a self-assessment from time to time to determine the number of his activities which may constitute leadership activities of an emergency nature. Too-frequent emergencies probably are caused by the leader rather than by those being led. The antithesis to delay is prompt action. As problem or critical situations requiring planning seem to emerge on the horizon of institutional activities, prompt action on the part of the administrators and supervisors tends to avoid the emergency. If the superior officer should enjoy the sense of dependence extended toward him by his subordinates because of the emergency, he may be inclined to permit emergencies—real or imaginary—to develop. Tolerance of this type of supervisory leadership behavior ought not to be expected either of superordinates or subordinates.

Suggest other conditions which influence choice of leadership type.

It has been stated many times earlier that the school is properly characterized as a group enterprise. It is unfortunate if those in the educational organization see the school purposes as existing primarily for individual enterprises. In a group situation, the problem of direction and control and their relationships to autonomy become extremely important. The school constitutes a group enterprise which means that it is organized. The problem of autonomy for the individual in a group activity should be raised. There exists what might be called group autonomy, but it exists because the individuals in the group have been granted certain permissions as separate entities. It does not seem inconsistent to conceive of a group, particularly a small organized one, as providing a situation in which each member has an opportunity to make some contribution to the group rules and regulations as well as to its purposes. Once these have been established, the rules and regulations for the group stand as directing and controlling factors over the individuals in the group.

Individual freedom need not be lost nor authoritarianism be usurped by a group rather than by a superior officer of the organization. Freedom comes from the opportunity to exercise it individually as a member of the group in which the individual has influenced the kind of environment or situation wherein his desires can be expressed and accomplished. For the person who is unable to find his individual satisfaction in the group enterprise, there is a question as to whether he would be successful in the school group or in any other type of organized activity. The group has a real capacity to influence the environment for the individual. As is indicated in the various theoretical models, particularly those which assume group action to be social action, any factor that can control the situation is important to the individual. In a sense, teachers can, through their professional groups, become their own role-definers, or, at least, have a part in determining the definitions and expectations. There are, of course, many theoretical and practical variations to this point of view. Those involved in supervision should review their perceptions of the relationship of the individual to his group and of the relationship of group membership to the factors of direction, control, and autonomy.[2]

How are individual judgments influenced by group behavior?

RELATION TO THE CHARACTERISTICS

The component of directing and controlling must be related in all respects to the characteristics of operational balance. As indicated in Chapter 12, certain of the characteristics seem more related to one component than to others. Thus, in this discussion of directing and controlling more emphasis has been placed upon autonomy than upon the other four characteristics of the operational balance. This has been because a maximum of individual freedom is sought in this component, while at the same time guarantees are assured that it is freedom with responsibility rather than an invitation to anarchy.

The characteristic of *perceptivity* also is important. The leader must relate the dimensions both of the situation and of the role-definers to the personality needs of the individual. As indicated in Chapter 12, a sensitivity to the needs, desires, and feelings of others is the key to keeping a balance in this respect. *Relativity* is essential in directing and controlling in that a conflict of purpose must be avoided because leadership is as much involved in this component as it is in the others.

[2] A more complete discussion may be found in a statement by Karl Mannheim, "Freedom Under Planning," *Man and Society in the Age of Reconstruction* (New York: Harcourt, Brace & World, 1941), pp. 364–381.

Leadership is involved in changing the purpose of those who are to be led and relativity becomes an important characteristic of balance. *Flexibility* on the part of the supervisor implies that he is willing to look at alternate behaviors and solutions. This characteristic indicates less likelihood that the directing and controlling behaviors selected will be weighted in the direction of only one behavior and consequently both obnoxious and ineffective to and for those who are led.

As directing and controlling are closely related to the sense of freedom possessed by the teacher, *creativity* as a characteristic of balance becomes a significant factor. It means that, in selecting the directing and controlling behaviors, there be a freedom from the excessively rigid bond of rules and regulations. There should be a premium placed upon the uniqueness of behaviors and outcomes, particularly of the outcomes. There should be continuous encouragement for those better behaviors which will help to accomplish the purposes of the school as an institution and of the professional staff members in the school.

An illustration of this importance of balance may be taken from the study of team teaching reported by Gilberts.[3] He discovered that the introduction and continuance of team teaching activities were not so dependent upon the type or quality of interpersonal relationships as upon the work done by the school principal in structuring the activity of the team members. He found that it was of primary importance for the team to know (1) the purpose of the particular organizational pattern, (2) the conditions under which it would operate, and (3) the assurance that the conditions of time scheduling and instructional material support would be forthcoming. This provided a situation in which people who might be termed incompatible by nature were able to work together and willing to continue working together in the team situation. That supervisor or administrator who chooses to ignore the balance in the characteristics of the team operation may use his powers of direction and control, combined with the wrong perception of what is important to the members of a team, to develop a situation in which team teaching would fail. Such failure, then, would be that of the supervisor or administrator rather than that of the idea of team teaching or of the team itself.

Frequently in this chapter it has been stated that the component of directing and controlling is not completely independent of the other three components; in fact, they may be the dependent causes or products of directing and controlling. The component of stimulating and initiating is a particularly apt illustration at this point. When the supervisor gives direction to an idea, it may cause a clearer definition or redefinition that will stimulate further action. It also may stimulate a new line or lines of actions. In turn, this may necessitate

[3] Robert D. Gilberts, "The Interpersonal Characteristics of Teaching Teams," unpublished doctoral dissertation (Madison: University of Wisconsin, 1961).

some controls which will limit the number of activities undertaken. In this sense, the supervisor is the agent assisting the individual or group in making those decisions which will give direction and control in working with an idea. This in itself may constitute both stimulation and the desire to initiate action on the part of those who are led. Thus, it will be discovered in the next three chapters that there are references to both preceding and succeeding chapters that cover specific components of process. Chapter 17 provides a synthesis of component processes which indicates that the four components are completely interwoven and yet are susceptible to separation for purposes of analysis, discussion, and planning.

SELECTED REFERENCES

1. Bass, Bernard M., *Leadership, Psychology, and Organizational Behavior.* New York: Harper & Row, 1960. Coercive leadership, pp. 221–235; persuasive leadership, pp. 161–177; permissive leadership, pp. 236–255.
2. Bennis, Warren G., Kenneth D. Benne, and Robert Chin (eds.), *The Planning of Change.* New York: Holt, Rinehart & Winston, 1961.
3. Dalton, Gene W., Louis B. Barnes, and Abraham Zaleznik, *The Distribution of Authority in Formal Organizations.* Boston: Harvard Graduate School, 1968.
4. Eye, Glen G. and Lanore A. Netzer, *School Administrators and Instruction: A Guide to Self-Appraisal.* Boston: Allyn & Bacon, Inc., 1969.
5. Gilberts, Robert D., "The Interpersonal Characteristics of Teaching Teams." Unpublished doctoral dissertation. Madison: University of Wisconsin, 1961.
6. Kemp, C. Gratton, *Perspectives on the Group Process.* Boston: Houghton Mifflin, 1964.
7. Mannheim, Karl, "Freedom Under Planning," in *Man and Society in the Age of Reconstruction.* New York: Harcourt, Brace & World, 1941. pp. 364–481.

14

The Component of Process: Stimulating and Initiating

It was stated in the introduction to this Part that four of the six chapters would be based upon one assumption. This assumption is related to those chapters dealing with the various components of the processes of supervision. Assumption thirteen in the list presented in Chapter 3 is:

Supervision encompasses the processes of directing and controlling, stimulating and initiating, analyzing and appraising, and designing and implementing those behaviors directly and primarily related to the improvement of teaching and, consequently, to the improvement of learning.

These four components might have been stated in four separate assumptions. It was the belief of the authors, however, that the components constitute *the processes* of supervision and, as such, they should be kept as interrelated as possible, even though it is necessary to separate them for the purposes of discussion.

The discussion in Chapter 13 was focused upon directing and controlling. It was indicated that there would be cross-referencing with this chapter, which deals with the component of stimulating and initiating. There are many instances in which directing and controlling, when accomplished in a threat-free manner, constitute supportive guidance that initiates behaviors. At the same time, directing can generate an atmosphere that stimulates action. Such are the interrelationships within and among the components of the processes of supervision. As experiences generate a mounting sense of success and satisfaction, the interrelationships will increase the reinforcement of one component of process with another. In order to make the more profitable contribution to change, there must be a balance within and among these components. This is the purpose of the cross-referencing so prevalent in these four chapters.

DEFINING THE COMPONENT

Just as the previous chapter differentiated between directing and controlling, so there is an effort here to identify differences between stimulating and initiating. Some pundit simplified this differentiation by summing it up in this way: "People tend to jump up and down to demand that something be done about something that is disturbing them. Others simply jump up and down." A possible liberal interpretation for such an observation is that when people are jumping up and down, they are showing evidences of stimulation. They may be stimulated to no purpose other than the personal affective awareness which accompanies emotions or the kinesthetic experiences that may be attached to the stimulation. On the other hand, if the stimulating is to lead to some practical result, a target purpose is selected and behaviors become characteristic of those which initiate a drive toward the accomplishment of that purpose.

What are some evidences of uncontrolled stimulation?

Any standard dictionary can give a number of words which add meaning to the concepts of stimulating and initiating. *Stimulate,* in one instance or another, may mean "to arouse to action," "to goad," "to spur on," "to incite," or "to excite." The word itself does not imply that action must be inherent in order for stimulation to exist.

The dictionary words associated with *initiate* are: "to begin," "to set going," "to originate," "to commence," "to introduce," "to inaugurate," "to crystallize," or "to formulate." These words are action words. "Initiate" means that one proceeds or progresses toward a purpose or a goal. Stimulating and initiating, then, are appropriately put together as one component of the processes of supervision.

One might drive others to initiate action toward a predetermined goal and achieve a practical purpose in the process. There is, however, ample evidence to indicate that actions or behaviors are more worthwhile and profitably consummated if the individuals who are to perform them are stimulated to initiate them. Consequently, in the area of supervision, each component of process is seen as a pair of action words, such as stimulating and initiating. In the vernacular, it is possible to say that to *stimulate* is to get up a head of steam, while to *initiate* is to convert the power into the accomplishment of work. On the other hand, perhaps one might say that stimulation is more glandular than intellectual while initiation reverses the two factors. *Stimulate,* then, is somewhat general and directionless, whereas *initiate* is specific and directional.

Those who have been engaged in school work for any length of time probably can recall many occasions on which the chairman of a program committee, an administrator, or a supervisor has indicated that he wanted an inspirational speaker for the opening meeting of the school year. Analysis of what is meant by the leader when the perceived need is that of an inspirational speaker would be an interesting task. If one would indulge in a casual conversation or a carefully structured interview with such a leader, he probably would find that the idea of "inspirational" is one primarily of stimulation. Inspiration seems related to the far-off goal and the desire to achieve it. Some emotionalism, which may be associated with whatever physical activity supports the achievement of an established purpose, is expected to generate enthusiasm.

What are the emotional effects of associating in large groups?

The assumption often is made that enthusiasm makes people work hard. Apparently, too, the concept of the inspirational speaker does not require the so-called practical or technical type of presentation. The inspirational speech can be a bit on the poetic side, or at least a series of anecdotes about people who have made a marvelous contribution to something or other. Their activities and accomplishments can be idealized. There is hope that the presentation will establish a determined disposition to support the general and specific purposes of the organization and will get people to work with enthusiasm. The hope is to get staff members to look beyond the "mire at the feet" and to look instead at the horizon for goals and experiences which possess the probability of satisfaction in a future that the leader envisions. So often, when an inspirational speaker is sought, there is little expressed concern about the kind of follow-up work that might characterize such a meeting. Apparently it is assumed that, once the staff is stimulated, it can be trusted to initiate action even though the direction and purposes are ill-defined by the leader who provided the inspirational touch.

What are the functions of an idealized perception of purpose?

Initiating, then, appears to go beyond the realm of the inspirational which apparently can be included in the concepts of stimulation. Initiation goes from the idealized perception of purpose to the efforts to accomplish the practical work of the world insofar as the school constitutes the working world. It is rather unfortunate and somewhat strange that few people seem to credit the real, practical, "here's how you do it" presentation as being so clear and so directive that the accomplishment of a purpose could be extremely secure. A positive anticipation, however, might be that the presentation of either the inspirational or practical type could result in the self-stimulation of some listeners and in this way have an observable reward.

INTERRELATING THE COMPONENTS

The component of stimulating and initiating is as directly and intimately related to the definition of supervision as were the components of directing and controlling or analyzing and appraising. The definition indicated that supervision is a phase of administration and that it is primarily concerned with the achievement of appropriate expectations. The term "school administration" implies management and leadership. Achievement indicates accomplishment. Accomplishment cannot take place without action of some type that constitutes the attainment of a purpose or goal. Normally, improvement implies that goals have undergone some change. Occasionally, there might be a situation in which the goal remains the same while the procedures by which its attainment is realized may vary and that, too, constitutes change. It is safe to speculate that improvement means change or, at least, a break away from the stereotype status.

If improvement is accomplished, both stimulation and initiation constitute essential ingredients of the action. This statement is made, of course, on the basis of an assumption that the school, as a group enterprise, ought not to be carried on by an individual but rather by the highest possible percentage of professional staff members that can be involved in the process of change. Chapter 4 dealt with management of change. It might be well at this point to turn back and review the extent to which the management of change involves the process of stimulating and initiating. The discussion of process and, specifically, this component of process—stimulating and initiating—is presented as one of the links between a statement of the purpose of supervision and the products toward which supervisory efforts are directed. The whole of Part IV constitutes a link between Part I and Part V, where the products of supervision are discussed.

Within the range of the concepts of the processes of supervisory behavior, stimulating and initiating mean that directing and controlling have found the target as a result of purposive behavior. They have found the target in the sense that the directing and controlling process elicited broad-scale cooperative and participatory efforts on the part of the professional staff. The patterns of leadership that might be involved in directing and controlling were discussed in Chapter 13. At that point, it was indicated that coercive leadership might not result in coercion. In other words, the attempt to force behavior upon subordinates would not be successful unless they recognized that the superordinate possessed the power of granting or withdrawing those satisfactions for which they would yield to coercion. With the two components so intimately interrelated, there must be a frequent review of the procedures of directing and controlling in order to determine their effect upon stimulating and initiating. Such review, at the same time, may reveal the need for frequent

What are the antagonistic effects of directing-controlling and stimulating-initiating?

periods of "recharging" the stimulant that brings about the initiation of behavior toward a desirable goal. This renewal of stimulating and, hence, initiating behaviors may come about as a result of the directing and controlling types of leadership.

In the absence of stimulation, there can be little successful initiation. The process of initiating takes place in the steps of crystallizing thoughts and formulating specific plans after the individual or group has been stimulated by an idea which could constitute either a pattern of behavior or a goal. Stimulation may be a general idea but initiation gives it specificity and precipitates action. Rewarding types of stimulation may be simple humanized interactions such as expressing confidence in potentiality, affirmation, assurance, and offers to share blame. The rewards of stimulation must be found in initiation.

The consensus of the group may indicate repeatedly that a given change is needed and desired. This group state may continue for a short or long period of time. When a proposal is introduced or originated with suggestions for group discussion as a basis for designing and implementing change, initiating action is taking place. The complexity of the plan and duration of the planning will determine what will be needed for stimulating increased and continuous action. In addition, the closer the individuals are to the impact of the decisions and involvements for change, the more vigorous and longer-lasting is the stimulation.

What, then, are the implications of these pressures or stimulations? The individual awareness of a need and a desire for a given change causes a state of natural disequilibrium between a current status and a desired one. Initiation and continued stimulation for change are inherent in this state of being. If the stimulation is strong enough, there will emerge an initiating force which will precipitate action. This intrinsic persuasion operates with equal strength in positive and negative directions. Leadership from within or outside the group that initiates action from positive stimulation will cause change to take place at a more rapid pace. If the stimulation results in a negative disposition toward change, the function of leadership is to channel such stimulation into a more positive direction. As natural disequilibrium increases in intensity, there may develop an anxiety on the part of the worker because of an urge to accomplish more than he is able to do while the emotional drive toward accomplishment remains strong. If disequilibrium is created or forced by the leader who is overenergetic in pointing out deficiencies, the subordinate may develop a keen sense of frustration and find one of a number of ways of adapting to it. When the forced disequilibrium has gone beyond the point of tolerance or acceptability, it becomes a hazard to the ongoing tasks of the group organization.

Analyze your most recent desires to be involved in decision and action. What characteristics in you and in the situation stimulated you?

Some administrators and supervisors may be inclined to use

Analyze your most recent desire to oppose decision and action imposed upon you. What characteristics in you and in the situation stimulated such opposition?

those behaviors which constitute forced disequilibrium for their subordinates because this approach appears to have all the effectiveness of autocratic controls over others. The advantage is rapidly lost, however, if the subordinate finds ways of striking back at the leadership of his superior or if he evades performance of the required tasks. The subordinate may also seek other employment or even attempt to destroy the organization. In any case, the behavior sought by the administrator or supervisor should not be destructive of the talents of people. The aim of administration and supervision should be the creativity that can be stimulated and preserved on the part of those subordinates who can respond to this type of leadership.

The discussion of the component *analyzing and appraising* in Chapter 15 relates to this problem of natural and forced disequilibrium. If effective leadership has taken place in analyzing the quality of the instructional program and in making valid judgments on the basis of the information developed in the analysis, the teachers will be confronted constantly with evidence of their acceptable or unacceptable performance. The supervisor who can give technical direction to analyzing and appraising and who makes the results of this process known to all of the professional staff through effective communication media will find that he has developed a way of stimulating and initiating action toward the improvement of an unsatisfactory situation or the maintenance of highly satisfactory conditions. When an individual or small group has an awareness of a need for a given change that is not as yet recognized by the majority, stimulation will have to be forced by some means. This may be called disequilibrium but, by whatever name, it must lead to a change in the purposes and procedures of the instructional program. This does not necessarily mean the creation of negative attitudes in the participants in the group operation.

TYPES OF PERSUASION

In forced or unnatural disequilibrium, an extrinsic persuader provides the stimulation that will bring about change. As long as the persuading agent is of an extrinsic origin, it will have to be repeated frequently to have a continuing effect. The extrinsic persuader, however, may be used to stimulate an awareness of a need for change and, in the process of problem identification, become an intrinsic persuader. This perhaps could constitute sufficient justification for the use of the forced disequilibrium and extrinsic persuaders. The position to be observed, however, is that such procedures are not pushed to the point where they no longer stimulate but rather exist as a barrier to free and creative action.

Leadership that stimulates and initiates action for change may come from designated leaders or from peer members of the staff. The encouragement of emerging leadership acts as a continuous stimulation and gives the individual or groups courage to initiate action for change. The question arises "How is leadership encouraged to emerge?" The underlying assumption here is that leadership is a function—it is not a given person, title, or position. This function should be performed in varying degrees along the hierarchy of staff positions. Before leaders can emerge and serve effectively, the perceptions of leadership functions held by the staff must approach congruency. A declaration of the functions of leadership must be supported by actions which give assurance that the administration has integrity in this policy. These evidences of assurance must be reinforced continually. A statement of policy distributed to the staff becomes of little worth if there is one instance of reprisal for any staff member who tries to function as a leader within the limits of the stated policy.

The assumption that leadership is a function that may be exercised by any member of the staff does not imply complete teacher autonomy or lack of designated leadership positions (see Chapters 9–11). The limits and types of leadership functions need to be defined. The relationships of the various leadership roles among members of an action group are seen in the case of a teacher acting as chairman of a committee, a supervisor, and a curriculum coordinator working in a common project. Coordination of these functions under operational policies does not negate the concept of emerging leadership but rather defines the limit of the operation.

In order to add meaning to the type of emerging leadership situations as indicated above, some illustrations are cited (see reference 1). In the case of a dependence upon natural disequilibrium, there is the implication that in initiating change the supervisor would do well to locate the areas where the staff has been wanting change. These identified change areas can be placed in some order of priorities. If committees are formed, membership should include those people who are most directly affected by the decisions. Such assignment practice will increase the probability of continuous stimulation of individual effort. If workshops are used, the planning should be in the hands of those most directly concerned with their outcomes. When a member of a group is stimulated to a high degree of action in the initiated activity and the direction is positive, the role of the supervisor becomes more that of a consultant and less a director of the action.

It is the responsibility of the supervisor to review the policies which define the limits of operation. The supervisor will also facilitate actions by providing needed facilities and materials that can be made available and by working as a liaison between the group and the central office. The purpose of this liaison is not only for communication purposes but also for encouragement of further activities of the group by supporting requests for additional funds, special assignments, outside consultants, and other types of assistance. As a consultant, the supervisor can assist the members in operating as a group as well as in drawing out the creativity of individual members. As a liaison between the working committee group and other members of the faculty, the supervisor's communication or progress reports may serve to stimulate other individuals and groups to action. All of these activities are techniques in the processes of supervision. When an individual or a group is stimulated to the degree that action is being initiated in either a positive or negative direction, the function of supervision is the same—in the latter instance, with the additional responsibility of trying to stimulate further action which will convert the negative to the positive.

If leaders emerge in a group enterprise, is that evidence that the relationships are either democratic or autocratic?

It appears, then, that a corollary to the development of emerging leadership is that the administrator and supervisor should develop techniques for identifying staff desires for improvement and that these desires should be regarded as more promising than external or artificial urges for change created by the supervisor. The supervisor can find his satisfaction in accomplishing the purposes of supervision rather than in exercising his will over the will of others. Supervisors often are overly concerned with the fact that one or more of the members of the staff fail to respond to their leadership efforts. There is some feeling that leadership efforts in the field of administration and supervision must achieve 100 percent response in order to be considered successful. Administrators and supervisors ought not to degrade themselves in this way. It is more important to catch the fancy and support of one person who might push ahead of where he would have been had the leadership and assistance not been available to him. Some have placed proper confidence in the "brush fire" tactic in supervision. This means that if you can set in motion changes that result in improvement in one particular spot in the instructional program, it will be seen, recognized, and emulated by other members of the staff. In this way of bringing about change, there is not the overwhelming satisfaction of seeing one recreate the world in a carefully selected image. It is better to be practical and to realize that some progress is good progress. It is not necessary to stimulate all members of the staff in *equal* amounts and in the *same* direction at any particular time.

A fascinating possibility is that the supervisor himself might become the "brush fire." If he is unable to catch the fancy of members of the staff who might join in his particular choice of the direction of improvement, he should proceed with projects of his own selection, as some are certain to be available. If, as the leader in the group situation, he proceeds with worthwhile studies—preferably the research type of attack—these will get attention. Eventually some colleagues, or hopefully all, will respond in varying degrees to the fact that here is one person working to create better instructional opportunities for the pupils in the classrooms. A wise technique of supervision, then, in this component of process is that of giving support to the ambitions and the energies of one or more of the staff members as interests in improvement emerge. This, essentially, is a different way of saying that disequilibrium of the intrinsic type can be encouraged by becoming interested, being supportive of the intent, offering suggestions that might constitute directions, keeping control at a minimum, and providing facilities that will keep the individual "fired up" with a desire to improve.

Initiation well may be mostly facilitation. Supervisors may profit by contemplating this possibility in choosing their supervisory behaviors. While this influence is interesting rather than precise, it suggests that the supervisor needs to be finding not the directions in which he wants to push his teachers but rather the directions in which they want to go and the kinds of facilitations which he has the capacity to provide. Basic to the "brush fire" technique is confidence in the fact that the individual influences the group and, conversely, that a group within the larger organization brings to bear on individuals a force for change that will conform to the group's perceptions.

How can the supervisor relate business management to the instructional program?

IMPACT OF CONTACT

A suggestion in the same spirit is that each supervisor might do well to develop in himself the art of leaving teachers alone. This is difficult for a person who has accepted a position that possesses known status and both real and imaginary prestige. The urge is to be continuously making an imprint upon the detailed activities of the school and upon the behaviors exhibited by members of the teaching staff. The attendant increased interruptions in a classroom may detract from the help that an administrator or a supervisor can contribute to the teacher. The interruptions referred to here are not the kind that would constitute an effort on the part of the leader to influence the behaviors of the subordinate directly. In this case of help or hindrance, the interruption takes place for the teacher regardless of its purpose. Frequent interruptions of this type can have an effect just the opposite of that desired from supervision, namely, the stimulation of change resulting in improvement.

How is the reduction of classroom interruptions a positive supervisory act?

One of the devices mentioned earlier used by supervisors is that of requiring all members of the faculty to "elect" assignment to a problem or a committee and thereby be forced into some sort of group action or assignment which continues through the entire school year. It seems a gross waste of time for teachers to withdraw their efforts from an appropriate improvement activity of their own choice and to divert these efforts to the assistance of a group working on a problem that has never become real or significant to them. Recently, a teacher was complaining that the supervisor called frequent

What is the teacher's responsibility in informing the supervisor about self-improvement efforts?

supervisory meetings to work upon certain problems selected by the supervisor. His comment was that it seemed such a waste of time to leave the extremely interesting things that he was developing in his science laboratory in order to join a group of colleagues in the general discussion of a problem that had never come to his attention as a problem. A teacher of this type can be more productive with respect to change if the supervisor remains sensitive to the teacher's self-motivated urges to pursue his own improvement program. Ideally, a supervisor should be delighted if all members of the teaching staff were so involved in the solution of problems of their own choice that they express reluctance to join in solving an artificially selected problem in order to experience a group effort.

Important stimulating and initiating behaviors can be characterized by supervisory action that gives recognition to and assures the consolidation of those improvements that have been made. It matters little at this point whether the gains were made on the basis of individual effort or of group action. It is particularly important in group effort that the leader have the skill to identify the essence of the consensus or actions that develop and to use them in summarizing the action so that common consent and understanding can be achieved. Such summary can constitute the directions to the next needed actions. This is the task of consolidating the gains that have been made. Substantial work done in the planning process can be preserved through the recording of the decisions made or plans developed. The time lapse should be limited between group sessions so that there will be a minimum loss of effort in following through on decisions or in returning to the solutions of the unsolved problems. The reporting function, then, both for individual and group achievement, is extremely important. This, in itself, may be the "brush fire" that will cause a substantial part of the staff to be stimulated to positive and worthwhile action.

EMPHASIZING PERCEPTIVITY AND CREATIVITY

One of the inexcusable situations that sometimes develops is that of a competitiveness among several members of the central office staff. This competitiveness develops in efforts to extend the purpose of the individual's office and its influence to various points in the instructional program. If the superintendent fails to achieve a balance between these influences, the teacher is put in the middle and that could result in the loss of a desire to initiate action of any kind. The members of the central office staff must be willing to exchange ideas about their purposes and their operational procedures in order that the different levels in the hierarchy will not create confusion for the subordinates at all levels.

The first chapter in this Part included a discussion of the

characteristics of operational balance. It was indicated that there are five characteristics in this balance—perceptivity, autonomy, relativity, flexibility, and creativity (see Chapter 12). It was also indicated that one or more of these characteristics might be more closely related to some components than to others. Following this declaration, the characteristic of autonomy was stressed in the discussion of the component of directing and controlling. In this discussion of the component of stimulating and initiating, the stress is placed upon the characteristics of perceptivity and creativity. These have been described in Chapter 12 and need not be repeated here insofar as the nature of the concept is concerned.

The above discussion of the various kinds of behaviors involved in the supervisory process of stimulating and initiating makes it sufficiently clear that the supervisor must have a sharp perception of the kinds of pressures playing upon the members of the staff that he would influence in his supervisory efforts. It is also important that he perceive the kinds of satisfactions that characterize the members of the staff. These will give the cues to the kinds of behavioral influences that will constitute stimulation and lead to the initiation of improvement activities.

Perceptivity is essential in the interpersonal relationships not only of members of the teaching staff who are peers but also in the relationships between superordinates and subordinates. There are many instances recorded in which the supervisor has failed to recognize when assistance is no longer assisting (see reference 5). In other words, when help is given to a teacher, it is important that the offering of help stop when the teacher has had all of the assistance needed and desired. Even though the level of performance is not satisfactory, the supervisor should perceive those reactions of the teacher which indicate that further improvement will not result from supervisory effort.

The suggestion that the supervisor should know when to leave teachers alone is related directly to the desire for stimulating teachers to behave creatively. One cannot require a person to be creative. He is creative because he desires to be and because he has the level of intellectual ability and technical skills which will support these desires (see references 3 and 4). The "brush fire" concept is also closely related to creativity. When a person has caused himself to seek improvement and is willing to apply both his ability and his efforts to the purpose of achieving improvement, the promise of creativity should not be thwarted by interruptions from those who systematically go about acting toward subordinates as superordinates. It means, then, that the supervisor must perceive all of the nuances of human behavior that will give him the cues to emerging creativity. It is less important to seek the stimulation of emerging leadership in a group than to encourage creativity even when it must be achieved as a lonely and individual type of activity. The perceptive and creative supervisor is the person who can adapt and select his own behaviors so that the purposes of supervision are achieved without causing others to lose the opportunities for achieving satisfactions equal to those found in the behaviors of supervision.

FAVORABLE CONDITIONS

There are conditions in the school operation that seem to support or thwart the efforts of the supervisor to perform the task of his office in such a way that the teachers will be stimulated and susceptible to initiating the procedures of change. Those conditions which support him are:

1. *The consistency of expectations that the teachers place upon those who are in administrative and supervisory positions must be supported by consistency of behavior by those holding such positions.* There is security in the sense of consistency. Teachers like the assurance of knowing the general probability of the superior officers' behaviors in events which have not yet occurred. Uncertainty breeds fear, and fear is not supportive to creative work of any type except that of personal survival. It is not probable that the fear of or confidence in survival in a school system is a component of superior instructional performance. Thus, the condition of consistency in the relationship between the superordinate and the subordinate is a significant condition for supporting stimulation and initiation.

2. *There must be a follow-up by superiors on group decisions which involve not only peers but also subordinates.* This means that if the supervisor chooses to submit a certain issue to the staff for decision, he must accept the consequences of its decision. The consequences might be that the group would make decisions not particularly palatable to the supervisor. If the outcomes of the decision reveal visible errors, correction must be treated as an experimental result. If the supervisor decides to ignore those unpalatable decisions, he will cause the individual members of the group to lose confidence in the group process. On the other hand, it can be a sobering experience for many teachers to have a supervisor who considers the action of the faculty as a command for implementation. If the supervisors submit major decisions to the faculty, they, at the same time, commit themselves to being the executive officers for the faculty in carrying out the intent and details of the decision. If the members of the faculty become careless in accepting the responsibility of this prerogative of participation in decision-making, it comes as a shock to them to find the actions implemented whether or not the decision was wise. The net effect is that this consistency on the part of the supervisor causes the individual members of the faculty to approach the decision-making procedure with profound respect. There is seldom an indication of

simply voting on an issue to have it settled; rather, voting on an issue has the purpose of accomplishing what the members of the faculty believe to be wise.

3. *A good system of recording and reporting decision is essential to the support of stimulation and initiation.* Nothing is more discouraging than finding that decisions are unclear and perhaps even forgotten in the future because good minutes of meetings were not kept. It is not enough simply to record the decisions. They must be distributed to all members of the faculty and be readily accessible in a central office should they be needed.

4. *Stimulation and initiation is supported when the leader begins the analysis of a problem situation or program possibilities from the perceptions of purpose of those who must carry out the details of decision.* This means that the superior officer must not predetermine an outcome and impose it on the group while expecting that group to apply its resourcefulness to the development of a plan to accomplish the purpose.

5. *There is need for periods of consolidation of gains for the individual as well as for the group.* The leader who feels that he must be continuously stimulating the group to move and move again may find that he is overstimulating the members of the staff until finally no stimulation takes place at all. When major effort has been made to design a change and the change has been implemented, it is not unreasonable to expect that the new procedures or processes might persist for a reasonable period of time. If the changes are complicated, they deserve a rather long period of time for trial. It is well not to divert interest quickly from one item to another by assuming that, as soon as one plan is instituted, the supervisor should turn to the development of another. Sometimes teachers become harried with the multitude of tasks involved in carrying on the existing program, in initiating new elements, and in sharing with colleagues the problem of discovering new ways for further introductions of change. Periods of quiet are not periods of loss. Periods of reflection in the security of a stable situation may provide the best foundation for those changes which are to be made next. This is not, of course, an invitation simply to "leave well enough alone" and use this as a means of avoiding the necessity for designing and implementing other changes.

6. *There are some individuals who find it difficult or nearly impossible to work effectively in group activities.* The supervisor needs to be sufficiently perceptive to identify these people and to provide opportunities for them to work under the conditions in which they can be the most creative. If an individually effective person is ill at ease in a group situation, why try to change him into a good group worker? This accommodation of an individual can be maintained provided his tasks are not preempted by a group. The contributions of the teaching staff are to such a large extent individualized

that there is no reason why the supervisor cannot make adaptations to the needs of most individual teachers.

7. *The established penalty and reward systems, even though constituting an extrinsic type of stimulation, do affect the conditions under which stimulation and initiation take place.* Insofar as the penalty and reward systems affect the attitudes of the workers, the ability of the individual to work at peak capacity is affected. Such aspects of the systems as salary involve the supporting public in the policy decisions. There are many program and facility considerations which do not involve the supporting public. The supervisor concerned with the component of stimulating and initiating is unable to isolate himself from all responsibility in the sanction systems as developed within the organization.

8. *There must be an agreed-upon manner and a periodic time set for what might be called an instructional audit.* There is no reason for any efficient teacher to shrink from the opportunity or even the necessity of having his outcomes evaluated. Every teacher needs the guarantee that all aspects of the teaching–learning situation and environment must be involved in the audit. The expectations placed upon the teacher must be realistic, not only with respect to his own capabilities but also with respect to the capabilities of the pupils and the conditions under which their learning is to take place. Those teachers who shun the responsibility of submitting to such an audit must be responsible for providing the kinds of evidence that the public and the pupils should have in being assured that the teaching performance is acceptable.

The polar opposite of the conditions described above are also those conditions which tend to thwart the realization of the component of stimulating and initiating. These authors believe that, when teachers and supervisors hold false assumptions, the first step to stimulating and initiating experiences is that of eliminating the false assumptions that constitute the thwarting probabilities. Some false assumptions with related brief discussions follow.

False Assumption 1. Others are responsible for my lack of opportunity to improve. It is reported that the treatment of certain types of mental illness involves getting the patient to see that the problem is within himself rather than with others. It is not implied here that educators are mentally ill. They must recognize, however, that the efforts to stimulate and initiate change lie within themselves rather than within the responsibilities of others. How often have teachers declared how well they would teach were it not for the lack of foresight and understanding on the part of the superior officers! Again, how often have administrators and supervisors indicated the kinds of leadership that they might perform if only they had teachers with better insight about the educational needs of the community! It is difficult to identify the responsibility for lack of personal stimulation and initiation. It requires a keen capacity for introspection if the false assumptions are to be identified and eliminated individual by individual. The suggestion here is that each person at any level in the operation of the school might from time to time assess the excuses that he is using for his lack of energy and effort directed toward improvement.

False Assumption 2. Self-improvement can be purchased in neat packages. There seems to be substantial belief on the part of professional workers that much stimulation and initiation of change follow professionalization. An unfortunate consequence of this belief is that individuals purchase membership in one or several professional organizations and expect that "joining" to constitute evidence that they are stimulated and are initiating change. The payment of dues to a professional society may constitute evidence of the professional loyalty and outlook of the individual. In itself, however, it can never be described as improvement. The professional organizations provide some assistance to the teachers but they should not pretend to be the major cause of stimulating and initiating activities that must be provided at the local level by the teachers themselves and by their administrators and supervisors.

False Assumption 3. We can identify and reward superior students but we must not identify and reward superior teachers. Boasts are made of the skills possessed in recognizing and accommodating the individual differences of pupils, but at the same time there is determined support of the single salary schedule for teachers. If merit salary policy is a naughty phrase, it should be sent to Semantica for some new words, but get on with the business nevertheless. It appears appropriate to socialize the support of the schools but, according to majority professional opinion, inappropriate to socialize the talents of teachers.

False Assumption 4. In-service development activities must be scheduled within the working day as defined in the employment contract. Teachers often protest the unpleasant fact that unskilled laborers earn as much money as many members of their profession. However, while insisting that they are members of a profession, many teachers want both the working conditions of the unskilled worker and the esteem and pay of the professional. A 50-hour voluntary work week for teachers will do more to professionalize the members of the "vocation of teaching" than negotiated, unlimited salary potential.

False Assumption 5. Self-improvement is directly related to financial support. A well-stocked library cannot replace a knowledgeable teacher; a high north light exposure in the room cannot endow the art teacher with creativity; a gold-leafed proscenium arch cannot conceal the teacher's lack of understanding of the great qualities in dramatic expression; and a plush office cannot undo the damage wrought by an insensitive autocrat in the administrator's chair. Financial support is a wonderful convenience, but it has limited therapeutic value in the area of self-improvement.

False Assumption 6. Uniqueness is the benchmark of progress in methodology, curriculum, and organizational patterns. There seems to be greater satisfaction potential in planning the new than in evaluating the old. People would rather initiate things than eliminate them. Teachers and supervisors cling to that which represents personal professional creativity even though its usefulness is long past. The easy assumption is that the spotlight always shines on the individual rather than the group in an organized enterprise. Uniqueness can be the benchmark of progress only if it can survive the scrutiny of valid and thorough evaluation.

Stimulating and initiating is the real test of effectiveness of directing and controlling. The authors intended to make it very clear in Chapters 13 and 14 that these components are highly interrelated. Directing and controlling may provide some types of satisfaction for those in the superior positions but there is little hope that this process alone will go far in changing the instructional program when many teachers are involved. Directing and controlling must include those kinds of supervisory behaviors that will help the teachers to become *stimulated* to *initiate* actions that will result in an improvement of the instructional program.

The discussion in the next chapter deals with the component of analyzing and appraising. A number of specifics are referenced to this chapter on stimulating and initiating. This chapter closes with the major premise that an honest look at the quality of the output on the instructional program always will constitute the best stimulation to the initiation of those changes which provide the maximum learning opportunity for pupils.

SELECTED REFERENCES

1. Association for Supervision and Curriculum Development, Yearbook, *Leadership for Improving Instruction*. Washington, D.C.: National Education Association, 1960. Chap. III, pp. 68–87. See bibliography on perceptivity, pp. 85–87.
2. Association for Supervision and Curriculum Development, Yearbook, "The Roles of Supervisors and Administrators," in *Individualizing Instruction*. Washington, D.C.: National Education Association, 1964. Chap. VI, pp. 125–158.
3. Association for Supervision and Curriculum Development, Yearbook, *New Insights and the Curriculum*. Washington, D.C.: National Education Association, 1963.
4. Bass, Bernard M., *Leadership, Psychology, and Organizational Behavior*. New York: Harper & Row, 1960. Emerging leadership, pp. 39–59, 139–157, and 194–205; esteem and leadership, pp. 277–300.

5. Bennis, Warren G., Kenneth D. Benne, and Robert Chin (eds.), *The Planning of Change*. New York: Holt, Rinehart & Winston, 1961. Emulation and identification, pp. 154–156, 511–516, and 602–605.
6. Gruber, Howard E., Glenn Terrell, and Michael Wertheimer (eds.), *Contemporary Approaches to Creative Thinking*. New York: Atherton, 1963.
7. Litwin, George H. and Robert A. Stringer, Jr., *Motivation and Organizational Climate*. Boston: Harvard University Press, 1968.
8. Miel, Alice (ed.), *Creativity in Teaching: Invitations and Instances*. San Francisco: Wadsworth, 1961. See bibliography on creativity in the appendix.

15

The Component of Process: Analyzing and Appraising

The component of the process of supervision—analyzing and appraising—is the major focus and emphasis in this chapter. In the total list of assumptions, it is related to assumption thirteen, which indicates that the processes of supervision are to be found in a group of four components of activities. Each of these is composed of two aspects. Consequently, each of the last two chapters dealt with one of these components. Chapter 13 involved the discussion of directing and controlling, while Chapter 14 dealt with stimulating and initiating. This and the following chapter deal with the remaining components.

DEFINING THE COMPONENT

The component *analyzing and appraising* is evidence of the fact that each single process of supervision as discussed in this book has two aspects. These two aspects are seen as complementary with respect to the nature of the behaviors involved on the part of the practicing administrators and supervisors. As in the discussion of other components, the dictionary definitions of the words involved offer substantial help in understanding the concepts of supervision being described.

Analyzing, and terms such as "separating," "breaking into parts in order to know about their nature," "proportions," "functions," "relationships," "resolving into constituent parts," "determining essential features," and "examining critically," give meaning to a constellation of actions that constitute the concept introduced as one of the important aspects of this particular component of the processes of supervision. On the other hand, the word *appraising* suggests expressions like "deciding the value of," or "estimating or judging the quality or worth." The complementarity of these two words as a single process of supervision is found in the fact that, when judging an instructional program in a school, significant parts of the teaching–learning operation must be identified and some judgments about the worth of such parts must be made. It is true, of course, that the judgments are made with respect to the individual parts, but finally an overall judgment is made about the total educational program.

MAKING JUDGMENTS

The working definition of supervision commits the tasks of supervision to the total array of instructional expectations. Since analyzing means separating into parts, it must be serviceable to the latter activity of appraising. Judging must be directed to those selected parts which are rewarding for the tasks of appraising. A book devoted to supervision, whether by these authors or any others, is divided into chapters according to the authors' desires for discussing the total array of responsibilities in a supervisory program. The very selection of chapter titles is evidence of an attempt to separate supervision into its constituent parts. The organization of a book by chapters usually is determined by the major objectives and perceptions of supervision as held by the person making the analysis. The fact that the presentation is made in parts does not presume that these parts are not to be integrated in the mind and in the behaviors of the student or of the practitioner.

The supervisor approaching the tasks of supervision with respect to the component of process categorized as analyzing and appraising needs to spend much time in planning his own attack on behavior selection. The selection of major process categories constitutes one of the important activities involved in developing the custom-built program of supervision. The categories of process have the power of predetermining the behaviors which will be consistent with the process category. Categories are not selected at random or by sheer chance. The selection of categories must be related to the intent and purpose of the total commitment. If this is not done, the selection of the parts, as dictated by the selection of the categories, will not be helpful later in making those judgments about the total operation of the program or about the purpose and intent of each component.

Decisions and judgments are made in each step of the process of supervision. They are made in selecting behaviors that are categorized as directing and controlling, or as stimulating and initiating. Even though the intent of those two components is not as specifically related to the assessment of purpose achievement as the component of process discussed in this chapter, they do nevertheless involve evaluative procedures at almost every stage of operation. The intent of this third component of process, however, is that of organizing abilities for the assessment of the instructional program in all of its aspects as the major purpose or intent of supervisory behavior.

The days of men are filled with the making of judgments. Judgments are made about people, things, situations, and ideas, hopes, and purposes. Because so much of man's time is devoted to evaluation, it is appropriate that careful thought be given to the quality of the judgments that are made. Those administrators and supervisors who are so careless in their judgment that they operate at about the level of a person who rises in the morning and comments, "It is the coldest morning of the year," will find that such levels of judgment are not serviceable to the duties involved in the supervisory program. In instances such as the cold morning remark, a referent point is necessary if a sound judgment is to be made. It is better to let the reporter on the radio or television make the judgment about the coldness or warmness of a morning, because in all probability he has taken the trouble to utilize the previous records of weather that are a matter of established knowledge.

Judgments made without a referent point seldom are valid. The level of supervisory judgment comparable to this might be the remarks made by administrators of some decades ago when they would say, "Let me have a few minutes in the teacher's classroom and I will tell you how good a teacher I have observed. All I need to do is to assess the atmosphere of the classroom." Many people have interviewed supervisors who have made such judgments in an effort to determine what criteria or referent points were used. It is almost impossible to analyze judgments made in this manner. Consequently, it is concluded that such judgments are not particularly serviceable to the improvement of the instructional program in the schools and that supervisory service is helped little by such faulty methodology.

Reliance upon clichés, prejudices, and superstitions is wholly unsuitable to the process of analyzing and appraising the procedures and outcomes of the instructional program. Judgments at this level are about as reliable as assuming that redheads are fiery-tempered people, that fat persons are good-natured, that an Englishman is of slow humor, that an Irishman is always looking for a fight, or that a Frenchman is extremely emotional. These are associations that have been made in a variety of ways and some people are inclined to substitute such clichés for responsible judgment. Anyone with a modicum of intellectual discrimination knows that such judgments possess little validity.

Above the level of clichés, there builds up from time to time a body of concepts about words that influence the judgment of people. The terms "conservative," "liberal," "progressive," and "modern" seem to carry a constellation of meanings that often are used in categorizing information about a particular observable activity or aspect of the instructional program. These meanings or concepts may or may not be serviceable for the tasks of evaluation. The extent to which the appraising has taken place in the selection of the categories for analysis determines the extent to which a self-proving type of thinking has occurred. Circular thinking does not support evaluation that offers direction for the future, a reliable evaluation of what occurred in the past, or useful observations about the present.

How does one distinguish between facts, notions, hunches, opinions, and prejudices?

There is too much impatience with the laborious task of collecting evidence or information. In other words, people want to look and judge rather than to go through the process of deciding on the procedures of evaluation that would give their judgments a high degree of validity. A part of the impatience may be due to the lack of sufficient help or facilities to collect evidence or to one's own ability to know how to go about the collection, organization, and presentation of data. This impatience often causes individual administrators and supervisors to seek other ways of accomplishing the evaluational tasks of supervision.

When has sufficient information been collected to support a judgment?

The belief often is expressed that one cannot collect evidence without being a master of the intricacies of statistics. A substantial knowledge of statistics is helpful; on the other hand, the inclination to feel that only a high level of understanding and sophistication in statistics is appropriate leads some to believe that they must operate at that level or not at all. Such false reasoning costs the profession much excellent work that could be done by the person who has a somewhat unsophisticated knowledge of statistical procedures. Each person must determine the level at which he can work with confidence and effectiveness. It seems axiomatic, however, that one of the in-service development responsibilities of the supervisor is that of raising his own level of competence in those statistical procedures which can help in accomplishing the inescapable responsibilities of the assigned work.

It is time that the prejudiced notions about statistical techniques be eliminated both on the part of the amateur in the field and by those who possess a high level of esoteric knowledge. Both extremes perform a disservice to the responsibilities of supervision. It is not an *either-or* proposition. There needs to be a much closer relationship between the sophisticates and the non-sophisticates. The practitioner in the local school system and the high-level scholar in the university can be mutually helpful. Such cooperation and coordination can bring together two essentials to good analyzing and appraising, namely, those practitioners who view the task from the operational necessities and the university representatives who approach the tasks from highly theoretical and statistical accurateness. One of the unfortunate outcomes of this apparent prejudice about the handling of data by statistical devices is that some people are willing to enter into discussions with an utter disregard for facts at all. Those who say facetiously "It is unfair to introduce facts when an argument is in progress," perhaps have made a serious and pertinent observation about general carelessness in appraising an individual's responsibility for an exchange of information and opinion when a problem situation is present. Above all, those persons who want to consider themselves as competent to operate at the professional level must not degrade their own professionalization by wanting to settle important issues at the "bull session" level rather than to apply technical devices to the determination of the most rewarding solution to problem situations.

Reference was made in the previous chapters to the fact that improvement in the instructional program involved changes of many varieties. The detailed discussion of the management of changes as presented in Chapter 4 indicates the respect with which these authors hold the responsibilities for stimulating and directing change in the instructional program of a school. There may seem to be inconsistencies between statements in the earlier chapters and statements of the early pages of this chapter in which it was indicated that people tend to avoid the responsibility for detailed analyses. This is not so much an inconsistency on the part of the presentation as it is an unhappy situation in the operation of the school systems and, specifically, in the fulfillment of the supervisory responsibilities. The unhappy fact stands that recognition of the need for stimulating and implementing changes in the instructional program has outrun the development of those statistical devices which make it possible to measure the amount of change that takes place. At the present time there is but slight evidence that the unsophisticated practitioner in the field of supervision has made contact with the highly sophisticated professor of measurement and statistics of the university campuses. More interchange is to be encouraged and this interchange must be considered the responsibility of both the field practitioners and the professors.

Define hypothesis, generalization, and conclusion.

The publication *Problems in Measuring Change* presents the formal papers from a 1962 conference sponsored by the Committee on Personality Development in Youth of the Social Science Research Council.[1] This book provides a record of the exchanges of information, the sharing of problems, the declaration of the limits of acceptance of current techniques, and the directions for future research, writing, and other scholarly efforts which may resolve some of the problems presented in the conference. It is by no means a book that will find popular acceptance by practitioners who basically are non-sophisticates in the area of measurement and statistics. It should be extremely helpful, however, for the practitioner to expose him-

[1] Chester W. Harris (ed.), *Problems in Measuring Change* (Madison: University of Wisconsin Press, 1963).

self at least to Chapter 1, "Some Persisting Dilemmas in the Measurement of Change." [2] While Bereiter made the presentation in the language of his colleagues at the sophisticated and scholarly level of the persons attending the conference, his presentation can be studied and appreciated by those who will never be able to share with him or his colleagues in the resolution of the dilemmas presented. At the very least, practitioners should become aware of the three major dilemmas presented by Bereiter in order that they will not, in their operational responsibilities, assume that such deficiencies or limitations do not exist.

Ignorance of the inability to master the instrumentation for measurement and the processing of data at the appropriate level is no excuse for going ahead blithely making decisions on the basis of the very thing that the scholars in the field declare to be unsound. The non-sophisticated practitioner must be held responsible for knowing his own limitations. He cannot discover those limitations by intuition. They must be studied and appraised in a coldly calculating manner if the individual stays within the reasonable bounds of basing his judgments upon data which can be available in the local school system. Those who are operating at the practitioner's level must work within the limits of the devices now known until the scholars in the field can present the next steps which sometime may become readily and easily available to the practitioner. Those who are unable to operate at the highest level of knowledge must, in addition to knowing the limitations of their own judgment-making, look hopefully and encouragingly to those scholars. The solution to the problem either at the field or the university level will never be achieved by making unkind statements about the opposite pole of what must be and continue to be a common responsibility. There is no time, within the professional array of obligations, to indulge in the luxury of being critical of those who have not yet mastered technical complication, as though such criticism would make the critic feel superior and develop the criticized into a contributor of solutions to the problem. The reliance upon a judgment which studiously avoids the techniques by which organized information can support a valid judgment is a major handicap to the practitioner in the field of supervision.

Who should be responsible for bringing together the practitioner and the specialist?

UNREWARDING STEREOTYPES

The purpose of this book is to offer assistance to those who have or want responsibilities in the field of supervision. One type of help is that of eliminating the blind spots, the ill-conceived concepts, and the outright errors of operation that can be identified. A more positive element is that of discontinuing

[2] Carl Bereiter, "Some Persisting Dilemmas in the Measurement of Change," in *Ibid.*, pp. 3–20.

or tempering ill-favored procedures as a first step in selecting new and wiser ones. One type of shortcoming is what might be called "the man of action" concept. This has developed in executive behavior at all levels as well as in all fields of endeavor. This may have grown out of the great respect for, and even worship of, efficiency in the early decades of this century. A part of this stereotype indicates that efficiency is related to observable vigor. Consequently, a person who has accepted this stereotype as the basis of selecting his own behaviors may be inclined to dash here and there in order that the kinesthetic awareness results in reassurance that he is being effective. Needless to say, the stereotype rather than the realities support this assumption. There are times when physical vigor has nothing whatever to do either with the quality of the operational procedures or with the validity of the judgments involved in those procedures.

What is meant by "stereotype"?

There has been some inclination to overrate experience as the origin of consistency in administrative and supervisory behavior. The assumption involved here is that experience causes persons to make the same judgments in identical or highly similar situations. Experience is supposed to assume that, when confronted with a situation with recognizable elements from a past experience, judgments will follow the previously established pattern. This position has observational support of some merit but it does not constitute a firm basis for the quality of consistency in judgment or values that practitioners often presume. The overlooked factor in experience-based judgment is that, while situations and persons appear to be similar to those encountered previously, there may be many subtle as well as gross variations that escape note and, thereby, are not used in tempering that judgment.

How would one identify and evaluate information secured from interviews if intellectual vigor were the major criterion?

An attendant aspect of the man-of-action stereotype is that strength is accompanied by a high level of positiveness and that weakness is evidenced by indecisiveness. This places a severe strain on those who wisely choose to withhold judgment when additional information is needed. It is not the fault of the supervisor who delays the finalizing of judgment, if those who created the situation requiring the judgment are demanding an immediate answer. Both the supervisor and the supervised need to be aware of the fact that decisions play an important function in the ongoing operation of the school as well as in the interrelationships of the two. Both the supervisor and the supervised might well study together how each and both can recognize the point in time when decisions must be made. It is recognized here that this discussion eliminates the decisions required in emergency situations. We are dealing here with the decision situation in which time is available for gathering, organizing, and evaluating information to support the judgment-making process.

The lowest level of group decision-making is characterized by those who are inclined to make and support their judgments on the basis of the recruitment of others to support a particular point of view. The possible future contests between teacher organizations and administrative officers of a school system will not lead to occasions wherein judgments must be a matter of political action or headcounting as a means of determining the validity of judgments and decisions. It is well to recall the statement of Galileo, who said, "The truth is not determined by the number of people who proclaim it." Thus, it seems wise to eliminate the operation by an ill-advised concept, the stereotype, or the man-of-action type of thinking as a type of supervisory behavior. Tempting judgmental expediencies should be shunted aside in favor of greater deliberateness on the part of both the supervisor and the supervised in order that more accurate judgments can be made. Accurate judgments are most probable when all parties to a decision have a high respect for facts and a high level of ability to acquire, organize, and interpret those facts.

There is yet another major precaution that needs to be established in the consideration of plans for analysis and appraisal. This precaution relates to the apparent basic differences in people. The reason for the importance of considering these differences at this point is that the selection of the categories for the analysis of any aspect of the educational program may have great bearing on the types of evaluation that may be made. It must also be recognized that, in addition to the categories used in analysis, the criteria by which appraisals are made may affect the types and validity of the evaluations. Those who provide group or individual leadership must be sensitive to the *in-sounds* as well as to the insights of all parties to interaction.

To what extent does the receiving audience affect the nature and quantity of data?

EVALUATING INFORMATION

Kleyensteuber, in his study on "Attitudes and Behaviors of Groups of School Administrators," gives some indication of the kinds of differences that may be found in people.[3] The differences may affect the process of evaluating the instructional program. Kleyensteuber found that people differ significantly in attitudes and behaviors with respect to a number of variables. Some of these are:

1. The number of years of experience in administration.
2. The pattern of educational preparation.
3. The age level.
4. The size of school in which experience was achieved.
5. Geographic location.
6. Experience patterns.

On the basis of his investigation, Kleyensteuber identified, in addition to his conclusions, the following six implications.

[3] Carl J. Kleyensteuber, "Attitudes and Behaviors of Groups of School Administrators," unpublished doctoral dissertation (Madison: University of Wisconsin, 1956), pp. 385–386.

1. Educators as individuals are subject to many influences. Different persons placed successively in the same administrative or teaching positions may reveal different patterns of attitudes and behaviors.
2. The objectives of education are interpreted differently by different educators.
3. Correlation of attitudes of the educators with their behaviors is consistently positive.
4. Administrators are consistently more social in attitudes and behaviors than the teachers and the education students.
5. Education students are consistently more theoretical in attitudes than the administrators and teachers.
6. Variation in attitude and behaviors between groups of administrators is consistently greater than for groups of teachers.

A major continuing task in evaluation is that of making the decision as to what kind of information is to be collected, how it is to be collected, where it will be sought, and what values are to be placed on each item collected. Any one of these or other aspects of evaluation might well command the attention of any scholar and supervisor over a long period of time. Practicality requires, however, that some simple but direct decisions be made with respect to the collection of information. When confronted with a problem requiring the making of judgments, supervisors and administrators, like many others, are tempted to seek out someone who has previously been confronted with a similar situation. In other words, the temptation is to solve problems first through interviews and library research. These are helpful sources of information. Often, regardless of the type of problem involved, one may go to the library and, with a careful search, find many extremely helpful published statements. However, one of the primary responsibilities for the person relying upon library research is to raise the question of who can be considered an authority with respect to the particular problem at hand. The extremely high respect that people hold for the published word becomes, at times, one of the most hazardous elements in seeking solutions to problems through library research. The mere fact that one finds discussions in the literature dealing with his problem does not mean that he is receiving advice from an authority. The practitioner expects to find the solution to an operational problem in a single research report whereas the practical problem may demand the synthesized findings of many pieces of research.

Authority often is overextended to those who have attained eminence of position. The field of politics provides many examples of these phenomena. The mere fact that a politician can maneuver into a high governmental post does not mean that he suddenly becomes qualified to speak with authority on some of the technical aspects of education. In a similar manner, those who have achieved eminence in the field of science often are considered authorities in many other areas of endeavor. While one may concede that eminence in one field is some reason to give credence to a person's views in other fields, it must not be assumed that he constitutes the source of the real or final authority that may be needed. When the solution to problems, which in this instance is that of evaluating a school program, is sought in the published word, there must be careful scrutiny and evaluation of the publication itself. Few educators would bother judging the quality of educational material that appeared in unsigned magazine articles or books. On the other hand, even the signed article must be studied to test the qualifications of the person making the statement. This immediately eliminates many of those who sell their evaluations of public education to the "slick" magazines. The mere fact that one is a good writer and can sell articles does not constitute proof of competence to the professional supervisor who is struggling with the task of analyzing and appraising the instructional program.

Concern must be exercised by the supervisor in determining whether that which appears to be a fact is genuinely a fact. Here again, whether it is the published word or information which the supervisor has collected by his own efforts and within his school system, he must raise the question of whether the information was collected in such a way and from such a source that it can be considered worthy. It is easy to quantify notions and invalid judgments but the multiplication of quantifications and invalidities is not a refinement of the source of information which is necessary if the information at hand is to be determined as acceptable. The collection of information requires technical skills which should be possessed by supervisors. There is not space here to review the literature which is available on the techniques of gathering, organizing, and analyzing data. Instead, the task is to identify this as a specific technical responsibility of the supervisor and to offer some directions as to where such technical information can be sought.

Does increased quantity of data tend to assure quality?

Basic to the preparation of supervisors is the development of skill in selecting criterion measures or areas of reference in evaluation. Too often, all phases of expectations are lumped together and evaluation is accomplished in generalities rather than in specifics. General evaluation results in generalized conclusions and generalizations are, too often, meaningless. In the general approach to evaluation, there is a tendency to combine the products of learning and the processes of teaching. The evaluator may become so enamored with the teaching–learning process that it is seen as the product. A well-designed evaluation program will be based upon carefully selected referents or criterion measures. As each criterion measure is broken into its component parts, the process of analysis is under way. In order to utilize each of the component parts in evaluation, sets of criteria need to be developed—preferably, through cooperative means—that will be applied both to products and processes. The information necessary for making judgments in terms of the criteria need to be determined. Having selected the kinds of data required, the procedures for collecting such data can be designed. The procedures for applying the criteria should be detailed in the design. The judgments made from the application of the criteria to the data become the appraisals.

The evaluation processes, then, are made up of the following steps:

1. Identifying and describing the criterion measures.
2. Analyzing the component parts into subcriterion measures.
3. Developing a set of criteria for each subcriterion measure.
4. Collecting data relevant to the criteria.
5. Applying the criteria to the organized data.
6. Making judgments or appraisals from this application.

Develop a similar analysis for another subject area in your school system.

Now for a specific illustration in the evaluational responsibilities of supervisors. Suppose that the long-range plan for a new mathematics program calls for an overall evaluation at the end of a five-year period. How does the supervisor go about it? The most obvious referent is the criterion measure of pupil achievement. Other criterion measures that might be enumerated are: the curriculum guide or plan, the objectives, the implementation of plans, and the teaching procedures in the area of mathematics. Because the evaluation of pupil achievement is the criterion measure which always draws the sharpest attention, the illustration here will be selected from the other measures just enumerated. The criterion measure to be analyzed is the Mathematics Curriculum Guide or Plan. This plan needs to be evaluated as a plan. In the analysis of this criterion measure, the following component parts may be selected to give direction to the evaluation of this plan as a plan:

1. The breadth of participation in the formulation of the plan.
2. The qualities of communication inherent in the plan.
3. The procedural design for implementing the plan.
4. The provision for evaluation of the effects of the plan when implemented.

In order to use each of these components in the evaluation process, sets of criteria need to be developed. Under the fourth component listed above, the criteria might be stated in the form of the following questions:

a. What provisions does the plan contain for the evaluation of change in student behavior?
b. What provisions does the plan contain for the evaluation of change in teacher behavior?
c. What provisions does the plan contain for the evaluation of the adequacy of teaching aids and supporting facilities?
d. What provisions does the plan contain for the use of the results of evaluation in planning the next steps in change?
e. What provisions does the plan contain for the evaluation of the plan as an agent of change?

Another criterion measure to be analyzed might be that of the objectives of the teaching program. In order to deal with the component parts of this criterion measure, it is suggested that a reference such as Bloom's *Taxonomy of Educational Objectives* be used.[4] This taxonomy relates only to the cognitive domain and does not include the similarly complex aspects of the affective and psychomotor objectives of educational effort. The six major classes in this taxonomy are raised in hierarchical order from the simple to the complex. The classes of objectives are:

1. Knowledge—Does the pupil have information?
2. Comprehension—Can the pupil relate an item of information to relevant knowledge?
3. Application—Can the pupil use the information in a new problem situation?
4. Analysis—Can the pupil break the information into its constituent parts and see their relationships?
5. Synthesis—Can the pupil use parts of several items of information to form a pattern not known before?
6. Evaluation—Can the pupil make judgments about the quality of the information? [5]

The supervisor has in this taxonomy a structure for designing an evaluation attack to determine the extent to which pupils achieve the expectations of the school as stated in the objectives. It could be a rewarding expenditure of leadership ability, time, and effort.

Another criterion measure to be analyzed might be the implementation of plans for the improvement of the mathematics program. This is much broader and will include an analysis of the in-service activity, the instructional materials, and the supervisory assistance to teachers. Yet another criterion measure might be the teaching procedures used in the mathematics program. This, too, has component parts, such as making assignments, directing discussions, organizing laboratory activities, selecting instructional aids, and reporting to parents.

A word of caution is offered at this point because of the power of tradition. The reluctance to differentiate sharply between process and product has led many supervisors to evaluate process without reference to product. A positive suggestion is that the evaluation of process may be more pertinent to the discovery of reasons for an unsatisfactory product rather than to stand as an evaluative end. Criteria evolving from the analysis of the criterion measures need to be developed and tested cooperatively. The appraisals based on these criteria constitute the composite evaluation of the effectiveness of the mathematics program and, similarly, support judgments regarding the quality of the evaluative effort. Then the cycle begins all over again. The composite evaluation should become a *must* as the basis for the short- and long-range planning—in this instance, of the mathematics program for the next set period of years. Similarly, evaluative procedures need to be designed for all areas of the curriculum. The evaluative em-

Does an evaluation necessarily suggest improvement needs?

[4] Benjamin S. Bloom (ed.), *Taxonomy of Educational Objectives* (New York: Longmans, Green, 1956).

[5] *Ibid.*, p. 18.

phasis by subjects should be rotated so as not to attempt an evaluation in depth in all curricular areas in the same year.

INVOLVING THE PERSONNEL

Because evaluation is a continuing process, it is essential that all professional personnel be informed about what is being done, when it is being done, the procedures used, the results, and what happens next. It is obvious that everyone on the staff cannot be involved in all the steps, but briefing sessions become *musts* as a communicating technique. The involvement of as many staff members as possible can be a positive influence. If the supervisor is to accept the function of evaluation in his leadership role, he will need to learn how to deal with the endless parade of demands on his time. He must learn to delegate authority in the same sense that the superintendent delegates authority to him. Many of the "musts" that supervisors list among the daily requirements of their positions can no longer receive top priority. The tasks that may be demanding time by way of managerial functions, often with respect to facilities and instructional materials, must be reappraised if the supervisor is to gain the time required by the program of evaluation (see Chapters 5–8). The effectiveness of the evaluative process is the measure of the supervisor's quality control over the instructional program. Neither quality nor control is achieved by shoddy planning and amateurish execution. A mastery of the techniques of evaluation can support the supervisor in making a unique contribution to the professional service of the total teaching staff. The increase in the uniqueness of this contribution to professional service will add stature to the supervisor's position and prestige to the supervisory skills demonstrated.

It should have become apparent in the earlier pages of this chapter that excellence in the process of analyzing and appraising requires many of the techniques necessary in carrying on more formal research. Analysis and appraisal are essentially research. Perhaps the suggestion that the supervisor in his day-to-day responsibilities should be doing research comes into conflict with some of the traditional notions about research. It is the aura of sophistication that seems to frighten many people from doing research and, at the same time, constitutes the reason why those who choose to become identified as researchers try to keep the required skills and abilities in "esoteria." In the most simple language, one might say that in our educational past the task of the supervisor in analyzing and appraising is *finding out* whereas the researcher chooses to *find out why*. Supervision should move to a higher level of sophistication in research procedures so that its analyzing and appraising function will pursue the level of *finding out why*. The processes of research need not be quite so frightening but their demands intellectually must not be discounted. The rigorous demands upon human insights and research skills perhaps best can be summarized by reference to the Multi-Faceted Strategies of Evaluation Model reproduced as Appendix A.[6] This model identifies many of the variables involved in the school personnel, tactics, and environment if justice is to be done to the classroom teacher. Teachers who gain confidence in the fact that non-teacher variables will be considered in the evaluation of instructional outcomes will be more disposed to cooperate in the analyzing and appraising functions of supervision.

There is no reason why more comprehensive planning should not go into the program of evaluation in the schools. The more planning that goes into evaluation, the more probable it is that research techniques of a sound variety are being approached. For instance, any supervisor can develop statements of hypotheses as a means of crystallizing thinking about a problem. The statement of an hypothesis in the simplest form is that of trying to get a statement that gives the best guess as to the relationships between two or more variables. There are many aspects to the testing of hypotheses that require complex skills, but many might or should be mastered by the supervisor to the extent that they would be serviceable in the local school situation. Supervisors who lack confidence in their ability to do research should be willing to secure consultant assistance to help design the research attack in the processes of evaluating the instructional program.

The responsibility of achieving objectivity in the collection of information is one that no person who intends to make judgments can possibly escape. There are different levels of achieving and testing the objectivity of collected information. It is something to be pursued not only by supervisors but by all researchers. Another skill which no supervisor or researcher can possibly get along without is the ability to generalize. One of the serious problems found in the literature of the profession is that of making certain that generalizations are based upon an adequate and proper amount of information. Reference was made earlier to the problem that one has in library research in determining who is or who is not an authority on any particular problem.

There are so many tasks involved in the processes of supervision that, in each of these chapters on the components of process, it may seem that a supervisor must be many persons. Such is not the case. The caution has been offered frequently that the supervisor must place a thoughtful order of priorities on the responsibilities to which his time is committed. The supervisor must do or cause to have done many things in a total supervisory program. The person who is unable to delegate to his peers or to his subordinates certain tasks involved in supervision will be unable to meet the full commitment of the supervisory position. A similar statement can be made

[6] Glen G. Eye, "Performance Evaluation: Measure of Education," *Wisconsin Journal of Education,* November, 1969, pp. 14–19.

about all administrative positions. The supervisor must involve as many of the teaching staff as possible in the process of evaluation. The supervisor, when involving teachers in this process, must be available to offer effective consultant assistance to those teachers as they proceed in the evaluational tasks. Directing group involvements becomes one of the skills demanded of the supervisor in designing and implementing a program of evaluation.

EMPHASIZING RELATIVITY

In each of the chapters dealing with a component of the processes of supervision, one of the characteristics of operational balance has been indicated as being particularly pertinent to the discussion. In the case of the component *analyzing and appraising,* the operational balance characteristic which seems most appropriate for emphasis is that of relativity. This characteristic was discussed in Chapter 12 and was defined as follows:

Relativity is the recognition of value and utility of one object, person, or situation as it relates to another with a different set of purposes, processes, and outcomes.

It seems unnecessary to present again an extended discussion of this characteristic as it is to be found throughout the chapter in the repeated cautions that judgments must not be made without a known and defined referent point (see Chapter 12). This is the essence of relativity. If one is to make judgments, those judgments must be made with respect to the facts as they compare to some level of achievement or criterion that will serve as the zero point for answering the question, "How good is this?" Thus, relativity becomes one of the major characteristics of balance in this component of process.

An excellent program of evaluation will, as an end product, provide information regarding the strengths and weaknesses of various aspects of the instructional program. When the program of evaluation includes the identity of those aspects which are being performed at a high level, it can become the source of great satisfaction for the supervisory and administrative staff, the teachers, and the supporting community. On the other hand, if the program of evaluation provides information which indicates a gross weakness of inefficiency in the instructional program, then, rather than having something to conceal, there is something that can trigger an improvement program. If evaluation has purpose at all, it is to determine the high points and low points in the instructional program. When the low points are identified they become the signal not only for designing but also for implementing a program of improvement. A program of improvement has two major aspects: (1) to plan a new or changed pattern which would substitute for or alter that which is being done presently, and (2) to provide an implementation of this plan once it is designed.

SELECTED REFERENCES

1. Bereiter, Carl, "Some Persisting Dilemmas in the Measurement of Change," in Chester W. Harris (ed.), *Problems in Measuring Change*. Madison: University of Wisconsin Press, 1963. pp. 3–20.
2. Bloom, Benjamin S. (ed.), *Taxonomy of Educational Objectives*. New York: Longmans, Green, 1956. p. 18.
3. Eye, Glen G., "Performance Evaluation: Measure of Education," *Wisconsin Journal of Education*, November, 1969. pp. 14–19.
4. Eye, Glen G. and Lanore A. Netzer, *School Administrators and Instruction*. Boston: Allyn & Bacon, Inc., 1969. Chaps. VII and VIII.
5. Harris, Chester (ed.), *Problems in Measuring Change*. Madison: University of Wisconsin Press, 1963.
6. Kleyensteuber, Carl J., "Attitudes and Behaviors of Groups of School Administrators." Unpublished doctoral dissertation. Madison: University of Wisconsin, 1956. pp. 385–386.
7. National Society for the Study of Education, Yearbook, Part II, *Testing Programs in the Schools*. Washington, D.C.: National Education Association, 1963.
8. Netzer, Lanore A., Glen G. Eye, Ardelle Graef, Robert D. Krey, and J. Fred Overman, *Interdisciplinary Foundations of Supervision*. Boston: Allyn & Bacon, Inc., 1970. Chap. VII.
9. Stanley, Julian C., *Measurement in Today's Schools*. Englewood Cliffs, N.J.: Prentice-Hall, 1964, 4th ed.

16

The Component of Process: Designing and Implementing

The component *designing and implementing* is designated in the form of two action words as are the other three components of the processes of supervision. All found their origin in assumption number thirteen, which indicated that there were four pairs of words constituting the various components. The three components discussed earlier were directing and controlling, stimulating and initiating, and analyzing and appraising.

DEFINING THE COMPONENT

"To design," according to dictionary definitions, means "to pattern," "to outline," "to plan," and "to devise a scheme for doing." These terms relate closely to the concept often repeated in this book that supervision should be custom-built for each school system. The concept of the custom-built program makes the design for supervision one of the first responsibilities of the supervisor. This entire book, as a matter of fact, is devoted to a design of the program of supervision. The emphasis has been that the design should be unique and peculiar to the particular person or persons responsible for the details of the program in a given school community. Designing, as a process of supervision, connotes more than the designing of a program of supervision. It extends beyond and, more specifically, to the point of designing improvement programs. These programs involve more of the things that teachers do with the pupils than what supervisors do with the teachers.

The term "to implement" means "to execute" or "to carry out." Frequent reference is made in the texts of school administration to the fact that there are executive functions that must be performed by line officers particularly, and occasionally by staff officers. The executive function is the responsibility of getting things done. It is unfortunate when the perception of executive functions becomes limited to the mere giving of directions to other persons. Such functioning could be implementation only to the extent that the communication or the directive is followed by attention and facilitation to the point of task completion. Thus, for supervisors going about the tasks of designing a custom-built program for supervision, there is the double implication that it is of little use to plan the program if it is never carried out to its intended end.

How is the supervisor's responsibility related to the organizational pattern when selecting, designing, or implementing behaviors?

Implementation, then, is that responsibility of the supervisor to pursue all of the processes of supervision in order that the purposes of supervision shall be accomplished (see Chapter 5). The implementing aspect in the design of supervision has identical responsibility with the making and carrying out of plans. Unless the plans for instructional improvements are carried out to a successful completion, the supervisory program itself falls short of that design which makes it unique as a custom-built program.

TRADITIONAL PREFERENCES

There has been a traditional preference for planning or designing as opposed to the responsibilities of implementation. School offices and classrooms are overflowing with statements of plans that have been developed, often with extreme care, by the members of the professional staff. They were reproduced and distributed to all members of the staff with the hope that they might bring about some changes in the instructional program. The feedback on the implementation of these plans has been woefully lacking in many school systems. This tradition in the practices of administration and supervision indicates a strong preference for planning activities which possibly can be explained as either an emotional avoidance or a technical inability to provide similar leadership in the implementation of plans.

The American people generally may have too much faith in the power of purpose. If this is a characteristic of the populace in general, it is well reflected by professional workers in education. It has long been recognized that religious faith must be expressed in daily behavior or the simple declaration of faith is an empty gesture. So it is in instructional improvement; the production of a plan must be followed by implementation. These instances of declaration without action are little different from the expectation that the state can be

Describe your perception of the power of purpose.

saved by legislating the title of a course to be offered in the schools. Legislation which indicates that a subject field is to be studied in the schools is nothing other than the declaration of an intent. No school subject will perform miracles with the pupils or for the country unless some teachers are able to devise those substantive aspects of the course that will result in accomplishing the intent of the legislators. This is not offered as a criticism of legislatures and legislators that express an interest in doing something for their constituencies through the schools. The point is that the declaration of purpose seems to be so sufficient that it is difficult to get those who made the declaration to be concerned with the substantive aspects of implementing a program. The purpose cannot be realized unless the declaration is only the first step in accomplishing the end desired. Other factors, such as financial support, suitable building or equipment facilities, length of the school year, length of the school day, capacity of the pupils to learn, and characteristics of the environment, will support or thwart the accomplishment of the purpose.

Another aspect of the traditional attraction to design and the avoidance of implementation is that designing seems to have the reputation for being the more intellectual activity, while implementing is the menial task. There is a long history of mankind's inclination to place higher values on the intellectual pursuits than upon the menial. While implementing a supervisory program or an improvement plan is far from menial, it does seem to represent the less exciting aspects of supervisory endeavor. This may result from the fact that implementation is a slow process, one that may require months or even years before the results of invested efforts can be seen. On the other hand, deciding or planning may be done quickly, even though haste often is unwise. Whether plans are good or bad, there is the possibility of going through the planning process and, within a reasonably short period of time, being able to announce for public consumption the plans that have been developed.

How can the implementation process be made more attractive?

Reference was made in an earlier chapter to the inclination on the part of some line and staff officers to make speeches to the teachers and to show great facility in declaring what is wrong with the current program, eloquently stating the direction that should be taken to reach the outcomes desired. They seldom provide an action model that joins the plan with an implementing process. Most anyone can make oral or written statements about the wrongs in any program and declare some new purposes or outcomes that appear to be highly desirable. However, the gap between the declaration of what should be accomplished and its actual accomplishment is a space filled with the prolonged, tedious, and technical process of implementation. Perhaps the inclination for planning as opposed to implementing is simply a choice between exhilaration and perspiration.

A part of the intellectual activity involved in planning is

imagination. We have heard concern expressed occasionally that, in this practical world, imagination has not been given its proper place. At the present time, imagination is high on the list of priorities for human effort. In part, the upgrading of imagination has been required in order to compete with other nations in space exploration. Science fiction in decades past was imaginative, yet not as exciting as the realities of the present. What the imagination of man will do in space exploration or in other fields of endeavor is hard to anticipate without a liberal application of the same ingredient, namely, imagination. Intellectual activities, particularly imaginative declarations, are attractive because of the reinforcement continuously given by those who readily observe and applaud the imaginativeness of the authors of ideas. An encouraging percentage of the population now is giving such reinforcement to the people who live by the mind. Fear for national survival and personal security has stimulated people to tolerate not only the extremes of the imaginative development of ideas but also the mundane, slow-moving, laborious task of implementing the suggestive directions of imagination. The amount of money directed to support the people who are applying their imaginations to the solution of practical problems and to the tasks of carrying out the emerging designs is an encouraging phenomenon of this era.

How is imagination related to creativity?

Education is only now emerging in the eyes of many citizens as a factor of as great importance to the future of the country as the fascinating but technical development of rocketry. More financial support is being provided for education so that some of the recent ideas for change can be implemented.

A contest must not develop between designing and implementing, because they are two elements of the same supervisory process. Skill in systems analysis is an excellent antidote to the neglect of balance in these processes. There must be equal responsibility applied to the realization of both aspects of the component. A good design is important because there must be something to implement; on the other hand, there is little use in providing a plan unless it is to be implemented. No plan achieves a status of goodness or badness until it has been implemented—thus testing its quality as a plan. Ideas that become the plans for improvement will be more responsibly organized if the designer is held accountable for suggesting the processes of implementation at the time the plan is released.

INTERRELATING THE COMPONENTS

As well as a balance between designing and implementing, a balance among all of the components of the processes of supervision is demanded. The authors declared a position on this matter when separating each component into two aspects of activity. Each component with its two aspects of activity is intended to be both complementary and supplementary. On the other hand, each component becomes a part of and is in balance with each of the other components of process. An example is found in the component stimulating and initiating. Stimulating is a starting device but initiating is a responsibility for getting a change process in motion. It was stated earlier that stimulating for the sake of stimulating can be nothing short of disastrous to a school program or any other group endeavor. There must be direction and there must be purpose; otherwise, stimulation becomes a hazard not only to the school activities but also to the individuals involved.

How can directing and controlling serve the component of designing and implementing?

Design cannot be held apart from the component of stimulating and initiating because it is in the design that purpose and direction are found. In a similar manner, analyzing and appraising are two aspects of a single component of process. Analyzing involves the task of looking at the parts, whereas appraising is the making of judgments. Designing is important among the tasks involved in the various aspects of analyzing. There must be a design for analysis. On the other hand, there is no point in taking things apart to see them as parts unless there is an intent to make an appraisal, thus justifying the expenditure of time involved in the process. Implementation of a design in analyzing and appraising would require that the supervisor move from analyzing to the appraising type of activities. So it is that the component of designing and implementing is not only a component of the supervisory process but also a part of the process by which a custom-built program is developed. As a matter of fact, whether or not the program is custom-built, the matter of designing and implementing is equally important in all of the various processes of supervision if any direction is given to activities. It is for this reason, namely, the interlocking relationships between the components of process, that assumption number thirteen involved all four processes of supervision. The combination of these into one assumption should obviate the probability that some readers see each component as a separate and distinct supervisory activity. This component—designing and implementing—can also be related to the *action pattern*. Assumptions, principles, objectives, and criteria determine the design. Procedure, as noted in the action pattern, is the matter of getting the job done.

LONG- AND SHORT-RANGE COMMITMENTS

The tasks of designing and implementing are many and varied. The fact that there are many and that they require an integration of the various procedures in a program indicates certain time considerations that must be involved in planning procedures. The tasks of designing and implementing are so varied that they demand a great deal of agility on the part of the supervisor in integrating his various skills and procedures with that selectivity which will bring the best of his abilities to bear upon the task at hand.

A man must plan his time carefully if he wants to apply his abilities in an organized way upon either the simple or the complex tasks which stand before him. Normally, those tasks which are more complex require more skill, more planning, and more time in execution. The most skillful supervisor possesses many different kinds of talents which must support his knowledge of the procedures of supervision. It is impossible, and it would be disastrous, if he were to exercise all of his knowledge and skills at one time regardless of the purpose of the activity. Selectivity, then, becomes extremely important to the supervisor in deciding how much time he requires to make discriminating judgments about particular behaviors which should characterize his attack upon supervisory responsibilities. The pressures of the day-to-day work for any member of a school system is such that, unless great effort is exercised, the time for planning activities may be usurped by the demands of the moment. This becomes a vicious circle in that the demands of the moment occupy the time that might better be used for planning—planning being the arrangement of those activities which would expedite the management of the tasks at hand. The failure to do the one makes the other all the more complicated.

The superintendent's office usually displays a detailed map of the school district with carefully designated locations of the present schools, attendance areas, and projected school sites. Usually well displayed on the walls of the central office are the population projections which facilitate planning for building needs as well as for staffing a school over an extended period of time. Strangely absent from this array of planning evidence are charts to indicate a similar attack upon the needs of the future, both near and far, which relate specifically to the instructional problems more than to either the population trends or building needs. Perhaps, in the one instance, the planning is more closely related to the economic impact of the educational program upon the taxpayers of the community. On the other hand, the needs of the instructional program are not easily visualized and usually are shunted aside until the more material and economic sides of future planning activities have been completed. Because the pressure for both financial support and building facilities increases year by year, the planning for the instructional program seems to be neglected.

How can the visibility of instructional accomplishments be improved?

An interesting note in the planning for population and buildings is that, if the projection is made for a ten- or a twenty-year period, the adjustment that is frequently made would simply extend the projection beyond the initial period and the years would be renumbered accordingly. This, as a principle of long-range planning, might well be emulated by those doing some planning in the improvements of the instructional program. There is no particular significance in the designation of a five-year program or a ten-year program. If one assumes that a decade is an appropriate unit of time for planning, he must at the same time recognize that when one year has gone by, another year must be extended beyond the original ten. In other words, if a ten-year span is a good planning unit, it is in a sense a rotating gift of time. At no particular point should the long-range plans be reduced to six or seven or eight. It must be recognized, however, that even though planning is being done by ten-year segments, the actual activities might vary, depending upon the type of planning required.

A master plan of ten years presumes that there would be short-range plans to pick up specific items within the long-range plan and to deal with them intensively for a shorter period of time. When the terms *long-* and *short-range commitments* are used, it does not mean that they alone are to be done or that they are to be considered as exclusive items in planning. One is a part of the other regardless of the pressure of the moment. When a plan is made for one particular element of the instructional program, the nature of the attack on that plan might vary from year to year. Just because a committee of ten is used to inaugurate a plan, there is no reason to assume that the plan must be completed in all of its details or implemented to the satisfaction of the district always with a committee of ten. There will be many occasions on which a committee of one might serve more successfully.

Planning, then, proceeds as a series of purposeful behaviors rather than as a continuing committee or a series of *ad hoc* committees. An important contribution of either the short- or the long-range plan is that, even though the procedures and emphases on a particular item may change from time to time, there is a constant reminder in the plan itself that the supervisor in charge must not forget the specific responsibilities of a plan.

The completion of a task is as essential as its initiation. It is not appropriate to say that designing and implementing require distinctively different skills. Both require the skill of being able to pursue a purpose until it is achieved. There is no justification in initiating the change process without knowing the direction of change or whether the anticipated change would be recognizable as a remedy to an unsatisfactory current situation. In other words, professional people who support the attempts for change, as well as the lay people who are asked to accept them, must see the attempted change as meritoriously possible. The problem requiring planning for change must have hypothetical solutions presented and these hypothetical solutions must appear suitable for testing. This is a practical requirement for those who would plan or design innovations for the instructional programs.

Another responsibility of the planner is to give attention to the time factors involved in the possible innovations. The extent to which the change is of an emergency nature must be determined. If it is of an emergency nature, there may be little time to develop a complete or extensive plan either of the long- or the short-range variety. Emergency usually calls forth the highest level of ingenuity, creativeness, and cooperative effort. This stimulating effect may become rather enticing for the persons responsible for directing change. It may be a temptation to create an emergency in order for action to be initiated and expedited. Emergencies are often the creation of the individuals involved in the responsibilities of the task itself. Thus, they become the ones who, if they do not want emergencies, can prevent them or keep them from taking on the pressures for speed usually shown in such situations. The more typical emergency situation is one in which a few teachers or a few laymen in the community become extremely excited about the quality of the instructional program.

Describe some emergency characteristics of an instructional situation.

Surprising as it may seem, laymen and professional workers often discover unsatisfactory situations with startling suddenness. To the supervisor, such sudden revelations appear to constitute emergencies. The supervisor who panics easily will design a plan that can be implemented quickly and will immediately publicize the fact that changes are being made. A more stable approach is that of giving proper weight both to the criticisms and to the real evidence of improvement needs in the instructional program. This provides a good base for determining the allocation of the specific responsibilities for planning. If the difficulty seems to be a self-initiated epidemic within a community in a particular year, one would not suspect that drastic changes need to be made on an emergency schedule. If the seeming epidemic of dissatisfaction is repeated over a period of time, then obviously there must be continuing evidence of inefficiency and a thoughtfully designed change is in order.

The designing and implementing of changes intended to improve the instructional program need to be viewed in terms of the number of years probably required. This is determined in relationship to the availablility of staff and financial support that may be involved. Determinations must be made as to what are the long- and short-range plans for improvement. In many efforts to revise instructional programs, it has been obvious that the attempt to do a general overhaul leads the staff members into a complex change of responsibilities that cannot be mastered or maneuvered in one action. The practical solution to this dilemma is to develop a series of short-range plans which will be coordinated within the master or long-range plan.

How long is long and how short is short? This must be resolved in view of the expectations established by the planners. As indicated above, a long-range plan might be five years, ten years, or more. In a similar manner, a short-range plan might be one unit of work, one subject in a self-contained classroom, one marking period, one year, or two years. The actual length of time which the planning covers is not nearly so pertinent as having the length of time involved obviously related to the kinds of tasks that are to be accomplished in the planning.

TASKS OF DESIGNING

If either the long- or short-range plans eventually are to produce the anticipated outcomes, it is necessary that some system be used in developing the designs or plans for implementation. The following seven tasks of designing are suggested:

1. Analyze and appraise the present status of designated areas to identify change needs.
2. Arrange the change needs in a priority order.
3. Select the action procedures for individual and group efforts.
4. Select the recording procedures.
5. Develop the content or activity sequence.
6. Plan procedures for implementing.
7. Outline procedures for evaluating.

What would you add or delete?

There now follows a discussion of each of these tasks with only enough illustrative references to aid in the communication of the intent of each specific task. As has been suggested in other parts of this book, the practitioner must feel free to select, reject, revise, or develop a task list of his own which will tend to systematize the approach in his own supervisory program. These steps or tasks of designing are offered as suggestions rather than as prescriptions.

The first task of designing is *that of analyzing and appraising the present status of designated areas to identify change needs.* The very selection of a particular area to analyze and appraise is in itself a step in the direction of acting upon some type of evaluation. This may have been very informal but sufficient to give the needed clue to the fact that more careful scrutiny is in order. The emphasis in Chapter 15 is on the component of supervisory process—analyzing and appraising. This is one of the best ways to identify the points at which an improvement program needs to be designed. The known points of weakness in the instructional program signal the need for improvement and these are found through the processes of analysis and appraisal. The identification of the starting points for improvement programs can be summarized from the content of the previous chapter in one word—research.

How can you determine the point at which a deficiency becomes a need for change?

Research is the best array of devices and techniques by which one can discover the goodness or badness of quality in the program of instruction in a school system. Many of the standard books on supervision and measurement provide ample illustration of the ways in which research procedures can be used in identifying the accomplishments of those endeavors identified as the teaching–learning effort. There are many ways in which research is used to discover the points at which the improvement program should be instituted. Some of the reported efforts, however, are not considered formal research by those who are highly sophisticated in the procedures of that discipline. It must be recognized that there are differing levels of sophistication in research and that it is not necessary to rely upon quantity and complexity of data treatment to defend a particular effort.

One of the very interesting innovations in recent years is that of modular scheduling in schools. Here is a type of innovation that some scholars would not see as based upon research. On the other hand, it is an innovation that was based upon a careful study of the social scene and a keen awareness of some of the aspects of current education that required attention and change. One may be inclined to conclude, primarily because of the manner in which reports have been made, that the reason for these innovations was the desire to be identified with change. This undoubtedly would do a serious injustice to the designers of modular scheduling. It appears that those who are aware of the radical changes of recent years and of the probabilities of the future have come to the general conclusion that traditional institutions cannot possibly serve either the recognized or the probable differentiations of the future. The general statements dealing with a need for excellence originally were stimulated apparently more by the fact that Russia put a satellite into orbit than by the need growing out of a desire for excellence as a prime vehicle of insuring the general welfare of our country regardless of Russian achievement. The impact of dramatic occurrences should not be depreciated.

The facets of a social scene that constitute the environment of education seem to constitute much of the research evidence that brought about changes, with some variations, in many schools. Efforts emphasizing the need for schools to break with tradition need not deemphasize the quality and the desirability of such innovations.

The second task of designing is that of *arranging the change needs in a priority order.* Reasonable, sincere, and efficient efforts at analysis and appraisal will identify numerous points at which improvement would be in order. It was indicated earlier that one cannot remake the world all in one glorious burst of activity. The person or persons who are directing the development of change must keep in mind the limitations of the staff involved so that overloading would not occur. The various improvements must be developed in some sequential arrangement. This requires yet another type of judgment—that of determining the nature of the priorities to be recognized in instituting the designs for change. In selecting the priority order, careful judgments must be made as to whether expediency is given a heavy weighting in terms of staff abilities and supervisor interest and, therefore, overrides other and more important considerations in the determination of priorities.

The third task in designing is that of *selecting the action procedures for individual and group effort.* The practices of recent years would dictate that almost everything be done by a committee. The inclination to want to assign every member of a staff to some planning or change committee is strong because of the length of time that this pattern has been encouraged and used. The decision as to whether standing or continuing committees with rotating membership through the years should be used, whether *ad hoc* committees of five or six should be used, or whether one person should be expected to carry forward certain aspects of the designing procedure is a matter that must be determined by the kinds of tasks that are to be done. It is quite possible that small committees, or even one person, might carry forward the procedures most effectively at certain periods during the designing procedures, no matter what the size of the school. Whatever the structure favored by the administrator or supervisor directing the planning activities, procedures should not be permitted to freeze into a standard pattern of activity. Flexibility in adapting the procedures is as important for designing as it is for the teacher who varies teaching procedures in hopes of catching the fancies, support, and learning efforts of the pupils.

What is the practical structuring of effective group action?

The fourth task of designing is that of *selecting the recording procedures.* Few would maintain that when planning efforts are put forth, no records should be made to provide continuity of the planning activity during the process of designing and on through the process of implementing. Some written record needs to be made of each step of progress in the designing process. This record may be minutes of committee meetings or summaries of small or large group discussions. The written material should indicate the purpose of the meeting, the conclusions made, and the next steps to be taken. As a very minimum, a written plan should include the following:

1. A brief description of how the need was identified.
2. A statement of the new purpose or outcome expected.
3. An identification of old practices worth continuing.
4. An identification of the changes needed either in content or practice.
5. A list of needs for facilities to support the staff effort.
6. Suggestions for judging decisions at some particular date.
7. A time schedule for the next activities.

Draft your own list of items that should be included in the written plan.

Whatever constitutes the minimum or maximum requirements for the recording procedure, its written form should be provided to all persons who may be concerned with the outcomes of the plan.

The fifth task of designing is that of *developing the content or activity sequence.* It is here that many of the cues for selection of the substantive aspects of a plan may have been deduced from the analyzing and appraising activities. The local studies involving analyses and appraisals, having revealed deficiencies, constitute one of the best ways to determine the direction of the design for a change.

Regardless of whether it is to be the one-man job of the supervisor or the cooperative efforts of all professional staff workers, a number of alternate solutions should be developed. There is always a danger in appraising a single proposed solution that might be used in the development of an improved instructional program. Even though one design appears to be better than any other, it can be adopted with greater security if it is compared with others, even if they are of known inferior quality. In all probability, there will be no great differentiation in the quality of the alternate solutions. The important thing in the designing procedure is to test one's own logic and imagination with two or more possible ways of instituting innovations that might provide remedies for the deficiencies.

What is the supervisor's responsibility in screening sources of information?

One of the sources for ideas is seeking the ready-made help which might be applied to the defined need for change. It is quite simple to make a library search for information about the kinds of deficiencies that have been discovered and defined in other school systems. There are inherent dangers in this source of assistance, however, unless the library researcher observes some simple but demanding rules in interpreting the information secured from published sources. There must be careful consideration given to whether published remedies or plans have been developed from comparable situations and whether the data came from sources of known and sound research procedures to support the particular conclusions or suggestions for change. The temptation to catch the quick answer must be resisted in favor of pursuing all of the information available from the most promising reports of innovations that seem to apply to the local school situation. The suggestions secured from library research must be carefully analyzed and appraised to determine whether or not they are adaptable to the local problems. There is little use in taking the suggestions from a district that has ten times the per-pupil wealth of the district under concern if wealth is a factor in effectuating the improvements. Further, there would be little advantage in taking the remedies for an instructional situation from a community with cultural characteristics extremely different from those of the community seeking the remedies and innovations. There must be a test of appropriateness for these ready-made suggestions for possible improvement.

Another aspect of the task of developing content in activity sequence is that of providing pilot opportunities for an emerging or an adopted plan. It is much safer to try the plan on one grade, one classroom, a few schools, or on any modest component of the total school system rather than to assume that the remedy is ready for complete implementation. The pilot run should be characterized by careful control of the problems attacked and of the innovations to be instituted. A thorough analysis of the trial run requires strenuous precautions in controlling the various factors that may affect the outcomes of the innovation. The supporting public, the necessary facilities, careful identification of pupil characteristics, the control over teaching materials, and other influential factors must be known when the trial is instituted. It is well to limit the liabilities at the time the controls are being instituted.

The sixth task of designing is that of *planning the procedures for implementing.* It seems sound that those who develop a design for change should give attention to its practicality and the procedures and facilities required for implementation. Freeing those with responsibilities for the development of the design from the obligations of implementation invites a careless or irresponsible type of idealistic and imaginative activity. While idealism and imagination are important ingredients in designing activities, they can deviate from the practical to a great extent if those possessing these qualities are relieved of all responsibility for future implementation. Later in the chapter, several tasks of implementing designs are suggested and these well might be surveyed by the groups designing a plan in order that proper concern can be given to implementation at the time the planning occurs.

The seventh task in designing is that of *outlining the procedures for evaluating the plan which has been designed.* There is little use in designing a plan based only upon an assumption of success at some future time. Those who develop the design are in the best position to know which elements are most significant to the proposals for improvement. These elements should be prominent in the design for the evaluation of the outcomes of the plan. The pilot run was indicated above as one of the useful procedures in screening the content and activity sequences of a design for change. At the same time, the pilot run can be useful in developing the evaluative procedures that will be needed to determine whether the new plan is really an improvement. Those who have been involved in the evaluation of instructional programs know how rarely they are able to measure all of the facets of the learning possibilities. It is necessary, then, that experience with the application of the plan for teaching and learning be studied continuously for the purpose of finding how best to evaluate the outcomes of that particular plan. The plans and procedures for evaluating should be considered an integral part of the pilot run activity.

TASKS OF IMPLEMENTING

Just as there were indicated above a number of specific tasks for the designing of improvement proposals and plans, so there are suggested here a number of tasks of implementation. Again, it is suggested that these not be considered as prescriptive but rather as a resource for those who must select the specific tasks of implementing a program of improvement in the local school situation.

The suggested tasks of implementing are:

1. Introduce the plan for acceptance.
2. Establish the time-order sequence of activities.
3. Assign specific responsibilities to staff members.
4. Carry out communication procedures.
5. Develop the needed in-service activities.
6. Assess the degree of implementing effort.
7. Evaluate the implementing procedures.
8. Evaluate the plan as a plan.
9. Evaluate the products or final outcomes.
10. Carry out the follow-up procedures.

What would you add to or delete from this list?

Several suggestions will be made with respect to each of these tasks in order that their intent may be clear.

The first task of implementing is that of *introducing the plan for acceptance*. There is little use in creating a design that is not accepted by a substantial percentage of the staff responsible for carrying it out. Further, acceptance of the plan becomes one of the resources of implementation because acceptance constitutes an important motivational factor. Acceptance in most instances will occur only if the members of the staff can see the worthiness of the plan or design and become convinced that it shows promise of resulting in improvement in the instructional program.

Acceptance of a plan should never be assumed. After the design has been communicated with all the effective procedures at the command of the administrative and supervisory staff, there should be some check on the extent to which the teaching staff has accepted the plan as a plan.

One of the ways of encouraging acceptance is through what might be called a series of briefing stages. The processes of communicating a design to all members of the teaching, supervisory, and administrative staffs will have resulted in a reasonably high level of understanding of both the purpose and the substance of the design for change. There needs, then, to be a series of intensive study, discussion, and decision sessions with respect to the specific individual responsibilities for implementation. The best place to start in the briefing of personnel about the respective responsibilities is within the central office. There should be a discussion at this level of the kinds of responsibilities that each member should assume as well as a thorough discussion of the tactics by which the implementation will be encouraged. The briefing type of activity is appropriate whenever communication procedures are required. In this first step of gaining acceptance to the plan, it is important that acceptance be accomplished generally by the administrators, supervisors, and teachers, the laymen and community groups, and the pupils.

What should be done about staff members who do not accept the adopted plan?

The second task of implementing is that of *establishing the time-order sequence of activities*. There are appropriate and inappropriate times to present the designs for change. There is no formula, however, which will make it simple for any supervisor to decide whether a plan should be presented in the spring, in the fall, or at various other periods during the academic year. In all probability, little progress would result from communicating the plan for change at a time when teachers, administrators, and supervisors are extremely busy with unavoidable routine tasks such as the change of semesters. On the other hand, it is quite possible that in the spring of the year, before teachers leave for summer vacations, a brief presentation might be made as a prelude to a complete presentation to be made in the fall.

Who should establish the time-order sequences?

An important part of the task of setting the time-order sequences is that of assessing the speed by which the teachers, after having accepted the plan, can make the appropriate preparations for their part in its implementation. The business office must determine when the budget will support the requirements. The parents of the children in the schools must gain sufficient understanding of the plan to support it. The supporting environment may be extremely important in the success of the innovation. The determination needs to be made at this point as to how much time will be allocated to each task of the implementing procedures.

The third task is that of *assigning specific responsibilities to staff members.* Here again, the briefing technique can be useful by starting with the superintendent of schools and moving through the various levels in the hierarchy of control in the school system with a complete briefing on the nature of the plan and its expectations. At the central office briefing level, the superintendent must make clear the specific assignments of each member of his staff as well as the relationships between the responsibilities of the individual school principal and the various central office administrative and supervisory staff officers. Agreement must be reached with respect to the various steps in the implementation procedures.

The next briefing level is that of the individual school. It is at this point that the principal must assume major responsibility for the leadership of his teaching staff and for constituting the liaison with the briefing outcomes at the central office. The principal must prepare the individual teaching staff members who will be responsible for the actual implementation of the design in the classrooms, and he needs to make certain that each of the teachers involved in the change shall gain a strong acceptance of the design for change. If only a part of the teaching staff is to become involved in the new plan, the principal must determine the extent to which those teachers not involved in the plan shall be informed. It is unfortunate to leave some members of the staff uninformed about plans for change since they, in turn, may influence the implementation of the design through their ability to affect the environment in which the change must take place. The principal should report the decisions that were made at the central office level—

Suggest some practical arrangements for allocating teacher time to planning.

particularly those agreements which involve central office staff personnel who might have direct contact with the implementation activities in the individual classroom.

The central office briefing stage should result in a clear understanding of the liaison procedures between the classroom and the building principal's office, as well as between the building principal and the central office. If the supervisory staff constitutes one of the major liaison factors between the individual school and the central office, these arrangements must be made known along with the procedures by which the liaison will take place. This information should be given by the principal as he briefs his teachers about their particular parts in the process of change.

The fourth step of implementing is that of *carrying out the communication procedures*. The reference to briefing procedures is not to be taken either as the best or the total of the appropriate devices by which communication may be completed. There must be carefully devised written directives as well as oral presentations. All of the facilities of audio-visual aids may be used to facilitate an understanding of the intent of those presenting both the design for change and the plan for implementation.

One of the aspects of communication often neglected is that of setting the stage for the feedback of information. There is a positive need to create a situation in which the classroom teacher who carries the major burden of the implementation of change feels support through reporting back first to the principal's office, then to the central office. Feedback procedures are appropriate, necessary, and appreciated when accompanied by a sense of involvement in the implementation process. Depending somewhat upon the complexity of the change proposal, there need to be frequent checks as to whether the steps as outlined by the central office are followed. More important, the frequency of the checks probably will identify certain elements in the plan that require change or supportive action that had not been anticipated at the time the design was developed.

The fifth task of implementing is that of *developing the needed in-service activities*. The briefing sessions and various other devices of communication can and do constitute in-service improvement activities. On the other hand, more may be needed as the demands of the design to be implemented become clear to those directing as well as to those carrying out the details of the plan. In the case of some of the newer developments in the content of the various subjects, much study is required if the teacher is to have a sufficient mastery of it to be able to teach pupils. It is unreasonable, then, to expect to implement a design which requires substantially new types of information to be taught without giving the teachers time and assistance in making preparations for the classes. In the more spectacular changes of content during the recent years, such as in mathematics, most teachers, supervisors, and administrators have not only recognized but also have supported in-service activities which helped teachers relearn the necessary mathematics to be able to carry out the new program.

There is another concept of in-service activity, however, which often is overlooked, namely, the in-service activities related to the supporting community. Careful steps must be taken to make certain that acceptance by a substantial percentage of the supporting public is achieved prior to the time that the outcomes of the changed instructional program begin to become apparent. This is often neglected on the false notion that it is easier to gain public support for a program which has demonstrated its success than to impress it with a design for change. The fault with such an assumption is that the implementation of a plan might not be successful because of lack of public support. The central office staff has no right to induce a classroom teacher to put into operation a new or changed instructional program without complete protection in case of possible failure. The teacher must not be required to bear the frustration and onus of failure alone. The importance of this step in the implementation procedure is that all of the prerequisites must be met before there is a commitment of total effort to implementing a design for change.

The sixth step is that of *assessing the degree of implementing effort*. This really should be a continuous assessment and made in terms of the sustaining enthusiasm that members of the staff have for the plan itself and of the evidences of an understanding on the part of all of the professional workers in approximating the intention of the plan. In other words, acceptance is not enough, although it is essential. Along with acceptance of the plan must be the kind of understanding in depth that will prevent the individual from drifting off at tangents to the original plan. Even though a plan is not intended to destroy the creative ability and opportunities for individual teachers, the point is that if creativity leads to a tangent, an assessment should be made as to whether the reason for this direction is the pursuit of a better way of carrying on the new program or whether it is an expediency occasioned by the lack of complete understanding.

Should teachers purchase instructional aids for pupils to support self-chosen improvements?

The seventh step is that of *evaluating the implementing procedures*. This is closely related to the assessment of the degree of implementing effort. As one proceeds through the time-order sequence set earlier, it is well to review whether this sequence proved wise. Here again is the pilot run of the implementing procedures. In a way it means going back through the previous six tasks of the implementation procedures and raising the question of whether the tasks have been carried out and, if carried out, have resulted in the anticipated outcomes.

The eighth task of implementing is that of *evaluating the plan as a plan*. Even though the design for improvement has been evaluated to some extent in terms of its acceptance by those who must implement it, there remains an additional necessity of making a more formal evaluation of the plan as a plan. At this point it is well to consider the evaluation of the procedures for designing as well as the design itself and the plan for implementing the design. A frequent review should be made but, at some point in time, a thorough evaluation should be made of the plans and their known effectiveness as of that time.

The ninth task of implementing is that of *evaluating the products or final outcomes.* This refers to the seventh task of designing which indicated that, as a part of the design, there should be developed the procedures for evaluation. Those who develop the design are in the best position to determine the criterion measures and the criteria by which the innovation should be assessed. This, then, is the point at which the procedures developed as the last task of designing should be applied to the results of the implementation of design.

The tenth task of implementing is that of *carrying out any needed follow-up procedures.* The outcomes of the application of the evaluation procedures will give an indication of the success of the plan. If this success is as anticipated, the cycle of tasks of designing and implementing may be considered completed at this point. On the other hand, if the outcomes are not satisfactory, the whole process of the tasks of designing must be reinstituted. It is important, then, to find out why the new design was not successful. Either it was because the plan itself was defective or because the procedures of implementation may have been faulty. On the other hand, it may have been for both of these reasons. At any rate, there may be follow-up procedures; if so, they must be considered a part of the implementing plan even though this might return the supervisor to item one in the tasks of designing.

DISTRIBUTION OF EFFORTS

There have been presented in the two preceding sections of this chapter a number of suggestions on the tasks that characterize the designing and implementing efforts which lead to innovations and improvements in the instructional program. These suggestions now may be put into a type of time schedule —in other words, integrating the tasks of designing and the tasks of implementing in time sequences—such that there will be a distribution of the human ability and effort available from the professional staff and the school's supporting community. Illustrations of the planning time sequences for designing and implementing can be chosen from any number of categories or areas for improvement. One might simply select at random the course or subjects represented in the curriculum from kindergarten through the twelfth grade. On the other hand, it might be possible to develop an illustration from a series of typical behaviors in teacher-pupil relationships. A number of items from the various aspects of methodology would support the illustration. Five areas of attention are suggested in Part V as serving the purposes of evaluating supervision as supervision; these categories are used as the basic reference for the illustration here of long- and short-range planning. Three of the five areas will be used in the illustration. *Curriculum developments* include all subjects or content areas such as mathematics, science, language arts, music, business education, art, and so forth. The first five of these areas will be used in the illustration presented as Figure 16.1. *Instructional improvements* include such things as methodology, evaluation, group structure, instructional aids, and so forth. For the purpose of the illustration, the instructional improvements chosen are team teaching, programmed learning, and television for foreign languages. Others might be added.

The third area is that of *school-community consolidations* and the specific tasks included are those of reporting to parents and sex education. It is helpful now to study Figure 16.1 carefully to see how this composite of the tasks of designing and implementing has been related to a program of long-range commitments. Note particularly, just after the tasks of designing and implementing are recorded, that there are illustrative areas and that in each one certain assumptions have been made. These assumptions, as recorded in the first half of Figure 16.1, must be kept in mind as one looks at the second half of the figure in which specific references are made by years. As indicated earlier in the chapter, one should remember that in long-range planning the fact of choosing ten years as the range is of little significance. Whatever the total span of years, when the first year in the plan is finished another year must be added.

Eventually there will be the tenth, eleventh, twelfth, thirteenth, and more years, or, if preferable, simply renumber and begin again with the first year of the long-range plan. The important thing is to structure the attack on the improvement program over a long enough period of time so that the efforts of the professional staff may be best applied to the change needs. In light of the assumptions indicated with respect to the plan, it will be noted that in the first year the tasks with respect to the mathematics program are keyed to task items 1, 2, 3, 4, and 5. While this is going on in the field of mathematics, keeping in mind the stated assumptions with respect to each of the illustrative areas, the work on the science program might be in the stage of implementation.

The first four or five task items in designing will be found at a diagonal from the upper left to the lower right of the figure. This means that the attack on designing is staggered with respect to all of its various tasks. In a similar manner, the tasks of implementing are staggered so that, in any one year, the number of activities involved in the enterprise of innovation does not become excessive. This is control over the use of the faculty and the commitment to a limited variety of change. Such a long-range plan does not provide for emergencies. On the other hand, it was indicated earlier in the chapter that emergency needs should not be subjected to long-range plans and often not even to short-range plans.

Short-range plans must be keyed to master or long-range plans. There is a short-range plan involved in each of the cells of Figure 16.1. For instance, in first-year mathematics there are five tasks of designing. This is a short-range plan of improvement within the long-range mathematics commitment. In all probability, those who are concerned with these five tasks in the first year may spell out in greater detail the actual involvements which will constitute meeting the commitment. The short-range plan, then, is an intensified plan of attack at any particular cell or stage of the long-range commitment.

In studying Figure 16.1 in terms of its possible suggestions for long- and short-range commitments, it must be remembered that an illustration can be nothing other than suggestive. Any particular supervisor in a particular school system may want to select a different array of tasks. At the same time, he may want to limit the long-range aspects of planning as well as the scope of planning in terms of the number of different tasks and in terms of the number of different fields to which a commitment is made or in which a concern is expressed for the designing and implementing of the improvement program. Again, it is suggested that one might select other areas or categories for organizing his own plans and efforts. The illustration is keyed to Part V of this text. It is offered as a pattern for developing long- and short-range plans rather than as a plan which might be adopted. In carrying out the tasks of designing and implementing, all of the concerns of each of the chapters in Parts I through IV play important parts. In fact, even Part V now becomes of some significance in the illustration for long-range planning. All the various aspects applied in different combinations and with different emphases become concentrated or integrated in the suggestions for commitments as detailed in Figure 16.1.

Draft long- and short-range plans for change in your particular assignment.

EMPHASIZING FLEXIBILITY

In each of the other three components of process a characteristic of balance has been related specifically to that component. The characteristic of *flexibility* seems more closely related to the component *designing and implementing*. This characteristic was discussed in Chapter 12 and was defined as:

The capability of a person or a situation to change patterns of being and behavior by adapting to newly accepted goals, to the different patterns espoused by others, and to the escape mechanisms for avoiding undesirable outcomes.

FIGURE 16.1
An Illustration of Long-Range Commitments

DISTRIBUTION OF EFFORT [1]										
	YEAR									
CURRICULUM DEVELOPMENTS [2]	I	II	III	IV	V	VI	VII	VIII	IX	X
Mathematics [3]	1,2, 3,4, 5	5,6	7,A,B, E,F, G	C,D,G, H,I,J	H	K,L	1,2, 3,4	5	5,6	7,A,B, E,F,G, H
Science [4]	B,E, F,G, H	C,D, H,I	H,I	H,I	J,K, L	1,2, 3,4, 5,6, E	A,B,C, D,F,G, H	H,I	H,I,J	H,I,K
Language Arts [5]	J,K,L	1,2,3, 4,5	5,6,7	A,B,E, F,G,H	C,D, E,H	E,H	G,H	I,J, K,L	1,2,3, 4,5	5,6,7
Music [6]	5,6,7	A,B, E,F, G,H	C,D,E	H,I	H	H	J,K,L	1,2,3, 4,5,6	6,7,8, A,B,C, D,H	H,I
Business Education [7]	H	H	J,K,L	1,2,3,4	5,6	5,6, 7,A, B	C,D, E,F, G,H	H,I	H	H
INSTRUCTIONAL IMPROVEMENTS [2]										
Team Teaching [8]	3,5,6, 7,A,B, H	C,D	H,I	H,I	J,K, L	Further planning will depend on results of J,K,L.				
Programmed Learning [9]	H	H	J,K,L	Continued application and expansion depends on results of J,K,L.						
Television for Foreign Language [10]	1	Plan long-range commitments from results of 1.								

SCHOOL-COMMUNITY CONSOLIDATIONS [2]

Reporting to Parents [11]	Continue present practices.	1,2,3	4,5,6, 7,A,B, E,H	C,D, F,G,H	H,I	H,I	H,I	J,K,L,M
Sex Education [12]	1,5	Plan further action from results of 1,5.						

[1] Tasks of designing: 1. Analyze and appraise the present status of designated areas to identify change needs. 2. Arrange the change needs in a priority order. 3. Select the action procedures for individual and group efforts. 4. Select the recording procedures. 5. Develop the content or activity sequence. 6. Plan procedures for implementing. 7. Outline procedures for evaluating.

Tasks of implementing: A. Introduce the plan for acceptance to the administrative and supervisory staff. B. Introduce the plan for acceptance to the teachers. C. Introduce the plan for acceptance to the community. D. Introduce the plan for acceptance to the pupils. E. Establish the time-order sequence. F. Assign specific responsibilities. G. Carry out communication procedures. H. Develop the in-service activities. I. Assess the degree of implementing effort. J. Evaluate the implementing procedures. K. Evaluate the plan as a plan. L. Evaluate the products or final outcomes. M. Carry out the follow-up procedures.

[2] The items below are examples. Actual items will be designated by the local school system.

[3] Assume that the mathematics area has been designated for analysis.

[4] Assume that the science area plan is ready for distribution to teachers.

[5] Assume that the language arts plan is ready for evaluation.

[6] Assume that the music plan is being developed.

[7] Assume that the business education plan is being used.

[8] Assume that team teaching is in the process of being introduced next year.

[9] Assume that the programmed learning project is continuing.

[10] Assume that television for the foreign language program has been designated for analysis.

[11] Assume that the present practices for reporting to parents are to be continued for three years.

[12] Assume that the sex education area is to be opened up for discussion.

The implications of this characteristic as related to this particular component of the processes of supervision are simply that of adapting to those requirements involved in the implementing of a design for change. In all probability, the purposes and outcomes of instruction will prove to be extremely stable insofar as intent is concerned. It must be remembered, however, that even though purposes remain the same, outcomes might vary because of the changed nature of the pupils and the situations in which learning takes place. Flexibility means that one might hold firmly to the purposes of education and to the hoped-for outcomes and yet provide great facility for adaptation. Because the greater probability of change will be found in the pupils and in the learning environment, there must be more frequent assessments of the appropriateness of plans and implementation procedures with respect to them. Another factor to keep in mind with respect to flexibility is that, as ten percent or more of the faculty change each year, new talents, new points of view, and the need for orientation and reorientation will be constant. Flexibility, as a characteristic in the process of supervision, means that supervisors must be ever on the alert to take advantage of the new talents and the changed situations that occur and which might affect the implementation of change. It is hoped, too, that flexibility can be established in the minds of all people as a desirable characteristic in order that each can feel comfortable in the face of the necessity for change.

An attendant attitude will be the ability to resist irritation at one's inability to feel that he "has it made" on the job. Those who seek to achieve a certain level or pattern of operation and hope that time and situations will never make it necessary to deviate from the familiar do not possess the flexibility needed to support the designing and implementing of changes. Flexibility is a characteristic that must occur as an aspect of the program but, more importantly, as a characteristic of all individuals who become involved in the change process.

Designing and implementing is the fourth of the major components in the processes of supervision. The next chapter has as its major focus the integration of the various aspects of the characteristics of balance and the specific processes of the components of supervision. This integration or synthesis involves suggestions for the choice of the techniques of supervision. Remember again that the philosophy held consistently throughout these chapters is that supervision at its best must be custom-built for each individual system. The next chapter is not intended to constitute a prescription for supervision but rather to indicate that techniques of supervision grow out of and are found in the various components of process, as well as in the purpose, patterns, and participants of supervision.

SELECTED REFERENCES

1. Association for Supervision and Curriculum Development, Yearbook, *Balance in the Curriculum.* Washington, D.C.: National Education Association, 1961.
2. Bennis, Warren G., Kenneth D. Benne, and Robert Chin (eds.), *The Planning of Change.* New York: Holt, Rinehart & Winston, 1961.
3. Feyereisen, Kathryn V., A. John Fiorino, and Arlene T. Nowak, *Supervision and Curriculum Renewal: A Systems Approach.* New York: Appleton-Century-Crofts, 1970.
4. Lucio, William H. and John D. McNeil, *Supervision: A Synthesis of Thought and Action.* New York: McGraw-Hill, 1969.
5. Neagley, Ross L. and N. Dean Evans, *Handbook for Effective Supervision of Instruction.* Englewood Cliffs, N.J.: Prentice-Hall, Inc., 1970, 2nd ed. Chap. IX.

17

Integrating the Procedures

The preceding sixteen chapters included references to and discussion of many related facets of supervision. The first ten chapters dealt with matters such as purposes in supervision, organizational and operational patterns for supervision, and participant involvement in the entire process. Even though the discussions centered upon the above major considerations, supportive attention was given to assumptions, purposes, principles, organizational patterns, specialized functions, and adequacy of staffing. Interspersed with all of these notations were direct suggestions of things to do. The early chapters are of greater significance than simply an enumeration of the processes by which a program of supervisory activities is planned. The procedures required for translating concepts and suggestions into operational accomplishments involve many specific supervisory behaviors. This constellation of behaviors, if well coordinated, is the program of supervision.

Review the Table of Contents for Parts I to IV.

SYNTHESIZING THE PARTS

In the first five chapters of Part IV the distinguishable components of the processes of supervision were dealt with separately and specifically. The chapters in Parts I through III included suggestions for the development of a program of supervision which in themselves constitute supervisory activity. The previous chapters in Part IV contained procedures for expediting a plan of supervision and for identifying specific procedural facilities and expectations of the program. The purpose of this chapter is to encourage a synthesis within, between, and among the first sixteen chapters. As indicated above, the emphasis in the earlier chapters was that of presenting those concepts of supervision which might support the supervisor who is interested in establishing a custom-built program for a particular school system. The earlier emphases also showed the interrelationships among the many aspects of the activities which constitute supervisory action. Illustrations were presented not only to suggest specific techniques but also to put the theoretical propositions into a practical setting. The order of presentation was designed to encourage the development of concepts of process for supervisory programs in a form that would be easily adaptable to the nature of the assignments of a supervisor in the field.

In this chapter, the situation is reversed in the sense that the practical situation is used as the starting point and the supporting illustrations of directions to action are drawn from the theoretical concepts. For the practitioner, a synthesis of previous discussions is better initiated and accomplished through the task attack. In other words, a specific and typical supervisory technique is analyzed in terms of its dependent relationships to the various supervisory activities which were described as components of process. For instance, if the concern is with a committee meeting, the question properly should be raised as to the intent of the meeting. Is the committee to direct, control, stimulate, initiate, analyze, appraise, design, or implement? Thus, the focal questions are drawn from the components of process. A question also properly may be raised as to whether the committee has structured itself and approached its task in terms of an analysis of the assumptions that seem to be involved in the committee problem and attack. If assumptions are identified, what principles, objectives, criteria, and procedures seem to follow in sequence by way of structuring the committee's actions? The action pattern is not only for the development of a supervisory program but also for the attack upon specific problems in any setting. Further, if the supervisor responsible for leadership in the committee's activities is to use the various characteristics of balance, the questions of autonomy, perceptivity, creativity, relativity, and flexibility may be raised. The test of balance will determine whether the committee's proceedings make use of the potential in the interrelationships of committee members, thereby achieving efficiency and effectiveness in pursuing the stated purposes.

Think of a supervisory experience of your own and indicate the component of process that seemed to dominate.

The supervisory program is a program of persons, behaviors, and situations. The definition of supervision gives recognition to the fact that supervision's intent is to influence all of these factors. Persons, behaviors, and situations should affect the teaching–learning activities so that pupil development shall be at its maximum. All of the items in the action pattern, all of the characteristics of balance, all of the considerations of patterns and participants, and all of the components of process cannot be brought to bear simultaneously upon any particular system or task situation which confronts a supervisor. Only a person who is utterly confused or determined to create confusion would presume that all of a supervisor's abilities should be exercised each time he is confronted with a problem situation or goal pursuit. The wise supervisor is one who has the common sense to evaluate the task at hand in terms of the abilities available and the identifiable situation. Many tasks which confront supervisors will require only a minimum of the total talent possessed. Unless the supervisor has a reservoir of understanding about supervision and a mastery of the skills required, he will be unable to draw upon an adequate reserve to meet problems which range from the simple to the complex, the near to far distant time, one person to many people, professional personnel to informed and uninformed laymen, and from the unsolved problem to the satisfactory solution.

SELECTIVITY IN SUPERVISORY TASKS

Analyze some community influence on the supervisory program in your school.

Several references were made in previous parts of the book to the effect of tradition upon the selection of the various elements of a supervisory program. One of the first steps in the development of a custom-built program of supervision is that of breaking the hold that tradition has not only upon the supervisor, his administrative and supervisory colleagues, and the teachers, but also upon the lay individuals and groups in the community. Many program characteristics of supervision as well as of teaching have been dominated by the environmental expectations which provide the cradle of tradition. A break with tradition offers the freedom to develop the kind of a program that seems more appropriate for a school system at a particular period in time; however, this is not to suggest that supervision is improved purely by breaking with tradition. Many of the so-called breaks with tradition are not burdens imposed by environmental influences but are a dependence of supervisors upon the convenient use of presently held notions about supervision and education. The environment may be friendly to change while the person who must initiate the change lacks either courage or ability to set it in motion.

From your experience as a teacher, describe discrete actions by your supervisor which illustrate each of the "five P's."

The five steps in the development of a comprehensive program of supervision as proposed in this book are what may be called "the five P's"—*purposes, patterns, participants, processes,* and *products.* The concepts and activities involved in each of the so-called "P's" constitute a constellation of supervisory acts. When confronted with a task situation—as all practitioners are continuously—the problem is to achieve the proper selectivity and interrelatedness to gain the maximum return on efforts in task accomplishment.

An important supporting facet of supervision is that of

recognizing a difference between the *doing* and the *causing* to be done. The principle of administration cited earlier—that authority but not responsibility can be delegated—was discussed at some length. The fallacy involved in this principle of administration if applied to supervision reveals an equally disastrous fallacy in practice. It has resulted in generations of supervisors and administrators who believe that if a thing is to be done well, it must be done by the person wanting it done. In other words, a supervisor operating on the basis of such an assumption will feel that few things can be delegated. The press of many tasks forces the supervisor to recognize that one person cannot do all things, but, having so concluded, he may follow the questionable alternative that one person can decide all things. Thus, there exists a single control of great power and influence over the instructional program. The increasingly well-trained professional personnel, then, would not be used in applying intelligence and judgment to the planning of improvement programs or to the specific solutions of problems. There is a difference between doing a thing and causing it to be done. Causing things to be done requires great skill in organizing efforts of others. These skills may be inferred from the discussion in Chapter 5, "The Structural Pattern for Supervision." The person who would cause things to be done is the one who has confidence in his ability to organize the efforts of others. The basis for this confidence is described in Chapter 6, "The Operational Pattern for Supervision." The person who recognizes his contribution in causing things to be done will be a thoughtful student of the interrelationships of persons and situations, particularly of persons as described in Chapter 7, "The Contributory Function of Supervision," and Chapter 8, "The Supportive Function of Supervision." Further, that person who is willing to accept the responsibility of causing many things to be done will be a student of available talent on the staff with which he works. As indicated in Chapter 9, he will, then, be concerned with "The Allocation of Talent." Also, because he is operating as supervisor on the basis of causing things to be done, he will be concerned about those individuals to whom he makes assignments. His concern will turn to "The Security of the Participants" as described in Chapter 11. This person, who is concerned with causing things to be done, will be a student of the characteristics of operational balance and of the four components of the processes of supervision. He will recognize the appropriateness of directing when directing is the best supervisory act, or of analyzing when analyzing will contribute the most to purposive behaviors. He will recognize in his organizational responsibility the task of providing a design for change and marshaling the skills for implementing those changes. Thus it is with almost any concept of supervision. It is clarified later in this chapter how specific task responsibility will command all the resources of supervision that can and must be brought to bear upon the task at hand.

In what ways have you seen staff officers confront a problem by "causing" things to be done?

The universality of the expectations that have been placed upon status distinctions well may be a concern of the supervisor as he sets about arranging functions such as stimulating, directing, and evaluating, not only for himself but also for those whom he would influence as a result of his supervisory efforts. Classroom visitation, traditionally and presently, is seen as the major symbol of the supervisory act. It is hoped that the above statement will indicate that these authors cannot subscribe to such a narrow view of supervision.

Even though the standard symbol of the supervisory act appears to be that of classroom visitation, there are many other activities commonly included in the lists of supervisory behaviors or techniques as they are identified in many quarters. The degree of importance and the amount of use put upon any particular technique of supervision vary immensely from region to region and from person to person. There is no one standard list of the techniques of supervision. The following items, however, will be found in most of the attempted listings of supervisory practices, behaviors, and techniques:

1. Classroom visitations
2. Orientation meetings for new teachers
3. Pre-term meetings for planning
4. Workshops of various kinds
5. Large group conferences such as conventions—national, regional, local
6. Institutes
7. Teachers' meetings involving the whole faculty or staff, the department, the grade level, or the subject area
8. Small group conferences, such as study groups and seminars
9. Committee work
10. Bulletins and other documentary aids
11. Audio-visual aids
12. Resource materials such as the central library, the browsing room, the curriculum library, or the curriculum laboratory
13. Extension or summer school courses—with or without credit
14. Local field trips, such as excursions, travel or visiting days
15. Local research problem attacks, such as the experimental trial of new materials, processes, and techniques
16. Directed reading, both for small groups and for individuals
17. Group counseling
18. Demonstration teaching involving small groups or individuals
19. Directed teaching
20. Individual conferences following classroom visits or by request
21. Follow-up conferences in a series based on a given problem or theme, involving the individual or small groups
22. Individual counseling related to personal or professional problems
23. Study councils
24. Exhibits
25. Interviews
26. Lectures
27. Panel discussions
28. Role playing
29. Tape recordings
30. Curriculum logs

Do you consider these as techniques unique to supervision?

31. Curriculum guides
32. Curriculum reports
33. Lesson plans
34. Testing
35. Buzz sessions
36. Brain storming
37. Briefing sessions
38. Sensitivity training

Obviously, a particular supervisor may use one or more, but not all at one time, of the above techniques and would select them as judgment dictates the probability of success for the task at hand. The supervisor who chooses to fancy himself as a master of one particular technique probably would not take advantage of the selective opportunity of a long list of techniques. Rather, he would force the persons and situations involved to fit the particular technique or device of supervision with which he has become enthralled. An awareness of the marked increase in the group attack in supervision over the past several years is frightening evidence that the day of individualized supervision as formerly conceived is practically gone. This is not to say that supervision, because of this, is less effective but rather that those supervisors who choose to use the group technique must be masters of certain skills that were not required of those who emphasized the individual or face-to-face type of supervision.

Any of the techniques listed above undoubtedly could be found operating in many different ways in different school systems. Any one of them could be subjected to an historical study which would reveal that it has gone through many stages of change. The group attack, such as large group meetings or workshops of various sizes, is a technique used for the past two or three decades with presumed effectiveness. Available historical evidence indicates that in the early stages of the workshop idea, a great deal of pre-planning was done by those who had decided that the workshop would be the technique of self-improvement. The leaders would structure the problem selection and attack. The workshop became the object of criticism because participation in planning was not sufficiently prominent among the workshop activities. If the teachers were the objects of the self-improvement, the workshop device must permit them to share in the planning. Consequently, there was a gradual shift from a highly structured, pre-planned workshop to one that was almost completely unstructured at the time the group was called together. This process, in turn, became subject to criticism, primarily because so much of the time was spent in helping each individual to "find a problem." It was thought that those coming to a workshop should have a well-identified problem at the time of entry to such an experience. Here is an indication of how a device that might have worked exceptionally well for a highly selected group became a rather weak instrument of self-improvement when applied on a broad scale. It is doubtful that the workshop ever should have been evaluated on the basis of the amount or nature of participation. There are many other criteria that should be applied.

How could you utilize the workshop technique profitably in a local school system?

The suggestion made earlier in this chapter is that the various components of supervision, the steps in the action pattern, as well as the items of the characteristics of balance would provide a very helpful checklist in analyzing not only the workshop as a device but the workshop as an effective instrument for self-improvement or whatever the supervisory objective may have been. There was at one time what might be called a workshop epidemic. Naturally, an epidemic of any type, if not the product of planning but rather something that encourages defense, is what must be considered an offender. Workshops at one time were offensive to a total and balanced program of supervision. Unfortunately, it stimulated the assumption that if people were working together for some purpose and were happy with the process, self-improvement and better teaching would result. Those who planned and directed the workshops, and who now direct many successful workshops, do not look upon the workshop as an overall device that will be successful in small group or large group situations when all other efforts may have proved inadequate.

One of the interesting outcomes, both of the workshop movement and of research and interest in group dynamics, has been the feeling that all meetings, to be successful, must begin with some kind of socializing. Of course, it may be argued that group dynamics research preceded the workshop and was the stimulant for such devices. This may be true. It is difficult to identify precisely whether these two phenomena were parallel or serial occurrences. That particular issue is not particularly appropriate to the point being made here, but it is true that the coffee hour seemed to become one of the essentials to any sort of group activity involving an interchange of ideas. This device was considered good for the individual if it was good for the group. Consequently, some supervisors adopted the philosophy, or at least the practice, that no conference could begin unless it was preceded by a cup of coffee. Several things happened as a result of this. Both supervisor and supervised used more time in the conference session than either may have desired. Too much coffee was disturbing to the digestive system of the supervisor, and this, in turn, did not improve either his ability or those characteristics which support successful supervision. The other thing was that it left both parties with the feeling that a certain period of parrying must be indulged in before one could get down to business. Apparently there existed an assumption that seemed to dominate the conference idea as well as the workshop idea, namely, that better work is done in informal than in formal situations. It must be obvious to all that some people respond in one way to a situation and some in another. Some persons would feel much more at ease by simply going into a workshop group situation or individual conference knowing its purpose

How do you like to have an individual conference conducted?

and its probable procedures, and then proceeding with whatever participation was required at the time. Some research has supported quite well the idea that participation is a means of achieving higher agreement as well as better conclusions. The point here is that participation should not be looked upon as therapy for the members of the group but rather as a device that may be used successfully in planning and implementing that change which constitutes an improvement in the instructional program.

IN-CLASSROOM AND OUT-CLASSROOM SUPERVISION

A question should be raised occasionally about the supervisor's perception of balance between in-classroom and out-classroom supervisory behaviors or activities. It is at this point that the thought is renewed that the common image of supervision is that of classroom visitation. It is unfortunate that supervision has been narrowed progressively in concept until it is perceived almost exclusively as classroom visitation.

Supervisory reports and the literature of the field bear witness to the fact that substantial efforts have been made over the years to improve visitation procedures. It is proper that such efforts should be made. The topics for study or consideration about classroom supervision include:

1. How many visits should there be per year?
2. Should these visits be scheduled or unscheduled?
3. Should the teacher be involved in planning the visit?
4. Should notes be taken during these visits?
5. Should a rating scale be used?
6. Should a written report be kept?
7. Should there be conferences related to the visits?
8. What items should be included in oral and written reports?

The emphases have been placed on these external aspects to the extent that the primary purpose of classroom visitations has been relegated to a minor role.

Should there be classroom visitations? Indeed there should! These visits, however, should serve only as one technique for carrying out a given purpose. Important in the process of successful classroom visitation is the cooperative pre-planning by the supervisor and the teacher. This planning should include a projected evaluative procedure which, in itself, is an excellent supervisory device. The implementation of new plans requires classroom visits but there can be only one answer as to the number, the nature, or the activities pursued during the visits. Both the best and the poorest of teachers need the assistance of the supervisor in the improvement of instruction. A gifted teacher, like a gifted student, should not be neglected. All teachers need consultation with the supervisor, but it will vary in amount and kind. Consider the variation in the needs of a beginning teacher, a highly

How might visitations vary between successful and unsuccessful teachers?

creative teacher, an experienced excellent teacher, and an experienced in-a-rut teacher.

There must be a focus upon the immediate purpose as well as upon the general objectives of classroom visitation. When the observer enters the classroom, what is the point of emphasis of the observation? Is it:

1. The pupils' reactions to one another?
2. The pupils' reactions to the teacher?
3. The pupils' reactions to the instructional aids?
4. The teacher's reactions to the pupils?
5. The teacher's procedures?
6. A combination of two or more of these?

Visiting a classroom to obtain a general reaction can result only in a general evaluation. If a teacher is having difficulty with group control, a series of visits may be necessary, with a specific purpose for each visit as enumerated above, in order to locate the causes of the problem. When the problem is defined, other visits, each with a specific objective, may be needed to assist in the solution of the problem. Further periodic visits may serve as reinforcements to the efforts at problem solution. All too often, classroom visits are made only when a teacher is having difficulty. A balance should be sought in the use of the available time to work with the teacher's problems and failures as well as with the improvements and successes. A teacher interested in developing a new idea may profit by a planned series of observations. Special behavioral directions and evaluative criteria need to be developed cooperatively in advance of each visit. A frequent reaction from supervisors goes something like this: "Cooperative planning sounds good, but what do you do when the teacher refuses help, never asks for assistance, or is unaware that help is needed?" Under these circumstances the question must be raised as to whether an isolated classroom observation might possibly accomplish anything by way of improvement in instruction. In such cases, other procedures need to be employed by the supervisor or administrator to develop the readiness on the part of the teacher for classroom visitation as a mutual effort to improve or develop an idea.

How specific should pre-planning be?

Pre-planning is essential for the success of most techniques. A classroom visit for the sake of a classroom visit lacks professional direction in much the same way as showing a film that has not been previewed. It may be argued that there are positive side effects and incidental advantages in unscheduled, casual visits. On the other hand, what about the negative side effects and incidental disadvantages? The no-schedule position is indefensible when long- and short-range lesson plans are required of teachers but no similar requirement is placed upon the supervisor to have long- and short-range plans in the selection and use of supervisory techniques.

The development of policy and procedure for classroom visitations might be the topic for a series of meetings in the in-service improvement of supervisors and administrators. In preparation for these sessions, it is recommended that the administrators and supervisors interview the teachers individually to survey the teachers' perceptions of the functions of supervisory positions. Questions such as the following ought to be included:

1. What can I do to assist you in improving your teaching?
2. What would you like to have me do when I visit your classroom?
3. How often would you like me to visit?
4. If you could design a supervisory program to your liking, what would you include?

A supervisor who would spend one hour a day interviewing a teacher a day until all have been interviewed, and then summarize these findings as a basis for developing policies and procedures, would be spending the days wisely in the improvement of instruction. He would, at the same time, be performing supervisory behaviors or techniques. In this developmental process, consider such guidelines as:

1. The teacher not only should know the purpose of the visit but also should have a part in planning the number of visits, the time of the visits, the criteria to be used in observation, what is to be done with the criteria, and any resultant evaluation.
2. The criteria will vary from visit to visit depending upon the specific purpose. No one set of criteria or checklist is sufficient.
3. The number of visits will vary depending upon the purpose.
4. The visit should be used as a means to improve instruction through mutual efforts.

Suggest other guidelines.

Such are the considerations that should characterize the supervisor's planning and performance processes. Numerous questions have been raised in the discussion of classroom supervision. Some suggestions were made as to what the answers to these questions might be. It is more important that each supervisor develop answers to such questions without accepting the ready-made answers supplied by another person. For instance, the first question raised was, "How many visits per year?" In this chapter, it is proposed that integration or synthesis takes place by bringing to bear the discussions of the previous five chapters as well as the first three parts of the book upon the particular question or decision at hand. In answering the question, "How many visits per year?" one might run through the four components of the processes of supervision, keeping in mind the question "To what extent will the desired accomplishment be supported by a particular component of process?" For instance, in determining how many visits per year, one must answer such questions as: "To what extent does he intend to *direct* the activities of the teacher and the teaching–learning activities in the classroom?" and "To what extent does he intend to dictate goals and teaching procedures?" If *directing* is the intent, it is possible that one visit would be sufficient to gain the orientation that would permit him to tell the teacher precisely what should be done in the classroom. On the other hand, if *control* is the purpose of the supervisory activity, it might require many visits during the school year for the supervisor to obtain a confirmation of the fact that the teacher is performing as directed.

One might turn to the second component of the processes of supervision in answering the question of how many visits should be made per year. If the intent of the visit is to *analyze* or to *appraise* some highly complex social phenomena, numerous visits as well as special observer assistance might be required. On the other hand, if the intent is simply to determine the nature of the lighting facility on the work surfaces used by the pupils, one visit might provide adequate time for such an analysis. If an appraisal is to be made, in all probability the number of visits becomes rather unimportant except with respect to the analysis which must provide the data needed to make the appraisal.

Using the third component of process, one may attack the question of how many visits per year in terms of whether the purpose of the visit is to *stimulate* or to *initiate*. In another attempt to gain a solution to the question of how many visits, one may provide an answer to the question of whether the fourth component of process suggests the intent—that of *designing* or *implementing* a plan. If the purpose is *designing* a plan for improvement, fewer visits might be required than would be necessary in *implementing* a plan in which many factors must be controlled if the implementation is to be complete and successful. Therefore, the four components suggest the attack for evaluating not only the success of the visit as a technique of supervision but also, and more importantly, the manner of planning such a visit so that it will be successful. This would accomplish the purposes of visitation as a supervisory technique.

The problem is raised as to what *action pattern* might be most appropriate at the same time that the evaluation of the above question is being made. If the dominant component of *directing and controlling* was the referent point for the problem at hand, one might raise a question with respect to the *assumptions* basic to the behaviors apparent in the classroom which had proven to be unsatisfactory. A question might also be raised about what assumptions seem basic to the selection of a new pattern of behaviors required of or adopted by the teacher or the supervisor. At some point, the *objectives* rather than the assumptions would dominate in the selection of the particular behavior of the supervisor in his direct contact with the supervised. There also may be times when *principles* or *criteria* become the major consideration. Whichever route and whichever emphasis may be given, the end to every action pattern is that of arriving at the most appropriate procedures which can be selected for the situation. At many points, the discussion is about the procedures to be used by the teacher in working with the pupils.

The consideration of how many visits per year might also shift from the components of process and the steps of the action pattern to a consideration of the characteristics of balance. It is at this point that one might wish to raise the issue about the effects of the number of visits upon the *autonomy* of operation as experienced by the teacher. On the other hand, the question might be raised as to what *perceptions* the supervisor has of what the teacher is doing and how many visits are required in order that the supervisor's perceptions of what the teacher is doing and the teacher's perceptions of what he is doing might approach congruency. Thus, each of the other items in the characteristics of balance may serve as guides to a choice of supervisory behavior. It can be seen in the above illustration related to classroom visitation that one question related to this supervisory technique might cause the supervisor to bring into consideration all the components of the processes of supervision in deciding which is to get the major emphasis, or even complete neglect, at any particular time. Further, he must decide how to involve his knowledge of an action pattern and the characteristics of balance as they may affect the procedures of classroom visitation.

Much space has been devoted to the discussion of just one supervisory technique—the classroom visitation. It is perceived as the most commonly used technique and thus has served as the best vehicle for illustrating the advantage of integrating the procedures of supervision. It has illustrated the in-classroom type of supervisory activity, but there is also the out-classroom type of supervisory contact and impact. The supervisor–teacher individual conference is the technique used for illustrative purposes here. Because many of the analyses of supervisory inferences are so similar to the above illustration, the discussion of the conference will be limited.

Earlier in the chapter it was implied that individual conferences are most appropriate as supervisory devices or techniques and that individual conferences almost always should follow classroom visits. This does not mean that a classroom visit is the only occasion for an individual conference. There could be many purposes, many occasions, and many precise procedures that might be used in the individual conference between the supervisor and the teacher which would make the conference effective. Many of the suggestions which have been made above in connection with the classroom visitation might be repeated in almost exact terms for the planning that goes into an individual conference or the appraisal of the value of such a conference. Achieving the idea of this integration of the *characteristics of balance,* the *components of process,* and the *steps in the action pattern* is the best means of synthesizing the above considerations for the purpose of selecting appropriate supervisory techniques. It is the belief of the authors that the supervisor, with a thorough knowledge of a theory of supervision and with clear-cut notions as to what the parts of that theory imply for behavior selection, will be able to face a particular situation and select the best techniques. This is a safer approach than turning to a textbook, reference book, or a neighbor to find a technique that, hopefully, might be successful in a unique and complex supervisory situation. The individual conference, if approached in this manner, can be planned, carried out, and evaluated through applying selectively the various components of process, the action pattern, and the characteristics of balance. Each problem situation will demand whatever emphasis the supervisor chooses to give that particular situation, which, in turn, dictates the supervisory techniques to be used.

Select another technique from the list and analyze it.

Any of the other specific techniques given in the list presented earlier can and should be subjected to similar treatment. Instead of individual conferences or classroom visitation, one might use the technique of the pre-term meeting for planning the year's activities. The procedures as indicated above should be followed by the supervisor as he plans such supervisory activities and selects the specific techniques which would be most appropriate for the task that he has set for himself. In the case of the pre-term meeting any of the components of process such as analyzing and appraising might be used very little. The products of analyzing and appraising a previous year might be used for the purpose of stimulating or initiating the year's activities. On the other hand, it might be more appropriate to let the component of process be dominantly that of directing and controlling. The point here is that every major task of supervision should be projected through this type of planning. The structure of the outline of this text can be used readily as a checklist against the situation and can help in the selection of supervisory techniques. Thus, in this text and in this chapter, in which more time is devoted to the discussion of techniques, there is no section on "here is how you do it." The commitment of the authors to the custom-built plan of supervision would be violated if such techniques were spelled out in detail and an indication given as to when they should be used. It is obvious in the discussion above that deciding when certain techniques should be used must result from the analysis made by the supervisor. Should some persons become disturbed at this point in feeling that their future supervisory activities have not been sufficiently structured, let it be recognized now that at no time should one presume that each little detail that presents itself to the supervisor for solution should be subjected to the kind of major analysis indicated in this chapter. Common sense can take care of most of the simple tasks that come to the supervisor even though that person has no previous training in supervision. The intent here is to indicate that the major techniques or behaviors of supervision should be subjected to careful analysis and planning.

THE INTEGRATION

The supervisor holds the responsibility of giving directions to the merging of *people* and *programs* in assuring a successful instructional program. Four components of process and a multitude of specific tasks are the substance of this responsibility. These constitute the variables, all of which recognize variability, diversity, and adaptability in the unique environmental milieu of a particular school system. The rationale of the supervisor brings cohesion to the processes when molded into a program. The interrelating of the processes provides the basis for designing the custom-built program of supervision when the integration takes place within the boundaries of the school system's purposes, patterns, participants, and expected products.

This summarized concept is supported by the matrix shown as Figure 17.1. The four components of process are shown graphically in interaction and the interaction occurs within the boundaries of the other four of the five P's of supervision as defined in this text. The matrix is generally self-explanatory and detailed description will not be indulged in at this point. The suggestion to the reader is offered, however, that a quick review of the six chapters in Part IV may be aided by frequent reference to the matrix, "Visualizing the Integration of Processes."

This summary and matrix are offered in lieu of a list of references. The reader will find pertinent literature cited in the selected references following Chapters 12–16.

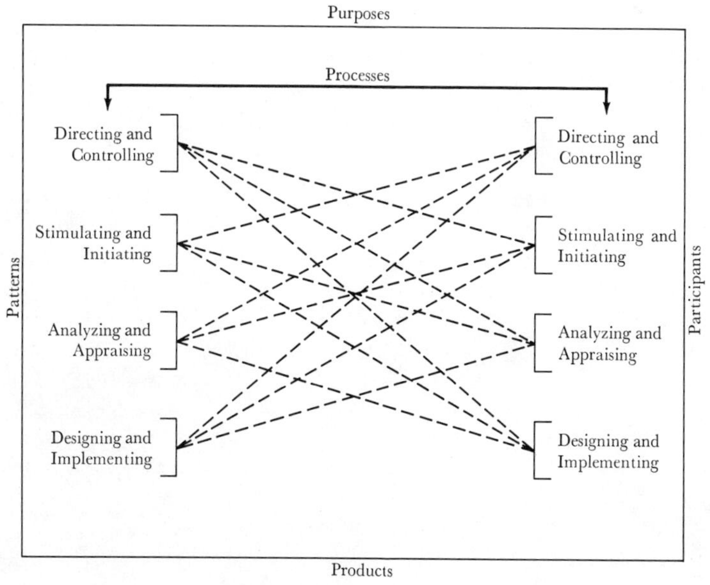

FIGURE 17.1 Visualizing the Integration of Processes

Part V

THE PRODUCTS OF SUPERVISION

The products of supervision are subject to multifaceted evaluation. They may be identified in broad categories or in specific detail. The former may be so general as to be meaningless in terms of the behaviors to be appraised; on the other hand, detail can be so minute that causal relationships cannot be assessed. Acceptable referent points must stand between these extremes. The approach taken here to the products of supervision seeks to identify broad categories that are meaningful as well as specific areas of causal relationships between supervision, teaching, and instructional outcomes.

Supervision should be evaluated by the supervisor's impact upon the teacher rather than by the teacher's impact upon the pupil. Pupil learning is an appropriate subject for evaluation, and it is a product of many agencies and influences. Products of supervision cannot be evaluated by secondary outcomes any more than the products of teaching can be evaluated by the achievements of middle-aged people. The products should not be too far removed from the influencing behaviors being appraised. Supervision should be evaluated by criteria appropriate to its proper expectations. Thus, it is mandatory that this evaluation be focused upon *its* products rather than on the products of teaching. This part attempts to identify those points of contact closer to the supervisor–teacher–learning environment relationships rather than the pupil outcomes in which the teacher stands between the supervisor and the pupils.

Throughout this book, assumptions pertinent to the various parts have been selected from the major list in Part I. Those appropriate to this part may be summarized as follows:

3. The major function of supervision is that of influencing situations, persons, and relationships for the purpose of improvement.

4. Planning is supported by systematically applied analysis.

6. Load-quality relationships must be considered in the expectations for teaching and supervisory personnel. . . .

10. Supervision of instruction and curriculum development must be cooperative and coordinative. . . .

11. The . . . functions of supervision include those policy determinations and implementations that deal with . . . improvement. . . .

13. Supervision involves the processes of directing and controlling, stimulating and initiating, analyzing and appraising, and designing and implementing. . . .

14. Professionalization is a result of individual and group maturation.

15. Professional personnel should be evaluated with specific reference to the declared primary expectations of the position occupied.

16. Leadership in evaluating . . . trends in the social, economic, physical, and ethical environment . . . is the responsibility of personnel assigned to the supervisory function.

17. The evaluation of . . . supervisory personnel is a responsibility of the chief administrator. . . .

These assumptions should make clear this book's basic position—that the tasks of supervision should be enumerated and that this responsibility rests with the superintendent of schools. Because supervision is a phase of administration, he should identify the kinds of evidence that will be accepted in analyzing and appraising supervisory efforts. He should participate in evaluation and study the *results* of the supervisory process. Often superintendents have been more inclined to make assessments on the basis of the *process;* its visibility is more convenient and immediate than that of the more elusive product. If the products rather than the processes are to be the focus, it is much more difficult to identify and control the various sources of evidence.

This part, then, centers upon the products of supervision, and suggestions for evaluation are based upon the idea that assessment is to be made of the products of those behaviors and relationships closest to the supervisory act. A basic concern in this part is that of providing a means for supervisors to meet the demands of accountability through a systematic study of relevant evidence. Just as teachers are held accountable for the teaching outcomes, so must supervisors be held accountable for supervisory outcomes.

18

Professional Maturity

Each occupational group seeks certain status symbols which represent to its members the kind and amount of prestige that give personal satisfaction. The most important realization is achieving a sense of personal worth. This sense of personal worth must have a referent point; that is, it must exist in the mind of another person. This person could be a member of the family, the peer group, or a supporting client group.

Professionalization must develop in terms of those characteristics which make one occupational group distinctive from others. Expressed personal and organizational views support the point that some occupational groups have established a concept of professionalization held generally by its members. This concept is based upon uniqueness of preparation and exclusiveness of services performed. Some occupational groups that either have not yet achieved such self-assurance or have not been accorded such client acceptance probably would prefer to base the concept of professionalization on a series of characteristics which various occupational groups hold in common. Dumont, however, takes the clear position that the realism of the current scene no longer supports the notion that credentialism is the determinant of professionalism.[1] The persistent demands now are related more directly to determination by the quality of performance.

How does the absence of criteria for determining the degree of professionalization affect the process of professional maturation?

[1] Matthew P. Dumont, "The Changing Face of Professionalism," in Lanore A. Netzer *et al., Education, Administration and Change: The Redeployment of Resources* (New York: Harper & Row, 1970), chap. II.

BOUNDARIES OF THIS CRITERION MEASURE

The members of each occupational group possess and exhibit a desire to have the sense of success through public or client acceptance because of the quality and importance of the service rendered. The professionalization of any group, however, is not a characteristic that can be set against an outside calibration to determine the specific point at which it has been achieved. There have been substantial efforts to identify the characteristics which could be described as marks of the achievement of professionalization. If there are characteristics held in common between and among occupational or hope-to-be professional groups, it would be that of the desire for the realization that such accord had been given to the skills and contributions of the group as well as the sense of achievement gained from the respect of client and colleague groups.

In order to locate the position of any group—in this case, the school staff—on a continuum of professional maturation, it is necessary (1) to decide on the characteristics of professionalization, (2) to develop the criteria for the assessment of the selected characteristics, and (3) to develop the procedures of assessment for both individual members and the group. Beach explored the various approaches to the matter of professionalization among school administrators and made some comparisons to other occupational groups. He expressed his point of view with respect to the essence of the achievement of professionalization in this manner:

> The evaluation that society places on a particular vocation is determined by (1) how the vocation meets the needs of society, (2) the knowledge and skills required to perform the tasks of the vocation, and (3) the standards set and maintained by participants in the vocation.
>
> The professionalization of an occupation or related occupations is in many respects a social and a political process. Professional status must be earned over a long period of time at both the individual and the organizational levels. In the development of any profession, individuals achieve status first. The respect duly won by dedicated practitioners provides the foundation for professionalization at the organizational level. A full-fledged profession is one that has reached the advanced stages of organization under which a pattern of self-government is adopted and enforced.[2]

Lieberman has written at length about the problems of professionalization in the occupational group of teaching. The characteristics of an occupational group which he accepts as being indicators of professionalization are as follows:

1. A unique, definite, and essential social service.
2. An emphasis upon intellectual techniques in performing its service.
3. A long period of specialized training.

[2] Fred F. Beach, "Professionalization of Educational Administration," *School Life,* XLII, October, 1959, pp. 5–8.

4. A broad range of autonomy for both the individual practitioners and for the occupational group as a whole.
5. An acceptance by the practitioners of broad personal responsibility for judgments made and acts performed within the scope of professional autonomy.
6. An emphasis upon the service to be rendered, rather than the economic gain to the practitioners, as the basis for the organization and performance of the social service delegated to the occupational group.
7. A comprehensive self-governing organization of practitioners.
8. A code of ethics which has been clarified and interpreted at ambiguous and doubtful points by concrete cases.[3]

In what respects have teachers made the most and the least progress in achieving professional status?

Lieberman's discussion of professionalization is impressive primarily because he declares the criteria by which he judges an occupational group and, secondarily, because he organizes his discussion in terms of the degree to which a vocational group may possess professional characteristics. While all of the stated characteristics are pertinent and of interest, one of the more intriguing points is that of the autonomy of individual members within the group organization. The granting or the denial of autonomy is not limited to the control of an occupational group in achieving what it perceives as autonomy. If the autonomy of one individual is achieved at the expense of the autonomy of another, conflict is certain to develop. This struggle for autonomy exists not only between competing occupational groups but also with the client public which the groups serve.

Distinctions are made between the occupational group and the client public on the basis of whether the group is a socialized service or a private enterprise and whether this makes a difference in the establishment of criteria for determining the aspects of professionalization. The more pertinent point of interpretation deals with the extent to which an organized group can and should achieve autonomy. Involved in this concept of autonomy is the exercise of group control over the entry of individuals into the occupation and the conditions under which the member is permitted to remain in or is compelled to leave. An alternative control would be that of the client group, such as the laymen of the community or the patrons of a school. The client group might retain selected controls while, at the same time, seeking the services of a nonsocialized service without demanding any controls over the performance of the group performing the services. In the one instance, the clientele is committed by social policy to the use of teaching services and does not seek the services of the teaching profession on a voluntary basis. On the other hand, persons seeking services of members of the medical or legal professions do so upon the self-appraisal of need and personal choice. The basic question is: Does socialized service or free enterprise make the difference in the determination of the

What is involved in the concept of "socialized service"?

[3] Myron Lieberman, *Education as a Profession* (Englewood Cliffs, N.J.: Prentice-Hall, 1956), pp. 2–6.

amount of autonomy that shall be given the individual to carry on the esoteric service as he perceives it or as his peer group controls it; or does the enterprise submit to the controls by a client population which has no mastery over the unique skills and services characteristic of the occupational group?

O'Brien analyzed the nature of the professionalization of a group in the case study of a small community where there had been violent differences of opinion among the lay people and, particularly, between the board of education and the professional educators at the local, county, and state levels.[4] He brings into question some of the criteria proposed by Lieberman, especially with respect to the nature of the autonomy that will be required if professionalization is to be claimed. He argues that there is a "stylistic" and a "standardistic" criterion to be used in making such decisions. "Stylism" means that one uses information as personal controls in terms of reference and deference on the part of the individual to those who are not members of his occupational endeavor. "Standardism" means that one defers or refers to other members of his profession, namely, his peers and their organizations. It is O'Brien's contention that there is no direct analogy between the members of the teaching profession and the members of the medical profession, a point which is emphasized in the Lieberman treatment. In surveying certain substantive issues in the community used for his case study, O'Brien discovered that there were wide differences in respect to stylistic and standardistic tendencies both among the lay people and the members of the teaching profession. He found, however, that there was an inclination on the part of the professional members in the controversy to be standardistic. He suggests that there are some areas of concern which are more properly the responsibility of the client public than of the teaching profession, but that there are other substantive issues which should be committed to the standardistic determination of the members of the occupational group. It is obvious that there can be several aspects to the concept of autonomy, both for individuals associated with and those separated from an organized vocational group.

Probably no occupational group ever achieves complete autonomy, and perhaps none ought to do so. The problem is one of the maturation of a profession to determine, within each occupational group and its associated clientele, the weighting of the various responsibilities that might be assigned to the substantive issues. There is no denying that there are certain esoteric characteristics of occupational activities over which complete control should rest with the members of the professional group. The development of the concept of relative responsibility and the identification of the uniqueness of each

[4] Dean W. O'Brien, "Reference and Deference to Authority as Factors Affecting Professional Autonomy in Education: A Case Study," unpublished doctoral dissertation (Madison: University of Wisconsin, 1963).

responsibility become the measure of the maturation of the professional group.

The superintendent of schools, who is to judge the achievements of supervision in terms of a developing professionalization of those with whom supervisors work, must make such an assessment on the basis of the criteria which he accepts. As has been characteristic of other positions taken in this book, the best program is that which is custom-built, meaning that it must be acceptable to the person or persons directing its use as well as to those who are subjected to it.

IMPLICATIONS OF THE ASSUMPTIONS

From the total list presented in Chapter 3, the specific assumption most closely related to the purpose of this chapter is number fourteen—"Professionalization is a result of individual and group maturation." It is obvious that these authors are committed to the notion that professionalization is a status that is achieved as a result of superior performance. Things which are achieved gradually need points of reference to determine the progress which has been made. Even though the commitment here is to gradualism, no precise and calibrated criteria which make it possible to determine the state of maturation at any particular time will be set. There can be no doubt about the possibility of identifying major achievements which would give some indication of the degree to which maturation has been achieved.

A complicating item in this perception of professionalization is the fact that group maturation is dependent not only upon the maturation of individual members but also upon the individual's capacity to be a productive member of the group. Many people, thoroughly competent in the skills of their own vocation, may be extremely slow in achieving those skills which make them productive group members. These, then, constitute some of the complicating factors in determining the extent to which the teaching profession has achieved professionalization.

Assumption number fifteen—"Professional personnel should be evaluated with specific reference to the declared primary expectations of the positions occupied"—is also closely related to the purposes of this discussion. It has been stated frequently that the superintendent is the one who must establish, communicate, and judge the expectations placed upon the supervisors as members of his staff. Similarly, the superintendent is an important factor in the determination of the professionalization of the classroom teachers. At the same time, it must be recognized that, because the teaching profession is a public service, the client group has some right to share in the establishment of the expectations placed upon any particular position. It is an obligation of the superintendent to consolidate the expectations placed upon the people in various school positions, whether the expectations are from professional colleagues or the supporting client public. In achieving this balance in the propriety of expectation, there could be three categories of determination. The first might be the prerogatives commonly recognized as being reserved for major determination by the client or lay group. The second might be that in which the responsibilities for control are shared. This would call for a well-defined working relationship between the professional and client group in terms of the procedures for the initiation of those ideas which might lead to policy decisions. The professional group might serve in an advisory capacity in the situation in which shared responsibilities are identified and determined. At the same time, the control over the determination of policy and procedures is not removed from the client group. The third category of determination would be those substantive areas in which the professional group performs tasks unique to their abilities. These tasks were developed through personal characteristics, specialized training, and experience. These tasks are so esoteric in nature that their performance could be placed safely only in the hands of a professional person.

In appraising the supervisor's effectiveness, the superintendent should attempt to assess the extent to which there exists a common understanding between the client group and the members of the teaching profession who come under the supervisory influence. Professionalization in this sense means achieving recognition of a dichotomy between the respective responsibilities of the client and the teaching groups. Once this dichotomy is established, each group should be able to operate independently within the agreed limits. It is well to observe at this point that a similar recognition of the substantive issues and the respective priorities of controls should exist among the various staff echelons as well as between the professional group and the lay-client group of a school community. The administrator must apply his criteria to the intra- as well as to the interrelationships existing for the teachers within the total professional group and within the client group.

A recent publication dealing with team teaching includes some pertinent observations on the place of the teacher in the organizational framework. Lortie has this to say:

> How do teachers get the authority which observers state they possess? What mechanisms grant them some ability to act in ways consistent with their work values? It is our hypothesis that the authority teachers possess stems from the spatial work arrangements found in most schools and from informal rules that are connected with those arrangements. The self-contained classroom, in this view, is more than a physical reality, for it refers as well to a social system, a set of recurrent and more or less permanent social relationships. Under this arrangement the teacher is separated from immediate supervision, and intrusion into his private domain is prevented by a set of understandings subscribed to by administrative officers and teacher colleagues. A set of norms exists which act to buttress the ecological separation: (1) the teacher should be free from the inter-

ference of other adults while teaching, (2) teachers should be considered and treated as equals, and (3) teachers should act in a nonintervening but friendly manner toward one another. Since these rules apparently re-enforce one another, they can be considered a pattern—a pattern which we call "the autonomy-equality pattern." This pattern, it must be emphasized, is not a formally accepted one and probably breaks down in crisis situations involving a teacher and the public. In the usual course of events, however, it seems to summarize how teachers strive to relate to each other and to administrative officials.[5]

FROM PROCESS TO PRODUCT

The product of supervisory effort, while related somewhat to many influences, is directly attributable to the processes of supervision. Each product of supervisory effort may be more dependent upon one set of processes than upon others. In the case of professional maturity, the component of process—stimulating and initiating—appears to have more contributory relationships to the product than do the other three components. The supervisor cannot command a teacher to act in a professional manner nor feel as a professional organizational member. Directing and controlling, then, as a component of process will not be particularly rewarding in a direct analysis of professional maturation. As a contributory component, directing and controlling can be important as a process in helping teachers to achieve distinction in effort in the responsibilities of the classroom.

Maturation professionally is so dependent upon the kinds of things that the individual is willing to cause himself to do that stimulating and initiating seem to be the best of the processes to support this particular product. A wise supervisor can relate himself to the teaching staff in such a way that its members will be stimulated not only to perform the expectations placed upon them as classroom teachers but also to perform as members of a group contributing to the institutional purposes. Initiating is really the evidence that the stimulation has been successful. Thus, teachers who are stimulated both to improve the teaching and learning efforts and to initiate innovations in attempting to improve the instructional program are persons who show evidence of professional maturation.

Those teachers who have responded favorably and aggressively to the supervisory processes of stimulating and initiating are persons who will, at some point, become aware of an acknowledgment of the successes of individual efforts. There probably is no therapy equal to acknowledged success for overcoming the ineffective efforts of teachers and stimulating them to select those behaviors which can be appraised highly.

[5] Dan C. Lortie, "The Teacher and Team Teaching: Suggestions for Long-Range Research," in Judson T. Shaplin and Henry F. Olds, Jr. (eds.), *Team Teaching* (New York: Harper & Row, 1964), pp. 274–275.

In the individual sense, this awareness of acknowledged success becomes one of the better motivators toward professional maturation. In a similar manner, individual members become aware of the achievements and successes of the organized group of which they are a part and, in this sense, gain professional maturation for the organized group. The acknowledgment of success for the teachers often is achieved, or at least the awareness is achieved, through the extent to which the higher echelons of administration and supervision permit them to participate in the policy decisions necessary to the organization. Such participation in policy formulation is another evidence of professional maturation. While teacher participation with the central office in decision-making is evidence of professionalization, the quality and product of participation also must be assessed. Concrete evidence is at hand when the higher echelons of control recognize the value of the contributions made by those in the lower echelons.

The desire for participation has been consummated at a high level of idealization on many occasions. Many administrators and supervisors have indicated a willingness to share the obligations of policy determinations with the teaching staff. It has been observed that this opportunity has been provided in several ways, some with unhappy results. If the teaching staff is asked to participate in policy determination, on the first such occasion the staff may not know how to respond. Some assistance will need to be given to the group to develop a readiness for the task at hand. This is comparable to the teacher using teacher–pupil planning with pupils who have never experienced the technique. It needs to be introduced gradually and carefully with the group being able to observe profitable results of the action in order for the situation to be successful. If the staff is asked to participate when there is a background of unsatisfactory experiences, the administrator will find the results unsuccessful unless assurance is given to the staff that this time their views really matter and will be reflected in the final policy. If the opportunity for participation in policy determination is granted and the group judgment is not agreeable to the supervisors, a crisis is at hand. There are many unpleasant examples in which the privileges of participation have been negated by the supervisor overruling the judgment of the group he invited to participate. On other occasions, the negation is accomplished by referring and re-referring the issue until the participating group is worn down to the point of abandoning its original desires and points of view. This makes democratic administration and participation in policy decisions nothing more than a hollow experience and a sham of the democratic process. Administrators and supervisors must not commit themselves to the sharing of decisions unless they are prepared to accept on some occasions group decisions that are not in accordance with their own wishes. Failure to observe this precaution and this commitment to the purpose of participation in itself becomes evidence of the lack of professional maturity on the part of the administrator and the supervisor.

The failure of leadership to exhibit professional maturation is prime evidence that little maturation has occurred among the staff committed to it. Public images, as well as self-images, possessed by members of the profession and the supporting public become conditioners of the awareness of the opportunities for maturing as a profession. The fact that caricatures about school teachers have often been developed has not encouraged members of the occupational group to possess the acceptable self-image which seems to be possessed by members of other occupational groups. The caricatures involve the possession of personal traits such as anemic physique, odd social traits, extreme sensitiveness to criticism and suggestions, and an absence of the ability to manage material wealth. Perhaps the fact that the caricature exists is due in part to the observed behavior of members of the profession as well as to a lack of understanding on the part of the client group. The process of supervision—particularly the component of stimulating and initiating—should help the members of the profession behave in such a manner that the unpleasant caricatures of the past are replaced by images which indicate a greater respect for the teaching profession.

There is yet another type of concern related to the determination of the degree of professional maturity. This is in the area of the status symbols that are available to all echelons of the staff and expressed in terms of the achievements of the particular position or position levels. Unfortunately, the concept of the educational system in this country is the ladder in which the pupil places his foot on the lowest rung and year by year progresses to the top of the ladder. The ladder idea, while useful for studying a total system of education, has done a serious disservice to those who are employed to perform the necessary functions at the lower levels. Only recently has progress been made in abandoning the notion that teachers at each successively higher level should be paid at a higher rate. The traditional practice implies that it is less important to teach successfully at the kindergarten or first grade level than it is to teach successfully and effectively at the intermediate, upper-grade, high school, or college level.

The amount and nature of training that teachers must possess to teach at these various levels have been defined in such a way that there is a differentiation. Factors of this type are gradually being eliminated in the attempt to see each member of the teaching profession contributing in an important and equal way. To the extent that the incumbents of the positions at the various levels use the positions as status-achievement devices, the progress toward total professional maturity will be deterred. The fact that the latter concept exists stimulates some persons in the profession to seek mobility upward as a means of achieving personal satisfaction, professional prestige, and more money. Mobility upward is a prerogative of the individual rather than evidence of professional development or maturation. The symbols of prestige, such as office gadgets, schedule advantages, parking privileges, travel support, and other major and minor appurtenances, if unrelated to the nature and quality of the service rendered, should not be used as evidence of increased professionalization.

SUB-CRITERION MEASURES

In each sub-criterion measure, how would you establish standards for making judgments?

Each of the criterion measures designated as chapter titles in Part V are broad areas of concern in supervision and, in order to be serviceable, must be broken into component parts. The component parts are designated as sub-criterion measures. These sub-criterion measures are sufficiently specific to facilitate the process of collecting information which would make possible the evaluation of the success of supervisory efforts. Under each of the sub-criterion measures specific questions are raised which will direct or structure the collection of information pertinent to facilitating judgments.

The first sub-criterion measure is that *the members of the faculty participate actively in professional organizational activities.* The following questions are offered as illustrative of the types of information needed to make judgments regarding this sub-criterion measure:

1. Do teachers in substantial numbers seek leadership positions in professional group activities?
2. Are there frequent intergroup exchanges of position statements and persuasions?
3. Will staff members attend professional organizational meetings on non-school time?
4. What questions would you ask?

The second sub-criterion is that *self-improvements proceed without the compulsion of local regulations and salary schedule benefits.* These questions may structure the gathering of pertinent information:

1. How many staff members reinvest one percent of the annual salary in self-improvements related to employment assignments?
2. What percent of the staff pursues advanced studies prior to salary schedule barrier arrangements?
3. What formal encouragements or requirements for self-improvements are placed upon the administrative and supervisory personnel?
4. To what extent are so-called self-improvement efforts identifiably related to position expectations?
5. What questions would you ask?

The third sub-criterion measure is that *organized groups discipline their inept members as vigorously as they defend the injured.* These questions seem appropriate to this measure:

1. How many times have organized groups openly supported a disciplinary action directed toward one of their members?

2. How many times have organized groups openly supported a member subjected to disciplinary action?
3. Are the organized group policies clear with respect to the employment of new colleagues and their dismissal for cause?
4. Are these instances of internecine conflict among peers?
5. What questions would you ask?

The fourth sub-criterion measure is that *subordinates state professional beliefs calmly and firmly even though the position is contrary to those held by superiors.* These questions are designed to gather needed information to support judgments in this area of measure:

1. Do subordinates perceive a sanction system operating in relation to superodinates?
2. Is there a free interchange of opinion between subordinates and superordinates in staff meetings?
3. Do individuals state their personal opinions in open meetings without seeking subgroup support?
4. Do the superordinates claim the prerogatives of veto power as inherent to status position?
5. What questions would you ask?

The fifth sub-criterion measure is that *the staff members give top priority of their energies and efforts to the obligations and expectations of the professional assignment.* The following types of questions may help secure pertinent information:

1. What percentage of the professional staff accepts additional employment which encroaches upon reasonable school time and energy expectations?
2. Do staff self-assigned tasks occur within the area of professional competence and commitments?
3. To what extent do staff members see community service properly included in the array of professional expectations?
4. How many curriculum developments and instructional improvements are initiated by administrative and supervisory expectations?
5. How many curriculum developments and instructional improvements are initiated by non-administrative and supervisory personnel?
6. What questions would you ask?

There is an assumption inherent in this discussion of the evaluation of professional maturation that professionalization is important to the improvement of instructional services. Those who are unable to accept this assumption must seek another criterion measure as a vehicle for evaluating this aspect of the supervisory program. Even though professional maturity as a criterion measure might be unsatisfactory or unacceptable, other measures can be substituted. The fact that five criterion measures are used in this Part does not imply that evaluation could not proceed on either more or less than five. Those who prefer to reject the measures suggested in this chapter may utilize one or more of the measures which are suggested in the next four chapters.

SELECTED REFERENCES

1. American Educational Research Association, "Teacher Personnel," *Review of Educational Research,* XXXIII:4, 1963.
2. Association for Supervision and Curriculum Development, *Supervision: Emerging Profession,* Robert R. Leeper (ed.), Washington, D.C.: National Education Association, 1969.
3. Beach, Fred F., "Professionalization of Educational Administration," *School Life,* XLII, October, 1959, pp. 5–8.
4. Dumont, Matthew P., "The Changing Face of Professionalism," in Lanore A. Netzer *et al., Education, Administration, and Change: The Redeployment of Resources.* New York: Harper & Row, 1970. Chap. II.
5. Lieberman, Myron, *Education as a Profession.* Englewood Cliffs, N.J.: Prentice-Hall, 1956.
6. Lieberman, Myron, *The Future of Public Education.* Chicago: University of Chicago Press, 1960.
7. O'Brien, Dean W., "Reference and Deference to Authority as Factors Affecting Professional Autonomy in Education: A Case Study." Unpublished doctoral dissertation. Madison: University of Wisconsin, 1963.
8. Shaplin, Judson T. and Henry F. Olds, Jr. (eds.), *Team Teaching.* New York: Harper & Row, 1964. pp. 274–275.

19

Curriculum Developments

The most common definition of curriculum is that it constitutes all of the educative experiences that come under the direction and control of the school. There is little doubt that this concept of the curriculum has been extremely serviceable, but it unfortunately causes many people to see the breadth of the curriculum as encompassing almost an unlimited universe.

BOUNDARIES OF THIS CRITERION MEASURE

There are, of course, extremes in point of view with respect to the above definition. The more idealistic would see it as being composed of the textbooks, libraries, laboratories, field trips, school rules and regulations, opportunities for leisure activities, sandbox in the kindergarten classroom, performance presentations for parents, and a host of other items that could be catalogued almost without end. One of the hazards of this broad definition is that those concerned with curricular development, direction, and promotion extend their concerns to practically all of the supporting facilities that are needed in order to provide an ever increasing number of activities which are school-sponsored. It seems that the person responsible for curriculum development might be encouraged by this broad concept of curriculum to see the construction of a building, the financial supports of the educational program, and the administrative procedures of the central office as being subservient rather than supportive to the controller of those activities labeled "curriculum." It should be remembered by those who see this definition in its broadest terms that, if responsibility or influence is claimed over the broadest range of supporting personnel and activities, the evaluations of the effectiveness of the person who controls the curriculum must include at the same time the success and failure of all of the presumed subservients to the curriculum.

Practical considerations eliminate the necessity for the person responsible for curriculum development to have other than specifically defined responsibilities with respect to the curriculum. By specific is meant that the design of curriculum support by other agents and agencies should be sensitive to the curriculum director's control but that, when any of these personnel or agencies fail, it is not a failure of the curriculum director. The person who claims control must at the same time accept responsibility for that which is controlled.

Is this undesirable? Why?

The other extreme to this concept of curriculum is that, no matter how many words are used in describing the various educative experiences sponsored by the school, in the end the teacher and the textbook constitute the largest part of the curriculum content. This, perhaps, is about as extreme in the conservative direction as the other definition was in the liberal direction. Neither extreme can be completely right and, perhaps, neither can that person who finds the middle ground be much more correct in his perception of what constitutes the curriculum. The advantage of the middle ground is that a reasonable number of categories of learning activities can be identified and these will be reasonable from the standpoint of analysis as well as the probability of control by one directing agent in the school organization.

The evaluation of the curriculum director in the first instance would be difficult because of the multiplicity of responsibilities. On the other hand, the evaluation of the curriculum director's activities in the more conservative instance would be substantially simplified, but only in the sense of a limitation of the number of items for which responsibility is accepted. Evaluation in the end must be defined in scope, depth, and character by the kinds of change induced in the student. These will give direction to a reasonable list of expectations which can be placed upon that person who is responsible for the development of the curriculum in the school program.

The chapter title indicates that there will be *developments*. Here, again, is a term that connotes change. As has been true in all other discussions in this book, change is presumed to be directional and the direction is toward a better way of doing those things which help the pupils to accomplish maximum development. One of the persisting problems in the organization and management of the instructional program in a school system is that of making reasonable differentiations between curriculum interests and those of the methodology of instruction. There is little doubt that curriculum and instruction, even though not necessarily the same items of activity and attention, do constitute two sides of the same coin. It is the matter of what to teach and how to teach it. If the two terms are combined, the total task of curriculum and instruction is that of selecting, organizing, presenting, and evaluating learning experiences which are designed to allow the student maximum possible development. This concept opens the possibility of seeing curriculum concerns related to the selection and organization of learning experiences, whereas the instructional concerns are with the presentation and evaluation of the learning experiences.

How may conflicts be kept at a minimum?

Two chapters in Part V have been established as vehicles of evaluating these aspects of supervisory activities. Chapter 19 is devoted to the concerns of curriculum developments and Chapter 20 to instructional improvements. If the considerations of curriculum and instruction are accepted as being closely related as indicated above, then it is possible to accept a division of labor with respect to each of these two functions. In many school systems both concerns are lodged in one person. This, at least, causes little difficulty with assignments if one person is responsible for both curricular and instructional procedures. As the school system becomes larger, there is an inclination to separate the assignments into two positions, so that one is primarily responsible for the curriculum and another for the instruction. A division of labor cannot be denied as a meritorious move on the part of those directing the total organization. However, the establishment of two offices with coordinate power and influence is an invitation to a conflict of interests primarily because of the possible overemphasis that may be encouraged in each area to the exclusion of the other.

If curriculum and instruction cannot be differentiated sharply in concept, they cannot be differentiated precisely with respect to the assignment of functions to central office personnel. Many of the larger school systems have resolved this staff problem by lodging both functions in an office such as an "assistant superintendent in charge of instruction" and creating subordinate positions which differentiate between the concerns of curriculum and instruction. The division of labor and assignment has been made successfully in other areas of the school operation and there is no reason to assume that such cannot be done in the organizational attention given to curricular and instructional activities.

One of the continuing basic problems of conflict in the understanding of curriculum is whether a reorganized experience is to be viewed as a new experience. The debate has been going on for some time and there is no apparent resolution of it. Some hold that a curriculum has not been revised, and therefore developed, unless the result of the revision is the introduction of all new content. In other words, the person who takes this point of view believes that periodically the old world must cease and a new one created. Idealistically, it is a wonderful thing to consider, but practically it can never happen. The point of view taken here is that the new curriculum should be built upon the most successful of the present ones and new experiences should be built continuously into and onto that structure. This point of view presumes curriculum adequacy in terms of continuing change. Reorganized experiences, then, will be considered *new* insofar as the curriculum is designed to influence pupil learning opportunities. The reorganization of the content is presumed to be for the purpose of establishing an organization or sequence of learning experiences which will result in more desirable pupil behaviors.

What are the virtues of "newness"?

The final implication in the title and subject matter of this chapter is that the learning experiences of concern here are identifiable, definable, predetermined, and controlled by the school. This means that the point of view applied in evaluating the supervisor's responsibility for curriculum development will be limited to those elements which approach the above characteristics. Further, it is assumed that only those elements of curriculum will become a part of the evaluative considerations which the school has selected under its own power or has accepted as its responsibility and admits to full control.

THE WITHIN AND AMONG RELATIONSHIPS

There are many curricular crosscurrents of interests, concerns, responsibilities, and people. It is well to enumerate some of these before moving directly to the main problem of the chapter, evaluation in terms of the criterion measure of curriculum developments. In all school systems, decisions are made as to whether, through organization and consequently curriculum, the responsibility will encompass kindergarten through twelfth grade. In many communities the responsibilities have been extended both downward and upward. Downward involves concern for the learning opportunities that might be provided in the nursery school. The upward extension includes a concern for certain types of post-high school opportunities either of a terminal or continuing nature. At any rate, these concerns in organization for education express a responsibility in curriculum for the coordination of a plan from the beginning of the school's responsibility until its declared termination of the formal provisions for learning experiences.

Regardless of whether the limits are N-14, K-12, or 1-6, there are both vertical and horizontal concerns with respect to curriculum responsibilities. The *vertical* means that a sequence of experiences is articulated well from one grade through a given number of succeeding grades or levels of work. The *horizontal* is the concern applied to the particular grade level which occurs at one time. Put simply, it means that the planning for the language arts might be viewed either as a responsibility from one grade to the next succeeding grade or as a program which cuts across all other subject areas at a particular time in the life of the student. Regardless of whether the curriculum attack is described as vertical or horizontal, there will be categorized areas of learning experiences usually called subjects or courses. Among these, interlocking fields or subject areas are recognized. The categorized learning experiences are called subjects and can be considered as standing alone among the many similarly organized bodies of learning experience or subjects to which the student is committed. Language arts can be studied as language arts, but to presume that language arts is completely separated from the social studies or other subject fields is sheer folly.

How would balance in the curriculum be in evidence?

The overlap of both content and procedures for learning is substantial. Even though it is theoretically possible to dichotomize these learning experiences into mutually exclusive bodies of knowledge, the fact remains that all will be integrated in the individual student as he proceeds with his learning. The student will behave as one person regardless of how he receives his opportunities to develop.

Another point of consideration in the evaluation of curriculum development is that of seeing it in a perspective of pupil capacity and learning pace. The curriculum cannot exist apart from the instructional procedures of the learning characteristics of the pupil. If there is, in this closely knit relationship, a way of identifying the sequence of learning relationships, it might be that of viewing them on a continuum in the responsibilities of the supervisor which extends from the *content* to the *methodology* to the *evaluation* of products. The content, then, would be the organized body of learning experiences; the methodology would be the means of communication or the instructional aspect of the curriculum; and the evaluation would be those responsibilities involved in determining what happens to the student after he has been committed to both the content and the instructional procedures.

The categories of input (curriculum content) have no identical categories of output (student behavior). This is a major complication in evaluating those responsible for developing the curriculum. The time lag between the input and output offers additional complications. Many professional educators are unhappy, and perhaps properly so, in the presence of such simplifications as input and output. There is no intent here, by choice of words, to indicate that a behavioral characteristic of a student at any particular time can be traced back with precision to elements of the content of the curriculum. The point is that there are two separate operations—one involving categorization for the sake of organization in the curriculum design and the other involving human behaviors which, even though subjected to categorization, cannot be held in a one-to-one relationship to the categories of curriculum.

How may a school staff know when curriculum change should be planned?

The responsibilities for the evaluation of instructional improvements (see Chapter 20) are somewhat more simple, even though their impact upon the instructional program is dependent upon the teacher as an intermediary. The curriculum is one more step removed from the final target of evaluation, namely, pupil development. It is important, then, that any evaluations of the supervisory efforts in curriculum developments be on a reasonably long-term basis. There is little justification and ought to be no tolerance for pressures placed upon those responsible for directing the curriculum to be evaluated on an annual basis, at least insofar as the final outcomes are concerned. If some elements of the periodic evaluation are espoused, there should not be emphasis on the organization of supervisor and teacher efforts to bring about curriculum changes which eventually may be determined as an improvement in the educational enterprise. There are then many crosscurrents and cross-fertilizations of ideas, responsibilities, and staff assignments. All have some responsibilities for change. The change should be in the positive direction which is so labeled because of its implication for better opportunities for pupil development. The responsibility for change, then, is for those curriculum developments which must be evaluated in the light of rigid standards of pupil learning opportunity and resultant outcomes.

IMPLICATIONS OF THE ASSUMPTIONS

As in the other chapters, certain assumptions in the basic list are especially appropriate to the discussion at hand. Assumption number ten—"Supervision of instruction and curriculum development must be cooperative and coordinative in operational functions"—deals with the establishment of a dichotomy of responsibility in curriculum development and supervision of instruction and thus makes this assumption of key importance. The two responsibilities are closely related even though assigned in the organizational pattern to different persons. Success for either incumbent will depend upon this ability and inclination to be cooperative and coordinative in professional activities. Even though, as indicated above, the same person is often responsible for both curriculum and instruction, there is the problem of a proper integration within that person which assumes that the selection and organization of learning experiences are not separated from the presentation and evaluation of those same experiences. In other words, there is no inclination here to encourage a professionalization of curriculum directors and instructional supervisors apart from the general professionalization of administrative and supervisory officers and responsibilities within the total organization.

Do professional associations encourage divisiveness among those of diverse responsibilities?

Assumption number eleven, dealing with contributory and supportive functions, is important to the consideration of curriculum developments. Here again, because of the broad scope of responsibilities and the difficulty of dichotomizing effectively among other functions within the school organization, the contributory and supportive functions have been emphasized both in the assumption stated and in two chapters of Part II.

Assumption number thirteen, dealing with the components of the processes of supervision, has important implications for curriculum developments but these implications are discussed in their relationships to evaluation more completely in the next chapter, which deals with instructional improvements. Assumption number sixteen constitutes the basis for the criterion measure of emerging expectations and is discussed in Chapter 22. The point of mentioning it here is that the assumption forcefully applies to the consideration of curriculum developments. The emerging expectations usually are stated less in terms of school services than in terms of pupil behaviors. Because the curriculum pattern is of substantial influence upon behavioral outcomes, it is obvious that the relationship between curriculum developments and emerging expectations is a close one. Success in the expectations described in Chapter 22 will indicate or signal the beginning of immediate and substantial concerns for the evaluative considerations presented in this chapter.

Assumption number four, while discussed and related to many other parts of the consideration of instructional supervision, carries substantial import for the concerns of curriculum development. It deals with planning as a primary factor in improvement programs. As already indicated, curriculum development implies change and change is equated with improvement. Because curriculum is an educative experience that cannot be altered as rapidly as some other service aspects of the school experience, it is essential that the long-range view be applied. "Long-range" is a fruitless term unless it is given specific meaning for planning; thus, the impact of assumption four upon the considerations of this chapter.

FROM PROCESS TO PRODUCT

Curriculum is not a process in the sense of supervision of instruction. Curriculum contains the plans developed by which instruction shall be guided in structuring and facilitating pupil learning. Curriculum, then, depends upon the term *developments* for the connotation of change or movement. The concern in this criterion measure is with the developments. It is impossible, however, to think of curriculum development without considering its static form at some point. There is an identifiable change when the planner makes the desired alterations or developments. Change in the curriculum, then, is the process which is the subject of evaluation in this chapter.

There are at least two stages to be considered in evaluation.

The first is that of the design of the curriculum itself. The second is the outcomes of the curriculum plan in terms of pupil behavior. The movement to be studied, then, is from curriculum content to the learning process to the products in terms of pupil behavior.

The procedures for instituting changes in the curriculum can be analyzed in terms of the four components of the processes of supervision. The division of attention between supervision and curriculum, as differentiated activities, makes little difference in terms of the analysis of the developments in the curriculum.

The first component of process in supervision is directing and controlling. In each of the components of process some illustrations of tasks will be given in order to clarify the way in which the components may be used in assessing curriculum developments as an outcome of supervisory effort. The supervisor is performing *directing* tasks when he arranges an in-service meeting at which a specialist in social studies presents an analysis of changing demands upon the school, with particular reference to the social studies curriculum. The supervisor is performing *controlling* tasks when he establishes the procedures for screening and selecting textbooks for the intermediate-level social studies program. Again, the attempt is to clarify the difference between the two words used as the processes of the component. Directing tasks are those in which the supervisor tries to guide the person being supervised to change his immediate goal and his ways of performing but does not impose his own predetermined goals and procedures upon that person. In the case of controlling, however, the connotation is more rigid with respect to the supervisor's demand that the teacher conform to a particular way of doing things—a way which may have been determined by the supervisor, by his subordinates, or by a cooperative action involving both superordinates and the teachers.

The second component of process is stimulating and initiating. Illustrations of the kinds of tasks that might be involved in this category of the supervisory process are offered. The supervisor may perform *stimulating* tasks when he reviews the case study information on transfer pupils. Upon release of this information gathered from case studies, the supervisor is in a position to inform the members of the staff and the people in the community. If the pupils find transitions from one school to another difficult, the problem is identified and the knowledge of the nature of that problem is designed to stimulate the staff to make the necessary corrections.

The supervisor is performing an *initiating* task when he identifies, announces, and encourages the observance of minimum common learnings in each grade which will bring about articulation horizontally and vertically. This is specific action which may have resulted from the above instance in which the stimulating task was illustrated. The difference between stimulating and initiating is the amount of specificity and rigidity of direction and control that is exercised by the supervisor over the supervised.

The third component of the processes of supervision is analyzing and appraising. The supervisor is performing *analyzing* tasks when he directs a grade-level committee in the analysis of the curriculum with respect to the facts and concepts involved in a unit of learning experience. This plan might follow an organization such as the taxonomy of educational objectives developed by Bloom.[1] In this instance, the supervisor is not offering this type of leadership for the purpose of stimulating, although stimulating may result. He is, however, structuring the analysis for the staff and, in this sense, is both initiating and controlling the activity. The process itself, however, is the analyzing process and need not be mutually exclusive of the other components of process. The supervisor is performing an *appraising* task when he develops the tests and norms for testing a pupil's ability to perform at each of the taxonomic levels which have been established. Here, then, is the technical ability of the supervisor being used to provide skills in the development of the curriculum which many of the teachers perhaps do not possess.

The fourth component of the processes of supervision is designing and implementing. The supervisor is performing *designing* tasks when he directs a series of committees and consultants in identifying the strong elements in "physical environment" education and drafting a plan for instruction. The tasks involved in designing are not necessarily all performed by the supervisor. In fact, the wise supervisor causes many things to be done rather than trying to do them all himself. The important point is that the procedures for designing be sound, that they meet the approval of the supervisor, and that the supervisor make them available to the staff as they participate in the development of some new curricular area. The decision remains with the supervisor whether the tasks are performed personally or whether they have been performed through the structured influence upon other persons.

The supervisor is performing *implementing* tasks when he delineates the tasks of the staff in putting into operation some plan that has been developed and accepted at all necessary approval points. The drafting of the plan for implementation and advising with respect to its use is the implementing responsibility. This occurs almost continuously whether the implementation is with respect to a broad and complicated design of curricular change or whether it is involved with converting some classroom methods such as "present and discuss" to another method such as the "laboratory approach" in the teaching of science.

[1] Benjamin S. Bloom (ed.), *Taxonomy of Educational Objectives* (New York: Longmans, Green, 1956).

SUB-CRITERION MEASURES

The final outcome of a curricular change effort may not be known for some time, as indicated earlier in the chapter. As a matter of fact, each school system should be engaged continuously in follow-up studies. These should be designed to look both at the judgments of the former students who were subjected to the curriculum and at how well prepared the students were for their vocational or advanced-schooling commitments. This does not mean that judgments cannot be made prior to that time. Some judgments can be made during the semester or the year in which the students are studying a particular subject. Further, the curriculum plan as developed can be judged as a plan before it has been put into operation at all. In this case, there is no point in studying pupil reactions or behaviors; rather, it is important to analyze the components of a plan and make judgments about them.

The items that should be included in a written plan were discussed in Chapter 16. This evaluation constitutes only a precautionary judgment which will give some assurance that the unsatisfactory aspects of a plan will not be put into operation, and, consequently, will not influence pupil behavior. In the end, however, all curriculum developments must be judged in terms of pupil learnings and behaviors. Thus, instruction that takes place as the intermediary between the curriculum plan and pupil learning must be taken into consideration. It is grossly unfair to assume that all curriculum plans will be handled with equal effectiveness by the classroom teachers, the most potent element in producing the successful pupil behaviors which later may be observed. In the process of changing the curriculum, however, even in the later stages when everyone can look back to make the evaluation, the teachers who are bound by the curriculum constitute the best source of information. The best information regarding pupil behaviors is gathered through the evaluation of teachers who have had the opportunity to use the particular curriculum plan. This judgment integrates the outcome and the curriculum facility based upon the teacher's obligation to teaching.

In each sub-criterion measure, how would you establish the standards for judgments?

The first sub-criterion measure is that *there is regular, continuing, systematized, and scheduled scrutiny of curriculum content and design.* These questions may give direction to the collection of information to support judgments:

1. Is there a description or a diagram of staff organization for curriculum study?
2. Do teachers report curriculum study as a continuing aspect of position expectations?
3. Is a time schedule in evidence which shows the distribution of study efforts and change attacks?
4. Are staff members conversant with the procedures for scrutinizing the long- and short-range plans for curriculum study and change?

5. Is there congruence in staff perceptions of the decision points governing curriculum change?
6. What questions would you ask?

The second sub-criterion measure is that *there are standardized procedures for selecting, organizing, and proceeding with known recurring tasks such as textbook selection.* These questions may suggest types of information appropriate for making judgments:

1. Have all staff members agreed upon the policies to be pursued in the choice of instructional aids?
2. Have printed copies of the dates of new textbook adoptions been distributed to staff and publishers' representatives?
3. How many staff members participated in establishing the criteria for the selection of textbooks?
4. Is there consensus regarding the recurring tasks which require review and decision?
5. Are reports of *ad hoc* and/or standing committees available for review?
6. What questions would you ask?

The third sub-criterion measure is that *there should be planned and operating procedures for coordinating school and non-school educative programs.* The following questions should assist in the collection of pertinent data:

1. Is there a system-wide council that is concerned primarily with the curriculum pattern?
2. How are laymen used in considering the needs of youth?
3. What communication facilities can be identified as intended to bring together professional and lay people?
4. Does a sample of the lay population give evidence of knowledge of the relationships between school and non-school educational programs?
5. Do members of civic, fraternal, and religious organizations ever discuss their impact upon the school programs as organizations?
6. What questions would you ask?

Sub-criterion measure number four is that *there must be functional knowledge of the existence, nature, and potential use of the broad scope of instructional aids and materials.* This embodies the research-oriented attack in the study of the curriculum. The following questions may be helpful in collecting information pertinent to making judgments in this sub-criterion measure:

1. Are there frequent demonstrations of new mechanical aids to teaching?
2. Are there specialist squads on the staff to identify, review, and evaluate instructional aids representing their major competencies?
3. Are there research plans and facilities devoted exclusively to newly marketed aids?
4. Is there a centralized local resource to receive teacher suggestions for undeveloped but needed aids?
5. Can a random sample of the teaching staff give accurate informa-

tion on the source of criteria for the adoption and purchase of newly developed aids?
6. What questions would you ask?

Sub-criterion measure number five is that *there must be evidence of long-range plans for evaluation of curriculum and the design for change.* The following questions may be helpful for those who are making judgments about the effectiveness of curriculum developments in the collecting of pertinent information:

1. Can the superintendent produce information regarding the curriculum changes introduced during the current decade?
2. Are any diagrammatic presentations of plans for curriculum change exhibited prominently in the central office?
3. Do classroom teachers seem to be knowledgeable about the probable changes scheduled for study in the next few years?
4. Are current efforts at specific curriculum change demonstrably related to a long-range plan?
5. Is there as much enthusiasm observable for curriculum designing as for implementing activities?
6. What questions would you ask?

The evaluation of curriculum developments has been limited to the supervisor's observable success in effecting curriculum changes related specifically to the selection and organization of learning experiences. It is reiterated at this point that these two aspects of curriculum change have been separated from the two supplementary aspects of presenting and evaluating learning experiences. The purpose of the separation serves the convenience of analysis and discussion, but these are not suggested as discrete entities. The activities related to the presentation and evaluation of learning experiences are the subject of the next chapter.

SELECTED REFERENCES

1. American Educational Research Association, "Curriculum Planning and Development," *Review of Educational Research,* XXX:3, June, 1960.
2. Association for Supervision and Curriculum Development, Yearbook, *Balance in the Curriculum.* Washington, D.C.: National Education Association, 1962.
3. Association for Supervision and Curriculum Development, Yearbook, *New Insights and the Curriculum.* Washington, D.C.: National Education Association, 1963.
4. Association for Supervision and Curriculum Development, Bulletin, *What Are the Sources of the Curriculum? A Symposium.* Washington, D.C.: National Education Association, 1962.
5. Bloom, Benjamin S. (ed.), *Taxonomy of Educational Objectives.* New York: Longmans, Green, 1956.
6. Feyereisen, Kathryn V., A. John Fiorino, and Arlene T. Nowak, *Supervision and Curriculum Renewal: A Systems Approach.* New York: Appleton-Century-Crofts, 1970.

7. Grobman, Hulda, *Evaluation Activities of Curriculum Projects.* AERA Monograph Series on Curriculum Evaluation. Chicago: Rand McNally & Company, 1968.
8. Krathwohl, David R. *et al., Taxonomy of Educational Objectives: The Classification of Educational Goals—Handbook II: Affective Domain.* New York: David McKay Company, 1956.
9. Sanders, Norris M., *Classroom Questions: What Kinds?* New York: Harper & Row, 1966.
10. Tyler, Ralph W., Robert M. Gagne, and Michael Scriven, *Perspective of Curriculum Evaluation.* AERA Monograph Series on Curriculum Evaluation. Chicago: Rand McNally & Company, 1967.

20

Instructional Improvements

The titles of Chapters 19 and 20 indicate that a distinction is made between curriculum developments and instructional improvements. The fact that the two are separated for discussion is not to be interpreted as an inclination on the part of these authors to see curriculum designs and instructional methodologies as separate entities. Their characteristics are sufficiently different that an analysis can be made of each separately.

BOUNDARIES OF THIS CRITERION MEASURE

What distinctions do you make between curriculum and instruction?

There long have been arguments about whether a pupil can be taught without *teaching him something,* as well as arguments over whether *what is taught* can be separated from *how it is taught.* The arguments along this line have perhaps been profitable as intellectual experiences for those participating, but they have led to little concrete assistance toward the improvement of the instructional program. One may think of the total instructional responsibility, which is borne by the teacher, as being that of selecting, organizing, presenting, and evaluating outcomes of learning experiences. The tasks and behaviors involved in the selection and organization of learning experiences are those which meet the distinct responsibilities of content or curriculum. At the same time, those tasks and behaviors related to the responsibilities for presenting and evaluating the learning experiences also have unique characteristics. It is in this sense, then, that a differentiation is made between curriculum developments and instructional improvements. Again, it is emphasized that even though this distinction is made, the two items are interwoven operationally.

Are changes in the closeness of the supervisor to the classroom caused more by the supervisor-teacher ratio than by the theory of supervision?

The responsibilities of the supervisors are identified readily but do not elicit so readily the sympathy of those who establish the expectations for supervision. The classroom teacher has an immediate contact with the pupil and has major control over the classroom operation. On the other hand, the supervisor has a remote contact with the classroom in the sense that, whatever he wants to effectuate there, he is dependent upon an intermediary person—the teacher—to carry out his wishes. Obviously, the supervisor is somewhat remote from the actual classroom operation if one considers not the fact that there may be frequent visits or observations of a single classroom activity but rather that the supervisor is responsible for some influence upon many teachers. Both time and ability to maintain contact with a multitude of people and things keep the supervisor increasingly separated from the actual classroom activity.

The title of this chapter implies the necessity for change. The word *improvement* itself declares that some of the things that are done now will be stopped and some things that are not done now will be started. Interwoven between these polar intentions are the many activities in which there will be slight or major changes. The term *instructional improvement* is superior to instructional changes in the sense that a direction is implied in the word improvement. It means, then, that the instructional procedures shall be subjected to change but, when subjected to change, should move in the direction of better outcomes. Further, the title implies that there is a broad view of the term *instructional.* It deals with more than the readily identifiable methods of teaching. Involved in the whole process of directing learning will be the selection and use of various types of teaching and learning aids as well as the selection and use of those techniques which provide an evaluation of the results of the teaching-learning activities.

Because the title of this chapter constitutes one of the major criterion measures for the evaluation of the supervisory program, it should be borne in mind that the referent point for the teacher is pupil improvement and that the supervisor has the same referent point. Its use for supervisors, however, is less serviceable in the sense that the supervisor's impact is upon the teacher or the conditions related to teaching. The teacher may institute some observable changes which can be called improvements, but they are improvements only in the case that the teaching effort results in the improvement of learning outcomes. Again, it is emphasized that supervision is the secondary line of contact with the pupil, because the teacher stands between the two referent outcome subjects. In evaluating supervision, the referent point of instructional improvement must be identified in those results of the supervisory facility relating to those processes of teaching which improve pupil learning. This constitutes an extremely complex type of evaluation.

As emphasized elsewhere in this book, it is grossly unfair for teachers to have the evaluation of the supervisory program based only upon pupil outcomes. This is more directly an evaluation of the teaching effectiveness and may be remotely indicative of supervisory effectiveness. In a sense, this major criterion measure for evaluating supervision as supervision is useful only to the extent that the evaluator can identify a chain of events initiated by the supervisor and find its conclusion in the learning outcomes of pupils.

IMPLICATIONS OF THE ASSUMPTIONS

Each chapter presentation has been related to one or more of the assumptions presented in the original list in Chapter 3. Assumption number ten, which indicated that the supervision of instruction and curriculum development must be made from the same pattern of operational relationships, was closely related to the preceding chapter, "Curriculum Developments." While this was discussed in Chapter 19, it is equally related to the considerations involved in this chapter. Even though the dichotomy has been made for purposes of analysis and discussion, it seems well to reunite the two aspects of curriculum and instruction in the one assumption which calls for cooperative and coordinative efforts.

Closely related to the content of this chapter is assumption number eleven—"The contributory and supportive functions of supervision include those policy determinations and implementations that deal with the improvement of the instructional program and its influential environments." In an earlier chapter, there was presented an extended discussion of the ways in which a supervisor or any other staff officer might perform certain supportive functions to selected line officers (see Chapter 8). There are also occasions when one supervisor may provide a supportive assistance to another supervisor. The intent of assumption eleven is to indicate that when decisions are being made, whether in terms of the policy development or operational design, the supervisor is concerned because of the potential impact upon the instructional program. Thus, in considering the impact of policy upon instructional improvements, those policies which deter or support the instructional program may well be considered evidence of the degree of effectiveness of the supervisor. Beyond the concerns with policy development in which the supervisor must perform directly, there are many other aspects of the total school operation which have instructional implications. In all of these the supervisor has responsibilities and these responsibilities become the objects of analysis in the evaluation of the effectiveness of supervision.

Some of the other assumptions deal somewhat less directly but still pertinently with the instructional responsibilities of the supervisor. It was indicated in assumption number four that one of the most consistent factors in all aspects of the operation of the school system is that of accomplishment of program improvements. There are improvement programs for buildings, for grounds, for financial arrangements, and for managerial accomplishments, as well as improvement program demands for instruction. All of these other areas are supportive of the instructional program, but at the same time they constitute unique, identifiable, but separate kinds of responsibilities.

Assumption number twelve indicates that there are both personal and situational factors which influence the behaviors of staff and pupils. In considering instructional improvements, there are situational factors which become direct responsibilities of supervisory behavior. The various sub-criterion measures discussed later in this chapter are directed to some aspects of the instructional program which are apart from the influence over the behavior of the teacher during the teaching act. There are non-school environmental influences which affect the instructional program of improvement but which may require that some responsibility be assigned to other officers, both in and out of the school, in order to effect the proper control and, therefore, to identify pertinent responsibilities. Assumption number thirteen is directly related to the outcomes of instructional improvement activities because it refers to the components of process which constitute the major program of impact as designed by the supervisor. The criterion measures, then, are closely related to the considerations of the components of process. The process leads to the product and this constitutes the referent point for the organization of the discussion here. Also, assumption number fifteen deals with the appropriateness of declared primary expectations of the various positions in the school system. This assumption indicates that there may be some points at which the supervisor ought not to be charged with responsibility. If he is not given the privilege of sharing in prior sequential decisions, he should not be held responsible for the behavioral results of others and thus lose the control over those factors essential to his own success.

FROM PROCESS TO PRODUCT

The major referent points for the evaluation of the supervisor's impact upon instructional improvement are found in the processes by which the supervisor attempts to influence the instructional program. This influence naturally involves teachers more than the inanimate objects and material which become a part of the instructional method. There is nothing inherent in a piece of equipment that will bring about better learning. The potential in a piece of equipment is realized only to the extent that some person can cause that potential to be converted into its instructional possibilities. The primary impact of supervision is upon the teacher if instruction is to be improved.

The supervisor, then, is in somewhat the same position as the person who wishes to communicate to a distant point via radio. The mystery of science now has brought about the possibility of a voice from one point being rocketed, in a sense, to Telstar and having the radio signal bounced back to another point on earth. For the nonscientific person this is a piece of magic that makes things seem to become extremely and simply automatic once the design is provided. For the scientists, it probably is not viewed in the same way because of problems in the control of the various scientific instruments used. Thus, the supervisor, when subjected to an evaluation of his supervisory successes or failures, may display the procedures by which the instructional program can be improved, but the supervisor must work through the teacher in order for that improvement plan to reach the pupil. The supervisor's idea does not bounce off the teacher but must be absorbed into the teacher's own knowledge and ability in order to be relayed in the form of teaching direction to the pupil. There is no doubt that the engineer-scientists have better control over the reflecting qualities of Telstar than a supervisor has over the reflecting or transmitting characteristics of a teacher.

What is the relationship of such situations to the mental health of the supervisor?

It is frustrating for the supervisor to wait for his ideas and plans to be realized after their relay to another person. These problems were discussed to some extent in Chapter 6, "The Operational Pattern for Supervision," in which a staff member plans and a line officer implements. The indirectness of the supervisor's influence is related more to his influence upon the teacher than to his direct influence upon the instructional materials which are less tractable than the personality of a teacher.

Because the outcomes of supervision must be the outcomes of the attempted processes of supervision, the consideration here is closely related to the four components of process as presented in Part IV. The discussion in Parts I through III are supportive or, at times, intimately involved in the successes and failures of supervision. The thought is proposed here that the outcomes of the processes of supervision are the dominant objects of evaluation. If the process does not produce satisfactory outcomes, diagnostic and remedial steps are needed. The diagnostic procedures should lead to an inspection of the elements of consideration in Parts I through III to determine the extent to which they may have conditioned the potential outcome of the components of process as discussed in Part IV.

There is no intent at this point to catalogue the four components of process by listing characteristic behaviors which can be categorized under each. The following statements will constitute only illustrations of the types of supervisory activities which might be characterized under each component, and then suggest that behaviors of these types must result in some observable outcomes. Again, the types of observable outcomes can be illustrative only because the total sweep of supervisory responsibilities and behaviors is so broad that no one has ever successfully brought into one listing even an acceptable representation of the possible total. It is hoped that, through the treatment by illustration, the individual supervisor will be helped in analyzing his own supervisory behaviors and that the supervisor and his colleagues will be in a position to identify the nature of their best potential efforts in the evaluation of the effectiveness of the supervisory program.

The first component of process is that of directing and controlling. In looking at the target of instructional improvement which is the major criterion measure under consideration, *directing* might involve activities such as assisting teachers in evaluating pupils' work through relating the evaluational techniques to the accepted objectives of education. Those activities which might be categorized as *controlling* behaviors might be those of administering system-wide standardized tests. In the two above illustrations, one is the intent to influence the teachers' judgments, while in the other, even though teachers' judgments may have entered into the decision, the supervisor is carrying forward under his own direction a testing program.

In the second component—stimulating and initiating—a typical activity of *stimulating* might be that of releasing factual information on the pupils' status and progress in the expected learnings for a particular grade or a segment of the school system. *Initiating* behaviors might be those of creating a committee to evaluate the science studies in the elementary grades and of structuring the committee attack upon the particular assignment. Here again, represented in the pairs of words of each component is the inclination to seek under the first word behaviors which are less restrictive and less supervisor-determinative than in the case of the second.

The third component of process is analyzing and appraising. The supervisor would be pursuing *analyzing* behaviors when he sought to identify the component parts of instruction in citizenship. The supervisor would assist the teacher to identify within the broad teaching purpose of citizenship the component parts and to evaluate those parts in terms of the contribution to citizenship development. The *appraising* behaviors, on the other hand, would involve activities such as developing the criteria for judging the quality of citizenship behaviors displayed by the pupils.

The fourth component of process is that of designing and implementing. The supervisor, in the instance of *designing,* might have behaviors characterized by planning the introduction of the use of teaching machines in an intermediate grade for the subject of social studies. The supervisor is responsible for developing a plan or causing a plan to be developed. In the case of the implementing activities, the supervisor might serve as consultant to the principal and teachers regarding the distinctive qualities of the newly developed learning, either by machines or by some other item of instruction. The supervisor might, on the other hand, consult with respect to the adoption or implementation of the new cumulative record of pupils. The point is that the supervisor becomes a consultant at the time of implementation. It is much more difficult to identify the effects of consulting than of those kinds of activities that have a more direct and observable outcome.

There could be many other types of activities performed by a supervisor which might be classified and categorized under the other selected components above. The important point is that the processes of supervision must have been performed or they should not be the subject of evaluation in terms of outcomes either of teacher behavior or of pupil learning. If there has been an absence of supervisory behavior on the part of the supervisor, there can be no attributable outcomes either to be identified with the teacher or the pupils. In such instances, the superintendent should assume full responsibility for judging whether the supervisor has been unwilling or unable to display supervisory behaviors of a nature that might be considered appropriate to the expectations of supervisory service. If there is reasonable evidence of neglect of responsibility, the supervisor is to be evaluated by what was not done rather than by the effect of what was done.

SUB-CRITERION MEASURES

In each sub-criterion measure how would you establish standards for making judgments?

In order to make further analyses of the major criterion measure of instructional improvement, several sub-criterion measures are suggested. The concept involved in each sub-criterion measure will be stated and a series of specific questions will be offered which might be useful in providing direction to the collection of information related to that measure. As discussed in other parts of the book, once the specific questions have been raised, they are in a sense criteria, but they are not stated in a form that would indicate the zero or referent point for evaluative judgment. They constitute the direction for the collection of those data which might be organized and used to determine whether, in terms of the expectations of the school, they are acceptable or unacceptable. One additional consideration should be kept in mind as the following subcriterion measures and their attendant questions are read—that is, that there is a unique time-schedule problem in judging the evidence of achievement of expectations for supervisors. As these measures and questions are considered, keep in mind that there is an intermediary, the teacher, between the supervisor and the measured outcome of pupil achievement when one is considering instructional improvements.

The first sub-criterion measure is that *the research approach is used in the solution of instructional problems.* This was discussed at some length as a technique or process of supervision in Part IV. It is closely related to the activities of analysis and appraisal. The identifying mark in the research approach to the solution of instructional problems is that the supervisor and others related to the task define the problem identified and make careful plans for the collection of data as well as for organizing and interpreting them. Practicality dictates that each individual problem identified might not be of a magnitude to require the research attack. On the other hand, the research approach to the solution of any problem can always be that of careful analysis, careful statement of findings, and a withheld judgment pending satisfaction with respect to information at hand. Those who would use this sub-criterion measure might be interested in using the following questions to give direction to their judgments about the degree to which it has been met:

1. Is there evidence of a written definition of an identified problem related to the instructional program and its outcomes?
2. Is there evidence that analyses have been made of previous problems which now appear to have been solved?
3. Is the supervisor able to give technical assistance to the teachers in designing an investigation of a particular problem area?
4. Is the supervisor familiar with resource personnel from colleges and universities who might assist in refining the research design or in the selection of appropriate statistical procedures?
5. Are there presumed solutions to instructional problems in different situations and locations within the school system that seem to be antagonistic in character, and does this antagonism stem from the difference or similarity in attack of problem identification or solution?
6. Can the supervisor cite with assurance the strengths and limitations of collected information?
7. Can the supervisor identify and state good hypotheses in selected study areas?
8. What other questions would you ask?

The second sub-criterion measure is that *there are rational transitions in testing, marking, placement, and promotion procedures.* It is easy for individuals within a school system to read about, hear about, or observe procedures used in some other school system. If those procedures have been well received, it is easy to fall to the temptation of simply appropriating that which has been successful in another system. The problem with this transplanting is that inconsistencies would develop within the school system making such appropriation. For instance, if a testing program is taken over and introduced in a local school system, it might be out of pace with the curriculum, with a marking system, with the reporting system, and with numerous other existing items of pupil management. This would indicate that there was a lack of rational transition from one type of program or practice to another. Rational transitions become evident when, with the changes of one item, appropriate changes are made in other parts of the program which are related and affected by the object of the major change. This, then, gives the evidence of careful planning and planning with the concern for relativity of influences upon other and attendant aspects of the instructional program. In order to make judgments with respect to this sub-criterion measure, these questions might be raised:

1. What changes have been made in the testing program over the past ten years?
2. Have changes been made in the marking system, reporting system, placement procedures, etc., which might reasonably have been affected by other changes?
3. Have the changes in testing, marking, placement, etc., been made after a written statement of a plan has been formally presented to some group or to the entire school staff, school board, and community?
4. Is there a file available which would indicate the kinds of plans that have been developed and which have been implemented in recent years?
5. Is there evidence that marks of pupils' progress are based upon some common criteria for all teachers in the system?
6. Are there extraneous items involved in the determination of grades for pupils?
7. Have there been follow-up studies which would indicate whether school systems receiving graduates find the pupils comparing favorably or unfavorably with graduates of other schools?
8. When discussing current change effort, does the supervisor refer with ease and surety to previous related actions and anticipated future ones?
9. What other questions would you ask?

A third sub-criterion measure is that *the revisions of teaching methodologies appear to conform with the evolving knowledge of the developmental characteristics of pupils.* The intent of this sub-criterion measure is that of determining the extent to which the teachers, as they choose the behaviors by which they deal with pupils, seem to be aware of recently reported research. If the teachers are knowledgeable, they must convert their knowledge of the characteristics or patterns of learning into an instructional design. Research in the psychology of learning and the developmental characteristics of adolescent pupils should find its way through the teacher to the pupils in the classroom. Supervisors must be on-the-job teachers of teachers in the identification and study of new information. In order to develop some evidence of how the teachers are meeting this type of criterion measure, these questions might be asked:

1. Are publications related to studies regarding the psychology of learning and developmental characteristics of pupils in evidence

in the professional library of the school or of the individual teachers?

2. Have some efforts been made in the in-service meetings of the staff to bring in consultants who might present and interpret recent research?
3. Are the difficulties encountered by pupils in the classroom approached by the teachers as though there was a science of treatment of school-age pupils?
4. Do the teachers perceive the supervisor as a reliable source of information about new publications and research reports?
5. Are variations in teaching method encouraged but controlled by clearly defined evaluative criteria?
6. What other questions would you ask?

A fourth sub-criterion measure is that *there is use of a broad base for guiding the selection of instructional aids.* It would be easy to expand this point to such an extent that it might seem to be of greater importance than the other sub-criterion measures. There is no intent either of indicating a weighting of the sub-criterion measures or of equating them. The point is that the success of the teacher in working with the pupil is either thwarted or supported in great measure by the kinds, quantity, quality, and use of the various instructional aids that are available. The supervisor has a responsibility not only of identifying the new and better instructional aids but also of making certain that these are accessible to the teacher. Once these are accessible, the supervisor has an equal responsibility in seeing that the teacher makes effective use of them. As indicated earlier, a teaching aid in and of itself can do nothing for the pupil unless that pupil has been well-assisted in making use of it. Computer Assisted Instruction is one of the newest of the items listed in the gadgetry of teaching, but the computer alone will not teach the pupil. A pupil must have good material put into the computer and he must have good direction if maximum learning is to take place from such a device. A similar statement can be made about the various other aids now available for the teacher to use in designing the pattern of classroom instruction. In order to judge whether the effectiveness of supervision is acceptable under this sub-criterion measure, these questions may be asked:

1. How are the new instructional aids identified and brought into use in the classrooms?
2. What is the basis for determining when a teaching aid is no longer satisfactory?
3. When new instructional aids are provided, is there an assumption that the old teaching techniques are still adequate or that they may need to be changed to adapt to the new aid?
4. Are the instructional aids made a part of the concern when new curriculum developments are being implemented into the instructional program?
5. Is there evidence that both the supervisor and teacher recognize the broad categories of instructional aids such as human resources, printed materials, mechanical aids, and many other items that might be considered miscellaneous?

6. Is there evidence of known criteria by which the teacher selects a particular aid for use at a particular time and for a particular purpose?
7. Does the supervisor express greater interest in analytical knowledge about a teaching aid use than for a personal mastery of the skill required by the aid?
8. What other questions would you ask?

A fifth and last illustrative sub-criterion measure to be used here is that *there is commonality in the use of the group process techniques that exists in supervisor-teacher relationships and also in teacher-pupil group situations.* This is not to suggest that the group process *per se* is a teaching technique; rather, it is a way by which people relate to each other so that tasks at hand have a better chance of being achieved. Thus, if it is important that there be certain types of participation between supervisors and teachers, there should also be determined those elements of participation in the group enterprise which are acceptable and profitable to the teacher-pupil interaction. If it is important that the records of the discussions and decisions in a supervisor–teacher meeting be kept for the purpose of giving continuity to the activity, it is also important that a record of certain of the shared planning activities between the pupil and teacher be kept and used for future direction. The questions which might be raised in relation to this sub-criterion measure are:

1. Is there evidence that the discussions have been interpreted in terms of the teacher-pupil interaction?
2. Is there a known policy related to participation in various types of decisions, whether it be at the central office, the individual school, or the classroom level?
3. Do all professional personnel participate with comparable ease in the presence of superordinates and subordinates as in peer groups?
4. What other questions would you ask?

A continuous caution to keep in mind in Part V, particularly in connection with this criterion measure on instructional improvement, is that judgments about supervisory behaviors be made in those areas in which the supervisors have a controllable responsibility. Because many of the judgments about instructional improvements must be made on the basis of the output as observed from the pupils, the supervisor is at a serious disadvantage unless those things for which he can be held responsible are carefully selected. There are many factors —both school and non-school—which become influential in the types of instructional outcomes as demonstrated by the pupils. It is necessary, then, to eliminate from the evaluation procedures those outcomes, whether favorable or unfavorable, which may be attributed to non-school influences. The only responsibility that the supervisor has for the non-school influence is to see that the community is alerted to such influences and to advise with respect to their control. Thus, fairness can be guaranteed by restricting the evaluation of the supervisor in this particular category of criterion measures to those things which can be directly attributable to his influence.

SELECTED REFERENCES

1. Association for Supervision and Curriculum Development, Yearbook, *Individualizing Instruction*. Washington, D.C.: National Education Association, 1964.
2. Feyereisen, Kathryn V., A. John Fiorino, and Arlene T. Nowak, *Supervision and Curriculum Renewal: A Systems Approach*. New York: Appleton-Century-Crofts, 1970.
3. Lucio, William H. and John D. McNeil, *Supervision: A Synthesis of Thought and Action*. New York: McGraw-Hill, 1969.
4. Neagley, Ross L. and N. Dean Evans, *Handbook for Effective Supervision*. Englewood Cliffs, N.J.: Prentice-Hall, Inc., 1970, 2nd ed.
5. Wilson, L. Craig, *et al., Sociology of Supervision*. Boston: Allyn & Bacon, 1969.

21

School-Community Consolidations

The title of this chapter perhaps needs some explanation because it is a word usage that has not been found normally in the literature of administration and supervision. The intent was to select words which give a meaning that extends beyond the popular use of the terms "public relations," "school-community relations," or "educational interpretation." All that is implied by such terms and more are included in the words "school-community consolidations." The intent of the term "consolidations" is to suggest a relationship that constitutes an integration of purpose and effort as an extension of pleasant intergroup relationships in which there occurs a frequent overlap of purposeful effort.

BOUNDARIES OF THIS CRITERION MEASURE

The school is a product of community desire, design, and support. There is some control involved in the relationship between the community and the school. Because public education is a service created and supported by a public agency, it is subject to many control factors designed by its creator. The state and federal governments exercise influences and/or actual controls over the schools, which means that such controls also are exercised over the community creating and supporting the schools. The state and federal influences make little difference to the intent of the concept indicated in the title because, with minor variations in the concept of community, the state and federal governments bear a relationship to the local school system in a manner comparable to the local municipality.

No educator has advocated or claimed that the schools should be stronger than the authority which created the system. It is acknowledged that the municipality has a broader range of powers, responsibilities, and expectations than have the schools. The schools constitute primarily a single-purpose agency and stand as one of several such agencies created and maintained by a municipality. For each of the single-purpose agencies there is an inseparability between its purposes and the community purposes. The purposes held by the school system should be highly congruent with the community educational purposes. If these come in conflict, there is evidence that a consolidation has not been achieved and the conflict will cause each agency to fail in a part of that which it set out to accomplish. At the same time, the inseparability of school and community purposes constitutes one of the reasons for the ease with which a community extends its expectations of the school beyond instruction and into other types of services. When the community expects the school to create and manage transportation systems or food services, or to accept police functions for non-school violations of school-age children, the community has extended its expectations of the school beyond the instructional expectations. When a community permits these expectations to invade the time and energies properly allocated to instructional purposes, it cannot then lose confidence in and withdraw support from the educational agency which has been forced beyond its proper function by the community.

Another idea in the term "consolidation" is that of unification. As indicated above, it is a unification of purpose. The unification must lead to a closer relationship between the parent community and the school system as well as a provision for the kind of relationship which will cause a better delineation of the expectations of the school as compared or contrasted to other single-purpose agencies within the municipality. There is a much closer relationship between the school and its parent community than between the municipality and a contracted service which the community wishes to have. A contracted service is exemplified by a construction company that is hired to build a new city hall or a parking ramp. This is a business-type transaction. The community determines that it wants a certain facility and simply contracts with a technical agency that can bring about realization of its desires. This is done through entering into a financial arrangement for certain services to be performed. Some exploratory actions related to contracted instruction are in evidence now, but it is too soon to venture judgment about them.

While the municipality, through its school system, does employ personnel to staff the various positions needed to carry on the educational program, it is not the kind of a relationship that a community would enter into if it were to contract with a private agency for professional services to its children. In this sense, the agency is not a public agency at all but a private agency that sells its services to the municipality. The point here is that the public school system bears a closer relationship to the municipality. Consequently, the idea of unification seems appropriate.

Does the development of professional negotiation alter this basic relationship?

In the relationship between the school system and the supporting community, the professional educators are not in a position to determine the tax rate, which is a way of telling the supporting citizenry what they must pay for the educational service. Even though the professional educators cannot determine this, they can help a community to be well informed about the facilities needed to accomplish the educational expectations and to advise about the costs of such provisions. On the other hand, the layman in a community cannot teach reading successfully although he can make judgments about the outcomes of the teaching of reading. Thus, there is always an opportunity for a mutual exchange of advice and judgment between school personnel and laymen of the community. When the facilities or relationships between professional workers and lay people do not provide this mutuality of exchange, there is a lack of school-community consolidation that should be of equal concern to both parties in the relationship.

What are some specific techniques for encouraging school-community cooperation?

The meaning of this chapter title in no sense indicates an abdication of the technical contributions of educators to the instructional program. Neither does it mean that there should be no individual, small group, or mass attempts on the part of the laymen of the community to indicate the kinds of expectations that they have for the schools. The important element in the concept is that there should be a melding of the individual and unique contributions of the professional educator and the supporting layman into a mutually supporting operation.

IMPLICATIONS OF THE ASSUMPTIONS

In all chapters of this book, one or more of the assumptions from Chapter 3 have been related. Two are particularly pertinent to the content and intent of this chapter. Assumption number three states:

The major function of supervision is that of influencing situations, persons, and relationships for the purpose of improvement.

The point of emphasis in this assumption as it relates to the intent of this chapter is that of influencing situations, persons, and relationships at the community level. The supervisor is responsible for influencing situations, persons, and relationships within the professional staff, but because a commitment has been made at various points to environment as a factor, it seems reasonable that those who are concerned primarily with the instructional program should accept some responsibility for influencing the community environment of the school. There are other professional workers who accept unique responsibilities for the impact of the community upon the educational program, but the supervisor must accept those which are more closely related to the curriculum and the instructional procedures. There are other important related and supporting types of concerns in the community environment such as financial support, school building sites, and improper moral influences. These are not as directly related to the instructional program, and, therefore, fall to the responsibility of some school officer other than the instructional supervisor.

Assumption number six states:

Load-quality relationships must be considered in the expectations for teaching and supervisory personnel if desirable change is to occur.

The impact of this assumption upon the criterion measure is related to "load-quality" relationships. It is one thing to have reasonable load expectations placed upon supervisors and other personnel by their professional colleagues, but it is quite another matter to have these expectations determined by the lay people in the community.

The expectations placed upon supervisors, either by the professional workers or by lay people in the community, often constitute the basis for action by the supporting community. It is important that the expectations placed upon all members of the professional staff be reasonable in magnitude and appropriate in nature. The lay people of a community sometimes place more unreasonable or ill-considered expectations upon the superintendent than upon any other member of the school staff. Improper expectations placed upon the superintendent can affect the outcomes of the instructional program. It is well to keep in mind that the expectations placed upon the superintendent, the principals, and the teachers have an influence upon the successful operation of the supervisory program. It is possible, however, to define community expectations to the point where those related more directly to supervision can be identified and used for evaluative purposes.

Why should teachers and supervisors be concerned with unreasonable expectations placed upon a superintendent?

FROM PROCESS TO PRODUCT

The concerns for the evaluation of supervision must be related to the preceding four parts of the book. The first three parts were more concerned with purpose, structure, and environmental factors affecting the processes of supervision. In a sense, the evaluation of the results of the processes of supervision may be the responsibility of some previous influence of structural or operational characteristics. The evaluation of supervision as presented in Part V is focused primarily upon the result of the application of processes. This means, then, that the four chapters dealing with the components of process constitute the reference points for the evaluation of the outcomes of supervision. If the outcomes of the supervisory processes are not satisfactory, a diagnostic study is in order and the causes may be sought in the items of consideration found in Parts I through III. The correction of deficiencies in the environmental structure for supervision, however, must so influence the processes of supervision that, once again, the outcomes of process become the focal point for the evaluation of the supervisory program.

Holding to the point of view that the processes of supervision are the focal points for evaluation, consideration must be given to the four major components of process. Following the order of the presentation in Part IV, there is first the component *directing and controlling.* If this component or its processes are viewed in terms of a school-community consolidation concept, a *directing* task on the part of the supervisor might be that of suggesting the design for satisfactory and appropriate reports to parents. This would involve marshaling the talents of the faculty for the purpose of developing a type of report that would accommodate both the needs of the school and the expectations of the community. This, then, would be a directing influence insofar as the supervisor is concerned. On the other hand, it may become necessary to provide some guides or regulations with respect to parents visiting the classrooms of the school. Classroom interruptions do possess some important implications for the success of the teacher in working with the pupils. This becomes a possible responsibility of the supervisor. A *controlling* task on the part of the supervisor, then, might be that of causing the enforcement of the conditions of parent visits which would provide both the opportunity for the parents to accomplish the purposes which stimulated visits and the protection that the teacher deserves in keeping classroom interruptions at a minimum.

The second component of process is *stimulating and initiating.* The focus here is upon the functions that the supervisor would perform in accomplishing school-community consolidations. These functions, when converted to specific tasks, become a basis for judging whether school-community consolidations have been accomplished. The supervisor performs a task of *stimulating* when he releases information on the status of instruction in the mathematics program. If it fails to measure up to norms, nationwide or otherwise, that have been selected, the release of this information to the teachers and to the community should stimulate the desire to improve the outcomes of the program.

The supervisor performs an *initiating* task by organizing and conducting—or causing to be conducted—parent classes on the content of the new mathematics. Many school systems have found this a practical necessity in meeting a keen desire on the part of the parents to learn the language of the new mathematics. Thus, the supervisor is selecting stimulating and initiating behaviors not only to fulfill his obligations to the instructional program within the school but also to fulfill his obligations for achieving school-community consolidations.

The third component of process is *analyzing and appraising* and it can be illustrated in a manner similar to the first and second components. The supervisor might pursue those tasks which lead to a survey of the pupils' home television habits. The purpose of such an analysis would be to decide whether the impact upon the instructional program within the school was such that the school and the community need to join forces in correcting or in reinforcing. Here, the supervisor is performing an *analyzing* task. The professional staff then establishes with the community the criteria by which judgments would be made about the effect of pupils' television habits upon the instructional program. It is possible that the community would not wish to make the judgments or be capable of doing so, but it can share in establishing the criteria. This is one of the important facets of the supervisory task of *appraising*. Here again, the supervisor has initiated behaviors of analyzing and appraising which are focused upon a common interest of the layman and the professional. The school and the community share in the acclaim of success or the blame for deficiency. In either case, it is a supervisory act that is intended to bring about school-community consolidation.

The fourth component of process is *designing and implementing*. In performing the task of *designing*, the supervisor might invite a group of lay representatives from the supporting community to help establish the purposes and expectations of the instructional program. This is a matter of determining general goals and purposes. It is appropriate to use the ideas and recommendations of the supporting public in determining the general direction in which the schools should go. In *implementing* the designs resulting from cooperative effort, the supervisor might distribute a statement of the specific parental supporting behaviors which are needed to reinforce pupil effort in a new instructional plan. In this instance, the consolidation is interpreted in terms of how much the parents are permitted to participate in designing the plan as well as in terms of how much responsibility they are willing to accept. The supervisor seeks the cooperation of the parents to perform in such a manner that they reinforce those teaching–learning efforts which seem most supportive of the accepted purposes of education.

The above illustrations involve the kinds of tasks that characterize a supervisor who is performing those components of process which are particularly related to the achievement of school-community consolidations. They involve a continuous process of dichotomizing the lay and professional educational roles within a community. The supervisor should know his specific responsibilities to the supporting public and, at the same time, have a clear view of the appropriate limits of lay contact with and influence upon the more technical requirements of the instructional program.

SUB-CRITERION MEASURES

It was indicated earlier that these authors selected five criterion measures for evaluating supervision as supervision. These are broad areas of observation and concern with respect to the impact of supervision upon the totality of the instructional program. Each of the major measures may be broken into sub-criterion measures which constitute an analysis of each broad field into some of its component parts. Several sub-criterion measures falling within the major criterion measure of school-community consolidations are suggested. Again, it is emphasized that these are for illustrative purposes. There is no intent to provide a catalogue of all of the potential sub-criterion measures for judging this particular area of outcomes of the processes of supervision. Each practitioner is urged to make his own list of sub-criterion measures with a series of related questions which will structure the collection of information. The illustrations supplied here will be supported by several specific questions. If these questions were chosen by a supervisor in a specific school system, they should cause pertinent information to be gathered. Even if hundreds of questions are used in structuring the gathering of information about the effectiveness of supervision, there still would be no automatic indication of how good or poor the supervision is. The point is that structuring the search for an evaluative type of information is an important step. In the absence of any reliable norms, each superintendent and his supervisory staff must arrive at their own referent points for deciding the quality of the supervisory program.

In each sub-criterion measure, how would you establish standards for making judgments?

The first sub-criterion measure is that *the competencies of the professional staff should result in participation in the non-school educative activities sponsored by the community.* This sub-criterion measure relates to the degree to which the educational staff is permitted some selectivity with respect to participation in non-school educative facilities. In order to make judgments about the effectiveness of the supervisory program in the freedom of selection and wisdom of staff choice in community non-school activities, questions such as the following might be raised:

1. Does the controlling agent of municipally sponsored youth clubs have regular consultation with the professional educators regarding the educational implications of the youth center?
2. Do the commercial radio and television stations of the community seek the help of professional educators in analyzing and appraising their impact upon educational outcomes?
3. Do the managers of local theaters seek opportunities to consult

with professional educators and school-related lay groups regarding the influence of the movie as an educative factor?
4. Do the city authorities who control the licensing of billboards consult with the professional educators regarding the influence of billboards placed near schools?
5. Does the management of the local newspaper seek to determine its policies by inquiring about the impact of its editorial and news policies upon the school-age youth of the community?
6. Do the fire department and cooperating insurance agencies in planning fire prevention programs consult with professional educators regarding the educational aspects of program planning and presentation?
7. Does the police department seek opportunities to exchange information on problems and policy determinations with those in the school program concerned with driver training as related to the police responsibilities of traffic control?
8. Do the representatives of the juvenile court seek opportunities for cooperative planning for delinquent youth as opposed to asking the schools to perform therapeutic functions?
9. Does the municipal health authority seek regular opportunities to advise and consult with school personnel in the maintenance of community health standards?
10. What other questions would you ask?

The emphases of the above questions are in the direction of the municipal agency seeking the cooperation of the school system's professional personnel. The purpose of stating the questions in this fashion is on the assumption that, if the municipal agency seeks the cooperation of the school, the school has so conducted its affairs that the municipal agencies see possible benefits in such cooperation. The supervisor, in order to achieve this type of school-community consolidation, may have to take the initiative in contacting these agencies if his professional colleagues are to be sought later by such agencies for cooperation. Because the concern here is with evaluation of outcomes, it seems more appropriate to make the judgments from the standpoint of the community seeking school cooperation than to encourage a listing of the school's efforts at outreach. The efforts at outreach are not to be disparaged, but they do not constitute the evidences of having achieved consolidation as the reverse initiation would indicate.

The second sub-criterion measure is that *the lay people and the professional educators of a community hold appropriate and common perceptions of the purposes, procedures, and products of the instructional program.* These questions might be asked in determining the extent to which this particular sub-criterion measure is met in school-community consolidations:

1. Could some nonresident randomly select twenty-five people on the main street of the community and get an intelligent and consistent response about what the school stands for, how the schools are organized, and some knowledge of the accomplishments of the instructional program?
2. Do the professional educators of the community have knowledge

about the desires of the various publics within the community with respect to educational outcomes?

3. Do lay people speak of school procedures in terms such as "teaching phonics" and seem able to carry a discussion beyond the title of the concern?
4. Do the members of the professional staff know the tax rate of the community and the percentage of the tax dollar devoted to various municipal services such as police, streets, health, and education?
5. Do laymen appear to be able to discuss the kinds of instructional procedures necessary to produce good citizens?
6. Do the professional educators understand the kinds of behaviors held in mind by lay people when they talk about the development of good citizens?
7. What other questions would you ask?

The third sub-criterion measure is that *the community members support the school program and the professional staff supports the community programs.* Questions such as these may be asked to determine whether this criterion measure has been met:

1. Do the activities such as a photographer's club or an artist's club receive organized special interest support from groups in the community comparable to the organized groups which support the band and athletic program?
2. Do the staff members serve on the committees promoting and expediting the subscription and collection of funds for activities of the United Givers type?
3. Are municipal trucks made available to school pupils who collect food for distribution to the needy at Thanksgiving and Christmas?
4. Will the school staff and pupils turn out in force and on non-school time to help in an annual parks clean-up program directed by the municipality?
5. Does the community support the school in efforts to discontinue night sports events when they appear to encourage juvenile delinquency?
6. Does the professional staff support the police and welfare departments in planning and carrying out supervised activities on Halloween to reduce the inclinations to destructiveness?
7. What other questions would you ask?

The fourth sub-criterion measure is that *there is coordination among the school, police, health, and welfare departments.* Questions such as the following may direct the collection of information to make judgments relative to the performance area of this sub-criterion measure:

1. Is there a central council or other clearing agency that is accepted in equal confidence by all agencies using the services of a referral center?
2. Is there an absence of quotations in news articles in which those concerned in each of the above-named public services blame one or more of the other services for their own difficulties?
3. Does the curriculum provide learning experiences intended to develop pupil knowledge about and appreciation for the other municipal services competing for the local tax dollar?

4. Are teachers conversant on the problems, policies, and aspirations of other municipal services?
5. How many annual occasions can be cited of conferences between the above agencies when a crisis situation is absent?
6. How many school principals has each police officer met in person?
7. What other questions would you ask?

The fifth sub-criterion measure is that *there is facilitation in the resolution of conflicts between school interests and non-school agencies.*

1. Are there dominant minority groups within the community achieving publicity even when discrediting the educational program?
2. Are there organized groups within the community being used as a continuing target of criticism by the school personnel?
3. Do parents who have questions or dissatisfactions about the instructional program tend to go to the educational, municipal, or lay agencies for satisfaction?
4. Do the parent-teacher organizations developed in each school seem to assume that the city council or any other municipal agency constitutes an opposing force which must be attacked?
5. Do the city officials feel that a part of their political strategy must be that of reducing tax support for the schools?
6. Do conflicts between labor and management in an industrial organization expect each to have none, some, or much involvement in the discussions in the classrooms?
7. What other questions would you ask?

It is well to return now to the thought presented in assumption number six. The above sub-criterion measures are indicated as being only illustrative. The number will vary by community and by school system. There is no intent to multiply illustrations and, by multiplying, imply that all of these things are the responsibility of the supervisor. The point emphasized is that supervisors have some highly definable and direct responsibilities to the instructional program. This major area in the evaluation of supervision relates to the extent to which the influence upon the instructional program gives consideration to the efforts and outcomes that are identifiable as school-community consolidations.

The reasonableness of expectations in terms of time and energy expenditures must be determined cooperatively by the members of the professional staff and the lay people of the supporting community. If all of the above sub-criterion measures plus those in the other major criterion areas suggested in Part V should constitute the expectations placed upon the supervisory program, there must be adequate provisions made for sufficient teaching and supervisory personnel. To do less than this would make this chapter, as well as all of Part V, constitute a hazard for the supervisor and his colleagues in any particular community. It is the belief of the authors that the professional personnel—particularly the supervisors—should help a community to establish proper expectations. Only this can provide freedom with security in pursuing evaluations in terms of known and acceptable criterion measures.

SELECTED REFERENCES

1. Burbank, Natt B., *The Superintendent of Schools.* Danville, Illinois: The Interstate Printers and Publishers, Inc., 1968.
2. Muniz, Arthur J., "But Citizens Committees *Can* Work," *The American School Board Journal,* November, 1969, pp. 41–43.
3. Savage, William W., *Interpersonal and Group Relations in Educational Administration.* Glenview, Illinois: Scott, Foresman and Company, 1968.
4. Wadia, Maneck S., *Management and the Behavioral Sciences.* Boston: Allyn & Bacon, Inc., 1968.

22

Emerging Expectations

The substance of this chapter cannot be made specific by predicting those expectations which may be placed upon the schools at some time in the distant future. The discussion must be limited to the problem of trying to anticipate the events that will occur either through projections of things that have happened in the past or that can be identified in the present.

The history of our schools includes many occasions on which the public, which created the school, appeared to develop dissatisfactions with the school's products. This does not mean necessarily that the schools were doing their work poorly, although such is a continuing possibility. Much of the dissatisfaction with the outcomes of education has been due to changes in the environment which alert people to some "wants" that they perhaps did not know that they possessed. The changing expectations placed upon the schools are closely related to the social, economic, and political changes in the environment. The supporting public, when it develops a new expectation for the school, does so not primarily because education needs to be changed but because some other change in society needs the support that only education can give.

Is this relationship between school and society good or bad?

BOUNDARIES OF THIS CRITERION MEASURE

Many of the observations of man have caused him to exclaim from time to time, "Why didn't I anticipate this?" or "Why didn't somebody tell me this would happen?" This, in a sense, is the implication of the title to this chapter. Things have happened in the past which found the schools unable to meet the needs or expectations placed upon them. There will, of course, be many similar situations in the future. The more rapidly that change takes place in the school's environment, the more probable it is that many new expectations will be placed upon it.

The determination of future expectations is not necessarily a supervisory obligation. The fact is, however, that someone in the school organization must be responsible for searching environmental horizons and determining the nature of the thunderclouds that may appear. There would be equal logic in charging this responsibility to the school principal or to the classroom teachers as in charging it to the supervisor. There is little support for arguing that one or the other or all should accept such responsibilities, although it is a practical certainty that someone in the school organization will have to accept it.

Does "everybody's business is nobody's business" apply here?

The assignment of such a responsibility to the supervisor has a rational basis of appropriateness. The supervisors are closely related to many of the factors controlling the quality of the classroom work. It appears logical that, if anyone in the school system has to be assigned the responsibility of detecting emerging expectations related to the instructional program, the supervisor would be most sensitive to these forces which may in the end directly affect it. The inclusion of this criterion measure among those used for evaluating supervision is in part logical and in part arbitrary.

IMPLICATIONS OF THE ASSUMPTIONS

The criterion measure suggested in the chapter title bears direct relation to assumptions four and six. These assumptions are:

4. Planning is supported by systematically applied analysis.

6. Load-quality relationships must be considered in the expectations for teaching and supervisory personnel if desirable change is to occur.

Much space in the book has been devoted to the function of planning and the subject will not be reviewed at this point. One of its most pertinent aspects in relation to this chapter is that planning cannot take place without the selection of a target. The facility of identifying emerging expectations is target identification. The discovery of the forces which may change the public demands placed upon the schools must be subjected to planning activities. This identification of the need for planning is well related to many of the other functions of supervision.

Assumption number six reiterates the point made frequently that the expectations placed upon school personnel must be reasonable. In the context of the meaning of this chapter, the expectations are more those that are placed upon the total program of the school rather than upon any particular member of the staff. Even though many functions needed for the successful operation of a school can be parcelled out to various professional employees, the matter of identifying emerging expectations is a function that cannot be delegated casually. The supervisor will not be able to summon a committee of teachers and turn over to them the matter of anticipating changes that might be needed in the instructional program ten or fifty years in the future. On the other hand, the supervisor must have the assistance of many specifically trained people if he is to develop the insight and foresight necessary for identifying emerging expectations with any degree of accuracy.

EMERGING EXPECTATIONS

What types of consultant service might be useful for this purpose?

Part of the demand placed upon the supervisor, then, is that he be on the alert to identify potential forces which might affect education and that he initiate interpretations of these forces in terms of instructional change. The supervisor who fulfills this criterion measure will be the one who is always seeking to know more about what is going on in the school's environment and is thoughtful about the environmental phenomena. Perhaps this is one of the criterion measures that will be satisfied best as the supervisor decreases the amount of time that he spends dashing here and there and increases the amount of time that he can reflect quietly upon education and the factors that may affect it.

FROM PROCESS TO PRODUCT

Reference was made above to the fact that this particular criterion measure of supervision is more related to what the supervisor does to himself than it is for use in judging the effectiveness by which the supervisor has influenced other people, particularly the teachers in the school system. The four components of process do not apply quite as easily here as in the case of the other criterion measures suggested in Part V. For instance, directing and controlling does not have a very prominent place in anticipating the emerging expectations. On the other hand, analyzing and appraising is extremely important to the processes by which the supervisor will meet the requirements of this criterion measure (see Chapter 15). The responsibility for anticipating future demands is a matter of the keenest analysis of the phenomena existing in society.

The types of analyzing that are most serviceable in this instance would be those of diagnosing the aspects of the phenomena which are most likely to affect education. Appraising must be done by projecting the values that presently exist to a rather uncertain future. Much of the information sought by the supervisor will be the judgments of other competent persons. It is possible that many of the phenomena appearing on the horizon may not develop at all or may develop very slowly. Analyzing and appraising seldom can be done as a crash-type activity. The phenomena must be watched over a period of years before they become sufficiently distinct to make certain of their potential influence upon the instructional program.

An example of this type of development is in the use of the various communication media that have been developed in recent years. These have had a gradual development and there has been much discussion of the impact of radio, television, and other mass media on the instructional program. Team teaching has also been developing in recent years. This development, perhaps, could not have started or certainly could not have made the progress that it has made without the use of the various audio-visual techniques providing support to the instruction of pupils.

How can you help the public to rationalize the necessity for secrecy and the determination of school expectations?

The first sputnik, as another example, is the type of phenomenon that catches not only the school people but also a whole society off guard. Looking back upon that surprise, many people now say that it could have and should have been anticipated by someone who could have alerted the schools to the probable need for a different type of instruction in some subject fields. The secrecy which seems to be necessary in developing the machines of defense and war as well as the secrecy necessary to outpace economic competition tends to withhold information that the schools need if they are truly to anticipate changing needs for the instructional program.

Many of the types of phenomena that must be analyzed are extremely sensitive from the standpoint of public opinion. There are areas of potential instruction that seem to carry a high charge of emotionality whenever they are mentioned. Sex education has stimulated strong differences of opinion and organized opposition.

One of these emotional characteristics is the matter of teaching thrift. In all probability, if the schools should turn back —as some reformers today believe they should—and seek to teach thrift as it was taught forty and fifty years ago, it might become charged with emotionality. Before deficit spending became the rule of the day in recent decades, schools were expected to give rigorous lessons in thrift. If a school today taught the kind of thrift that Benjamin Franklin emphasized, it would be running contrary to many of the present economic and banking policies. The business agencies of a community, who do everything possible to entice people to spend more money than they earn by making credit extremely liberal, might consider the schools as anti-business if they again taught the old brand of thrift. Thus, the supervisor, in analyzing and appraising the phenomena that surround a school, is dealing with explosive problems at almost every point. When the process of analyzing and appraising brings a change factor into focus and causes it to become more distinct, then the supervisory component of designing and implementing becomes the dominant one. The supervisor must know the points at which help is needed. He must be able to detect the kind of help that is essential. In the increasingly technical society, all specializations must be brought to bear upon many of the problems that perhaps earlier could have been solved by one person.

SOME ILLUSTRATIONS OF EMERGING EXPECTATIONS

In reviewing the past, one can identify occasions on which the schools perhaps should have been more alert in discerning the kinds of demands that would be placed upon them because of changes in society. Reference was made above to the first sputnik. Even though that would have been extremely difficult to anticipate and even though the achievement was highly spectacular, this event caused the people of this country to turn upon the schools as though the schools should have anticipated it. Sputnik was a Russian achievement, and Americans apparently expected more from the schools in responsibility for anticipation than they expected of the Central Intelligence Agency. Sputnik was interpreted by our people as being, in substantial part, the product of the educational system of Russia. There is little doubt that the educational system of Russia had much to do with the fact that a sputnik could be put into orbit. Society's demands were that the schools in this country should adopt the kind of instructional program which characterized the Russian and the European schools on the assumption that their standards were higher and therefore standards must be raised in this country. This has resulted, during the past several years, in demands for more rigorously applied standards at all levels of education than had been demanded a few years earlier.

The schools reacted favorably to public demands that more rigorous standards be applied and, in the process, began to group pupils for instructional purposes to an extent that the same public had not permitted a few years earlier. Associations representing organizational interest in mental health have had much influence upon the expectations placed upon the schools with respect to the mental health of pupils. When people demand that youngsters know more mathematics and know it better or know more science and know it better, their concerns have been replaced by something other than the mental health of the child. Even though the recent pressures upon the schools have constituted a campaign on raising standards for only these few years, there now are appearing words of caution that pupils are being asked to work too hard. It has become a popular radio, television, and platform topic to express anguished concern about the fact that elementary school pupils are required to do homework, that high school students are deprived of the opportunity to play because of the pressures

What makes public opinion change so rapidly?

of competition in the classroom, and that college students are losing too much sleep in order to meet the demands of their professors. So it is that any campaign for added expectations soon stimulates a counteracting group and, at that point, the schools stand between the opposing forces without knowing quite how to resolve them.

Automation has been a phenomenon of our society that has gone through a rather long period of development. During recent years there have been increased warnings about the changes in the demand to be made upon education as a result of automation. For instance, if the schools had not previously given much attention to the responsibilities of leisure time or recreational activities, it is obvious that they may have to do so now. There is no doubt that automation is making it possible to reduce the length of the work-week in many businesses and industries. When the work-week becomes shorter, leisure time use becomes a problem for many people who did not grow up knowing what to do with it. There are many other implications for education—such as the need for training and retraining the technicians to tend the machines—that can be attributed to the development of automation.

Another illustration of the kinds of changes that have taken place in society and hence in the schools is in the field of science. The discovery of new knowledge in the field of science has been so rapid in recent years that the pace has created a very real problem for the textbook writers. One successful science textbook writer recently made the statement that he had finally to rewrite his book in terms only of the principles of science because the facts were coming so rapidly that the book was out of date before it got off the press. Much of the emphasis now is in the direction of teaching pupils how to think about science problems rather than teaching them the cataloguing of facts. There are other subject areas in the school where the problem of having development and discovery hold still while people learn the facts has not been so much of an issue.

The urbanization of our society is now becoming a topic of concern for many thoughtful people. An urban society, in developing new social problems, will make demands on the schools quite different from those made by a rural society. An example of one of the types of demands that might be made upon the school as we move from the rural to the urban society is the problem of conservation. People in a rural society grow up with the knowledge of plants and animals that do not characterize the experience of city dwellers. There may soon be a need for bigger and better zoos, bigger and better museums, and opportunities for field trips as well as other ways of teaching children about nature. The point should be kept in mind again that the supporting public has a way of looking back at something that has been concluded unsatisfactorily and of finding someone to blame for having let it happen. In the anticipation of many of the demands of the future, the schools must do it in the loneliest possible way, that is, at a time before a supporting public has developed.

The editors of *Education, U.S.A.* publish each year a pamphlet carrying the title, "The Shape of Education." This publication lists numerous items which constitute concerns that may become major in forthcoming months and years. Each topic receives very brief treatment, but the important thing for the supervisor is that the list of items chosen can constitute a reasonably good checklist for stimulating one's imagination in anticipating the problems that may appear in the local school system. In "The Shape of Education" for 1962–1963 a few of the topics indicated which may have an impact upon education are: "Math Isn't Square Anymore," "It's the Program, Not the Machine," "Modern Magic Lantern," "An Assessment of Team Teaching," "Moonlighting in Michigan," "The Affluent Teenager," and "Big Questions for Junior Colleges." [1] Almost a decade later, in the table of contents for 1970–71, there are found topics of this type: "Schools without Walls," "Drug Crises," "Accountability," "Differentiated Staffing," "Sensitivity Training," and "Environmental Education." [2] Again, the treatment of these topics is very brief, but they can serve, as indicated above, to alert the supervisor to the kinds of phenomena that might be affecting education and, therefore, are deserving of his attention.

Do these titles stimulate your imagination about future change?

The above illustrations are not intended to be in any sense a cataloguing of possibilities of things that may have great impact upon education. They are to illustrate the fact that one must be always alert to the current scene in order to detect those things which can be anticipated and cared for prior to the time that neglect can be charged against the educational program.

SUB-CRITERION MEASURES

The emerging expectations constitute the last of the criterion measures suggested in Part V. As in other chapters of this Part, each criterion measure is broken into several sub-criterion measures with specific questions raised under each. Five sub-criterion measures are suggested for structuring a list of questions that might elicit the kinds of information that would help one to evaluate the supervisory outcomes in terms of this particular criterion measure. These sub-criterion measures are the forces that might change: (1) the purpose of

[1] National School Public Relations Association, Bulletin, "The Shape of Education" (Washington, D.C.: National Education Association, 1962–1963).

[2] National School Public Relations Association, Bulletin, "The Shape of Education" (Washington, D.C.: National Education Association, 1970–1971).

In each sub-criterion measure, how would you establish standards for making judgments?

education, (2) the length of the pupil's time commitment in school, (3) content and method, (4) evaluative procedures, and (5) control structures.

It should be noted that these five are only illustrative of the type of sub-criterion measures and criteria that might be developed in the local school system and made particularly pertinent to that system. In assessing the extent to which each of the sub-criterion measures is met satisfactorily, these questions will lead to the type of information that can be helpful in judging the effectiveness of supervision.

The first sub-criterion measure is that *the purposes of education are altered or reinterpreted as the supporting environment shifts basically in nature.* These questions may direct the efforts of gathering pertinent information:

1. Do the written statements of school philosophy and purpose reveal developmental characteristics?
2. Are teachers conversant with relationships of changes in subject purposes to general educational purposes?
3. Are lay representatives of the community informed about major program changes in the local schools?
4. How many public statements during a recent school year were made by school personnel for the purpose of interpreting the educational changes in relation to environmental factors?
5. Can the supervisor discuss, imaginatively, the long-range probabilities of educational change?
6. What other questions would you ask?

The second sub-criterion measure is that *the length of the pupil's time commitment in school is based on educational requirements.* The following questions might give direction to the collection of appropriate information:

1. Do business, industrial, and labor leaders consider the school an appropriate facility for controlling labor supply?
2. Do lay and professional people seem to see a relationship between the expectations of education and the length of the school year?
3. Do major local industrial changes take place with or without an exchange of personnel training demands between industrial management and school instructional leaders?
4. Does the recorded design of curriculum change include estimates of time requirements?
5. What other questions would you ask?

The third sub-criterion measure is that *the changes in curriculum content and instructional method are related to anticipated as well as past environmental influences.* These questions may help structure the search for pertinent information:

1. Are there pilot applications of curricular and instructional innovations?
2. Are the pilot efforts focused both on the testing of established practices and anticipated future demands?
3. What devices are in evidence which are designed to organize lay opinion about future changes and demands?
4. What other questions would you ask?

The fourth sub-criterion measure is that *the evaluative procedures are sensitive to the gradually emerging knowledge about the human mind and techniques of measurement.* The following questions may help secure pertinent information:

1. Is the supervisor knowledgeable about recent research on the use of published tests?
2. Are the teachers conversant with the criteria of evaluative procedures?
3. Have there been explorations into the use of data processing equipment in developing measurement technology?
4. How often have laymen been consulted regarding the establishment of criterion measures for judging pupil accomplishment?
5. Is there evidence of an "eyes-on-the-future" squad for surveying the future evaluative procedures?
6. What other questions would you ask?

The fifth sub-criterion measure is that *the control structure of the instructional program is undergoing continuous improvement.* These questions may give direction to collecting appropriate information:

1. Do the supervisors have evidence about the changing controls of the curriculum?
2. Are school board members willing to give careful consideration to the purchase and use of modern instructional aids?
3. Are the professional staff members sometimes overruled on instructional procedures by the board of education?
4. Does the supervisor have information on the internal as well as external controls of the instructional program?
5. What other questions would you ask?

The evaluation of a supervisor's accommodations to things "yet to be" can never be very precise. Considerations of the future are inescapably anchored to the past and the present. Imagination must be applied to the task of evaluating imagination. The criterion measure considered in this chapter is primarily an invitation to every supervisor to consider the necessity of keeping the door to the supervision of instruction wide open and looking into the future.

Supervision is that phase of school administration which focuses primarily upon the achievement of the appropriate instructional expectations of educational systems.

SELECTED REFERENCES

1. Cartwright, Gene J., "A Study of Lay Motivations to Influence Public Schools." Unpublished doctoral dissertation. Madison: University of Wisconsin, 1971.
2. Chandler, B. J., Lindley J. Stiles, and John I. Kituse (eds.), *Education in an Urban Society*. New York: Dodd, Mead, 1962.
3. Kast, Fremont E. and James E. Rosenzweig, *Organization and Management: A Systems Approach*. New York: McGraw-Hill Book Company, 1970.

4. Muller, Herbert J., *The Children of Frankenstein.* Bloomington, Indiana: Indiana University Press, 1970.
5. National School Public Relations Association, Bulletin, "The Shape of Education." Washington, D.C.: National Education Association, 1962–1963, 1970–1971.
6. Rogers, Everett M., *Diffusion of Innovations.* New York: The Free Press, 1962.
7. Stoltenberg, James C., "Indications of Tolerance and Change Potential from an Analysis of Current Educational Practices in the Merrill Area Public Schools." Unpublished doctoral dissertation. Madison: University of Wisconsin, 1969.

COMPOSITE BIBLIOGRAPHY

1. Allport, Gordon W., *The Nature of Prejudice.* Garden City, New York: Doubleday, 1958.
2. Allport, Gordon W., "Psychology of Participation," *Psychological Review,* LIII, May, 1945, p. 126.
3. American Association of School Administrators, *The School Administrator and Negotiation.* Washington, D.C.: National Education Association, 1968.
4. American Educational Research Association, "Curriculum Planning and Development," *Review of Educational Research,* XXX:3, June, 1960.
5. American Educational Research Association, "Teacher Personnel," *Review of Educational Research,* XXXIII:4, 1963.
6. Ardrey, Robert, *The Territorial Imperative.* New York: Atheneum, 1966.
7. Association for Supervision and Curriculum Development, NEA, Yearbook, *Balance in the Curriculum.* Washington, D.C.: National Education Association, 1961. Chap. VIII.
8. Association for Supervision and Curriculum Development, NEA, Yearbook, *Individualizing Instruction,* Washington, D.C.: National Education Association, 1964. Chap. VI.
9. Association for Supervision and Curriculum Development, NEA, Yearbook, *Leadership for Improving Instruction.* Washington, D.C.: National Education Association, 1960. Chap. III.
10. Association for Supervision and Curriculum Development, NEA, *New Insights and the Curriculum.* Washington, D.C.: National Education Association, 1963.
11. Association for Supervision and Curriculum Development, NEA, *Perceiving, Behaving and Becoming.* Washington, D.C.: National Education Association, 1962.

12. Association for Supervision and Curriculum Development, NEA, *To Nurture Humaneness: Commitment for the 70's,* 1970 Yearbook. Washington, D.C.: National Education Association, 1970. Part III.
13. Association for Supervision and Curriculum Development, NEA, Bulletin, *What Are the Sources of the Curriculum? A Symposium.* Washington, D.C.: National Education Association, 1962.
14. Ayer, Fred C., *Fundamentals of Instructional Supervision.* New York: Harper & Row, 1954.
15. Bartky, John, *Supervision As Human Relations.* New York: Heath, 1953.
16. Bass, Bernard M., *Leadership, Psychology and Organizational Behavior.* New York: Harper & Row, 1960.
17. Bass, Bernard M. and Harold J. Leavitt, "Some Experiments in Planning and Operating," *Management Science,* IX, July, 1963, p. 584.
18. Beach, Fred F., "Professionalization for Educational Administration," *School Life,* XLII, October, 1959, pp. 5–8.
19. Beckhard, Richard, "The Confrontation Meeting," in Warren G. Bennis, Kenneth D. Benne, and Robert Chin (eds.), *The Planning of Change.* New York: Holt, Rinehart & Winston, 1969, 2nd ed. pp. 478–485.
20. Benne, Kenneth D., "Democratic Ethics and Human Engineering," in Warren G. Bennis, Kenneth D. Benne, and Robert Chin (eds.), *The Planning of Change.* New York: Holt, Rinehart & Winston, 1961. p. 142.
21. Bennis, Warren G., Kenneth D. Benne, and Robert Chin (eds.), *The Planning of Change.* New York: Holt, Rinehart & Winston, 1961.
22. Bereiter, Carl, "Some Persisting Dilemmas in the Measurement of Change," in Chester W. Harris (ed.), *Problems in Measuring Change.* Madison: University of Wisconsin Press, 1963. pp. 3–20.
23. Bloom, Benjamin S. (ed.), *Taxonomy of Educational Objectives.* New York: Longmans, Green, 1956.
24. Briggs, Thomas H. and Joseph Justman, *Improving Instruction Through Supervision.* New York: Macmillan, 1952. pp. 126–142.
25. Browning, Robert, "Andrea del Sarto," in *Complete Poetical Works of Browning.* Boston: Houghton Mifflin, 1895, Cambridge ed. p. 346.
26. Burbank, Natt B., *The Superintendent of Schools,* Danville, Illinois: The Interstate Printers and Publishers, Inc., 1968.
27. Burton, William H. and Leo J. Brueckner, *Supervision: A Social Process.* New York: Appleton-Century-Crofts, 1955.
28. Butts, R. Freeman and Lawrence A. Cremin, *A History of Education in American Culture.* New York: Holt, Rinehart & Winston, 1953.
29. Button, Warren, "A History of Supervision in the Public Schools 1870–1950," unpublished doctoral dissertation. St. Louis: Washington University, 1961.
30. Callahan, Raymond E., *Education and the Cult of Efficiency.* Chicago: University of Chicago Press, 1962.
31. Campbell, Roald F., Luvern L. Cunningham, and Roderick F. McPhee, *The Organization and Control of American Schools.* Columbus, Ohio: Charles E. Merrill, 1965.

32. Carlson, Elliot, "Education and Industry: Troubled Partnership," *Saturday Review*, August 15, 1970, pp. 45–47ff.
33. Carlson, Richard O., *Executive Succession and Organizational Change: Place-Bound and Career-Bound Superintendents of Schools.* Chicago: Midwest Administration Center, University of Chicago, 1962.
34. Cartwright, Dorwin and A. F. Zander (eds.), *Group Dynamics: Research and Theory.* New York: Harper & Row, 1960, 2nd ed.
35. Cartwright, Gene J., "A Study of Lay Motivations to Influence Public Schools," unpublished doctoral dissertation. Madison: University of Wisconsin, 1971.
36. Cass, James, "Profit and Loss in Education," *Saturday Review*, August 15, 1970, pp. 39–40.
37. Castetter, William B., *Administering the School Personnel Program.* New York: Macmillan, 1962. Chap. III.
38. Chandler, B. J., Lindley J. Stiles, and John I. Kituse (eds.), *Education in an Urban Society.* New York: Dodd, Mead, 1962.
39. Clark, James V., "Authentic Interaction and Personal Growth in Sensitivity Training Groups," in Warren G. Bennis, Kenneth D. Benne, and Robert Chin (eds.), *The Planning of Change.* New York: Holt, Rinehart & Winston, 1969, 2nd ed. p. 406.
40. Coch, Lester and John R. P. French, Jr., "Overcoming Resistance to Change," in Eleanor E. Maccoby, Theodore M. Newcomb, and Eugene L. Hartley (eds.), *Reading in Social Psychology.* Chicago: Holt, Rinehart & Winston, 1958. p. 250.
41. Commission on the Reorganization of Secondary Education, *Cardinal Principles of Secondary Education.* Washington, D.C.: United States Bureau of Education, Bulletin No. 35, 1918.
42. Cremin, Lawrence A., *The Transformation of the School: Progressivism in American Education, 1876–1957.* New York: Knopf, 1961.
43. Curti, Merle, *The Social Ideas of American Educators.* Paterson, New Jersey: Pageant, 1959.
44. Dalton, Gene W., Louis B. Barnes, and Abraham Zaleznik, *The Distribution of Authority in Formal Organizations.* Boston: Harvard University Press, Division of Research, Graduate School of Business Administration, 1967. Chap. III.
45. Deutsch, Morton and Robert M. Krauss, *Theories in Social Psychology.* New York: Basic Books, Inc., 1965.
46. Dumont, Matthew P., "The Changing Face of Professionalism," in Lanore A. Netzer *et al. Education, Administration and Change: The Redeployment of Resources.* New York: Harper & Row, 1970. Chap. II.
47. Eye, Glen G., "The Importance of Decreasing Classroom Interruptions," *American School Board Journal,* June, 1955.
48. Eye, Glen G., "Performance Evaluation: Measure of Education," *Wisconsin Journal of Education,* November, 1969, pp. 14–19.
49. Eye, Glen G. and Martin Gray, "Expectations Behavior Inventory," unpublished document. Madison: University of Wisconsin, 1960.
50. Eye, Glen G. and Willard R. Lane, *The New Teacher Comes to School.* New York: Harper & Row, 1956.

51. Eye, Glen G. and Lanore A. Netzer, *The Lost Quantity-Quality Criterion in Staffing Administrative and Supervisory Positions,* unpublished research study. Madison: University of Wisconsin, 1959.
52. Eye, Glen G. and Lanore A. Netzer, *School Administrators and Instruction: A Guide to Self Appraisal.* Boston: Allyn & Bacon, 1969.
53. Feyereisen, Kathryn V., A. John Fiorino, and Arlene T. Nowak, *Supervision and Curriculum Renewal: A Systems Approach.* New York: Appleton-Century-Crofts, 1970.
54. Filley, Alan C. and Robert J. House, *Managerial Process and Organizational Behavior.* Glenview, Illinois: Scott, Foresman and Company, 1969.
55. Franseth, Jane, *Supervision as Leadership.* New York: Harper & Row, 1961.
56. Getzels, Jacob W., "Administration as a Social Process," in Andrew W. Halpin (ed.), *Administrative Theory in Education.* Chicago: Midwest Administration Center, University of Chicago, 1958. Chap. VII.
57. Gilberts, Robert D., "The Interpersonal Characteristics of Teaching Teams," unpublished doctoral dissertation. Madison: University of Wisconsin, 1961.
58. Grobman, Hulda, *Evaluation Activities of Curriculum Projects,* AERA Monograph, Series on Curriculum Evaluation. Chicago: Rand McNally & Company, 1968.
59. Gross, Neal, Ward S. Mason, and Alexander W. McEachern, *Exploration in Role Analysis.* New York: Wiley, 1958.
60. Gruber, Howard E., Glen Terrell, and Michael Wertheimer (eds.), *Contemporary Approaches to Creative Thinking.* New York: Atherton, 1963.
61. Harris, Chester (ed.), *Problems in Measuring Change.* Madison: University of Wisconsin Press, 1963.
62. Hicks, Hanne J., *Educational Supervision in Principle and Practice.* New York: Ronald, 1960.
63. Holt, Fred R., *Allocation of Administrative Functions.* Janesville, Wisconsin: Janesville Public Schools, 1963, 1967, and 1970.
64. Homme, Lloyd, "A Modern Concept of Motivation," in Lanore A. Netzer *et al., Education, Administration and Change: The Redeployment of Resources.* New York: Harper & Row, 1970. Chap. III.
65. Hunt, Herold C. and Paul R. Pierce, *The Practice of School Administration.* Boston: Houghton Mifflin, 1958.
66. Johansen, John H., "An Investigation of the Relationships Between Teacher's Perceptions of Authoritative Influence in Local Curriculum Decision-Making and Curriculum Implementation," unpublished doctoral dissertation. Evanston, Illinois: Northwestern University, 1965.
67. Johnson, Richard A., Fremont E. Kast, and James E. Rosenzweig, *The Theory and Management of Systems.* New York: McGraw-Hill, 1967.
68. Kast, Fremont E. and James E. Rosenzweig, *Organizations and Management.* New York: McGraw-Hill, 1970.
69. Kemp, C. Gratton, *Perspectives on the Group Process.* Boston: Houghton Mifflin, 1964.
70. Kennedy, John F., *Profiles in Courage.* New York: Harper & Row, 1961, Inaugural Edition. pp. 1–21.

71. Kleyensteuber, Carl J., "Attitudes and Behaviors of Groups of School Administrators," unpublished doctoral dissertation. Madison: University of Wisconsin, 1956.
72. Knezevich, Stephen J., *Administration of Public Education.* New York: Harper & Row, 1969, 2nd ed.
73. Knezevich, Stephen J. and Glen G. Eye, *Instructional Technology and the School Administrator.* American Association of School Administrators, Washington, D.C.: National Education Association, 1970.
74. Koopman, G. Robert, Alice Miel, and Paul J. Misner, *Democracy in School Administration.* New York: Appleton-Century-Crofts, 1943.
75. Krathwohl, David R., *et al., Taxonomy of Educational Objectives: The Classification of Educational Goals—Handbook II: Affective Domain.* New York: David McKay, 1956.
76. Krey, Robert D., "Factors Relating to Teachers' Perceptions of Curricular Implementation Activities and the Extent of Curricular Implementation," unpublished doctoral dissertation. Madison: University of Wisconsin, 1968.
77. Leeper, Robert R. (ed.), *Role of Supervisor and Curriculum Director in a Climate of Change.* Washington, D.C.: Association for Supervision and Curriculum Development, National Education Association, 1965.
78. Lieberman, Myron, *Education as a Profession.* Englewood Cliffs, N.J.: Prentice-Hall, 1956.
79. Lieberman, Myron, *The Future of Public Education.* Chicago: University of Chicago Press, 1960.
80. Litwin, George H. and Robert A. Stringer, Jr., *Motivation and Organizational Climate.* Boston: Harvard University Press, 1968.
81. Lucio, William H. (ed.), *The Supervisor: New Demands–New Dimensions.* Washington, D.C.: Association for Supervision and Curriculum Development, National Education Association, 1969.
82. Lucio, William H. and John D. McNeil, *Supervision: A Synthesis of Thought and Action.* New York: McGraw-Hill, 1969, 2nd ed.
83. MacKinnon, Donald W., "What Makes a Person Creative," *Saturday Review,* February 10, 1962, p. 69.
84. MacMillan, Velma J., "A Study of Procedures Used in Establishing New Intermediate Administrative-Supervisory Positions in Public Schools," unpublished doctoral dissertation. Madison: University of Wisconsin, 1969.
85. McGregor, Douglas, *The Professional Manager.* New York: McGraw-Hill, 1967.
86. Mannheim, Karl, "Freedom Under Planning," in *Man and Society in the Age of Reconstruction.* New York: Harcourt, Brace & World, 1941. pp. 364–481.
87. Miel, Alice (ed.), *Creativity in Teaching: Invitations and Instances.* San Francisco: Wadsworth, 1961.
88. Miller, Van, *The Public Administration of American School Systems.* New York: Macmillan, 1965.
89. Morphet, Edgar L., Roe L. Johns, and Theodore L. Reller, *Educational Administration.* Englewood Cliffs, N.J.: Prentice-Hall, 1959.
90. Munitz, Arthur J., "But Citizens' Committees *Can* Work," *The American School Board Journal,* November, 1969, pp. 41–43.

91. Muller, Herbert J., *The Children of Frankenstein.* Bloomington, Indiana: Indiana University Press, 1970.

92. National Education Association, Educational Policies Commission, *The Purposes of Education in American Democracy.* Washington, D.C.: NEA, 1938. Chap. II.

93. National Education Association, Educational Policies Commission, *The Central Purpose of American Education.* Washington, D.C.: NEA, 1961.

94. National School Public Relations Association, Bulletin, *The Shape of Education.* Washington, D.C.: National Education Association, 1962–1963, 1970–71.

95. National Society for the Study of Education, Yearbook, Part II, *Testing Programs in the Schools.* Washington, D.C.: National Education Association, 1963.

96. Neagley, Ross L. and N. Dean Evans, *Handbook for Effective Supervision of Instruction.* Englewood Cliffs, N.J.: Prentice-Hall, 1970, 2nd ed.

97. Netzer, Lanore A. and Glen G. Eye, "Checklist Inventory of Supervisory Functions," unpublished document. Madison: University of Wisconsin, 1960.

98. Netzer, Lanore A. and Glen G. Eye (eds.), *Education, Administration and Change.* New York: Harper & Row, 1970.

99. Netzer, Lanore A. and Glen G. Eye, "Instructional Supervisory Interview Instrument for Supervisors," unpublished document. Madison: University of Wisconsin, 1961.

100. Netzer, Lanore A. and Glen G. Eye, "What Is the Supervisor's Position in the School's Program," *Wisconsin Journal of Education,* January, 1962, pp. 8–9.

101. Netzer, Lanore A., Glen G. Eye, Ardelle Graef, Robert D. Krey, and J. Fred Overman, *Interdisciplinary Foundations of Supervision.* Boston: Allyn & Bacon, 1970.

102. O'Brien, Dean W., "Reference and Deference to Authority as Factors Affecting Professional Autonomy in Education: A Case Study," unpublished doctoral dissertation. Madison: University of Wisconsin, 1963.

103. Olmsted, Michael S., *The Small Group.* New York: Random House, 1959.

104. Overman, J. Fred, "Perceptions of the Role of the Instructional Supervisor in the State Department of Public Instruction," unpublished doctoral dissertation. Madison: University of Wisconsin, 1968.

105. Peter, Lawrence J. and Raymond Hull, *The Peter Principle.* New York: William Morrow and Company, 1969.

106. Plato, *The Republic* (trans. O. D. Shorey). Boston: Harvard University Press, 1935.

107. Pope, Alexander, "Essay on Criticism," in *The Pleasures of Pope.* London: Hamish Hamilton, 1949. p. 25.

108. Presthus, Robert, *The Organizational Society.* New York: Alfred A. Knopf, 1962.

109. Rogers, Everett M., *Diffusion of Innovations.* New York: The Free Press, 1962.

110. Sanders, Norris M., *Classroom Questions: What Kinds?* New York: Harper & Row, 1966.

111. Saunders, Robert L. and John T. Lovell, "Negotiations: Inevitable Consequence of Bureaucracy?" in Robert R. Leeper (ed.), *Supervision: Emerging Profession.* Washington, D.C.:

Association for Supervision and Curriculum Development, National Education Association, 1969. pp. 241–244.
112. Savage, William W., *Interpersonal and Group Relations in Educational Administration.* Glenview, Illinois: Scott, Foresman and Company, 1968.
113. Schein, Edgar H. and Warren G. Bennis, *Personal and Organizational Change through Group Methods.* New York: Wiley, 1965.
114. Shaplin, Judson T. and Henry F. Olds, Jr. (eds.), *Team Teaching.* New York: Harper & Row, 1964.
115. Spencer, Herbert, *Education: Intellectual, Moral, and Physical.* New York: Appleton-Century-Crofts, 1860.
116. Stanley, Julian C., *Measurement in Today's Schools.* Englewood Cliffs, N.J.: Prentice-Hall, 1964, 4th ed.
117. Stewart, Harold G., "Criteria Used by Superintendents in the Selection of Beginning Building Principals in Certain Wisconsin Schools," unpublished doctoral dissertation. Madison: University of Wisconsin, 1963.
118. Stoltenberg, James C., "Indications of Tolerance and the Change Potential from an Analysis of Current Educational Practices in the Merrill Area Public Schools," unpublished doctoral dissertation. Madison: University of Wisconsin, 1969.
119. Stone, Howard Lee, "A Conceptualization of Professional Autonomy in the Context of Emerging Negotiated Relationships," unpublished doctoral dissertation. Madison: University of Wisconsin, 1970.
120. Teague, Wayne, "An Evaluative Analysis of the In-Service Program for Teachers and Administrators in DeKalb County, Georgia," unpublished Ed.D. dissertation. Auburn, Alabama: Auburn University, 1962.
121. Tagiuri, Renato and Luigi Petrullo (eds.), *Person Perception and Interpersonal Behavior.* Stanford University Press, 1958.
122. Thompson, Barbara Storck, "A Study of the Synchronization of Behaviors Related to Selected Tasks of Elementary School Supervisors and Principals," unpublished doctoral dissertation. Madison: University of Wisconsin, 1969.
123. Tobin, John M., Superintendent of Schools, *Annual Report of the School Committee and the Superintendent of Schools.* Cambridge, Massachusetts, 1961.
124. Torrance, E. Paul, *Guiding Creative Talent.* Englewood Cliffs, N.J.: Prentice-Hall, 1962.
125. Tuttle, Frederick, "The Theory of Supervision of Instruction, 1875–1920," unpublished doctoral dissertation. New Haven: Yale University Press, 1942.
126. Tyler, Ralph W., Robert M. Gagne and Michael Scriven, *Perspective of Curriculum Evaluation,* AERA Monograph Series on Curriculum Evaluation. Chicago: Rand McNally & Company, 1967.
127. Wadia, Maneck S., *Management and the Behavioral Sciences.* Boston, Massachusetts: Allyn & Bacon, 1968.
128. Wesner, Gordon Eugene, "A Study of In-Service Education Programs for Secondary School Teachers in Selected Large-City Systems," unpublished Ed.D. dissertation. Lawrence, Kansas: University of Kansas, 1963.
129. Wilson, L. Craig, T. Madison Byar, Arthur S. Shapiro, and

Shirley H. Schell, *Sociology of Supervision*. Boston: Allyn & Bacon, 1969.

130. Young, William F., "Curriculum Negotiations: Present Status—Future Trends," in Robert R. Leeper (ed.), *Supervision: Emerging Profession*. Washington, D.C.: Association for Supervision and Curriculum Development, National Education Association, 1969. pp. 238–241.

APPENDIXES

APPENDIX A
Multifaceted Strategies of Evaluation *

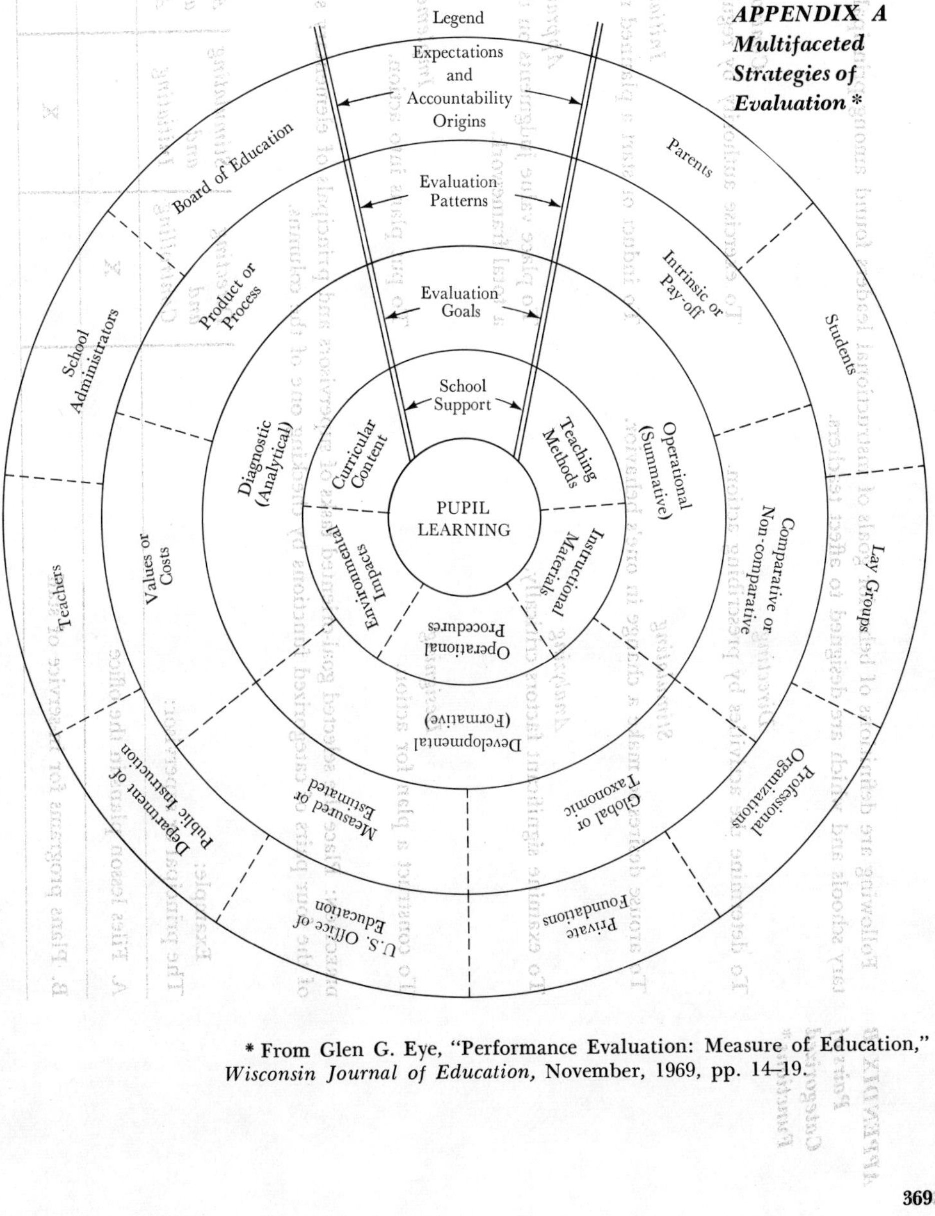

* From Glen G. Eye, "Performance Evaluation: Measure of Education," *Wisconsin Journal of Education,* November, 1969, pp. 14–19.

APPENDIX B Pairs of Categorized Functions*

Following are definitions of behavior goals of instructional leaders found among principals and supervisors of elementary schools and which are designed to affect teachers.

Directing
To determine the activities by prescribing action.

Controlling
To exercise authority by regulating behavior.

Stimulating
To arouse desires to make a change in one's behavior.

Initiating
To induct or start a planned movement of change.

Analyzing
To examine significant factors critically.

Appraising
To place value judgments on the various dimensions within a total framework.

Designing
To construct a plan for action.

Implementing
To put plans into action.

DIRECTION: Place the selected goal-oriented tasks of supervisors and principals of elementary schools listed below into one of the four pairs of categorized functions by checking one of the columns.

Example: The principal or supervisor:	*Directing and Controlling*	*Stimulating and Initiating*	*Analyzing and Appraising*	*Designing and Implementing*
A. Files lesson plans in the office	X			
B. Plans programs for in-service of staff		X		

The principal or supervisor:	*Directing and Controlling*	*Stimulating and Initiating*	*Analyzing and Appraising*	*Designing and Implementing*
1. Informs board of education of faculty progress in curricular development				
2. Encourages teachers to use audio-visual materials and equipment				
3. Recommends pupil grade-placement to parents				
4. Guides the production of curricular guides				
5. Screens requests from outside special interest groups for student participation in activities such as essay contests, spelling bees, and debates				
6. Sees to it that statutory requirements are met				
7. Helps teacher diagnose a child's reading problem				
8. Prepares written reports of classroom visits for superintendent				
9. Carries out research in cooperation with classroom teachers				
10. Informs agencies such as welfare, health, and guidance clinics of needed information				

* Barbara S. Thompson, "A Study of the Synchronization of Behaviors Related to Selected Tasks of Elementary School Supervisors and Principals," unpublished doctoral dissertation (Madison: University of Wisconsin, 1968).

Appendix B (Continued)

The principal or supervisor:	*Directing and Controlling*	*Stimulating and Initiating*	*Analyzing and Appraising*	*Designing and Implementing*
11. Conducts individual conferences with children who have behavior problems				
12. Holds class enrollments within a reasonable pupil-teacher ratio				
13. Confers with teachers about results of first-grade reading readiness test				
14. Approves daily class schedules				
15. Plans long-range curricular plans with faculty				
16. Plans the fall pre-school orientation meeting for new teachers				
17. Holds individual conferences with teachers concerning instructional improvement				
18. Executes follow-up reporting concerning evaluation of classroom visits to individual teachers				
19. Demonstrates new methods of teaching to individual or small groups of teachers				
20. Approves the scheduling of school parties for pupils				
21. Assists teacher to improve class discipline				

The principal or supervisor:	*Directing and Controlling*	*Stimulating and Initiating*	*Analyzing and Appraising*	*Designing and Implementing*
22. Makes suggestions to teachers pertaining to enrichment and remedial activities for certain children				
23. Schedules parents for conferences with teacher(s)				
24. Makes a final edit of curricular guides before they are published				
25. Visits classrooms to observe teaching				
26. Evaluates need for and recommends plant development				
27. Plans with teachers a camping experience for children				
28. Reports pupil progress and problems to superintendent				
29. Leads teachers in the revision and writing of a common philosophy of education				
30. Circulates newly acquired professional literature				
31. Enforces the legal length of the school day				
32. Conducts orientation meeting for new teachers				

Appendix B (Continued)

The principal or supervisor:	*Directing and Controlling*	*Stimulating and Initiating*	*Analyzing and Appraising*	*Designing and Implementing*
33. Plans and puts into effect curricular changes in instructional field				
34. Files qualifications and licenses of staff				
35. Plans with the kindergarten teachers for prekindergarten enrollment day				
36. Schedules psychological services				
37. Evaluates semester course outlines				
38. Makes arrangements for teacher visitations to other rooms or schools to observe innovative practices				
39. Coordinates schedules of staff specialists and teachers				
40. Works with teachers as they apply research findings				
41. Evaluates teachers for re-employment				
42. Organizes curricular study committees				
43. Encourages teachers to participate in professional organizations				
44. Studies with teachers in the interpretation of test data				

The principal or supervisor:	*Directing and Controlling*	*Stimulating and Initiating*	*Analyzing and Appraising*	*Designing and Implementing*
45. Arouses interest of teachers to plan pilot projects and innovative experiments				
46. Schedules student teachers with host teachers for practice teaching				
47. Outlines resource units for use by teachers				
48. Sets up short-range curricular plans with faculty				
49. Arranges for representative of publishing companies to discuss with teachers the products offered for purchase				
50. Assists teachers in the identification of talented students				
51. Interviews prospective teachers				
52. Enforces standards for dress and behavior of students				
53. Regulates visitors to the school				
54. Introduces to teachers newly prepared curricular guides intended for their use				

Index

INDEX

INDEX